MW00791920

# POLITICAL MERITOCRACY

# IN RENAISSANCE ITALY

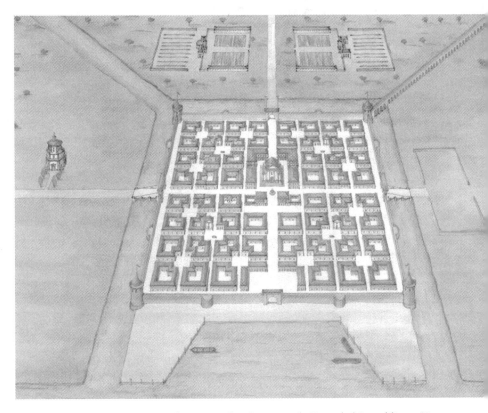

Reconstruction of Patrizi's Plan for a Newly-Founded Republican City.

# Political Meritocracy
# in Renaissance Italy

## THE VIRTUOUS REPUBLIC OF
## Francesco Patrizi of Siena

## JAMES HANKINS

HARVARD UNIVERSITY PRESS
*Cambridge, Massachusetts • London, England • 2023*

"Reconstruction of Patrizi's Plan for a Newly-Founded Republican City"
used as frontispiece and Figure 3 on page 225 courtesy of Duncan G. Stroik,
Architect, LLC. All rights reserved.

Cataloging-in-Publication Data is available from the Library of Congress
ISBN: 978-0-674-27470-9 (alk. paper)

To the memory of Mark Kishlansky

# Contents

NOTE ON SOURCES    ix

TIMELINE OF EVENTS IN PATRIZI'S LIFE    xi

Introduction    1

1 The Formation of a Political Philosopher    14
The Young Patrizi: Poet, Teacher, and Statesman—The Crisis of
1456: Condemnation and Exile—Governor of Foligno—Calm after
the Storm: Gaeta, 1464–1494

2 The Great Political Treatises    55
The Humanist Synthetic Treatise—How to Found a Republic—Aims in
Writing the *De republica* and the Meaning of *Institutio*—On Kingship
and Kingly Education—Patrizi's Historico-prudential Method

3 Principles of Republican Government    92
The Defense of Republics—Republican Values: The Rule of Law—
Republican Values: Equality—Republican Principles: Liberty—
Ranking Constitutions—Practical Wisdom in Warfare

4 Meritocracy and the Optimal Republic    126
Meritocracy and the Best Regime—Which Citizens Should Be
Admitted to Political Office?—How to Keep the Best Men in Charge—
Deliberation and the Virtue of Free Speech—Preventing Corruption
and Revolution—Magistracies in the Best Republic: General Princi-
ples, the Senate, Consuls—The Legal System—Censors, Quaestors,
Overseers of Provisions, Aediles—Summary: The Patrizian Republic

5 The Virtuous Society 172

Educating the Virtuous Citizen—The Roles of Wife and Husband—
The Role of the State—A Scheme of Public Education—The Moral
Economy: The Household, Unfree Labor, and Marriage—The Moral
Economy: The City-State—Republican Architecture and Urban
Planning—Piety and Religion in the Best Republic

6 Citizenship and the Virtuous Citizen 242

Two Models of Citizenship—Who Should Be a Citizen in a Republic?—
Inclusion of Workers among the Citizenry in a Republic—Admitting
Foreigners to Citizenship—The Virtues of a Good Citizen—Royal
Citizenship

7 Virtuous Absolutism: Patrizi's *De regno* 272

Rethinking Monarchy: The View from Gaeta—The Argument for
Monarchy—Can Monarchical Power Be Virtuous?—The Ideal Prince—
The Sources of Royal Legitimacy—How the King May Become
Virtuous—Civil Friendship, Humanity, and Piety—Monarchy,
Dyarchy, and the Future of Republics

Conclusion: Patrizi and Modern Politics 318

*Appendix A: List of Patrizi's Works (Compiled with
the assistance of Caroline Engelmayer)* 331

*Appendix B: Editions, Translations, and Compendia
of Patrizi's Political Works, 1518–1702 (Compiled by
Victoria Pipas)* 335

*Appendix C: Patrizi's Epigram 14: "What Would
Make Me Happy" (Latin text)* 345

*Abbreviations* 347

*Notes* 349

*Bibliography* 393

*Acknowledgments* 411

*Index* 413

# Note on Sources


Patrizi's political works were written in humanist Latin and have never been translated into modern English. The only work of his available in English is an Elizabethan translation, published in 1576, by one Richard Robinson, of a Latin epitome of the *De republica* (see Appendix B). A slightly modernized version of this text will be published in 2023 by the Library of Liberty with an introduction by the present writer and Victoria Pipas and with source notes compiled with the assistance of Caroline Engelmayer, Molly Goldberg, Carolina Elizondo Moya, and Maya McDougall. All translations from Patrizi's Latin in the present volume, however, are mine.

The Latin texts of Patrizi's two great political treatises, which date from the sixteenth century, are not wholly reliable. The dozens of printings of the *De republica* and *De regno* that appeared in the sixteenth and early seventeenth centuries all descend from the Paris editions (1518–1519) prepared by a minor French humanist, one Jean de Savigny. Savigny was more concerned with rendering the contents of the treatises usable by his contemporaries than he was with faithfully reproducing Patrizi's *ipsissima verba*. Collation with fifteenth-century manuscripts produced under Patrizi's supervision discloses enough variants to make a careful scholar uneasy about citing Savigny's texts.

For this volume, the Latin text of all quotations from Patrizi's *De republica* has been checked against the dedication copy to Pope Sixtus IV (*V*) and the partial autograph in the Biblioteca Laurenziana in Florence (*F*). Aside from cases where the text has been corrected,

I have not included the Latin original of either the *De republica* (1518) or *De regno* (1519) in the notes. Those editions may be readily consulted through the website *Early European Books*, published by ProQuest. A provisional edition of the *De republica*, corrected against V and other authoritative manuscripts in the Vatican, will soon be made available at the website of the Patrizi Project (see the Acknowledgments), along with other hitherto unpublished texts by Patrizi, annotated lists of his other works, manuscript lists, and bibliographies. See https://projects.iq.harvard.edu/patrizisiena.

# Timeline of Events in Patrizi's Life

1413    Francesco di Giovanni Patrizi is born on 24 February to Giovanni di Franchino Patrizi and his wife, Lorenza. He is baptized on 25 February.

1426    He delivers the academic prolusion *Oratio de laudibus philosophiae* for the opening of the school year at the University of Siena.

1435–1438    He studies Latin eloquence and Greek with Francesco Filelfo at the University of Siena.

1436    His first surviving letter, dated 19 April, is written to Lapo da Castiglionchio the Younger.

1440    May–June. First term as prior of Siena for the *terzo* of San Martino.

1441/1446    Professor of rhetoric at the University of Siena. His *De metris Horatii* is likely written during this period.

1446    He writes the letter-treatise *De gerendo magistratu* for his pupil, Achille Petrucci.

1446    Elected chancellor. He resigns this office in favor of Achille Petrucci in March 1447 on being elected as prior.

1446    March–April. Second term as prior of Siena.

1446    *Podestà* (governor) of the fortress-town of Radicofani.

1447    Marries Bartolomea di Antonio Gori, by whom he has four sons, Giorgio, Camillo, Alessandro, and Giulio.

1447    August. Appointed Sienese ambassador to Pope
        Nicholas V in Rome.

1450    Ambassador to Florence. Ambassador to Rome for a
        second time.

1450    Signs along with 144 other Sienese a sworn pact
        (*coniuratio*) to uphold the government of the "Tre
        Monti."

1452    Ambassador to Emperor Frederick III, then in Bologna.
        He accompanies Frederick on his progress to Rome,
        where Frederick is crowned Holy Roman Emperor on
        1 April 1453.

1452    September–October. Counselor of the Capitano del
        Popolo in Siena.

1453    March–April. Third term as prior of Siena.

1453    September. He serves, together with Goro Lolli, as
        ambassador to the duke of Calabria, the future King
        Ferrante of Naples, who is in Tuscany in command of
        the Neapolitan army.

1454    Second ambassadorial mission to the duke of Calabria.

1455    July. The condottiere Jacopo Piccinino invades Sienese
        territory.

1456    June. Halley's comet appears in the skies. An outbreak
        of plague and a famine follow. Emergency government
        (*balìa*) in Siena. Antonio Petrucci is exiled.

1457    January. Antonio Petrucci sponsors a coup against the
        emergency government, which fails; 164 of Antonio's
        political allies, including Patrizi, are arrested.

1457    Patrizi is tortured and condemned to be executed, but
        he is saved by the intervention of Cardinal Enea Silvio
        Piccolomini.

1457    3 September. Patrizi is sentenced to twenty years of
        *confino,* a particularly strict form of exile, in Pistoia.

1457    October. Patrizi is invited to teach in Lucca but the
        Sienese government refuses its permission.

1457    November. With plague breaking out in Pistoia, Patrizi
        is allowed to withdraw to the estate at Montughi
        belonging to the Milanese ambassador, Nicodemo
        Tranchedini, outside Florence. He becomes tutor to
        Nicodemo's son, Francesco. He remains at Montughi
        until June 1459.

1457/1459   Probable date of Patrizi's epitomes of Quintilian's
            *Institutes* and Priscian.

1458    7 May. Alamanno Rinuccini invites Patrizi to meet
        other members of Giovanni Argiropolo's "academy."

1458    3 September. Enea Silvio Piccolomini is crowned Pope
        Pius II.

1459    February. Pius II visits Siena for the first time since
        becoming pope. Patrizi composes a 104-line hexameter
        poem (*Poem.* 4.5) for his *adventus*.

1459    15 April. Patrizi is tonsured and ordained a priest. He
        is given a rich benefice at Campoli in the Val di Pesa,
        north of Siena.

1459    1 June. The Diet of Mantua, called by Pius to organize
        a crusade against the Turks, opens.

1459    22 July. Patrizi is ordered to go to Verona by the
        Sienese authorities, where he arrives by 6 July with his
        pupil, Francesco Tranchedini.

1459–1460   Early December. The Sienese authorities, under pressure
            from Pius II, allow Patrizi free movement within Italy on
            condition that he remain outside Siena and its territory.
            It is likely that he visited Mantua during the final weeks
            of the Diet, which ended on 14 January 1460.

1460    March. *Ecloga de Christi nativitate,* Patrizi's most
        successful poem, is dedicated to Pius II.

1461  January. Letters dated from Rome document Patrizi's presence in the city.

1461  Before 23 March. Patrizi's first collection of Latin poetry, the *Poematum libri IV,* is dedicated to Pius II. He likely begins work on the *De republica.*

1461  23 March. Patrizi is elected bishop of Gaeta, a see in the Kingdom of Naples.

1461  13 April. Patrizi's exile from Siena is rescinded and he is restored to full citizen rights.

1461  27 May. Patrizi is appointed governor of Foligno in the Papal State.

1461  October. First mention of the *De republica* in Patrizi's correspondence.

1461  Shortly before 1 December. Patrizi's mother dies.

1462  March. Patrizi visits Siena for the first time since his exile.

1462  15 October. Patrizi mentions in a letter that he has reached the fifth book of his *De republica.*

1463  September. Patrizi states that he has reached Book 8 of the *De republica.*

1464  Spring, summer. A conspiracy is organized to expel Patrizi from the governorship of Foligno.

1464  14 August. Pius II dies. A rebellion breaks out in Foligno while Patrizi is in Nocera, and he is unable to return to the city.

1464  October. Patrizi is charged by his enemies in Foligno with maladministration and corruption; a cardinalatial commission formed to investigate likely clears him of wrongdoing.

1464  December. Patrizi leaves Rome for his diocese in Gaeta.

1465  May–June. Patrizi represents the Kingdom of Naples at the marriage ceremonies for Alfonso, duke of Calabria, and Ippolyta Maria Sforza. He delivers the *Oratio ad Hippolytam Mariam Sforzam (De matrimonio)* and renews his ties with Francesco Filelfo. He becomes tutor and adviser to Alfonso of Calabria.

ca. 1467/ 1488   Earliest and latest datable poems in Patrizi's second collection of Latin poetry, the *Epigrammata*, likely left unfinished at his death.

1471   9 August. Sixtus IV is elected pope.

1471   Scribal publication of Patrizi's *De republica*, dedicated to Sixtus IV.

1476/1478   Commentary on Petrarch's *Canzoniere* is finished, dedicated to Alfonso of Calabria.

1481–1482   Outbreak of popular rebellion in Siena.

1483/1484   Scribal publication of Patrizi's *De regno*.

1484   September. Ambassadorial mission representing the king of Naples to congratulate Innocent VIII on his election as pope. His *Oratio ad Innocentium VIII* is printed in Rome.

1491   Patrizi refounds the sanctuary of the Madonna della Civita in the hill town of Itri, near Gaeta.

1494   22 August. Baccio Ugolino replaces Patrizi as bishop of Gaeta after the latter's death.

1518   First edition of *De republica* published in Paris, edited by Jean de Savigny.

1519   First edition of *De regno* published in Paris, edited by Jean de Savigny.

# POLITICAL MERITOCRACY

# IN RENAISSANCE ITALY

You must try to find out what sort of knowledge it was that enabled Themistocles to give Greece liberty; you must try to find out what kind of knowledge it was that got Pericles recognized as his country's best counselor; you must reflect, further, how it was that Solon by deep thought established in his city the best laws; you must search out what kind of practices they are that give the Spartans the reputation of being preeminent military commanders.

Xenophon, Symposium 8.39

There is a voice within us, which seems to intimate, that real merit should govern the world; and that men ought to be respected only in proportion to their talents, virtues, and services. But the question always has been, how can this arrangement be accomplished? How shall the men of merit be discovered? How shall the proportions of merit be ascertained and graduated? Who shall be the judge?

John Adams, Discourses on Davila

# Introduction

Most historians of political thought have never heard the name Francesco Patrizi of Siena. Specialists in Renaissance studies are likeliest to find it filed under *trattatistica,* the Italian name for a group of Renaissance political treatises, mostly of the late fifteenth century, written by men with even more unfamiliar names: Bartolomeo Platina, Diomede Carafa, Giovanni Pontano, Giuniano Maio. The vast legion of Machiavelli scholars may recognize Patrizi as a shadowy "forerunner" of their hero, an author they all too readily dismiss as a compiler of interminable works stuffed with moral bromides—written in Latin, no less!—to be contrasted unfavorably with the profound and pungent analysis of the great Florentine.

The thesis of this book is that Patrizi does not merit his present obscurity. Let me make this claim in a more provocative form: Patrizi deserves to be recognized as the most substantial and influential voice of Italian humanist political thought between the time of Francesco Petrarca in the fourteenth century and Niccolò Machiavelli in the sixteenth. In a recent book I have labeled that tradition of thought "virtue politics," and if what I argue there is correct, it is Patrizi, not Machiavelli, who is the more authentic representative of Renaissance political thought.[1] He was, indeed, specially chosen to fill that role by Pius II, the humanist pope, who charged the Sienese scholar with creating a synthesis of ancient political wisdom for the use of humanist reformers. What Patrizi produced in his two great treatises on republican and royal government were no mere compilations, but powerful statements of contemporary political ideals. As such they deserve to rank alongside other canonical writings on

I

politics produced by better-known Renaissance thinkers such as Erasmus, Francesco Guicciardini, and Jean Bodin. They merit study as indispensable reference points for contextualizing the Renaissance's arch-realist, Machiavelli, and its arch-idealist, Thomas More.

To appreciate the originality of Patrizi's political philosophy, we have to step back and take a wider view of the way political power was ordinarily legitimated in Europe between the medieval and modern periods. From that perspective it is evident that Patrizi's mer-itocratic way of justifying political power, inspired by classical Greek philosophy, is fundamentally different from the theological-legal modes of legitimation characteristic of the medieval *ius commune,* reinvigorated in the sixteenth century.[2] The latter tradition, which was to remain dominant down to the age of democratic revolutions, justified political power by appeal to its *sources.* Patrizi focused instead on its *ends.*

Medieval justifications of political power were based on the concept of *dominium,* a term which, crucially, combines ideas of lordship (the power of commanding others, *imperium* or *dominatio*), jurisdiction (a power of declaring and enforcing laws), and ownership (ultimate rights over the disposition of property). Medieval lords were owners of the power they wielded and could pass it down as a hereditary possession to their children or other members of their lineage. They could alienate it for a fee to counter-parties, as when entire towns were sold by their proprietors to other lords. Or, like city-states, they could invest their *dominium* in a signorial institution whose public goods (*res publica*) could be shared among citizens. The whole range of proprietary claims to lordship, from local fiefdoms and signories to the whole of Christendom, could be arranged in a "tree of jurisdictions" ultimately depending on divine authority: either the temporal authority of the Holy Roman Empire or the spiritual authority of the Church. The legitimacy of this scheme was authenticated through the universal, transtemporal, and providential wisdom of Roman law, which was *ratio scripta*—reason in written form—*vera philosophia,* or even (as Dante claimed) an inspired, sacred body of texts revealing knowledge of things human and divine.[3]

In the modern West, by contrast, political legitimacy relies above all on the principle of popular sovereignty, which in turn is based on a belief in the natural dignity and equality of all human beings. That belief can be traced back to theorists such as Locke, Rousseau, and Kant, whose notions of human dignity and equality were derived from Stoic philosophy and New Testament Christianity—from Nature and Nature's God, as the designers of the United States' federal government were wont to say.[4] Sovereignty is legitimate when a government within a defined geographical area reflects the will of the people living there, or of all qualified citizens. The will of the people may be expressed via a fictive contract, an unwritten tradition of governance, a revolutionary act, or a written constitution that counts as fundamental law.

In the early modern period, the transition to popular sovereignty was motivated by tyrannical abuses of power committed by those enjoying hereditary privileges of rule. Popular sovereignty was designed to constrain and ultimately replace the principle of heritable lordship. In the liberal version of popular sovereignty that became dominant in the nineteenth century, human flourishing in the wider sense was held to be best secured when individuals were permitted by the state to choose their own goods. The individual "pursuit of happiness" came to be understood as the freedom to accumulate material goods or to challenge traditional moral standards and settled ways of life. In the illiberal version of popular sovereignty that currently dominates Western societies, the people authorize scientific experts to dictate and enforce optimum modes of living.

In contrast with these dominant modes of legitimation, which focus on the sources of power, Patrizi's way of justifying rulership— as was only natural in an age of governments with weak claims to legitimacy—focused on achieving the *ends* of political power. The principal end of political power for Italian humanists was human flourishing and the goods associated with it. These included liberty, civil peace and order, security from foreign threats, material prosperity, and above all, virtue, meaning the full flourishing, physical and spiritual, of human beings. Liberty in republics, defined as self-rule, was secured through relative equality of citizens, rejection of any lordship permanently invested in a single individual, and wide participation in government. In kingdoms, liberty, construed as personal freedom, was to be secured through humane and moderate government.

Equality in republics was not based on any concept of individual dignity—*dignitas* in the Renaissance referred to deserved rank, not to an ascribed respect for all persons *qua* persons.[5] Equality was instrumental to liberty and, according to Patrizi, should be achieved by institutional or customary regulation of social, economic, or political power. The ends of government were to be secured by human prudence, informed by the study of history, literature, and philosophy. Patrizi, who was among other things a Catholic bishop, values traditional religion but nowhere appeals to divine authority, whether of the Church or the Empire, in order to legitimate government. Roman and canon law for him are rich repositories of wisdom but nevertheless imperfect, historically contingent creations of human practical intelligence. Human laws are more effective when endorsed by the vote of all the citizens, but they do not derive their legitimacy from the people. What makes laws and customs legitimate is their success in enabling individuals, families, and communities to flourish in the fullest way possible.

Virtue, for Patrizi, is both the principal end of good government and the principal means of securing it. A good government, as both Plato and Aristotle taught, is one that makes its citizens good, but only virtuous magistrates can create the conditions for a virtuous citizenry. A virtuous citizenry, in turn, can make its rulers better. Good character, competence, and a fine education in princes, magistrates, and citizens were for humanists the principal solution to the failures of government in their time. For Renaissance literati the greatest obstacle to full flourishing in political communities was the corruption of human nature and culture that had occurred after the fall of ancient Rome. In decayed modern times, power was too often found in the hands of persons driven by lust for wealth and status, men who abused their inherited power or diverted the shared resources of the community to benefit themselves at the expense of their fellow citizens.

More seriously than any other humanist of his time, Patrizi addressed the question of structural reform in social and political life: the changes to existing institutions that would be necessary to promote fully flourishing human communities. What was the best way to raise the most meritorious and public-spirited men to leadership positions in the state? And how could ordinary citizens be brought to recognize and respect true merit in their leaders? These are the classic challenges of all meritocratic forms of government. Patrizi advanced solutions to these fundamental problems that drew on earlier humanist thought but went well beyond it.

Humanist political reform since the time of Petrarch had sought to exploit the transformative power of literary and philosophical education in order to improve the character and practical wisdom of elites. Patrizi laid out two complete systems of education—one for republics and another for princes—expressly designed to foster civic virtue. The best republic, he argued, will offer some degree of participation in office to all qualified citizens. But no citizen could be expected to perform well in office without some education. By a natural process of thought Patrizi became the first author in European history to advocate universal literacy among the citizen class as well as public funding for teachers of the liberal arts and humanities. Responsibility for educating the young should be shared, he believed, between families and the state. Through education the whole city would possess a common culture and history, leading to greater social cohesion.

Other humanists had written treatises and orations on republican government advocating meritocratic principles, but Patrizi was the first to devise institutional measures to elevate the worthy. He laid out specific procedures for discovering and promoting merit in the citizen body and for insulating the order of magistrates from the power of wealthy individuals of high status. He recommended best practices for public deliberation in assemblies that would amplify the voices of the wisest citizens and prevent partisan suppression of good counsel. He proposed new standards for the legal profession to reduce venality and a system of appeals courts to provide recourse for those mistreated by unfair judges. He was the first political thinker since Aristotle to devote sustained attention to the concept of citizenship, and he proposed a form of merit citizenship, inspired by Aristotle, to optimize rights-based conceptions of citizenship inherited from the medieval popular *comune*.

Patrizi's boldest proposals for reform addressed inequalities in private wealth and the misuse of the city's collective resources. Setting moral standards for the use of wealth had been a concern from the beginning of the humanist movement in the Trecento, but Patrizi went well beyond his predecessors.[6] In this respect he was far more radical than his more famous successors, Machiavelli and Guicciardini. For theoretical daring his proposed measures can be compared only to the fictive institutions of Thomas More's *Utopia*.

Patrizi proposed that, when founding a new republic, the collective property of the state be divided into thirds: two thirds would belong to the state, and the final third would be assigned to private proprietors. The first public third would be given over to religious uses and the second public third would support the poor and the military. This ideal distribution would accomplish four objectives. It would ensure that private wealth could never challenge or corrupt the public power. It would allow the state to support the poor by offering them opportunities for honest labor and help protect them from becoming debt slaves of the rich. It would provide support for an independent military so that the republic would not need to rely on hiring mercenaries, which empowered the wealthy. And by making the republic's ecclesiastical institutions economically dependent on the state, potential conflicts between church and state would be reduced.

In the case of existing republics, Patrizi's counsels were less radical. He defends private property but recommends that the city-state should place limits on the total amount that any one citizen can accumulate. It should regulate profits and outlaw usury. In general, the pursuit of mercantile gain was to be subordinated to the needs of family and community. A moral economy, Patrizi held, could be achieved by fostering in merchants and bankers the virtues of frugality and generosity and by teaching them to disdain greed and luxury. The republic could help by building strong civic norms of acceptable behavior. Among these, Patrizi emphasizes the importance of work for all citizens and the avoidance of idleness. No one should live entirely on rents or devote himself wholly to pleasure.

Patrizi was, finally, as a true representative of the larger Renaissance movement, an advocate of what I have called elsewhere the "virtuous environment." Following the lead of Leon Battista Alberti and of his own patron, Pope Pius II, he was the first political theorist, to my knowledge, to explore the potential of urban planning to shape civic values and to facilitate a free way of life. Drawing on the expertise of architects and on classical antiquity for inspiration, magistrates and founders of new cities should make their cities strong and beautiful. Public and private spaces should remind citizens of their glorious Roman ancestors. The fine arts were to be cultivated with a view to forming virtue, piety, and love of country. The city should also encourage the study of poetry, oratory, history, and philosophy to ennoble the minds of its citizens.

*       *       *

Patrizi's status as the most substantive theoretician of humanist meritocracy does not exhaust his significance for the history of Western political thought. He was also the first political theorist in European history to have access to almost the entire corpus of ancient Greek political thought we possess today.[7] A highly accomplished Hellenist himself, he was able to study and synthesize the newly available Greek literature that was rapidly filling the shelves of Italian libraries in the quattrocento, both in the original and in new Latin translations made by his fellow humanists. Medieval scholastics had been able to study Aristotle's *Politics* after the Dominican friar William of Moerbeke translated the work into Latin around 1260, and the encounter with Aristotle made a deep impression on theorists from Thomas Aquinas to Marsilius of Padua. But the translation movement of the Renaissance vastly extended the Latin West's access to the heritage of ancient Greece. The medievals had not possessed any of the political works of Plato, Xenophon, Isocrates, Polybius, Dio Chrysostom, or Plutarch. They had no access to the political history of the Greeks written by Herodotus, Thucydides, or Xenophon, nor to the Greek historians of the Roman Empire such as Polybius, Appian, Dionysius of Halicarnassus, Diodorus Siculus, and Arrian. Patrizi read and excerpted all these authors, and many other Greek and Latin writers as well.

Patrizi is also worth studying as the principal inventor of a new style of political writing based on the collection and analysis of ancient literary, historical, and philosophical texts. His manner of composition is apt to disappoint modern readers, especially if they come to him from the study of Machiavelli. Patrizi is not a pithy writer, and he does not display the Florentine's analytical brilliance. That is in part because, unlike Machiavelli, he is not trying to be clever and provocative, but judicious and learned. He writes in what I have labeled, somewhat cumbrously, the historico-prudential mode. That manner of writing was pioneered by Petrarch in his letters and treatises, where historical examples and authorities are marshalled to prove some moral point. Patrizi takes over this method but is far more exhaustive in his use of historical examples and far readier to engage in debate with his authorities, pitting some against others, sifting out the best views after a careful weighing of goals and consequences. He consulted well over 150 Greek and Latin authors—an astonishing number in his day—in compiling his treatises, and cites thousands of classical examples and dicta. The result is that his treatises seem very long-winded to us moderns, who are less prone than our ancestors to luxuriate in banquets of erudition. Like other authors who wrote in this tradition, such as Bodin, Lipsius, and Grotius, the weight of learning sometimes threatens to obscure the original elements in his thought. Later writers in the historico-prudential tradition, like Montesquieu and the authors of the *Federalist Papers,* understood that to influence a wider range of readers they would have to wear their learning more lightly.

In his own time, standards were different. Though Patrizi is almost unknown today, that has not been always the case. His fame in the later Renaissance, as is shown by the printing history of his works, was enormous. In the sixteenth century his political writings were published more often than either More's *Utopia* or Erasmus's *Education of a Christian Prince*. True, printings of Machiavelli's three great political treatises—*The Prince*, the *Discourses*, and *The Art of War*—slightly outnumbered the printings of Patrizi's two major works, *How to Found a Republic* and *On Kingship and the Education of a King*. But on the evidence of their printing history, Patrizi was arguably more influential among the highly educated. Editions of Machiavelli were mostly in Italian, a European language of culture by the later sixteenth century, but Patrizi's works were far better known in Latin, the international language of scholarship. They were also translated into Italian, French, Spanish, and German, and epitomes of his works circulated in Latin, French, and English.[8] After 1610 his works ceased to be attractive to European publishers and readers and explicit citations from his works are hard to find. Presumably his form of virtue-based meritocracy was less relevant in a world where states increasingly sought to base their legitimacy and their principles of public order directly on religious doctrine.

There are also other reasons his voice has been absent from political discourse over the last four centuries. Patrizi lived quietly in a small port town in southern Italy for most of his later life while composing his major works, and he was evidently unskilled in the arts of self-promotion. He had difficulty applying the *ultima manus* to his writings and, once finished, preferred to circulate them in manuscript form among a select few. Like other refined literary spirits of his day, it would seem, he was reluctant to submit his writings to the vulgarity of print. It was almost an accident that Patrizi's works were printed by an obscure French humanist in 1518–1519, even though, once printed, they obtained immediate celebrity. They, not he: for no contemporary had written his biography and the sixteenth century knew nothing about the life of the man who became known to the reading public as "il gran' Patritio." Crucially, he was not included in the authoritative collection of *elogia* written in 1546 by Paolo Giovio, the most imporant source for the lives of quattrocento literati used in early modern reference works.

The absence of a biography helps explain why Patrizi and his great political treatises have been neglected in modern scholarship. It is widely accepted today that, to understand political thinkers who lived in other times and places, we need to set their writings in the context of their life experience. In Patrizi's case we have no biographical study that takes advantage of all the sources now available. The last substantial study devoted to Patrizi and his thought was written in Italian in 1936.[9] Since then there have been only brief sketches of his life in a few reference works.[10] No studies of Patrizi before the present one have considered the key insights provided by his two major poetical collections: the *Poemata* in four books, scribally published in 1461, and the collection of 345 Latin epigrams composed between 1467 and 1488. Only a handful of these poems have been printed, and the complete collections had to be consulted in manuscript for this study. Patrizi's familiar letters have also been largely neglected. Fortunately, in 2014 Paola De Capua published, again in Italian, a major study of his correspondence, which provided ample quotations and analyses of 66 familiar letters scattered in miscellaneous manuscripts, along with summaries of 153 archival documents.[11] Thanks to her work, we now have for the first time the ability to look into the mind of this minor nobleman from Siena, a city which he himself described as ranking "if not second, at least third among the republics of our time."

The study of Patrizi's life offers us not just a background for interpreting his political thought, valuable though that is. De Capua's research also surveyed in print for the first time a remarkable dossier of 175 letters compiled by Patrizi himself, an almost weekly record of his experiences during his three years serving as governor of Foligno, a major urban center in the Papal State. To my knowledge this is the only sizable set of sources surviving from the Italian Renaissance that documents in real time, as it were, the efforts of a humanist to reform a government over which he had full authority.[12] It provides a priceless witness to the interplay of thought and action in the work of a humanist reformer and lights up for us as never before the pages of his two great political treatises.

⚬        ⚬        ⚬

A final word about the use in these pages of the modern term "meritocracy," invented as recently as 1958 by the British sociologist and politician Michael Young. There is no ready equivalent for this term in Patrizi's Latin, and strict historical practice might shun it as anachronistic.[13] Yet some such term is surely needed. Quattrocento humanist usage takes political merit to be a function of "true nobility," a term of art in humanist writing of the Renaissance. True nobility is an attribute of persons who deserve to rule others because they possess good character and a good classical education, including an education in "eloquence," meaning high-level communication skills.[14] The opposite of true nobility is a merely hereditary nobility, consisting of persons who have done nothing to deserve rule over others, and whose rule will therefore be experienced as tyranny by the ruled. True nobility, in other words, needs to be earned, not only by the upwardly mobile but also, and especially, by those who have inherited elite status from their ancestors.

True nobility was earned through virtue (*virtus*) or human excellence. As defined by Aristotle, the virtues were stable habits of action and thought that enabled one to live the best possible human life and to serve one's community in the best possible way. Through virtue both the individual and his or her community flourished and achieved the highest kind of human happiness. A virtuous person who had the capacity to benefit the community had merit or merits (*meritum, merita*). Patrizi routinely used these terms and their derivatives. Those whose meritorious public service had earned them a leading position in the community had *dignitas*, personal rank or standing or prestige. A political system that selects for the most meritorious persons to act in leadership roles is properly called meritocratic.

"Aristocracy," rule of the best in Aristotle's theoretical language, might seem at first sight a less anachronistic alternative to meritocracy. The term "aristocracy," however, suffers from two defects. First, most people today take "aristocracy" to mean hereditary aristocracy, titled lords and ladies, the sort of people who appear in Debrett's *Peerage* or the *Almanach de Gotha*. But this sense of aristocracy is the opposite of Patrizi's meaning. Second, readers familiar with Aristotelian constitutional analysis are likely to think of "aristocracy" as a type of regime, one of the canonical six constitutions of *Politics* 3. Such an understanding would also be foreign to Patrizian meritocracy, a concept that is conceptually prior to and distinct from regime type.

Using the term "meritocracy," moreover, permits constructive engagement with modern Chinese political theory, which for a generation now has been mining a particularly rich vein of thought running through the intellectual history of imperial China. Recent studies of Chinese meritocracy see it as a characteristic product of the Confucian governing tradition going back to the Han dynasty, but also as a source of inspiration for the reform of modern Chinese govenment. Imperial Chinese meritocracy presents many interesting parallels with the aims of quattrocento humanists, and as I have argued elsewhere, modern Chinese meritocratic theory can often be illuminating for students of Renaissance political thought.[15] Contemporary Chinese political philosophers, for example, distinguish two senses of virtue politics (*dezhi*): (1) as a type of constitution and (2) as a type of political excellence to which any regime may aspire—meritorious governance in a general sense.[16] The latter sense is how I am using the term here, and it well describes, I believe, Patrizi's own goals as a political reformer.

◦      ◦      ◦

But enough of terminological quibbles. Patrizi is an author who deserves many more readers, perhaps especially so in our time. To indulge for a moment in further anachronistic language, he is, in our terms, both liberal and conservative. He is liberal in wanting to limit the influence of wealth and hereditary privilege in politics as well as in his deep belief, shared with most other Renaissance humanists, in the power of education to improve humanity. Though no utopian, he held that human beings are not necessarily subject to natural patterns such as the rise and fall of states but can get control of their own political fates through knowledge and the power of human virtue. But he was a conservative in the finest sense of wanting to preserve what was beautiful and good in the Western tradition, and he understood that it is far easier to destroy good things than to preserve them. He feared revolutions, whether instigated by a mob, an oligarchy, or a tyrant. His ideal state was built above all for stability and peaceful flourishing, not for conquest. He thought the most important political virtue was prudence and the most important resource of the prudent statesman was the wisdom of classical antiquity, which for him included the wisdom of ancient Egypt, Persia, and India. He is never dogmatic and opposes the scholastic approach to political theory as too theoretical, too much reliant on knock-down arguments that change no one's behavior. Unlike the scholastics he is deeply aware of the importance of restraining unruly passions in politics and the need for sound customs, learning, and piety in both statesmen and in the citizen body. In short, he is a writer of great sanity, balance, and wisdom—qualities not always found among political theorists but ones that in all times and places, especially our own, are as needed as they are rare.

ONE

# The Formation of a Political Philosopher

## The Young Patrizi: Poet, Teacher, and Statesman

Francesco Patrizi's experience of politics, diplomacy, and government, for a man destined to become the greatest political philosopher of the humanist movement, could hardly have been bettered.
A comparison with Machiavelli's career may help underscore the
point.

Machiavelli has often been praised (not least by himself) as a man
of action, no mere armchair theorist. Before setting up as a political
writer, he had been a second-tier official in the Florentine republic
with extensive experience in diplomacy and the military affairs of
the republic. Thanks to his father's illegitimacy, he could never hold
political office himself, but he was able to observe the workings of
government at close hand, across the open balustrade separating the
office of the Florentine chancery from the apartments of the Priors
in the Palazzo Vecchio.[1]

Patrizi's political experience, by contrast, was far more extensive
and varied, and he held a number of high offices with real executive
powers. He was born on 24 February 1413 into the most important
hereditary bloc of political families in Siena, the *Nove,* which remained the dominant force in Sienese politics for most of his lifetime. He held numerous offices in the Sienese republic, including the
priorate—the republic's governing body—and other executive posts
in the city's territories. He headed at least six major ambassadorial

missions in the decade before the coup that led to his exile. He also enjoyed a prominent social position in the city. He married, had four children, and maintained a large household with an urban palazzo and rural properties. He was a professor of literature in Siena's public *Studio* (or university) and private tutor to Achille Petrucci, offspring of the city's most important political family of the quattrocento and a future civic leader.[2]

After his exile from Siena in 1457, Patrizi supported himself for a while as private tutor to the son of the Milanese ambassador to Florence. In that capacity, he met leading statesmen and princes from Tuscany and northern Italy. When his friend Enea Silvio Piccolomini became Pope Pius II in 1458, Patrizi took holy orders and was made the bishop of Gaeta. Soon thereafter, Pius appointed him governor of the city of Foligno and its territories, a key post in the Papal State. After Pius's death in 1464, Patrizi's position in Foligno became untenable owing to a popular uprising, and he retired to administer his diocese in Gaeta, a port city in the Kingdom of Naples. The Kingdom was ruled by Ferdinand I of Naples (known as Ferrante), the most powerful monarch of the peninsula. In Gaeta Patrizi finished his two major political treatises, *De institutione reipublicae* (finished 1471 / 1472) and *De regno et regis institutione* (1483 / 1484). His life in that small city was mostly a retired one, but even so he was called upon to advise the heir to the throne, Alfonso of Calabria, and to represent the Kingdom as the Aragonese *orator* (or ambassador) on at least two major public occasions—the marriage of Alfonso with Ippolita Maria Sforza in Milan (1465), and the ceremonies for the coronation of Pope Innocent VIII (1484).

*     *     *

Such is Patrizi's life in outline. But to understand the context and therefore the intent of Patrizi's political writings, we will need a much more fine-grained account of his life experiences in Siena, Rome, Naples, and elsewhere. In particular we can profit from understanding the development of the Sienese republic in the Renaissance, which produced institutions quite different from those of Florence, more familiar to English-language students of the Renaissance. We will also consider the large body of unpublished Latin poetry Patrizi left behind, which has hitherto not been exploited by students of his thought.

As the scion of an old and established family in Siena, Francesco must have known from childhood that he would be expected to take part in the political life of his native city. Later in life he claimed that his family was descended of ancient Roman patrician stock and that he had the documentation to prove it.[3] But when we first catch sight of him in the historical record as a university student during the 1420s and 1430s, it seems that his fondest aspiration was to distinguish himself as a poet, writing in classical Latin. The Sienese elite in those early decades of the quattrocento had begun to embrace the gospel of Renaissance humanism, first proclaimed by Petrarch in the mid-fourteenth century and afterward spread by his followers and admirers throughout northern Italy and down into Tuscany, Rome, and the Kingdom of Naples.[4] In the early decades of the humanist movement, Latin poetry written in a classical style was the most prestigious accomplishment of those who, inspired by Petrarch's example, devoted themselves to the renaissance of ancient education, literature, and philosophy.

In the early fifteenth century, while Florence under the leadership of Leonardo Bruni was mastering the art of classical prose, Siena was becoming a center for the revival of ancient Latin poetry. A powerful impulse came from two young Sicilians who had come to Siena to study law with their fellow Sicilian, the famous jurist Niccolò de' Tudeschi. Antonio Beccadelli, called Panormita (b. 1394), composed in Siena the first book of his notorious poetical cycle, *The Hermaphrodite,* a celebration of the brothels of Florence, later dedicated to an embarrassed Cosimo de'Medici. In 1430 he received his reward and was appointed court poet to Filippo Maria Visconti, duke of Milan.[5] The other Sicilian was Giovanni Marrasio (b. 1400/1404), who revived the Latin love elegy in his poetical cycle, called *Angelinetum* or *Angelina's Garden* (1429). The cycle was set in Siena and portrays a *sodalitas* or coterie of aspiring young Latin poets who would gather at the Fonte Gaia—built by the sculptor Jacopo della Quercia in the new classical style—that stood opposite the vast Palazzo Pubblico on the Campo. There they would declaim their poetry publicly, sometimes with young ladies looking down on them from the windows of nearby palazzi.[6] Most of the young poets were, however, Sienese, including the young Enea Silvio Piccolomini, later Patrizi's chief patron, and Andreoccio Petrucci, who became a leading politician in Siena as well as Patrizi's main sponsor in public life. As in the case of Panormita, Enea Silvio's poetical accomplishments won him fame and fortune when in 1442 he was named imperial poet in the court of Emperor Frederick III. Marrasio, by contrast, tried unsuccessfully for well over a decade to win a post as a court poet before returning reluctantly to his native Sicily to practice medicine.

Patrizi must have drawn inspiration from this new cultural phenomenon, for as he wrote much later in his *De republica,* he had "cultivated poetry from his earliest youth."[7] Like Machiavelli, he studied and wrote poetry long before dedicating himself to political philosophy. As late as 1460 he still thought of himself, and was thought of by others, primarily as a poet.[8] He ultimately assembled two major verse collections, the *Poematum libri IV* (*Four Books of Poems*), dedicated to Pius II around 1461, and the *Epigrammaton liber* (*Book of Epigrams*), containing 345 epigrams collected during his Gaeta period.

Both of these collections contain a few poems that look back to the erotic interests of the Fonte Gaia group.[9] But the *Poemata* in particular reveal a more exalted poetical ambition. That collection deals with a wide range of subjects in a variety of ancient meters, including difficult Horatian meters on which Patrizi was a scholarly expert as well as one of their first Renaissance practitioners.[10] The richness of its vocabulary, much of it drawn from Silver Latin models, is dazzling. The collection was modeled on Statius's *Silvae,* an ancient poetical cycle rediscovered by Poggio Bracciolini in 1417. The *Poemata* included long poems in the epic manner celebrating the famous men of his day; a didactic poem on the origins of music; and poems on love and married life. It also contained poems reflecting on personal experience—describing, for instance, the cruelty of plague, the sufferings of exile, the hostility directed at poets, the pleasures of country life and learned leisure—and a poem of self-criticism for his own idleness and low spirits. There are also three highly innovative religious poems: two sapphic odes to the Blessed Virgin and an *Ecologue on the Nativity of Christ,* a pastoral dialogue that has been described as "the first pastoral treatment of a Christian theme" in the Renaissance.[11] Some poems also bear on politics, such as the poem "On the Injustice of Peoples" addressed "to Italians." There and elsewhere in the collection Patrizi presents himself as a peace-loving *vates* or poet-seer who reluctantly predicts the decline of Italy into war and tyranny owing to its moral corruption and thirst for riches.[12] The *Epigrammata,* written contemporaneously with his political treatises, occasionally reflect on those works and their audience, and also shed light, as we shall see, on his milieu and the evolution of his political opinions.[13]

This considerable body of poetry is far more accomplished and innovative than anything composed by the other poets working in Siena during the first half of the early fifteenth century, and is in no way inferior to the best Latin poetry of the early Renaissance. Yet Patrizi's poetry has been almost entirely neglected by scholars and remains mostly unpublished. Why? Patrizi's descent into obscurity can be explained in various ways. One is the undue neglect of Sienese humanism in general: *Senensia non leguntur.* Patrizi also committed the cardinal sin of not writing any original works in the vernacular, thus escaping the attention of students of Italian literature.[14] His self-imposed isolation in Gaeta during his later life may well have played a role, as well as his tenuous connections with humanist circles in Rome and the papal curia after the death of Pius II in 1464. Patrizi seems to have been inexpert in the arts of self-promotion, and, like many humanists, always wrote for small groups of powerful men rather than for *le grand public* (which of course hardly existed in his day). He never learned to take advantage of the printing press and its potential for generating fame.[15] The same general circumstances also

help explain the neglect of Patrizi's political writings in the two
decades following his death.[16]

◆     ◆     ◆

That Patrizi's Latin poetry scaled new heights of excellence and innovation was in large part due to the profound effect upon him of a
great teacher: Francesco Filelfo, Italy's finest Latin poet and Greek
scholar in the middle decades of the fifteenth century. Filelfo taught
in Siena for only four years (1434–1438), and his presence in the
city was far less transformative than the teaching of Manuel Chrysoloras had been in Florence during the last years of the Trecento.
Still, it was significant. Filelfo came to Siena from a teaching post in
Florence. There he had sided with an aristocratic faction against
Cosimo de'Medici, and when Cosimo returned to power in 1434 after
his brief exile, Filelfo was obliged to decamp to Siena. (He later claimed
to have survived there an assassination attempt orchestrated by
Cosimo.)[17] Filelfo's teaching in Siena was sponsored by Andreoccio
Petrucci, Patrizi's patron, and Andreoccio's ally, Barnaba Pannalini,
later the humanist chancellor of the city.[18]

Patrizi, then in his early twenties, turned out to be the principal
beneficiary of Filelfo's teaching in Siena. What Filelfo had to offer
the Sienese, above all else, was the opportunity to learn Greek. Before the regular teaching of Greek in Italian classical schools was established during the later quattrocento, knowledge of the language
was rare and hard to come by.[19] Western scholars who knew Greek,
like Leonardo Bruni and Guarino of Verona, enjoyed immense prestige. Though Filelfo's tenure in Siena was brief, it was long enough
to transmit to Patrizi a high degree of proficiency in the language as
well as a lifelong devotion to Homer. After Filelfo's departure, Patrizi tried in his turn to pass on his knowledge of Greek to his own
pupils, among them Agostino Dati, who later composed the most
popular textbook of Latin style of the quattrocento. Patrizi and Dati
remained the only two native Sienese scholars of the fifteenth century
to master Greek.[20]

Patrizi, to be sure, never scaled the highest peaks of Hellenism that some other Italian scholars of the Renaissance attained. Unlike Guarino, Bruni, and others, he published no translations from the Greek. We have no compositions in Greek prose from his hand. Filelfo was one of the very few native Italians—Angelo Poliziano, later, was another—to leave a body of poetry in Greek, but from the Sienese poet we have only a single, awkward couplet.[21] Study of the sources for his great political treatises, however, shows he was not entirely reliant on the translation movement of the quattrocento for his access to Greek sources.[22]

Even more important for his later career as a political philosopher was the attitude he absorbed from Filelfo about Greek studies. Filelfo was a tireless champion of the value of Greek literature and philosophy—often proclaiming, with questionable tact, that those who knew no Greek were half-educated and could never really hope to write Latin well. Patrizi too became a champion of Hellenism. It is surely through Filelfo's influence that he became the first Latin writer on politics since Cicero to draw upon a wide range of Greek political history, biography, geography, oratory, poetry, and philosophy in order to stimulate his own thinking about the best republic and the best kingdom.

Thanks also to Filelfo, Patrizi was able to improve his already considerable mastery of Latin eloquence, a subject he would later teach in Siena's university. He acquired from him as well an interest in the less common Latin poetical meters, where Filelfo's own poetry eventually would provide models.[23] But for our purposes it was Filelfo's deep knowledge of Greek philosophy, a knowledge that went well beyond the marquee names of Plato and Aristotle, that was to prove most valuable for Patrizi's intellectual development. Filelfo's vast and learned correspondence is studded, enticingly for a humanist, with citations and allusions to a whole lost continent of philosophy to which quattrocento Latinists did not have access—yet.[24] Patrizi would be among the first humanist literati to explore that continent and mine its riches for political philosophy. Particularly innovative was his able reconstruction of Academic Skepticism in a long letter of 1445, using materials from Cicero's philosophical writings and Diogenes Laertius's *Lives of the Philosophers,* the latter recently translated by Ambrogio Traversari (1431). According to the great authority on Renaissance skepticism, Charles B. Schmitt, Patrizi was among the first to recognize the Platonic paternity of the skeptical tradition and "to view the critical, quasi-skeptical, and probablistic elements of the teachings of Socrates and Plato as an integral part of the tradition."[25]

Patrizi's fascination with philosophy, however, had begun long before Filelfo arrived in Siena. We can trace it back at least to the year 1426, when as a precocious youth of thirteen he was induced to give a speech for the beginning of the academic year before the Sienese priors and members of the Studio or university. As Paul Grendler has shown, the mid-1420s were precisely the period in which humanists throughout Italy were just beginning their long campaign to introduce humanistic subjects such as rhetoric, poetry, and moral philosophy into university curricula.[26] They had met with some success already at the most prestigious Italian university, Bologna. Siena's hated rival Florence had also been experimenting with special lecturers to teach Greek, poetry, and moral philosophy. Patrizi's speech can be seen as opening a Sienese front in this campaign.

In one of the two surviving manuscripts the work is called *In Praise of Philosophy;* in the other it is called *In Praise of Study of the Finest Arts.*[27] In the speech the *bonae artes,* a synonym for the humanities, are said to be all included under the name of philosophy. As it develops, however, the speech shows that Patrizi understood philosophy in the broadest sense of the word, as the *fons et origo* of all subjects taught at the university, including the professional studies, theology, law, medicine; the quadrivial studies, arithmetic, music, geometry, astronomy; and the arts of speech: grammar, dialectic and rhetoric.[28] Of these studies, theology, law, and Latin eloquence are given the most praise, but all the finest arts are said to flow down like rivulets from the fountainhead of philosophical wisdom. Though most of its allusions to Greek authors are taken (silently) from Cicero and Quintilian, the speech reveals how Patrizi was already seeking to move from the brackish waters of Roman philosophy upstream to the pure fountains of Hellenic wisdom.

In the *De laudibus philosophiae* Patrizi offers his hearers three grounds for studying philosophy, also called "the arts of gentlemen" (*ingenui*). Philosophy in its purest form transforms the soul, making it finer, more virtuous, more resilient to the blows of fortune, and better able to bear mental suffering. Secondly, mastering the best arts gives one fame and personal distinction and opens the way to earthly glory. Finally, and most significantly for this study, Patrizi emphasizes theology's role in maintaining a peaceful, harmonious, and flourishing city—theology here being understood as instruction in piety. Patrizi also emphasizes the civic functions of civil law—reformed so as to model itself anew on ancient Roman law—and above all the ancient art of eloquence. The speech presents a unified vision of learning that joins professional studies to the seven liberal arts and makes a case for the inclusion of humane learning and eloquence in the university curriculum as instruments of good government.

To be sure, it is implausible to suppose that so mature a vision of civic education proceeded from the head of a thirteen-year-old.[29] It undoubtedly reflects, rather, the governing philosophy of those around him: Andreoccio Petrucci, a humanist and statesman, and his faithful lieutenant, Giovanni di Franchino Patrizi, Francesco's father, himself a man of considerable humanistic culture.[30] We would not go far wrong to see in the speech an expression of the cultural politics of Siena's leading alliance of political families, the *Nove*, to which both Andreoccio Petrucci and Giovanni Patrizi belonged. Indeed, we cannot understand the shape of Francesco Patrizi's career or the context of his mature writings without some grasp of the regime in control of the Sienese republic for most of his lifetime.

⸱　　⸱　　⸱

The Nove was the most eminent of the five hereditary blocs, or *monti,* of families that had formed regimes for different periods of time in Siena during the thirteenth and fourteenth centuries. The others were the Noblemen or *Gentilhuomini*, the Dodici (the Twelve), the Riformatori, and the *Popolo* or People. (*Popolo* in Sienese politics had a broad and a narrow sense: in the broad sense it meant non-nobles; in the narrow sense it referred to one of the five *monti*, a delimited group of families able to hold office in the regime.) For most of the fifteenth century the nobles were excluded from the highest offices in Siena, though admitted to some lesser magistracies. The Dodici—historic enemies of the Nove—were excluded from all offices, despite the wealth and prominence of some of its members. Offices were thus shared principally among the remaining "trinity" of *monti*, with leadership, after 1402, coming as a rule from the ranks of the Nove. The virtue politics of the humanists was embraced most eagerly by some of the excluded noble clans, such as the Tolomei and the Piccolomini, but also by leading Nove families like the Petrucci and the Patrizi.[31]

The Nove had by far the most prestige owing to the memory of its *buon governo* of Siena during the city's golden age, from 1287 to 1355. It was under the Nine Governors and Defenders of the City, the Commune, and the People of Siena that the city solidified its position as the great rival to Florence in the international banking system of the day, servicing above all the financial needs of the papacy and other ecclesiastical institutions. It was under the Nove that Siena came firmly into the Guelf Party, with its historic commitment to city-state liberty and its traditions of political loyalty to the pope. It was under the Nove that Siena became a major capital of European art, with great artists such as Duccio di Buoninsegna, Simone Martini, and the Lorenzetti brothers. It was Ambrogio Lorenzetti who painted the famous *Allegory of Good and Bad Government* (1338) in the Communal Palace, a visual representation of the political ideals of the regime. The Nove built or began to build what are still the most notable monuments of the city: the Palazzo Pubblico with its extraordinary bell tower, the theater-like Piazza del Campo (built for the *recreatio civium*) fronting the Palazzo Pubblico, and Siena's magnificent Duomo, the most beautiful in Tuscany. The

Nove, indeed, for longevity, prosperity, and stability was arguably the most successful example of republican government in the Italian Middle Ages. In a period when the vast majority of Italian communes were exchanging popular government for signorial rule, Siena stood alongside Venice, Florence, and Lucca as the sole survivors of the great age of the city-republics in thirteenth-century Italy.

The Nove is often described as a mercantile oligarchy, but the term is misleading in several respects. Siena's largest banking families were surely powerful forces within it, but the regime was nevertheless a broad and relatively inclusive one. Minor nobility—like the Patrizi—as well as middle-class artisans and tradesmen could also hold the highest offices, and some members of the greater noble *case* were permitted to serve on lesser magistracies. Only the high nobility from families judged incapable of civil equality in the proscriptions of 1277, like the Tolomei and Piccolomini, as well as the poor and wage-earning classes at the bottom of society, were formally excluded from office. Naturally the high nobility found indirect ways to exercise political power, and one of Patrizi's ancestors, Niccolino di Buonaventura Patrizi, a factor for the Tolomei, must have served their interests when holding high office. He and his two brothers Tino and Tizio are known to have been seated on the Nove many times between 1306 and 1338.[32] The term "mercantile oligarchy" is also inaccurate in that Siena, unlike Florence, never possessed a large manufacturing base producing textiles for international markets. And because banking wealth in Siena tended to end up invested in agricultural property, large landowners in Sienese territory were also well represented in its ruling regime.[33]

There is a third respect, too, in which "oligarchy" is a misnomer. The regime of the Nine was not only socially inclusive; it also had formal meritocratic elements that set it apart from republican regimes like those in Florence, Lucca, and Genoa, which relied more heavily on sortition to select magistrates. Although there was some limited use of the lot after 1318, co-optation and election remained an important mode of filling Sienese magistracies well into the fifteenth century. The practice of election made it possible for the Consistoro, the supreme governing body of the Nine, to create an informal *cursus honorum,* testing officials in lesser offices like the *Biccherna* (state finances) and the *Gabella* (tax collection) before promoting them to the highest offices. Furthermore, in seeming imitation of the Roman Senate, former chief magistrates automatically became *riseduti,* members of the Council of the People, the chief deliberative body advising the Consistoro. This may be contrasted with the Florentine practice of choosing the Signoria's advisory bodies by lot from electoral lists, without considering its advisors' political experience or competence. Finally, the Nove was careful to isolate judicial from political decision-making. This was a version of judicial independence that went further than the modern variety, in that judges and lawyers were prohibited entirely from holding political office. That measure did much to prevent the legal system from becoming politicized. As elsewhere in Italy, the chief judicial officer of the city, the Capitano del Popolo, by law could not be a Sienese citizen. Political parties, as usually in premodern republics, were branded as *conventicole,* or potentially seditious factions, and prohibited. In principle, political debate was supposed to happen in public and never in secret, as in other premodern republics.

By the fifteenth century the political system established by the Nove and their allies had undergone certain modifications, but its ideals and institutions remained largely unchanged. It had become somewhat less inclusive: it now prohibited from office the *monte* of the Dodici, formed in the late Trecento. This was a group of around five hundred powerful people who as a result of their proscription became permanently resentful and alienated from the regime. The proscription of such groups would later be strongly condemned by Patrizi in the *De republica.* On the other hand, thanks to border disputes, the regime was under continual pressure to grant Sienese citizenship rights to elites originating in the towns of its territory. Patrizi would also later criticize the broadening of citizenship rights in this way. By the quattrocento, too, lawyers, judges, and other university-trained professionals were regularly admitted to important roles in the regime, and the office of the foreign Capitano del Popolo had sunk into insignificance.

In the fifteenth century, moreover, Siena, like its rival republic Florence, began to experience more strongly the pull of one-man rule. Within the *monte* of the Nine, the Petrucci family, under the leadership of Siena's military hero Antonio di Ceccho Rossi Petrucci and his brother Andreoccio, appeared to be seeking a position in the city analogous to that of the early Medici in Florence. Popular and traditionalist opponents accused Antonio in particular of aiming at tyranny. Except for brief periods of populist resistance in the 1450s and again in the 1480s, the Petrucci remained a dominant force within the Sienese republic. In the end Pandolfo Petrucci—praised by Machiavelli for his political skill—succeeded in establishing his "quasi-lordship" over the city in 1497.

＊　　　＊　　　＊

Like other rulers of questionable political legitimacy, the Petrucci were attracted to the virtue politics of the humanist movement. No doubt they (like the Medici) saw the new kind of moral legitimacy it offered as a means of justifying their preeminence. They had groomed Francesco Patrizi since boyhood to be an exemplar of virtuous leadership. He was eloquent and deeply learned in the humanities—an ideal avatar of what they stood for as the managers of a political alliance: wise government in the service of the common good, inspired by ancient models.[34] He rose quickly in the republic's *cursus honorum*. Patrizi first held the office of prior in 1440 at the age of twenty-seven. Thanks to the influence of his Petrucci sponsors he eventually succeeded Filelfo as professor of rhetoric at the Sienese Studio (1441–1446), teaching Ciceronian virtue and eloquence to the youth of Siena while awaiting higher public responsibilities. This was no mere academic appointment, since for the humanists, eloquence—the study of how to motivate one's fellow citizens through argument and study of the passions—was a key part of political education.

While teaching at the Studio, Patrizi also served as a private tutor to Achille Petrucci (ca. 1427–1499), son of Antonio and a future leader of the Petrucci clan in the second half of the quattrocento. In this role the young humanist composed his first work on politics, the letter-treatise *De gerendo magistratu* of 1446, addressed to Achille. It already contained numerous themes *in ovo* that would later be deepened and elaborated in his great works of political philosophy. The work was never published, and is still unpublished, but it enjoyed some circulation in manuscript form.[35]

In the letter, young Achille, aged nineteen, has just been elected a prior of Siena, the city's highest honor, defeating two older and more experienced candidates in their forties and fifties. This is a great mark of distinction, writes Patrizi, for you now hold the magistracy that all other officials must obey. You should realize the gravity of your task. You now rule in a city that has long stood as the domicile of Tuscan liberty and has had many excellent senators. Our city has long been the only one not to be vexed with the factions and wars that have afflicted the rest of Italy. Other peoples call us an abode of true peace and tranquillity. Your job is to keep it that way.

You have achieved the highest civic distinction at your age thanks to your study of the Greek and Latin philosophers, who have nurtured the roots of virtue in you. You know that there is nothing evil except what seems shameful to the best minds, and that virtue alone is enough to live well and blessedly in all things. Virtue is the most important quality in a magistrate. It will win you praise, glory, and a favorable reputation among the people. A leader should want nothing more than to be heeded by all and to procure the favor of the people for himself. Leaders who are dear to the people rule them in safety and easily persuade them to do whatever they want. But their rule is brief who try to be feared rather than loved. Fear causes hatred. That is why the maxim *oderint dum metuant* ("let them hate so long as they fear"—the motto of the monstrous Roman emperor Caligula) is badly said. It violates the basic principles of physics. Violent motion is inherently unstable, hence violence cannot last as a principle of rule. Nobody wants hatred for themselves rather than love, and if you do, you are an enemy to yourself despite your deep learning. The magistrate who is dear to the citizens, who is loved and praised by them, achieves lasting fame and influence. Though strictly speaking you should not care about popular opinion, especially the opinions of bad men—conscience alone ought to be the theater of true virtue—Cicero reminds us that glory follows virtue like a shadow. Glory should not be the motive of virtue, in other words, but virtue wins glory nonetheless. Your magistracy will reveal your character to all, as the wise Greek Bias of Priene teaches us. So keep before you the image of every famous and brave man of antiquity you have ever read about. Know that those who deserve well of the republic are remembered forever and rewarded in heaven.

Patrizi follows these Ciceronian sentiments with an exhortation to observe the city's laws and preserve them unchanged. He imparts a good many other *sententiae* on fairness and care for others, as well as on the speech and deportment expected of a magistrate. A civic official should also encourage learning and virtue in others. He should show the highest honor to the best men, the men of virtue, the learned men who distinguish themselves in the *bonae artes*, for it is impossible for any regime to be strong and stable where men of virtue are not honored. He should avoid war like the plague, because war always threatens a regime with instability. Let him use public funds wisely and avoid high taxes, which will make him hated. "Citizens hate to be stripped bare by persons from whom they rightly expect profit and advantage." Scarcity and high bread prices are to be avoided at all costs as a peril to the state. City guards and the backing of condottieri will count for nothing if the people are angry and there is no food in the markets. Nothing can calm a famished mob and no statecraft can prevail against it.[36]

Wise words, which Patrizi might well have remembered in 1456, when famine contributed to the political instability that nearly led to his execution for treason. But they are not the only prophetic words in the letter. In the *De gerendo magistratu* Patrizi addresses young Achille at the point when he is leaving the palaestra for the line of battle (i.e., leaving school for political life). He could have applied the phrase with equal justice to himself, for later in 1446 he left his teaching post in the university and entered his most intense decade of public service to his native city. He had already held the highest office in the republic in 1440, and would hold it twice more, in 1447 and 1453. As a former prior he was automatically a member of the Council of the People, the city's highest deliberative body. He served briefly as chancellor, the chief cultural-bureaucratic office of the republic. He was also appointed by the city as *podestà* (mayor) of at least two important towns in Sienese territory, the fortress-towns of Radicofani and Montalcino.[37]

But by far Patrizi's most important role in Siena's civic life during this decade was his service on a series of diplomatic missions. These placed him at the center of Sienese foreign relations. As in the case of Machiavelli, the missions would introduce him to the highest potentates of Italy and Christendom in his day. In 1447 he headed an ambassadorial mission to Rome to congratulate the new pope, Nicholas V. Nicholas was the pope who began the secular project of the Renaissance popes to restore the physical fabric of Rome to its ancient glory, and who built the first library dedicated to Greek literature in the Vatican. In 1450 Patrizi was ambassador to Florence, where he met the patrician and diplomat Gino Capponi, who later gave him material help during his exile, as well as other Florentine humanists. In the same year he was ambassador again to Rome. In 1452 he went to Bologna as Siena's representative to the court of Frederick III and accompanied the Hapsburg king on his journey to Rome, where Frederick was crowned Holy Roman Emperor. Following the emperor's court, he must have became better acquainted with a man who would later play a decisive role in his life, his fellow Sienese poet Enea Silvio Piccolomini, later Pope Pius II.

## The Crisis of 1456: Condemnation and Exile

In 1453, the year Constantinople fell to the Turks, Alfonso of Aragon was invading southern Tuscany with his army and navy, trying to put pressure on the Florentines and their Sforza ally in Milan. He expected his friends in Siena to support him, given the long dedication Antonio Petrucci had shown to his house, but the Sienese government had different ideas. Their policy was to preserve the city's friendship with Florence and neutrality toward the House of Aragon. Patrizi was sent with the jurist Goro Lolli—a close friend from his school days and later his chief ally in the household of Pius II—to represent the Sienese position to the King. But as Patrizi and Lolli were both closely aligned with Petrucci interests, their failure to discourage Alfonso was construed by critics of the Petrucci in Siena as *voulu,* a result of bad faith. It was an impossible situation for Patrizi and Lolli, one that required them to serve two masters. Their failure was remembered a few years later when a major uprising against Petrucci dominance in Siena erupted.

The year 1450 was key in Sienese foreign relations, since in that year the condottiere Francesco Sforza established himself as duke of Milan after the short-lived episode of the Repubblica Ambrosiana. Sforza had long been an ally of Cosimo de'Medici, and their close alliance soon led to a general political realignment in the peninsula. One effect was to strengthen the hand of pro-Florentine elements in the Sienese government and to weaken pro-Aragonese interests, traditionally supported by the Petrucci. In an effort to shore up his position within the three ruling *monti* of Siena, Antonio Petrucci induced 144 of his political allies, from all three *monti,* to swear privately an oath to uphold the current regime. This would, it was claimed, increase the prestige of the republic and give it "a secure and perpetual peace." Such an oath, though called in Latin a *coniuratio,* a word with inevitable echoes for humanists of the Catilinarian conspiracy, was not necessarily at the time regarded as a *facinus* or outrageous, disloyal act. In fact, oath-taking was a common tool of political alliances of the day. In this case the oath of 1450 was regarded as treasonous only in retrospect, after the violent events of 1456 that led to the expulsion of Antonio Petrucci and his supporters from the Sienese regime.[38]

Among the signers of the oath was Patrizi himself: "I, Francesco di Giovanni Patrizi, having understood the aforesaid statement [introducing the oath] to be just and for the salvation of the city and regime, promise and swear so to uphold it and thus subjoin my signature." The document was undated, but can be placed, thanks to the later history of Sigismondo Tizio, in the year 1450.

The first person to sign the document was Antonio di Ceccho Rosso, who since the death of Andreoccio in 1449 was the undisputed head of the Petrucci clan. Though a popular war hero who had helped foil Florentine attempts at territorial expansion during the war with Lucca (1429–1433), Antonio Petrucci was also criticized for his high-handed behavior in politics and for a general lack of respect for communal traditions. His aristocratic ways aroused the antagonism of traditionalists, as did his reputation as a libertine. Pius in his *Commentaries* wrote of him that *nullam Venerem intentatam relinquit:* he left untried no form of sexual indulgence. The suspicion that he aimed to make himself *signore* of Siena was widespread. Opposition to his dominance and that of his allies came to a head in 1456 when the condottiere Jacopo Piccinino invaded Sienese territory and began seizing towns and laying waste to agricultural property. Piccinino was widely believed to be doing the bidding of Alfonso of Aragon, who was said to be punishing the Sienese for their failure to take his side in the war against Florence.[39]

The year 1456 in any case was inauspicious for the stability of regimes. It began with an appearance of Halley's comet and continued with an outbreak of plague and famine, resulting in high grain prices. As Enea Silvio Piccolomini noted in a letter, these extreme conditions led immediately to *seditiones* in Siena.[40] Opponents of the Petrucci in the Sienese government came into the open, led by Giovanni di Guccio Bichi, Cosimo de'Medici's agent in Siena, and Ludovico Petroni, a humanist follower of Leonardo Bruni and a member of Francesco Sforza's secret council. The faction they headed was markedly less aristocratic than Petrucci's political alliance. Taking advantage of popular discontent, they were able to get authorization for a *balìa* or emergency commission to take control of the city and break the power of the Petrucci. On 13 October, Antonio was condemned to perpetual exile and his property confiscated. Antonio responded in January 1457 by mounting a coup against the *balìa*, aided by soldiers of Jacopo Piccinino and accomplices within the city. The coup failed and Antonio was condemned to death. Though he himself escaped with his life, 164 of his political allies were arrested, Patrizi among them. Many were executed or exiled.

In accordance with the usual practice of the time, Patrizi was tortured to obtain a confession. The instrument of torture was probably the *strappado,* the usual method for extracting confessions in communal Italy. The *strappado* involved hoisting the victim into the air by his wrists, tied behind his back, then allowing his body to fall toward the floor until the torturer yanked him back upward. Having submitted to this procedure, Patrizi was found guilty, put in chains, and sentenced to death.[41] In Milan, Filelfo was shocked and grieved to hear that the sentence against his former student had actually been carried out.[42] But in fact Patrizi was saved at the last moment through the intercession of Enea Silvio Piccolomini, the bishop of Siena, recently created a cardinal, who had many close personal ties with the Petrucci and their supporters. As a fellow student of Filelfo and a fellow Latin poet, Enea Silvio pleaded with the *balìa* to spare Patrizi, describing him as "a famous man who has been no small ornament of your city hitherto. You should weigh his misdeeds against his good ones, and leave the man his life. He has already brought fame to your city through his writings, and in the future can bring to it the greatest splendor."[43]

The Sienese government relented, and on 3 September 1457 Patrizi was sentenced instead to twenty years of *confino,* the strictest form of exile which required him to confine his movements to particular places, to report twice daily to an accredited representative of the republic, and also to send documentation of his reports twice monthly to Siena. He was stripped of civic rights, had to pay a large fine, and was forbidden to correspond with any of the other conspirators.[44] Violation of his sentence would lead to confiscation of the goods of his parents and children. He was to begin his exile in the town of Pistoia, a small city near Florence, by the end of September.

Patrizi's exile was the greatest disaster of his life. In his poem *On Exile (Poemata* 2.1) he reported that he had lost *divitias, patriam dulcesque penates,* "riches, his country and his household gods." His wife had died some years before, probably in childbirth, but he had four small boys, whom he was obliged to leave behind in the care of their grandparents.[45] He was in severe straits financially, and he felt his poetic inspiration drying up. The divine fire requires serenity of mind but all he can think of, he writes, are his shipwrecked fortunes. Fortunately, he had many friends and admirers among men of culture. Gino Capponi of Florence was among his first benefactors, providing him with a house and furniture in Pistoia. Soon, however, the diplomat Nicodemo Tranchedini, a personal representative of Francesco Sforza and a confidant of Cosimo de'Medici, came to his rescue.[46] With the plague breaking out in Pistoia, Tranchedini was allowed to host Patrizi on his private estate at Montughi, just outside Florence. The two men became close and Tranchedini appointed Patrizi tutor to his son Francesco. It was to Francesco that Patrizi dedicated his epitome of Quintilian, a work that was later to enjoy a certain success.[47] At Montughi Patrizi also was able to have contacts with Florentine humanists belonging to the "academy" of the Greek émigré John Argyropoulos, and particularly with Alamanno Rinuccini, an accomplished Hellenist who translated Plutarch, Isocrates, and Philostratus.[48]

In September 1458, just a year after his exile, Patrizi's prospects changed dramatically for the better when Enea Silvio Piccolomini was crowned Pope Pius II. Within six months Patrizi had resolved to take holy orders, and on 15 April 1459 he was tonsured and ordained a priest. It seems Patrizi took his new responsibilities more seriously than many, for he arranged to receive careful instruction in theology beforehand from a Franciscan friar, Matteo di Domenico Ferranti da Fucecchio, with whom he maintained cordial relations. Once ordained, Patrizi was able to receive a major benefice, and at the instance of Tranchedini Pius conferred on him one of the richest benefices in his gift. This was the *pieve* of Campoli in Val di Pesa, the heart of the modern Chianti region, a few miles north of Sienese territory, with seventeen *popoli* or parish churches under its jurisdiction.[49] Patrizi's economic woes were at an end.

Around this time, when he was still living in Tranchedini's villa, Patrizi wrote a poem expressing his desire for a quiet life and an end to political involvements. The poem, entitled "De vita quieta," was dedicated to Goro Lolli, now Pius II's private secretary.

Este procul, miserae ciuilis praelia rixae,
urbibus exitium magnis extremaque labes!
Sit procul ambitio rabidaeque insomnia mentis,
dum studet optatos tribuat plebecula fasces
atque soporiferae per saeua silentia noctis
murmure sollicito repetit discrimina rerum.

Away with the strife of wretched civic quarrels,
The ultimate corruption and ruin of great cities!
Away with ambition and the nightmares of a rabid mind
Scheming for the rabble to give it the power it longs for,
And through the fierce stillness of sleep-bearing night
Seeks crisis after crisis, driven by their agitated cries.[50]

He himself no longer has any taste for the litigiousness of civic life; he doesn't care about riches or fine clothes; he doesn't envy men with large crowds of supporters following them. He is content with the simple country life and the beauties of nature. Were these sentiments mere poetic *topoi* or was Patrizi tempted, like Petrarch and Boccaccio before him, by the lure of rural retirement and solitude?[51]

However genuine the feelings this poem may reveal, as a man of deep culture Patrizi could not long absent himself from urban life.

Later, in his *De republica* (5.1), he was to equate rustic life with boorishness and the life of the civil man with urbanity, wit, and *savoir faire*. In the summer of 1459—perhaps under pressure, once more, from the pope—the Sienese government again changed the terms of Patrizi's exile, and he was permitted to take Francesco Tranchedini to Verona to further the young man's education. At Verona, a great center of humanist culture, Patrizi was welcomed by Battista Guarino, son of the famous educator, who composed an elegy in his honor, a *consolatio exilii*. A less famous schoolmaster of the town, Antonio Brognanigo, dedicated an elegy to him. He met other famous Veronese, including (probably) the young Domizio Calderini, who later won renown as a commentator on the classics, and Fra Giocondo, the humanist architect and first editor of Vitruvius, who influenced Patrizi's ideas about city planning. He formed a friendship with Niccolò Fontanelli, better known as Ilarione of Verona, that lasted until the latter's death in 1485.[52] It seems likely that he met another famous schoolmaster and scholar, Ognibene da Lonigo, who taught in nearby Vicenza; Patrizi composed an epitaph for him after his death in 1474.[53] The distinguished exile, it now seemed, had a typical humanist career before him as a teacher of ancient literature. He began to attract new students.

Siena, too, continued to call to him. When Pius II made his first visit to Siena as pope in February 1459, Patrizi composed a celebratory poem (*Poem.* 4.5) in hexameters describing the festivities for the pope's *grande entrée,* which, of course, as an exile he could not personally have witnessed. At the end he described his own love of his native city, offering to write a verse history of Siena should he be allowed to return:

O dulcis patria, o vita mihi carior ipsa,
Incipiam tua gesta libens numerisque per aeuum
Extendam, priscis non inferiora tropheis.
Me quamvis toruo dudum spectaris ocello,
Tu mihi, tu mater, tu mores dura flagello
Egregios firmas pignusque innectis amoris.

O sweet land of my fathers, dearer to me than life itself,
Let me begin a perennial history of your deeds in verse,
Deeds no less trophied than the triumphs of the ancients.
Although but a short while ago you looked on me askance,
You, you are my mother! Harshly do you strengthen morals
With the lash and bind me with proof of your tender love.[54]

Whatever had been her earlier rigors, mother Siena continued to loosen the shackles of exile. In December 1459 the pope arranged for the Sienese government to allow Patrizi free movement throughout Italy so long as he did not enter Siena or its territory. Sometime after this date we find Patrizi in Rome, now part of the papal court, that great fountain of honor and profit.

In Rome Patrizi seems to have played the role of a court poet, like Enea Silvio before him in the entourage of Frederick III. He had already composed occasional poetry for Pius, such as his long poem celebrating the cultural achievements of Ludovico Gonzaga, the host for Pius's Council of Mantua (May 1459–January 1460).[55] He continued to write poetry in classical Latin and experimented with the treatment of Christian subjects in ancient meters and genres. Before March 1460 he composed *On the Nativity of Christ,* an imitation of Vergil's *Fourth Eclogue,* dedicated to Pius II. This was his most successful work, surviving in eighteen manuscripts and an edition printed in Padua in 1482. It was one of only two works by Patrizi to be printed in his lifetime and was later included in anthologies of humanist Latin poetry.[56]

By early 1461 he was able to assemble his first collection of poetry, the *Poematum libri IV.* He dedicated it, inevitably, and surely with genuine gratitude, to Pius II.[57] Some of these compositions were later polished and included in a poetic anthology in Pius's honor, the *Epaeneticorum libri V,* a volume celebrating the rise of a Latin poet to the spiritual pinnacle of Christendom and the inauguration of new Golden Age.[58] In this collection Patrizi's poetry stood side by side with the work of the finest Latin poets of his day. Living in the capital of Christendom, surrounded by men of high culture who valued his learning and accomplishments, Patrizi's prospects for a happy life must have seemed fair indeed.

## Governor of Foligno

Pius, however, had other plans for him. The Piccolomini pope would soon become notorious for practices that were to be normalized by the High Renaissance popes: using members of his own family and Sienese cronies to carry out his bold policies while bypassing existing personnel and structures in the papal curia.[59] Francesco Patrizi, as a former Sienese diplomat and high official who owed his life to Pius, was an ideal recruit for the pope's network of personal power. In March 1461 Pius elevated his protégé in ecclesiastical rank, making him bishop of Gaeta, while allowing him to retain his rich benefice in Campoli. On 13 April Siena, at Pius's instance, revoked Patrizi's sentence of exile entirely, and he and his sons were restored to full citizen rights. Finally, on 27 May, Pius appointed Patrizi governor of the city and province of Foligno in the Papal State.

This was an important post. The city held a strategic position on the routes from Rome to Tuscany and from the Adriatic coast inland. It controlled a large and rich territory, about one-quarter the size of the Sienese republic, including the towns of Trevi, Montefalco, Bevagna, Assisi, and Nocera, among others. Patrizi was granted full powers of "reforming, ruling, and governing" the province, including broad judicial powers, supervisory authority over other magistrates, and general oversight of the city's political life. On June 1 he made his solemn entry into the city as governor, accompanied by a great crowd of citizens and the ringing of church bells, and "was accepted humbly and reverently by the magnificent lord priors and all the citizens and common people."[60]

That moment was probably the high point of Patrizi's career as governor. He soon found himself plunged into an intractable political situation, one not uncommonly found in towns of the Papal State in the fourteenth and fifteenth century. In these centuries the papacy engaged in a long struggle to reestablish its authority, dangerously weakened during its "Babylonian captivity" in Avignon. The default setting for papal government had fallen into a weak version of the Italian system of provincial government known as "dyarchy." In this system the relations of a city and its province with the central government and with outside powers were controlled by a governor appointed by the prince, who also retained some powers of taxation, while internal governance of the city was left in the hands of local authorities, especially the appointment of magistrates as well as control of local courts and finances.[61] Foligno until the time of Eugene IV had long been allowed to rule itself under the signory of the Trinci family (1305–1439), something of a golden age for the town, which reached its apogee of wealth and culture in that period. The Trinci had recognized the nominal overlordship of the pope until the last of their line, Corrado III, tried foolishly to declare the city's formal independence. The pope responded by sending an army under the military cardinal Giovanni Vitelleschi, who put down the revolt and had Corrado strangled in 1441 while under arrest in the castle of Soriano. The town seethed with sedition for the next half century. The death of popes was regularly an excuse for an outbreak of open revolt—for example, in 1447, 1455, and 1458, following the deaths of Eugene IV, Nicholas V and Calixtus III, respectively. In 1445 a working compromise was reached between papal claims and Foligno's desire for self-rule via the so-called *Santissima Unione,* brokered between the city and Cardinal Vitelleschi by the the Franciscan preacher Giacomo della Marca, later declared a saint (1726). The *Santissima Unione* provided for an uneven dyarchy that strongly favored local authorities. In return for recognizing papal overlordship, the city was conceded rights to choose its own ruling magistracy, the Twenty, as well as its consultative council of one hundred local worthies; it could control the legal system, including the right to appoint its own *podestà* or chief judicial magistrate; and it could rule its own territory. Papal taxes were reduced and the city was given permission to coin its own money, a strong marker of civic independence.

This unequal accord was destabilized by the activist government of Pius II and his loyal servant, Francesco Patrizi, which aimed to establish much tighter papal control over the city.[62] Pius's larger goal, which Patrizi may not have shared, was to exploit Foligno's wealth and resources in his two great political causes: the crusade he was organizing against the Turks, and his bitter struggle against condottieri princes like Jacopo Piccinino, Sigismondo Malatesta, and Federico da Montefeltro, each bent on carving out territorial principalities of their own from the soft flesh of the Papal States. In order to get control of Foligno's financial resources, Pius needed to establish greater political authority over the city, and that is what Governor Patrizi set out to do. Patrizi reasserted the Church's claim to appoint judicial officers and local officials in the countryside and enforced Pius's revocation of Foligno's right to coin money. He was obliged to carry out Pius's orders, bitterly resented, to supply *corvée* labor and draft animals to build the Castello Piccolomini in Trevi. He also had to execute Pius's most unpopular measures of all, the burdensome crusading taxes he levied on the city and its province.

Patrizi's own perspective on his role as governor was typically high-minded. Thanks to several inquisitions into his governorship that were demanded by his enemies in the city, we possess an extraordinarily detailed dossier, compiled by Patrizi himself, containing 173 letters and reports that give his side of the story.[63] From these documents it appears that Patrizi saw his own goal as imposing moral order on a city corrupted by wanton, seditious, and power-hungry individuals resistant to the rightful authority of Holy Church. Already on 9 June 1461 he writes to his friend Goro Lolli, Pius's secretary, who was his principal liaison with the pope:

License has invaded the minds of this city's citizens and its provincials thanks to the heedlessness (not to give it another name) of its leaders, so severity will be necessary. I hope that in a few days I can bring them back to much better behavior [*mores*]. If there should be those who try to undermine our power, you must drive them out completely, for you can surely recognize that I am not going to injure anyone but treat everything in an upright and proper way.[64]

His illusions did not last long, for, in a sign of things to come, the city immediately sent a delegation to Rome to complain of Patrizi's "innovations" (always a negative word before modern times). Patrizi tried to forestall them with another letter to Lolli.

> If they complain that I have innovated in the city, please shut them down. For I've decided to suppress their insolence and bad behavior and gradually to reduce them to stricter moral control [*censura*]. They are used to taking counsel without the governor knowing anything about it. From now on I shall not permit them to take counsel or to propose anything or even to breathe without my permission. I have abolished the laws and mandates they have rashly made and taught them that this jurisdiction belongs to Our Holy Lord Pope and is not the free republic [*respublica libera*] they have already put into place.[65]

As Patrizi soon learned, the key to successful administration was competent and loyal personnel. Here his success varied. He appointed many of his own subordinates, including the *podestà* as well as judges and and treasury officials, but he also was obliged to take on other officials he did not know personally who were sent to him from Rome. Some of them, he later wrote, he would prefer to pay salaries for *not* serving, given the slack way they performed their duties. Others, like Pacino Pacini, a member of a minor Sienese noble house, proved competent and reliable.

His greatest disappointment, however, was his own first choice for *podestà* of the city: his former student, Achille Petrucci, the dedicatee of *De gerendo magistratu,* whom Patrizi appointed on 22 July 1461. Petrucci, however, now thirty-four years old, aspired to higher things than to serve as a police magistrate in a provincial town. By autumn Achille had abandoned his post in Foligno, "driven by a frivolous fear of pestilence," as Patrizi wrote to Lolli, causing the justice system to break down. The governor wrote the young man a sharp letter, ordering him to return immediately:

> I can no longer bear the rebukes of the court and the citizens on account of your absence, or, beyond that, that you are abusing our friendship and patience, and especially when I have exhorted you over and over again in letters and mandates that you return to your magistracy. Since I have already discharged the duties of friendship towards you more than enough, I am instructing you in this letter to return within eight days and present yourself before me in the city of Foligno, at which time we shall order what is fitting and execute the mandate of His Holiness, whose favor we hold far more dearly than life itself.[66]

For a couple of years, the city seemed be settling down under Patrizi's stricter rule. The bishop soon felt secure enough in his position to stand up to powerful figures in Pius's entourage like Cardinal Jacopo Ammanati when his actions as governor were questioned in Rome.[67] Recurring to his old role as a diplomat, he tried to broaden his scope and broker a peace between the pope and Sigismondo Malatesta. But he was ignored: the pope was not interested in peace.[68] Within his own province Patrizi's authority grew increasingly assured, but he was nevertheless careful to protect himself from predictable slanders by sending detailed reports of his activities in almost bi-weekly letters to Lolli, keeping careful copies for his own records. Rome, on the whole, gave him reliable backing, even for his more unpopular actions.

By October 1461 Foligno was already calm enough that Patrizi was able to embark on another project that Pius had laid on his shoulders: the writing of a treatise *De republica* that would collect and synthesize the political wisdom of the Greeks and the Romans for the use of modern times. For a while Patrizi made great progress with the treatise, which he continued to work on throughout 1462 and 1463.[69] He even found time in March 1462 to visit Siena for the first time since his exile, where he was received with great affection, as he told Lolli, while reporting also on the resentments that were stewing in the city thanks to the pope's political meddling.

But, as so often in the past, the stability of papal government depended on the health of the pontiff. In the spring and summer of 1464 rumors began to circulate in Foligno about the pope's physical decline and imminent death. This was the signal for malcontents who wanted to throw off papal rule and re-establish the old dyarchy to spring into action. According to Patrizi's long and detailed account of the conspiracy, composed in order to defend his reputation in Rome, the ringleader of the plot was one Niccolò della Tacca, a notary who had been imprisoned by previous popes for his seditious activities.[70] Della Tacca schemed with the city priors to form a board of twenty men with the apparently religious purpose of creating a *monte di pietà,* a pious foundation that would give interest-free loans to impoverished Christians. The inspiration for this initiative had come the year before when a traveling Lenten preacher, the Franciscan Alberto da Perugia, had delivered some fiery sermons against Jewish moneylenders, mixed with political criticism of the pope who (as usual) was accused of protecting the Jews in order to finance his crusade. According to Patrizi's ironic account, "this good man ensnared the minds of certain citizens, who decided to establish a kind of free republic [*quasi liberam rem publicam*]. To facilitate this they caused to be created, with the approval of the Council, under the cloak of religion, a board of twenty men to act on [the question of] the Jews and usury."

This board, meeting in secret, became the vehicle of an anti-papal conspiracy, as Patrizi learned from informers. The governor followed their activities but waited to act until he had clear proofs of their treason. He learned that the conspirators were telling prospective followers that if they rose up, as they had so often before, the governor would be forced to compromise with them and they could restore the terms of the *Santissima Unione* of 1446.

Eventually the conspirators came out into the open with their demands and presented Patrizi with a copy of their *capitula,* the proposed terms of a new agreement with the papal government. He instantly saw that the terms would spell the complete ruin of Pius's project to consolidate his authority in Foligno and advance the *reconquista* of the Papal States. The conspirators also, simultaneously, sent their preacher (presumably the same Alberto da Perugia) to beg everyone to urge upon the governor "this holy work, as they called it, that fra Giacomo [della Marca] had accomplished elsewhere." Patrizi told the conspirators he could not give them an immediate answer to their demands and would have to consult the pope. The next day the conspirators returned with their preacher, who harangued Patrizi in a long sermon, urging him to accept the *capitula*. Cross-examining the Franciscan, Patrizi established that the man had not even read them, but "had been assured by certain good citizens that they were excellent." Patrizi satisfied himself that the friar was simply a useful idiot being exploited by the plotters.

The governor then moved to quash the seditious movement. The conspirators responded by sending two ambassadors to Rome to accuse Patrizi of corruption. Patrizi in self-defense composed the long memo from which we have been quoting, vigorously defending himself and accusing the "faction of ser Niccolò [della Tacca]" of aiming to establish a tyranny in place of papal government.

> If I have acquired any judgment at all from my age and experience, this affair has an evil foundation, and should be stamped out now while it is still drowsy, rather than waiting to see how it turns out. For as the Roman proverb has it, a fire that is badly extinguished can be turned by a light wind into a great conflagration. I send attached to this letter the *capitula* being sought by the conspiracy.

In another letter of April 1464 he expressed his willingness, even eagerness, for a papal commission to come to Foligno and investigate his actions.

> The orators from Foligno have been barking a great many things against me that are entirely false, like people who, in order to cover their own crimes and foul misdeeds, calumniate others . . .

snd surely, unless Our Lord Pope takes notice of these criminals and crushes their rabid behavior, they will seize the occasion to cause a great conflagration. I'm not saying this to escape their calumnies, and I promise I will undergo any judicial process you like.

A few days later, in another letter to the same correspondent, he added:

I am perfectly conscious of my innocence and am evading no inquiry and seek no favor but rather the most severe justice, and nothing could happen that would cause me more distress than if the matter were allowed to drop without discussion.[71]

But the conspirators had struck too soon. Pius II looked as though he might recover, and a blue-ribbon panel of ecclesiastics, including two cardinals, was sent to Foligno to investigate the charges against Patrizi. The Foligno conspirators threw all the mud they could at him, charging him with foul crimes and acts of wickedness that would be unthinkable, Patrizi remarked drily, in the Greek tyrants Phalaris and Dionysius of Syracuse and the famously corrupt Roman governor Verres all combined, let alone in a blameless bishop and governor. Patrizi called for a thorough inquisition in order completely to clear his name and to punish those who had slandered him, but the papal commission was determined to work swiftly. They declared him innocent of the charges and left the city.

The conspiracy was over, for now. "The rebels now hung their heads and were deserted by their supporters." Patrizi gradually reestablished his control over the city. The pope fortified the governor's position further with a bull of 1 July endorsing his policies. Patrizi's first step after receiving this document was to amend the electoral lists of the city government so that Niccolò della Tucca's faction would be excluded permanently from office and majorities favoring the pope would in future be drawn from the urns. Order had been restored, or so it seemed.

In late July Patrizi decided to take a well-earned rest and escape the summer heat to the near-by hill town of Nocera. The decision saved his life. On 14 August Pius suddenly passed away, and when the news reached Foligno, a new and terrifyingly violent rebellion broke out. A crowd of rioters ran into the streets, stormed the governor's palace (the former Palazzo Trinci) and set fire to his apartments, burning or looting Patrizi's possessions. The acting governor escaped to a nearby house but was tricked on false promises into coming back out into the piazza. He was struck from behind, beaten and left for dead; dragged into a nearby church he was decapitated by one of the rioters before the very altars of the church. The rebels then broke into the palace of the *podestà*, slaughtered all the officials friendly to the papal government and destroyed any documents that might incriminate their faction. The chest that held the new elcctoral lists, a sacred object decorated with a Virgin and Child and the papal arms, was burned by the seditious crowd. Even private citizens known to be sympathetic to the pope suffered reprisals.[72]

Patrizi, having by good fortune escaped the violence, fled back to Rome. But the rebels' hatred of their governor was not so easily sated. In October 1464 the new rulers of Foligno sent more representatives to Rome, charging Patrizi with maladministration and corruption. This time Patrizi found it much harder to clear his name. The new pope, Paul II, a Venetian, had won election thanks to an oath sworn by twelve of the twenty cardinals not to elect any Piccolomini cardinal as pope. They were determined to keep Pius's Sienese mafia out of power. Nor was the new pope known to be a friend to humane letters, so he could not be appealed to on Patrizi's behalf in that way. The pope put a hostile French cardinal in charge of his case, Richard Olivier, who was determined to try Patrizi in Foligno. Patrizi and his supporters begged to have the trial held in Rome. Given what had happened in August, Patrizi's life would surely be in danger in the Umbrian city. Olivier thought the Folignati would not dare harm Patrizi in his own august presence. Cardinal Ammanati in his response insinuated that Olivier's long service in France had made him naïve: "Most reverend father, I am an Italian and have lived fourteen years among the subjects of the Church. Believe me, they do not respect rulers the way French subjects do."[73]

Unfortunately, it is precisely at this point that our documentation fails us. We have no reports of Patrizi's second trial, and even no way of ascertaining whether it was held in Foligno or in Rome. The most plausible hypothesis is that he was exonerated in Rome sometime in the fall of 1464. He was surely helped by the careful dossier he had compiled of all his doings in Foligno, a copy of which was no doubt put into the hands of Olivier's commission.[74] However critical the new pope was of Pius II's nepotistic practices, to make an example of Patrizi would come at a high cost. It was hardly to the pope's or the curia's advantage to accept the word of local malcontents over that of a papal governor. There is some evidence, indeed, that the college of cardinals stood by Patrizi, who was, after all, still a respected literary figure in the Roman court with powerful friends.[75] The Piccolomini interest in Rome, still potent if no longer dominant, energetically defended him. Most telling of all, a few months after Patrizi's retirement to his diocese in Gaeta, which probably occurred near the end of 1464, he was appointed by the king of Naples to head an ambassadorial mission to Milan to celebrate the marriage of the king's son and heir, Alfonso, duke of Calabria, to Ippolita Maria Sforza, the duke of Milan's learned daughter.[76] This highly visible occasion in June 1465 marked an alliance between the two most powerful rulers of Italy. It is inconceivable that Patrizi could have received this appointment had he been recently convicted of corruption by a papal tribunal. It also seems unlikely that Patrizi could so quickly have won the role he was soon playing in the Kingdom of Naples, that of tutor and advisor to the young duke of Calabria, had he been living under so dark a cloud.

## Calm after the Storm: Gaeta, 1464–1494

Whatever the outcome of the trial, the papal court under Paul II was no longer a place that welcomed humanists, particularly those so closely associated with Paul's predecessor, Pius, or with the Kingdom of Naples, with whom Paul had poor relations. The judgment about Paul's hostility to the humanist movement comes above all from the highly prejudiced attacks on the new pope by the papal biographer Bartolomeo Platina, a major source for the cultural life of the curia in Paul's pontificate. The future Vatican librarian was outraged, first of all, at Paul's prompt dissolution of the College of Abbreviators—a body according to Platina full of "good and learned men," jurists, orators, and poets, "who certainly conferred no less distinction on the Curia than they themselves received from it."[77] A few years later, in 1468, Pope Paul struck again, this time at a group of humanist intellectuals around Pomponio Leto, whom he suspected of being inspired by "Epicureanism" and (rather inconsistently) with accepting Plato's heretical belief in reincarnation, all the while plotting against himself and Holy Church. According to Patrizi's friend Agostino Patrizi, who had slipped nimbly into Pope Paul's camp, the adherents of the so-called Academic conspiracy were

> hyper-elegant men [*elegantioli*] . . . [who] seemed too learned and too much in love with antiquity, and they appeared to take not only their language and literary style [from the ancients] but also their opinions about the ends of good and evil and about the highest God Himself, not from our philosophers, as would be fair, but from the ancient gentile [pagan] philosophers.[78]

Pope Paul did not hesitate to jail and persecute several participants in the "conspiracy" (if there was a conspiracy). According to a report of the Milanese ambassador, the pope declared that "they would be considered heretics who hereafter shall mention the name *academia* either seriously or in jest."[79] It is no wonder that Patrizi himself saw Paul II's papacy as a time infelicitous for political philosophy, especially when based on ancient pagan sources.[80]

It probably did Patrizi no good, either, that his teacher Filelfo chose the months after his trial to attack the memory of Pius II, drawing down on himself thunder and lightning from the Piccolomini clan in Rome. One of the furious responses to Filelfo was written by his rival at the court of Milan, Lodrisio Crivelli, who may also have attacked Patrizi, as Filelfo's student, into the bargain.[81] Filelfo claimed as much in his reply to Crivelli, and defended Patrizi, excepting him from his rhetorical carpet bombing of Pius II's former officials. (Goro Lolli, for example, Filelfo portrayed as a corrupt fixer who enriched himself by embezzling crusade taxes.) By contrast, "Francesco Patrizi, Bishop of Gaeta, a most eloquent and learned man, my former student—an extremely gracious man whose morals are utterly unlike your own—I gladly hear praised, so that I cannot but be grieved on his behalf to hear his great and distinguished virtues being twisted in your stinking mouth."[82] The humanist invective is not a genre that inspires trust as an historical source—among Filelfo's charges against Crivelli were those of being a thief, a perjurer, a sodomite, and (the horror) a fat man overly fond of food and drink—but an atmosphere filled with flying mud was clearly no place for a man trying to rebuild his reputation.

Gaeta, on the other hand, was a welcoming and attractive port city surrounded by interesting ancient ruins both Greek and Roman.[83] It had a mild climate, provided fresh fish and olives, and enjoyed abundant sources of clean water. As Patrizi wrote in an epigram, perhaps with allegorical intent, it was a place whose gently curving harbor offered sailors shelter from stormy seas and whose position on a spur of the Apennines protected it from rough winds.[84] It jutted out into the sea a few miles away from the coast road from Rome to Naples, but not so far away that the occasional learned visitor could not be induced to stop a few days there and perhaps drop off a book that the bishop needed for his work. It was also an Aragonese naval base, and thus offered a second line of communication with the Kingdom's capital city of Naples to the south, as well as maritime links to the Sienese republic's port, Talamone, and to Porto Ercole to the north.

Eventually Patrizi's patron, Duke Alfonso of Calabria, a great builder of beautiful villas, constructed a palace in Gaeta for his own use. It may well have been designed by his favorite architect, Fra Giocondo, the great expert on Vitruvius, who was consulted when the builders found ancient ruins while digging its foundations.[85] Another humanist man of religion, Patrizi's old acquaintance Ilarione of Verona, a Benedictine monk, took up residence in the city for a few years in the monastery of S. Angelo after the death of his patron, Cardinal Bessarion. In his *Dialogus* of 1473 Ilarione offered a glimpse of intellectual life in the town that showed it to be by no means a desert for men of learning.[86] Gaeta, it seems, offered the same kind of isolation from, yet proximity to, political power that Petrarch had sought in his later life when finishing his many literary projects.[87] Patrizi, now fifty-one, had spent his entire life as the instrument of other men's political designs, while never quite mastering the arts of the courtier.[88] In Gaeta he could be his own man and build his own cities—in his mind and on paper.

A poem from that early period in Gaeta gives us some insight into Patrizi's state of mind after a tumultuous decade of public life. In his *De republica*, as we shall see in Chapter 2, the Sienese philosopher, while defending republican freedom and equality, wrote that if it were possible to live one's life always under a good prince, the republican alternative would never have been invented. In his poem "What Would Make Me Happy," he tells his reader that if his youth could return to him again—a thing never to be hoped for—and Jupiter would grant all his wishes, he would choose to live under a just king who would offer him a compliant ear, protect the good, and destroy the bad. "Let me have a little house with a little well, a dim little kitchen lit by an ever-burning hearth, a fat little flock pasturing in a field, some land giving grain and good wine, a hill thick with olive trees, and a wood with trees for cutting, to give me firewood for the rest of my life."

Then comes the epigram's pivot. Belying the *topos* of the simple life, the poet continues: "Let me have these little gifts and one truly great one: a library rivaling that of Pergamum!" A library, in the manuscript age, that would require an immense fortune to collect. It would have all the poets of Greece and Rome in order, with grammarians and rhetoricians standing among them, along with the great orators who tamed the people with their eloquence.

Across from them on the shelves would be ranged the historians who remember the past and are the witnesses of mankind. Then mathematicians and astronomers and musicians, natural philosophers and those "who are able to set out the laws of the soul, and men deeply learned in Chaldaean lore who know that great God created all things from nothing." Then the moral philosophers who, having established the ends of the good, laid down mores and the blessed life for men. "Among these books I would wish for the years of Tithonus and Nestor, and I would vanquish Argos with all his eyes."[89]

The poem suggests that the way Patrizi seems to have to lived the rest of his life was no accident. As far as we know, apart from two ambassadorial missions in 1465 and 1484, Patrizi spent the last thirty years of his life in Gaeta, working quietly on his literary projects, only episodically in touch with the outside world.[90] These years are by far the least well documented years of Patrizi's adult life. We have a few unrevealing records generated by the administration of his diocese, which seems to have been careful and responsible.[91]

Our best record by far of this last period of Patrizi's life is a collection of 345 epigrams by him, which survives in only one manuscript, rediscovered at the end of the nineteenth century.[92] Only twenty-three epigrams from the collection have been published, together with a list of titles of the individual poems, which range in length from one to forty-one couplets. None of them carry dates, but the earliest of the few datable pieces come from around 1467 and the latest from the end of the 1480s. Patrizi intended to dedicate the collection, perhaps rearranged in four books like the *Poemata*, to Cardinal Francesco Todeschini Piccolomini, and a copy was also to have been presented to the city of Siena. A dual dedication of the *Epigrammata* to a Piccolomini and to Siena would then have constituted a poetic gift corresponding to the dual dedication of the *De republica*, originally intended for both Pius II and Siena. Patrizi, it seems, had written no poetry in the years after his appointment as governor of Foligno, but in Gaeta he meant not only to finish his great political treatise but to renew his service to the muses of poetry.

Nevertheless, the *Epigrammata,* unlike the *De republica,* remained unfinished at the end of his life.[93]

The epigram was a genre that experienced a great revival in Renaissance Italy, being practiced by all the major Neo-Latin poets of the age from Panormita to Poliziano, Marullus, and Sannazaro.[94] In the early quattrocento, exponents of the epigram imitated the sharp-edged wit and obscenity of their Roman models, Catullus and Martial. Panormita's collection of epigrams, the *Hermaphroditus,* influenced also by the pseudo-Vergilian *Priapeia,* was so scandalous that it was censored and even publicly burnt by the authorities. Enea Silvio Piccolomini's youthful *Cinthia,* a cycle of love poetry influenced by Propertian elegy, was also frankly erotic and proved an embarrassment to the later pontiff.

Patrizi, by contrast, participated in the general tendency among poets in the second half of the fifteenth century to elevate the genre and mix *hilaritas* with *gravitas, ioca* with *seria.* Although (so far as we know) he did not explicitly criticize Catullus, Martial, or Panormita like some later poets—Andrea Navagero paid homage to the Muses each year by burning a copy of Martial—Patrizi was clearly dissatisfied with the triviality of the genre as currently practiced. He devoted two poems to investigating its Greek origins. Epigrams were once noble and solemn, he wrote, like the ancient epigram for the Spartans slain at Thermopylae, and were aimed at inspiring virtue, but they have become frivolous, erotic, and full of bitter humor. Poets today should restore the epigram to its ancient dignity.[95]

His own collection of *Epigrammata* show that Patrizi for his part succeeded in making the epigram a more serious vehicle of expression. Many of his verses, to be sure, are devoted to love and its discontents. One epitaph mourns the death of a puppy; another celebrates the coming of spring; another praises the taste of ripe melons. There are jokes and satiric send-ups of unnamed contemporaries. But many poems in the collection reach for a more elevated tone. Some celebrate the achievements of humanists he had known, sometimes in the form of moving funerary epitaphs. A number mix courtly themes with moral advice for his pupil and patron, Alfonso of Calabria, who is often reminded of the enduring fame that comes from virtue.[96] Some have political themes, such as Epigram 38 on the miserable life of the tyrant Dionysius of Syracuse. A series of ten epigrams from the 1480s condemns the Sienese populist regime for its cruelty and ingratitude to its senators and leading men.[97] Others are addressed to humanist friends in Rome and Naples or give affectionate comfort and counsel to his sons and grandsons.[98] He gives advice on love, festivity, and penitence, and writes verses inspired by mythology and ancient history. A number discuss classical authors: Strabo on how kings should persuade (by gifts, not words); the insanity of Lucretius; Homer's *Odyssey* as an education in virtue, wisdom and felicity; on a low character in Plautus; on Plato's view of hermaphrodites in his *Symposium;* praise of Propertius's elegance; and on Greek authors little known to his contemporaries such as Aeschylus, Anacreon, and Epictetus.

If the picture of Patrizi's literary network conveyed by the epigrams is accurate, there is one surprising absence. Not a single epigram mentions Antonio Panormita, Giovanni Pontano, or any of the eighteen core members of the Neapolitan academy.[99] This academy (or Porticus as it is more properly called) was at the center of literary life in Naples; its complete absence from Patrizi's poetry and correspondence probably indicates conscious avoidance on his part. In part, to be sure, this is a question of chronology. Though the origins of the academy are supposed to go back to the last years of Panormita (d. 1471), most of its documentable activities come from the last decade of Pontano's life (d. 1503), after the latter's retirement from his official duties as prime minister of Naples.[100] Given Panormita's reputation as a salacious author, Patrizi may well have preferred to keep his distance from the Porticus in its early stages, but the total absence of any connections with Pontano, who like Panormita and Patrizi was proud of his role as *praeceptor* of the king's heir, Alfonso, is harder to explain.[101]

In general, Patrizi seems not to have been one of nature's academicians. His relations with other literary academies of his day—those of Cardinal Bessarion and Pomponio Leto in Rome, Ficino's academy

in Florence—were tenuous at best.[102] His closest connections in the
Kingdom of Naples were with his pupil and patron, Alfonso of
Calabria, heir to the throne, who maintained a court of his own in
Naples at the Castel Capuano that included his diplomat brother
Federico and his humanist wife Ippolita Maria and their daughter
Isabella.[103] The prince's court was attended by the highest nobility
of the Aragonese kingdom and it may be that Patrizi appreciated the
social distance between the duke of Calabria's residence, with its fine
library (assembled by Ippolita Maria), and the Porticus Antoniana,
an open arcade in the center of the city (now Piazzetta del Nilo)
where the Neapolitan academy met.[104]

Though Prince Alfonso clearly had high esteem for Patrizi's literary gifts, their relationship was not always cordial, as we learn
from Epigrams 86 and 87, the first addressed "To the illustrious
Duke of Calabria who is angry with him without cause." The epigrams do not tell us why the prince was upset with the bishop,
though in Epigram 87 a slanderer is blamed for spreading false reports
about him.

But we can point to at least one occasion—perhaps even the one
alluded to in the epigram—when Patrizi's independence from the
Castel Capuano required the intervention of a mutual friend to
smooth ruffled feathers. This occurred in 1476 or 1477, when Patrizi, no doubt hard at work on the *De regno* for Alfonso, was asked
by the prince (or perhaps by his wife Ippolita Maria in Alfonso's
name) to write a *commento* on Petrarch's *Canzoniere*.[105] The assign-
ment was not at all to Patrizi's taste, and he protested that the ama-
tory subject matter was not suited to his white hairs, but he agreed to
comply with the prince's request. He produced a draft, which was sent
to Giovanni Albino, Alfonso's secretary and librarian, with whom
Patrizi was on good terms.[106] Albino gently suggested to him that
unnamed members of the household of Alfonso had found his treatment too summary and selective, and that he had failed to open up
the deep mysteries of the text. Writing for once in Italian, Patrizi
replied that he had "applied his mind in obedience to the illustrious
duke, for whom he would offer his life, but not because he recognized

any *excellente doctrina* in the works of Petrarch." In his view the *Canzoniere* was full of metrical errors and willful obscurities; it contained more flowers than fruit. He had simply avoided drawing attention to its many blemishes, like a portrait painter covering up the imperfections of his sitter. He would take the criticisms under advisement. Patrizi continued his disobliging line, however, in the preface to the final version of the commentary, where he continued to complain about being forced at his age to comment on the amorous whingeing of the Florentine poet. He did this only to please His Highness, the Most Illustrious Duke, to whom he had devoted not only his goods of fortune but his very life. But he had decided after due consideration not to go on at great length after all, despite objections from certain quarters, as he did not want to bore the Duke, who was occupied with far more exalted concerns.[107]

The message was clear. Alfonso was a busy man absorbed in his great affairs, but Patrizi had his work to do as well. As the retiring bishop must have realized, he was devoting his time to composing what would count as the most important treatises on political philosophy yet written by a modern humanist author.

# TWO

# The Great Political Treatises

## The Humanist Synthetic Treatise

The great Renaissance project of restoring the lost civilization of classical antiquity unfolded in a number of stages over the course of several centuries. The groundwork was laid by the scholar-poet Petrarch (1304–1374), who first dared to hope that Christendom might overcome the patent failures of its recent past and its present misery by returning to the wisdom of Greece, the virtue of Rome, and the uncorrupt Christianity of the early Church. By the first half of the fifteenth century Petrarch's followers had turned themselves into a movement, called today the humanist movement, and the scholar-official Biondo Flavio (1394–1463), in a famous passage of his *Italia illustrata* (1448/1458), was able to boast of its successes.[1] In the "shipwreck" of Graeco-Roman culture caused by the barbarian invasions of late antiquity, much—far too much—had been lost, but thanks to the collaboration of humanists throughout Italy, following Petrarch's example, the scattered literary remains of the ancients had been brought together again. They were being cured of their textual corruptions and copied in elegant literary hands inspired by the antique. The books of the ancients were being collected in great libraries such as the Library of San Marco created by Niccolò Niccoli and Cosimo de'Medici in Florence and by Pope Nicholas V in the Vatican. Thanks to these books, and the unremitting efforts of teachers all over Italy, a new generation of scholars had arisen who could write and speak Latin with something approaching the beauty, power, and precision of the best Roman writers. The damage inflicted on the Latin language by the barbarians of the north was being repaired. Furthermore, wrote Biondo, thanks to help from Byzantine scholars, the Latinate culture of late medieval Italy had acquired the ability to read and even compose poetry in ancient Greek. Humanists of the Renaissance knew that elite Roman culture in its best period was bilingual, a fact abundantly illustrated in the works of their great model, Cicero. They accepted as unquestionable the view of their revered Byzantine teacher, Manuel Chrysoloras, that it was impossible to achieve eloquence in Latin without knowledge of Greek. Or as Biondo put it even more emphatically: in his time, if you did not know Greek, you appeared ignorant of Latin as well. [1]

By the second half of the fifteenth century, the humanists were ready to take the next step and carry forward the transformation of Italian city-states and principalities on the model of antiquity. By then, much of Italy's political elite had enjoyed a classical education, and Italian arms had begun to win new glory. According (again) to Biondo, Italian military success was the main reason that wealth, magnificence, and elegance had returned to public and private life. [2] Italy was mostly at peace, united for once by the common threat emanating from the Ottoman armies, made vivid by the fall of Constantinople (1453). The empire of the Greeks had come to an end, but the study of Greek was becoming a regular part of the curriculum in the best humanist schools. The Renaissance, it seemed, was enjoying considerable success. Hence, in this period the humanists began to turn their efforts to works of synthesis, excerpting and analyzing their large and growing corpus of ancient writers, bringing ancient knowledge and wisdom to bear on particular aspects of contemporary life that could benefit from renewal all'antica.

Probably the most famous example today of this new trend was Leon Battista Alberti's On Architecture (ca. 1452). Alberti's aim, as Angelo Poliziano wrote in his preface to the first printed edition (1485), was "carefully to examine the vestiges of antiquity so that he might grasp all the rational principles of ancient building and recover them as examples."[3] This involved, as Alberti himself wrote (1.1), gathering both physical and literary evidence and using his own experience as an architect to interpret the best writings of the ancients, adapting them to the needs of modern Italian building.

Other examples of humanist synthetic treatises help illustrate the goals of the genre. The most ambitious of the lot was surely Biondo Flavio's massive study of Roman religion, politics, customs, and mores, *Rome in Triumph* (1456). You can't revive antiquity unless you know what antiquity was like, and the *Roma Triumphans* collects, sifts, and compares hundreds of ancient literary sources as well as selected legal, archeological, epigraphical, and numismatic evidence—whatever was useful to recover what ancient Rome had been and still had to offer the modern world.[4] Roberto Valturio's *De re militari* (ca. 1460, first printed edition 1472), similarly collected material from more than a hundred ancient Greek and Latin authors, adapting their lessons to the challenges of contemporary warfare.[5] Johannes Tinctoris in his *De inventione et usu musicae* (ca. 1481) brought together a vast body of ancient sources, including biblical sources, to investigate the Greek and Hebrew origins of music, musical practices in ancient times, famous singers of antiquity, the various types of instruments used in antiquity, what sort of repertoire was considered appropriate for each, and their relationship to modern instruments. The medieval inheritance could be vastly enriched and ennobled by placing revered antiquity before the mind's eye. Again, Tinctoris's purpose was to refound modern music as far as possible on the "classic" or best practices of the ancients.[6]

One might also include in this group of humanist syntheses Marsilio Ficino's *Platonic Theology on the Immortality of Souls* (ca. 1474, first printed edition 1482). Ficino's work represented a direct challenge to medieval theologians' reliance on Aristotelian philosophy, and his work synthesizes, for the first time, hundreds of ancient Platonic and other philosophical sources surviving from antiquity. His aim was to reestablish Platonism as the premier tradition within Christian theology, a position it had enjoyed (according to Ficino) before the fall of the Roman Empire in the West and throughout the history of the eastern empire of the Greeks that had come finally to an end in 1453. Aristotle's failure as a theologian was nowhere better illustrated than in his flawed analysis of the human soul, whose weaknesses, exacerbated by the influence of his great Muslim interpreter Averroes, had corrupted Western teachings on human immortality. This was a doctrine that, apart from anything else, was key to maintaining the social order, since without wide belief in rewards and punishments in the afterlife, no government could hope to discipline the behavior of its citizens.[7]

Francesco Patrizi's two great works of political philosophy, *How to Found a Republic* (scribally published ca. 1471) and *On Kingship and the Education of a King* (1483/1484), clearly fall into the genre of the humanist synthetic treatise. Whereas medieval political theorists since the thirteenth century had relied overwhelmingly on Aristotle, with only occasional citations of Justinian's compilation of Roman law and a smattering of Roman histories, Patrizi had a far wider source base. He not only brought Western political thought into dialogue with Greek philosophers, poets, geographers, historians, and orators, but also, via his Greek and Latin sources, was able to draw on the historical experience of ancient Persia, India, Egypt, and Carthage as well as Greece and Rome. He presents his project, as so often in the Renaissance, as resuming the interrupted literary activity of antiquity and remediating its losses. In *On Kingship* (*Reg.* 1.4) he writes that most Greek literature on kingship did not survive the recent shipwreck of Byzantine culture after the fall of Constantinople: only Isocrates and Dio Chrysostom had survived, and both of them wrote far too briefly. Thus, his own work in Latin on kingship, however imperfect, could help supply the losses of time. Similarly, in the preface to *On Republics* addressed to Sixtus IV, he says he was tempted to write his book because Cicero's *De republica* had disappeared in a still greater shipwreck, that of the Western Roman Empire in late antiquity. As Cicero was the only Latin author who wrote about republics, Latin literature demonstrably needed such a treatise as he has tried to provide, unworthy though it might be. If his contemporaries should find it inadequate, he might at least be praised for having aroused other writers of greater intelligence and learning who will sail with a more favorable wind and bring back from the distant past a more polished and brilliant account (*Rep.* 1.1).

## How to Found a Republic

The *fons et origo* of Patrizi's decision to write a treatise on republican government, as he later claimed, was an exhortation from his savior and patron, Pius II. In a letter sent after August 1471 to Cardinal Francesco Todeschini Piccolomini, Pius's nephew and heir, who had been inquiring about the status of the project, Patrizi wrote,

> Your uncle, Pope Pius II . . . often exhorted me with many arguments that I should undertake the task of writing on the civil order [*de institutione civili*] and used to say that he thought I would be doing something valuable if I should carefully transplant what the Greeks said on this subject and include what I thought useful from our [Latin] authors as well. I took on the burden of writing [the book] and started in under his auspices, less in hope of finishing, since the subject matter was huge and extremely difficult, than of denying him nothing; for I recognized that I owed him everything. But soon after that, having left Rome to launch an army and a huge fleet against the Turks, he was stricken by disease and died, throwing not only all Italy but the whole Christian religion into consternation. For my part I became hopeless, having been frustrated of all the help and protection I was counting on, and in grief and depression abandoned the work I had begun—and indeed nearly finished—like a man who realized that the infelicity of our times had no place left for virtue and humane studies. Now, however, owing to the marvelous virtue of Pope Sixtus and his divine learning and wisdom, hope revived somewhat, and I took the abandoned work again in hand, revised it, finished it, and dedicated it to

Sixtus's divine spirit, since from the beginning it had been intended for a pontiff.[8]

This letter seems to place Pius's exhortation to write the *De republica* shortly before the pope's departure for Ancona on 18 June 1464 and its near completion by the time of his death in August of that year. But this cannot be correct; Patrizi, writing a decade after the fact, must be telescoping his dates. The project in all likelihood goes back to his time in Rome (1460/1461) before his term as governor of Foligno began in June 1461. If Patrizi finished his *Poematum libri IV*, dedicated to Pius II, in early 1461, that could well have been the moment when he committed himself to a major new project.

But the letter to Cardinal Francesco is surely accurate in stating that the project was inspired by Pope Pius. The *De republica*'s fundamental commitments to the participation of all citizens in government and to meritocracy echo Pius's own political ideas. In February 1459, on his progress to the Council of Mantua, Pius had made a grand entry into Siena, his first since becoming pope. After a magnificent welcome by the city fathers, the pontiff made a speech in which he urged the city to embrace justice and civic harmony. This could be done, he said, by restoring the nobility to full citizen rights and observing a principle of merit in assigning offices:

And this one thing shall keep you forever united and your state secure: if justice, the mother and queen of the virtues, shall prevail among you. Justice is a certain principle of equity which distributes penalties and rewards among men according to their deserts. Happy is the state guided by justice. And you too will be happy, people of Siena, if you distribute public offices to those who deserve them [*si honores publici inter merentes partiemini*]. It is a principle you have allowed to fall into neglect. For more than fifty years you have treated your noblest citizens like slaves—those whose ancestors founded this city, those who were not forced, but by their own free will handed over the reins of government to you. Now you must return to the path of justice. The nobles must be respected; they must be elected to the posts held by those you cast out and killed.[9]

Pius's interest in reforming the civil order and even the physical design of city-republics in this period is well known. The most famous example of his urbanism, the "ideal city" he created in Pienza, was begun in 1459; its cathedral, rebuilt by the Florentine architect Bernardo Rossellino, was consecrated in 1462. The city's design, "one of the masterpieces of Renaissance urban planning," may well reflect the ideas of Leon Battista Alberti, at that time a member of the papal curia and a close collaborator of Rossellino. Pius also planned to renovate Siena itself in a more classical style.[10] It is easy to imagine the pope asking his devoted follower Patrizi, already known from the *De gerendo magistratu* to be an authority on political philosophy, to write up a comprehensive treatise in order to set out the pope's ideals, and perhaps the ideals of Sienese literati in general, on how to perfect the government of free states in modern times by applying the lessons of antiquity.[11]

In fact we know from Patrizi's correspondence that he had begun the treatise before October 1461, when he wrote from Foligno to his former student and longtime literary collaborator, Agostino Patrizi, asking him to forward a volume of extracts that he, Francesco, had already compiled, which included passages from a Greek historian of the Roman Empire, Diodorus Siculus. He also asks Agostino to procure for him from the bishop of Ferrara a copy of Vitruvius. A year later, writing again to Agostino, he reports that he has reached the fifth book of his treatise and asks Agostino to obtain copies for him of Columella and Ammianus Marcellinus. By September 1463 Patrizi has reached the eighth book of his work and is asking Agostino to find him books by Aulus Gellius and the medical author Celsus.[12]

After that we hear no more of Patrizi's work on the project until the later 1460s. An epigram datable to 1467 complains that his *De republica* has not found a patron to reward it, and says that he has stopped working on it for that reason.[13] In a letter written between

1467 and 1471 Agostino Patrizi reports that for some time extracts of the work have been circulating in Rome, and many eager readers are demanding from him daily the complete text of his *Republic*. Cardinal Francesco Todeschini Piccolomini and Leonardo Dati, the learned bishop of Massa, having had a taste of the work, are ordering him to finish it and publish it under their names.[14] Agostino doesn't know how to answer them anymore, since his old teacher has already exceeded the Horatian limit for polishing a literary work, i.e., nine years.[15]

> So I beg you finally to publish those books and emancipate your son, who has now grown up, and who, I trust, possesses the virtue to protect himself everywhere in the world. And no excuses about the lack of scribes! If you send the work to me, I'll see to it that it's transcribed faithfully and correctly.[16]

It was probably around this time that Patrizi composed another epigram in which he takes himself to task for his incessant revisions to the work and his inability to let it go into the hands of readers. He counsels himself that no work can please everyone and he should be content if the learned and those who cultivate the Muses approve of it. He should be getting on with other writing. He has kept the work hidden for nine years; let it go and meet its fate, Patrizi! Let it fly throughout the world and with good fortune undergo the journey it has long desired to make.[17]

In August 1471 Cardinal Francesco della Rovere was elected Pope Sixtus IV after the sudden death of Paul II. Patrizi still seemed to be apprehensive that his book would be savaged by detractors. After his experiences in Foligno, his trial in Rome, and the continuing fallout from the "academic conspiracy," some paranoia on behalf of his "son," however grown up and virtuous, would be understandable. Who then better to protect his work than the pope? But who would help him present the work to the new Della Rovere pontiff, a man with few ties to the Piccolomini network in Rome that had supported him hitherto?

Fortunately, another old friend, Ilarione of Verona, a client of Cardinal Francesco Todeschini Piccolomini, offered to act as a go-between. Ilarione's own relations with Sixtus seem to have been uncertain in the 1470s, though by 1479–1480 he held an appointment as Sixtus's private secretary.[18] In any case Ilarione's representations seem to have borne fruit and Sixtus agreed to become the work's dedicatee. This must have occurred in late 1471 or 1472. Ilarione also composed an epigram addressed to Patrizi, probably intended as a liminal poem, urging him to publish his distinguished work and to "let a new Plato arise in the earth." There is no reason to fear insolent and shameless tongues, Ilarione wrote; his work will be honored as divine. His language is grave and eloquent, and he has opened up the records of history in both Latin and Greek. The learned will revere his work as the extraordinary accomplishment it is. So come, let the work prostrate itself at Sixtus's feet, and, with me as its guide, set out on its happy journey.[19]

The work, as it was eventually published in several elegantly written and decorated manuscripts during the 1470s, was truly a remarkable one. It represented a major advance in both the range and depth of humanist political thought. Its originality emerges when one considers Patrizi's models and predecessors. Given that Patrizi intended from the first to write a systematic treatise, he could not use Plato's *Republic* or *Laws,* both dialogues, as literary models. As already noted, Cicero's *Republic* did not survive, apart from the cosmological *Dream of Scipio* and a few fragments, and it too, like the Roman orator's *Laws,* was in dialogue form. The only possible model from antiquity was Aristotle's *Politics,* the text that had dominated formal theory in Europe for two hundred years and was the principal authority used in Giles of Rome's *On Princely Rule,* the scholastic text Patrizi aimed to supplant.[20] Aristotle's treatment was too analytical for Patrizi's purposes and was addressed to philosophers; Patrizi's approach was prudential and sought to persuade literate citizens of modern republics to embrace a particular ideal of civil life. The remit Pius had imposed on Patrizi, in any case, was to enrich contemporary political thought by integrating into it a wide range of Greek and Latin sources. Hence, in the end, the structure of Patrizi's treatise, though it echoed Aristotle at certain points, was completely different from the *Politics*.

Patrizi's *De republica* was also unlike any treatise on politics of more recent times. Giles of Rome's treatise—setting aside its preference for monarchy—was divided into three large books: on princely virtues; on "economics" or household management and child-rearing; and on the governance of cities in peace and war. Three humanists before Patrizi had written treatises with the title *De republica:* Uberto Decembrio (ca. 1420), Tito Livio Frulovisi (1435), and Lauro Quirini (1449). None of these treatises circulated widely, and Patrizi may not have read any of them. Decembrio's *De republica* was a dialogue in four books, surviving in one manuscript, that marshalled arguments from Aristotle, Cicero, and Plato's *Republic* (which Decembrio had translated) in order to advocate an idealized form of signorial government.[21] Frulovisi's treatise, which survives in two manuscripts, was a dialogue in three books dedicated to Leonello d'Este, Marquis of Ferrara. Despite its title, the treatise, of broadly Aristotelian inspiration, favored monarchy.[22] Quirini's two-book treatise, dedicated to the doge of Venice, Francesco Foscari, favors a virtuous popular regime led by aristocrats but authorized by the people; it has been described by Guido Cappelli as a "creative rewriting" of Aristotle's *Politics*.[23]

Patrizi's work, by contrast, is by far the most comprehensive and innovative treatise on politics written in the fifteenth century. It was ultimately divided into nine books, but there is some evidence that the design of the work gradually expanded to accommodate new ideas and new source material as the work progressed. It may have begun as a treatise in two books like Quirini's, the first on principles of republican government and the second on the education of magistrates.[24] It is noticeable that, on a doctrinal level, Patrizi seems to have been more positive about popular participation in deliberative and legislative processes in book 1 than he was to be in book 3 and in the later books. Were his experiences in Foligno as he was writing *De republica* altering his attitude to republican government?

His discussion in book 3 of magistracies in the best republic, which he claimed was based on Roman practice, is markedly more aristocratic in tendency than the description of republican institutions given in book 1; book 3 omits, for instance, any mention of popular assemblies or popular tribunes.[25]

At the end of book 3 we get one of the few clues Patrizi himself gives us about his conception of the work's structure:

> So much for the magistrates; for that which relates to military affairs we will speak of in another place when we treat military service and war. We have said a great deal in the first volume that pertains to the constitution of the republic; in the second about the arts and disciplines in which civic leaders should be educated. In this third book we have set out the civil magistracies, imitating the Romans rather than the Greeks.

This does not sound like a man who knows he has another six books ahead of him, though he already plans separate treatment of military affairs, ultimately included at the end of the whole treatise as book 9. The rest of the work, however, does have a reasonably clear structure. Book 4 is concerned with household management and contains a treatise-within-a-treatise on early childhood education, highly innovative for its attention to the psychological development of young children. Book 5 is about citizenship and the virtues and comportment of the good citizen. It contains the first sustained discussion of citizenship written by a political theorist since Aristotle.[26]

Book 6 is the key book for meritocratic theory and introduces the fundamental distinction between political hierarchy based on true nobility (i.e., virtue and education) and social hierarchy based on wealth and heredity. In it Patrizi proposes a series of institutional devices designed to prevent a republic from being dominated by the wealthy and ambitious. But there are several passages in the book that look like afterthoughts, chapters that would have fit more naturally into previous books but were inserted here instead.[27] There are also a number of subjects, like elections, that had been introduced in earlier books but are further developed here.[28] Moreover, Patrizi was no stranger to the pleasures of learned digression, and the phrase "but to return to my main point" occurs a bit too often, in this book and elsewhere, for those readers looking for an orderly exposition.[29]

Books 7 and 8 make a pair.[30] Book 7 deals with the best site for a city and the natural resources needed for it to flourish. The topic is treated both in Plato's *Laws* and Aristotle's *Politics,* though Patrizi's exposition is far more wide-ranging and incorporates much more practical information, especially from Vitruvius, the Roman agricultural writers, and the elder Pliny. Book 8 is on the built environment appropriate to and supportive of the best republic. To my knowledge it is absolutely unexampled in earlier political literature, ancient and medieval. It was inspired by Aristotle and Vitruvius and surely reflected also Pius II's interests in urbanism. But we know that Patrizi on his own account was deeply interested in architecture and the role of the arts in creating a "virtuous environment." As he wrote at the end of book 1, in a chapter on painting and sculpture,

> indeed, by looking at pictures in which famous deeds are depicted we are aroused to desire praise and to undertake great affairs, as though we were reading historical accounts. Let painters therefore have a place in the republic, and an honorable one, that we may be set aflame with the desire for glory and induce the young to seek equal praise. . . . On this account we ought not to fear staining the hands of youths with colors, since painting is proximate to learning.[31]

While both Plato and Aristotle put great emphasis on the kind of music performed in a state and its influence on mores, and many ancient authors consider the influence on politics of poetry and the art of rhetoric, Patrizi, appropriately enough for a Renaissance author, may well be the first political philosopher to pay sustained attention to the role of the fine arts and architecture in shaping the souls of citizens. Patrizi's political thought in general has a striking aesthetic dimension, absent from earlier Western political thought, that is perhaps related to his earlier calling as a Latin poet. He believed that civic harmony and tranquillity are strengthened when citizens enjoy their life together, and this enjoyment of life (*iucunditas vitae*) can be enhanced by imposing symmetry, order, and classical beauty on public and private spaces. Patrizi's sensibility, linking good government with a built environment embodying ideals of beauty and rational planning, was shared by the artists and architects who in the following decade built Federico da Montefeltro's castle and apartments in Urbino, with its famous depictions of ideal cities.[32]

## Aims in Writing the De republica and the Meaning of Institutio

As a citizen once exiled for betraying the republican government of Siena; as a former papal governor of Foligno who had tried to quell a populist uprising against its lord, the pope; as a former chief magistrate accused of corruption; and as a bishop resident in the Kingdom of Naples who had served its king as an ambassador, Patrizi was not at first blush the ideal candidate to appoint himself a teacher of republican government. The two prefaces to *De republica* addressed to his fellow Sienese hint at the awkwardness of his position.

In the first he excuses his long absence from the city by pleading the burdens of his office as bishop of Gaeta. He longs to return to Siena and enjoy its "delightful homely charm." Still, he wants his fellow citizens to know how happy he is in his new home, that pleasant and welcoming city by the sea, where Scipio Africanus went to collect seashells and "became a boy again." Instead of his person, he is sending to the illustrious Senate and famous People of Siena his words in the form of a book. Since words best express a man's nature, he is really sending himself. He hastens to add that *of course* he is not so arrogant as to think his native city needs instruction from him about politics. "I am entirely persuaded that I can teach nothing about human society that is not already found, perfect and finished, in your own institutions and laws." I am just going to review a few old things (*vetera nonnulla*) which you may perhaps find pleasant to hear, as they confirm that your current enactments have been drawn from the fonts of ancient wisdom.

Considering that the *De republica* is full of political advice that, taken seriously, would have required radical reform of Siena's popular regime as well as its economy and system of education, Patrizi's flattery of his fellow citizens is disingenuous, to say the least. He then flavors this tasty carrot with more than a dash of stick. After the first preface to the Sienese he inserts a long dedicatory epistle to his new patron, Pope Sixtus IV, explaining why the book deserves the pontiff's protection. Patrizi then adds a second preface to the Senate and People of Siena, describing how the ancient lawgivers Rhadamanthus and Minos, according to Plato's *Laws,* credited their legislation to Jove himself in order to have it accepted more readily by the people. Inspired by this thought, he had asked Pope Sixtus to be the *auctor* of his book, to give it his authoritative sanction. The pontiff accepted this responsibility, read it with great care, approved it, and strongly recommended its publication.[33]

To the Sienese the implications would have been obvious. In the feudal *imaginaire,* still valid in fifteenth century Italy, Sixtus IV was Siena's spiritual overlord. Any Sienese who read the two prefaces would surely remember how, in the previous decade, the first *auctor* of Patrizi's book, Pope Pius II, had come to Siena and imposed radical political change on the city. Pius was no observer of niceties when it came to distinguishing spiritual and temporal power. He had forced Siena's popular government, against bitter resistance, to accept back into its ruling Concistoro and its sovereign Council of the People the class of nobles or *Gentiluomini*—the class to which Pius's own family, the Piccolomini, belonged—which had been excluded from office for more than half a century.[34] Whatever Pius's intention, the reform did not succeed in making Sienese government more aristocratic in tone, and it was reversed shortly after Pius's death in 1464. Still, the Sienese could hardly doubt the ability of a potentate like Sixtus IV to force unwelcome political changes.

As we shall see, the constitution recommended by Patrizi in the *De republica* also inclines toward the aristocratic, though his is an aristocracy of virtue and learning that maps imperfectly onto the hereditary nobility of Siena. But the prefaces to the Sienese raise the question of Patrizi's goals for his work. Did he expect his advice to be accepted and implemented by the republic of Siena, perhaps under pressure from the pope, perhaps by better-educated Sienese in future generations?[35] A number of passages in the *De republica* addressed explicitly to the Sienese could support that argument. There are many more places where his criticisms of Sienese customs and institutions are only implicit but would have been obvious to its citizens.[36] Or did he, as a man tried and convicted of joining a coup against Siena's popular government, as a man who had been restored to citizenship only through the strong-arm tactics of Pius II, perhaps have another agenda? Did he want to show the Sienese that his real ideals of republican government were generous and high-minded, far above their own grubby party politics, driven as they were by suspicion, greed, and ambition? Did he perhaps want to show the estranged citizens of Foligno that he was not simply a tool of papal autocracy but had genuine sympathy for well-ordered republics?

Whatever his personal motives may have been, on any reasonable reading of the *De republica* it is clear that Patrizi intended his book to apply far more widely than just to the immediate Sienese context. It was meant to help reform and improve the quality of republican governments generally. Especially in the later books Patrizi sometimes considers what a lawgiver should do, should he be granted the great good fortune and resources to found a new city, unencumbered by the refractory political compromises of past regimes. This was no utopian dream—numerous new towns had been founded in Tuscany since the thirteenth century, and, as we have seen, the composition of Patrizi's *De republica* proceeded *pari passu* with the radical reconstruction of Pienza by his patron Pius II. In such cases, "if fortune smiles on us and we can found a city from the ground up," one can hope to design something closer to an optimal civil society, though all human polities will have built-in natural limits owing to climate, geography, and the nature of its people.[37]

This is what Patrizi thinks happened in Venice a thousand years ago: the city's founders gave it an excellent set of laws and institutions, thus setting it on its path to the exceptional harmony and stability it had enjoyed ever since. In 3.2, arguing against the contemporary practice in Italian city-states of bringing in foreign judges as a prophylactic against partisan justice, he writes:

> If the republic is constituted in the best possible way, and everyone properly heeds its laws and mores, [it will not need foreign magistrates]. It is far better to have citizens rule than foreigners, a practice that may be observed not only among the Romans, Carthaginians, Athenians, Spartans and many others, but also in the celebrated republic of the Venetians, which has no place for foreigners and yet experiences no discord or severity, nor do any discords, seditions or hatreds arise in its courts. Indeed, we can say one thing of this republic that I don't remember hearing or reading anywhere else: that the city's constitution, as laid down by its first founders, has always remained the same and never changed. For those who built that city divided its magistracies among themselves as a kind of reward for their labors, and left this inheritance to their posterity, so that they never admitted an immigrant, colonist or foreigner to any magistracy, and this practice has been maintained constantly for nearly a thousand years. Hence the posterity of those who founded the city have always had charge of it, and are called senators, patricians and nobles; all the rest are plebeians. Custom has a great deal of power and it is hard to depart from it, but if it is established from the beginning, the principle of citizen rule will be the safer one, as we said.[38]

Patrizi was wrong to believe that no one had ever noticed before how the Venetian constitution had never departed from its founders' initial design—George of Trebizond had said much the same in 1460/1462—but it was characteristic of his realistic idealism to

believe that statesmen had been able in the past to found lasting institutions and that these could be used as models by others today.

Patrizi, to be sure, was no utopian. He did not believe perfection
was possible in human things. But he was an optimist in this sense:
he believed that, by consulting the wisdom of the past, existing political regimes could be greatly improved and the customs, physical
arrangements, and institutions of new cities could be optimized. Like
Thomas More in *Utopia*, he claimed to be designing an *optimus
status reipublicae*, a best constitution for a state—though in his case
not in jest but in earnest. Like Alexander Hamilton, he held that
human beings were not "forever destined to depend for their political constitutions on accident and force," but had the capacity
"to establish good government from reflection and choice."

In the rest of this book I will use the term "optimal republic" to
specify Patrizi's "best possible republic," analogous to the polity optimized by Aristotle in books 4–6 of the *Politics*, as opposed to an ideal
republic such as is set out in Plato's *Republic*. The latter was widely
understood by Renaissance thinkers to be an ahistorical model—and
therefore not subject to prudential verification—which might be full
of impractical thought experiments but which nevertheless might
have heuristic value in designing better institutions.

Both the reform and the founding of republics *de novo* are implied in Patrizi's use of the Latin word *institutio*, always difficult to
translate into English. The word can mean an ordering or arrangement; it can be an abstract noun meaning "founding" or "instituting," or it can refer to a particular statute or ordinance. But it
also means "education" in the widest sense. Patrizi, like other humanists, uses the word to translate both *politeia*, Aristotle's word
for constitution, and *paideia*, the Greek word for education and
learning. *Paideia* can also suggest, more broadly, acculturation or
civilizing, and it retains this sense in Patrizi's usage.[39] The complex
connotations of the term explain why Patrizi's work on kingship,
*De regno et regis institutione*, is best translated as "On Kingship and
the Education of a King," while *De institutione reipublicae*, the full
title of the *De republica*, could be translated as either "On Ordering

a Republic" or "On Founding a Republic." But Patrizi does not let us forget that *institutio* means education and culture too, because for him, as we shall see in Chapter 5, ordering a republic is inseparable from the task of educating its citizens and optimizing its mores, customs, and built environment. *Institutio,* in other words, implies both statecraft and soulcraft.

## On Kingship and Kingly Education

Once the *De republica* was off his desk after 1471, Patrizi seems to have turned immediately to his next great project, the *De regno et regis institutione,* a title we will henceforth shorten to *De regno* for convenience. While sources for the composition of the *De republica* are abundant, we know almost nothing about the genesis and progress of Patrizi's work on the *De regno.*[40] The treatise was dedicated to Patrizi's new patron, Alfonso, duke of Calabria, and contains, in addition to the dedicatory letter, proemia to books 2 through 6 that are also addressed to the duke. These allude to biographical details of Alfonso's career that allow completion of the work to be dated to 1483/1484.[41]

Patrizi's *De regno* was not the first Renaissance treatise on kingship, nor would it be the last, but it was the longest, most comprehensive, and—before the late sixteenth century—by far the richest in its use of Greek sources for ideal kingship.[42] Still, it was only one of a number of humanist works on kingship and government written in the second half of the quattrocento, the so-called *trattatistica* of *umanesimo politico* that has received a good deal of attention in recent scholarship.[43] These works included Giovanni Pontano's treatise *De principe* (begun in the later 1460s, published in 1490); Bartolomeo Platina's twin treatises *De principe* (1470) and *De optimo cive* (1474); the Bolognese humanist Giovanni Garzoni's treatises *De eruditione principum* (1488–1490) and *De principis officio* (1499);[44] Diomede Carafa's *Memoriale sui doveri del principe* (before 1476), twice translated into Latin but not published in Italian until 1668; Giuniano Maio's *De maiestate* (1492); Filippo Beroaldo the Elder's

*Libellus de optimo statu* (first published 1497); and Giovanni Francesco Bracciolini's *De officio principis liber* (dedicated to Julius II and published in 1504). Like Patrizi's *De republica,* the *De regno* was intended in part as a humanist alternative to the most popular scholastic guide to princely education, Giles of Rome's *De regimine principum,* and by the early sixteenth century it had successfully driven Giles's work out of the market.[45]

We will postpone to the beginning of Chapter 6 a fuller consideration of the extent to which Patrizi may have modified his theoretical commitments between finishing the *De republica* in 1471 and publication of the *De regno* a little over a decade later. But even a cursory examination of the later work reveals it to be a very different sort of project. The *De regno* represents a markedly different approach to meritocracy, one more in line with Giles of Rome and the long-established genre of the *speculum principis,* or mirror of princes, stretching back to Seneca's *De clementia.* Yet the *De regno* also breaks new ground, even within that tradition, and not only because it deploys a much wider range of ancient sources than any previous work of its type.

In his *De republica* Patrizi had argued for the superiority of republics to monarchy because of the moral dynamics of princely government. Even if a prince was a good man, holding monarchical power usually corrupted him, and the children of good princes as a rule were worse than their forebears. Monarchy was in principle the best form of government so long as the prince was virtuous, but the rule of a virtuous prince was rare and short-lived. That was how republics arose. Citizens oppressed by bad princes would band together and share power, and by cultivating a respect for the supremacy of law and a spirit of equality could achieve freedom from arbitrary rule. The political philosopher could optimize republican rule by designing good institutions and an educational curriculum that would prevent ignorant, greedy, and ambitious men from holding power. Good institutions and a properly educated elite would "elevate the worthy" (in the Confucian phrase), making sure that the governing class would continue to be men of virtue and practical wisdom. That in turn would secure the stability and flourishing of the republic.

In the *De regno* Patrizi took on the challenge of optimizing the monarchies of his day. If the problem with monarchy was princes who were morally bad or good princes who were corrupted by power, what resources could the humanities and the liberal arts provide to prevent those outcomes? Could a form of education be devised that would improve and stabilize a king's character? Could study of the ancient world and its experiences of rulership help kings and their advisers anatomize the psychological challenges experienced by powerful individuals? Could humanistic study help them form behavioral patterns that would enable them to serve their countries well? Patrizi, now, thought all of this was possible. If his *De regno* represents an advance on earlier mirrors of princes, it was precisely in its presentation of the psychology of rulership and the dynamic aspects of character formation. Patrizi aimed to give kings a refined understanding, based on history, of the innumerable ways bad behavior—both their own and that of their courtiers—could threaten their rule, and how acquiring the virtues would preserve it. He admitted from the outset that ruling other men was the most difficult of all human tasks, not least because, of all species of animals, the human species was the most ungrateful to its rulers. The man who sought power over others was taking a wolf by the ears, as the ancient maxim had it. But it was not an impossible task, and the rewards of successful rulership were the greatest that a human being could aspire to.

Patrizi laid out the problem in his preface to the work and in the first book.[46] Kingship was the hardest thing in the world, and a king needed to learn how to be a king, but what could he learn from a mere scholar and private citizen? Wouldn't a humanist adviser be like the hapless Aristotelian philosopher Phormio, who made a fool of himself lecturing Hannibal on how to be a general? Wouldn't it be better for a king to be taught by another king, as the Persian Cambyses instructed his son Cyrus? Yet all the great ancient rulers kept around them men of letters to advise them. Why? What men of letters could do for the king, it turns out, was to demonstrate the superiority of kingship to other forms of government, teach kings that they are not playthings of fortune but can control their own destiny through virtue, help future kings understand the rewards of good kingship, and remind them that their office is favored by God, whose divine power will uphold their just rule. But that is only the beginning.

In book 2 Patrizi offers a definition of kingship as the just authority of one man over others. Without justice a king is no better than a tyrant. If the highest goal imaginable for human life is to be like God, the king in dispensing justice is the human being who has the power to be most like God. Justice implies meritocracy. The king should elevate men to high office in the state who have virtue and merit. "Virtue, indeed, should be the measure of all things." His goal should be to make everyone in his kingdom blessed, "so that the city wins moral goodness through virtue, great glory, riches, and resources." Justice also implies benign treatment of other nations. The tyrant seeks to harm them, the just king benefits them; kings liberate, tyrants enslave.

To acquire the supreme virtue of justice, along with the other virtues, a king needs education. The rest of book 2 lays out a program of liberal education for the king that includes the trivium and quadrivium, but also emphasizes, in line with humanist theory since Petrarch, the study of noble poets, historians, and orators. A king should cultivate a royal manner of speech. He need not study abstruse philosophy but should learn wise maxims and sayings that are salted with prudence. The king also needs vigor and a fine physical presence, and book 3 is occupied by describing the best types of physical exercises for a king. It also advises the king to travel and learn about geography.

Books 4 and 5 contain an anatomy of the passions harmful to royal rule. Patrizi presents these as enemies of virtue, but above all they are enemies of truth. A king cannot rule without truthfulness both in his own mind and speech and in that of his courtiers. He needs truthful information about what is going on in his own kingdom and in neighboring regions. He should act to muzzle the bearers of lies—flatterers, slanderers, yes-men, informers—and he should curb verbal incontinence and license in his courtiers. For himself, he needs to know how to weaken and control malign perturbations of soul. The list of such perturbations is a long one: avarice, anger, erotic love, excess of joy, malevolence, excess pleasure, boasting, over-spending, ambition, fear, laziness, excess of fear, depression, envy, grief, anxiety, desperation, and many others. These perturbations are each treated in detail, and examples from antiquity are given both of those who have yielded to them and those who have successfully reined them in. Patrizi's mastery of ancient Latin poetry is often tapped to illustrate the nature and force of the passions.

Books 6 and 7 discuss how and why the king should cultivate the virtues he needs, which will bring him personal felicity as well as strengthen his authority. Book 6 emphasizes general civil virtues while book 7 focuses on the great kingly virtues: courage, magnanimity, trustworthiness, constancy, forbearance, and patience. Book 8 discusses further means to stabilize the character of a king and his subjects: obedience to the laws, cultivation of true friendship and the social virtues, maintenance of religion and piety. The work ends in book 9 with two final topics: the duties of citizens toward their king, and a description of the rewards a king can expect for excellent rulership: in this life, in the memory of future generations, and in the life to come.

Like the *De republica*, the *De regno* draws on an immense range of sources, and Patrizi, here as in his earlier work, is as much concerned with describing the actual institutions and functioning of ancient governments as he is with presenting classical political philosophy. Here as in the earlier work his interests range well beyond the Graeco-Roman world. He found much to admire in the customs and institutions of other civilizations, such as the gymnosophists or "naked wise men" of India, and the Persians, Parthians, Babylonians, and Lydians; in the *De republica* he even elaborates on Ammianus

Marcellinus's account of the "Silk People"—the *Seres* or Chinese. The ancient, pre-Hellenized Egyptians, known from Herodotus and Diodorus Siculus, are of particular interest, especially as the greatest ancient poets, political thinkers, and teachers of the disciplines went to Egypt as their school.[47] Even barbarians, such as the British and the Gauls, have things to teach the serious student of government.

Patrizi's use of sources, to be sure, would not satisfy modern scholars. He was not above embroidering, sometimes extensively, on his sources, as will be illustrated several times in the rest of this volume.[48] Historical writing, in the Renaissance as in antiquity, was a branch of rhetoric, and began to be understood as an independent literary *ars* only toward the end of the quattrocento.[49] There were no societies of historians to organize anything like professional standards, and the temptation, conscious and unconscious, to manipulate ancient accounts to serve present purposes must have been hard to resist, much as it is for modern journalists. Patrizi had few or no reference works to help him when he got into a muddle, but however one judges his work, he should be given immense credit for his efforts to assemble and apply, in many cases for the first time, recently recovered ancient sources to the analysis of contemporary political problems.

Those efforts were truly impressive for a someone living in the age before print vastly facilitated access to old books. Preliminary research on Patrizi's sources in the *De republica* disclose his study of the following ancient authors:[50]

* Agricultural treatises. *In Latin:* Cato the Elder, Columella, Varro.
* Biographers. *In Greek:* Diogenes Laertius, ps. Herodotus (*Life of Homer*), Plutarch. *In Latin:* Cornelius Nepos, Jerome, Suetonius.
* *Corpus iuris civilis.* Many jurists are cited, including Florentinus, Modestinus, Papinian, Paulus, and Ulpian. Particular laws are also cited (sometimes from historical and grammatical

authors), such as the Law of the Twelve Tables, the Lex
Aemilia, Lex Cincia, Lex Didia, Lex Fannia, Lex Licinia
Sextia, Lex Voconia.

- Dramatic writers: *In Latin:* Plautus, Seneca, Terence.
- Epistographers. *In Greek:* ps. Phalaris, ps. Philip of Macedon,
  ps. Diogenes Cynicus, ps.-Plato. *In Latin:* Cicero, Pliny the
  Younger.
- Geographical writers. *In Greek:* Pausanias, Strabo. *In Latin:*
  Pomponius Mela.
- Grammatical and antiquarian writers. *In Greek:* Philostratus
  (*Heroicus*). *In Latin:* ps. Asconius Pedianus, ps. Caesar,
  Censorinus, Donatus, Festus, Aulus Gellius, Nonius Mar-
  cellus, Pliny the Elder, Solinus, Varro, Vibius Sequester.
- Historians. *In Greek:* Appian, Arrian, Cassius Dio, Dio-
  dorus Siculus, Dionysius of Halicarnassus, Herodotus,
  Polybius, Thucydides, Xenophon. *In Latin:* Ammianus
  Marcellinus, Caesar, Curtius Rufus, Eutropius (with the
  continuation of Paulus Diaconus), Florus, the *Historiae
  Augustae Scriptores,* Justinus, Livy, Sallust, Tacitus, Valerius
  Maximus.
- Military writers. *In Greek:* Polyaenus. *In Latin:* Frontinus,
  Vegetius.
- Orators and works of rhetorical theory. *In Greek:* Aeschines,
  Aristotle (*Rhetoric*), Demosthenes, Isocrates. *In Latin:*
  Apuleius (*Florida*), Cicero, Quintilian.
- Poets: *In Greek:* Apollonius of Rhodes, Homer, Hesiod,
  Pindar, Theocritus. *In Latin:* ps. Cato (*Distichs*), Claudian,
  Horace, Juvenal, Lucan, Lucretius, Macrobius, Martial, Ovid,
  Persius, Propertius, Silius Italicus, Valerius Flaccus, Vergil.
- Philosophers, including political philosophers: *In Greek:*
  Aristotle, Dio Chrysostom, Plato, Plutarch (*Moralia*), Proclus,
  Sextus Empiricus, Xenophon. *In Latin:* Apuleius, Calcidius,
  Cicero, Macrobius, Seneca.
- Patristic writers. *In Latin:* Augustine (*City of God*), Jerome,
  Tertullian.

- Technical treatises, including medical works and natural philosophy. *In Greek:* Hippocrates. *In Latin:* Celsus Cornelius, Pliny the Elder, Vitruvius.

Similar work on the sources of the *De regno* has not been done, but readers of that work will find Patrizi using more or less the same dossier of sources, with a few exceptions. The most important change is a newfound respect for Plato. In the *De republica* Patrizi mentions Plato mostly to disagree with him, whereas in the *De regno* he seems readier to diffuse the kind of Platonism radiating from Florence and the circle of Ficino in the 1470s and 1480s. Patrizi in his early letter from the 1440s to Achille Petrucci on the history of the ancient Academy had inclined to a skeptical reading of its history. In the *De republica* he explicitly denied a doctrine crucial for Ficino's whole revival of Platonic theology—that philosophers had had knowledge of the true God before the time of Christ.[51] In the *De regno,* however, he shows from time to time a much greater sympathy for Platonic metaphysics. He invokes Plato's theory of ideas (via Cicero) to explicate his account of the ideal king.[52] The bishop has also, clearly, spent more time with Plato's *Laws* and has read the *Symposium,* a dialogue not cited in his earlier work, as well as Ficino's translation of Hermes Trismegistus, a text the Florentine believed to stand at the root of a lost ancient tradition of theology.[53] In the *De regno,* moreover, Patrizi is less inclined to conceal his debt to Aristotle, drawing particularly in books 6 and 7 on the *Nicomachean Ethics.* Though Giles of Rome, in common with all other modern authors, is never named, his presence too on Patrizi's bookshelf is revealed in the structure and topics of these books.[54]

Neither of Patrizi's great treatises found many readers in his lifetime. Only eleven manuscripts of the *De republica* have so far been identified, and only six of the *De regno.* The limited circulation of his works may be by design, however. Patrizi was an author who throughout his life wrote for small coteries consisting of his patrons and other like-minded people—"fit audience though few," as Milton would say. In the era before printing, most literati, particularly Latin poets, wrote for such restricted audiences. This is difficult for modern writers to comprehend; for us, having more readers is almost always more desirable. But the book world was different in the age before the commercialization of the written word. Even after printing became the dominant mode of written communication, scribal publication continued to thrive in certain milieu where mutual trust between author and reader was important.[55] Like Bartolomeo Scala and some other humanists and book collectors of the incunabular period, Patrizi may well have regarded the printing press with disdain and distrust.[56] Machiavelli's *Prince, Discourses,* and *History of Florence* were likewise intended for private circulation, probably owing to their controversial, even scandalous content.[57]

Nevertheless, by the time of his death, sometime between June 1493 and August 1494, Patrizi might well have wondered whether the seeds of his intellect had fallen on sterile ground. Had he lived just a little longer, he would have witnessed the military collapse of the Aragonese kingdom in southern Italy and the expulsion from Naples of his former pupil, now King Alfonso II, by the French king Charles VIII. The same Charles in 1495 would capture and sack his beloved Gaeta. He would have seen his native city of Siena fall in 1497 under the tyranny of Pandolfo Petrucci, the ruthless nephew of his former student Achille Petrucci. He could hardly have anticipated the tremendous success his works would begin to enjoy two decades later, during the sixteenth century, when they were printed more than seventy times in various forms, including French, Italian, German, Spanish, and English versions, between 1518 and 1610.

Some of Patrizi's sixteenth-century readers were surely responding to his teachings about meritocracy. Thomas More, Erasmus, and Juan Luis Vives may well have been among them, though this remains to be demonstrated.[58] The great classical scholar Denis Lambin, who wrote a preface to the 1567 edition of the *De regno,* praised "not only the gravity and majesty of the argument, but the writer's brilliant mind, learning and elegance." Patrizi's *De republica,* via an epitome translated into English in 1576 by Richard Robinson, played no small role in the history of early modern English republicanism.[59]

Other readers, like the two works' first editor, the obscure Joannes Savigneus, were perhaps more attracted by its encyclopedic qualities, its value as an armature on which were systematically arranged, under various heads, an extraordinary array of anecdotes and quotations relevant to the governance of cities and kingdoms. But the reception of Patrizi's writings in early modern Europe must remain a task for other hands.

## Patrizi's Historico-prudential Method

However the two works were utilized in later times, Patrizi's amassing of classical authorities both Greek and Latin cannot be explained as a product merely of antiquarian zeal or a desire of encyclopedic "coverage." It was the consequence of his new way of writing political philosophy, which I shall label the historico-prudential method. The method is undertheorized in Patrizi's own works, so its assumptions must often be inferred from scattered remarks and from his practice. But they are worth teasing out in some detail, as Patrizi's method counts among his most original and valuable contributions to political thought.

The nature and goals of his method can be brought out by a comparison with the most influential work of scholastic political theory in Patrizi's time, Giles of Rome's *De regimine principum* (1277–1280). Patrizi certainly knew this work, which was "among the most widely-read books of the late Middle Ages." It was often used as a university textbook and had been translated into the principal Western European vernaculars. Patrizi must have regarded it as the chief rival of his own treatises, which aimed—successfully, as it turned out—to displace it.[60] Giles's work, despite its ubiquity in Renaissance libraries, is unfamiliar even to specialists today; like both of Patrizi's treatises, it has never been critically edited or translated into modern English.[61]

Giles was a theologian of the Augustinian order, trained in Aristotelian philosophy, and a student and follower of Thomas Aquinas. He wrote commentaries on many of Aristotle's works, including the *Ethics, Politics,* and *Rhetoric.* His *De regimine principum,* intended as an exhaustive treatise on rulership, was divided into three sections: how princes should rule themselves, how they should rule their families, and how they should rule states in peace and war. Though Giles was a convinced monarchist—the *De regimine* was written for Philippe IV of France, whose tutor Giles may have been—the book was intended to be of use to other *principes* as well, including nobles, civic leaders, and prominent citizens of medieval city-republics who had rule over families and country estates. Giles's exposition relies almost entirely on Aristotle's *Ethics, Politics,* and *Rhetoric,* with only a light sprinkling of citations from other sources, such as Valerius Maximus, Justin, and Palladius's *De re rustica.*[62] The non-Aristotelian work most frequently cited was Vegetius's *De re militari,* used mostly in the final section of the book on military science. Like Patrizi, Giles avoids citing the Bible and the Fathers, but he ignores the jurists, whom he regards with contempt as "political idiots."[63]

Giles takes Aristotle's point that reasoning in the practical sciences, including ethics and politics, is less precise than that of the theoretical sciences. But he attends less to Aristotle's equally important doctrine that the practical sciences should proceed inductively, moving from reflection on experience to classification, then to formulating general but flexible rules. Giles's scholastic training makes it natural for him to proceed instead from definitions, then make analytical distinctions, and finally produce reasons or accounts that enable readers to say why one course of action is the right one. Historical examples play little role in his reasoning. Like most scholastic interpreters of Aristotle, he anchored moral decisions in the eternal law of God, to which human beings had direct access through "synderesis," conceived of as an innate human ability to recognize the principles of moral reasoning, analogous to conscience. This introduced an *a priori* element into practical reasoning, foreign to the method advocated by Aristotle, who discovered the best patterns of ethical and political action via prudential judgments based on human experience, personal and historical.

The difference between Giles's scholastic method and Patrizi's historico-prudential method can be illustrated from the arguments each author makes in favor of monogamous marriage. Giles begins his treatment of the issue (2.1.9) by saying that "some sects" think it rational to have more than one wife, but right reason dictates that all citizens—and kings and *principes* most of all—must be content with a single wife. This is a conclusion that "we can pursue in three ways: on the part of the man himself, on the part of the wife, and on the part of the offspring." If a man has too many wives, he will have too much concupiscence, just as having too much food makes him overeat. Excess concupiscence will cloud his mind and over-whelm his reason, and that is obviously bad. Furthermore, politi-cally, it's bad for citizens to devote themselves to venery, making it necessary for them to withdraw from acts of prudence and civic activity, and particularly bad for kings and princes, who should be attending to their public duties and the safety of the realm. Polygamy harms women too, since it necessarily involves the dilution of a hus-band's love for his wife, which ought to be great ("as is proved in *Ethics* 8") in order to strengthen the fundamental bond of society. On the other hand, the need for polygamy cannot be proven by the need for offspring in cases where the wife is infertile, as Giles proves using a complicated argument from natural philosophy.

This is precisely the sort of argumentation—and it is far more long-winded and intricate than I have represented it—that Patrizi finds fault with in both his political treatises. In the *De republica* (2.5), discussing the usefulness of dialectic in the education of re-publican citizen-magistrates, he tells us that there are two kinds of argument, dialectical and oratorical. Both are necessary, one to prove, the other to persuade. Oratorical argument is more civil, "because it draws minds toward one's will in a softer way, by per-suasion and dissuasion," but dialectic "seems more to extort (*extorquere*) what it tries to prove, and by certain abrupt speeches drags us into [the speaker's] own way of thinking, and compels us to confess things in words which we by no means assent to in mind." He makes a similar point in *De regno* (2.2) but relates it to the audience for political argumentation. Severe logic may appeal to those living a contemplative life, he writes, but ordinary human beings, those who live in civil society, require "gentler belief" (*mitior opinio*), which indulges our softer mores. "For those harder arguments are more suited to contemplation than to action and cannot easily persuade readers, but through shrewd argumentation extort (*extorquent*) confessions that those beliefs are true rather than [producing voluntary] assent to them." They might dazzle for a moment, but soon the undertow of the audience's prepossessions and social commitments will cause them to lapse back into their customary beliefs.[64]

This attitude to formal argument, derived ultimately from Cicero's skeptical *Academica* (which Patrizi cites), was a common one among humanists. It was made most elaborately in Petrarch's influential invective *On His Own Ignorance and That of Many Others* (1367/1371), directed against the arrogance of scholastic natural science.[65] Petrarch complained that the overwhelming reliance of scholastics on Aristotle gave them a mental formation that was not so much Christian as Aristotelian. He believed that their rebarbative language and pseudo-demonstrative style of argument made them, paradoxically, unable to persuade. Only a mind immersed in the writings of all the ancients would be able to preserve its sovereignty over each of them; to follow one author only enslaved the intellect and undermined Christian faith. Demonstrative argument in ethics was also ineffective; it might produce temporary assent but it would not fundamentally change anyone's behavior. For that, eloquence would be needed, an eloquence like that of Cicero—informed by the wisdom of Greek philosophy and Roman tradition but able to appeal to reason, the imagination, and the passions all at once. Dialectic could be a useful weapon of eloquence, but it did not by itself yield the sort of humane prudence that could change lives—and, as Patrizi would later add (*De republica* 2.4), societies.

It is not surprising, then, that Patrizi's argument for monogamy, though its conclusion is the same as Giles's, follows an entirely different path. His point of departure is Plato's notorious proposal in *Republic* 5 that the male guardian elite of his ideal polis should forsake normal family life, seek sexual satisfactions nonexclusively from guardian women, and reproduce itself via temporary, secret couplings. These would be arranged on eugenic principles, in such a way that fathers and mothers would not be able to identify their own children, who on birth would be turned over to common nurseries to be raised by the whole community.[66]

Patrizi understands Plato's reasons for proposing such an institution—to eliminate occasions for factionalism among the elite—and he seems to know (without mentioning their source) Aristotle's rather abstract criticisms of Plato's *communio mulierum* (*Politics* 2.2–4). But his own criticisms of Plato do not follow Aristotle's lead.[67] Instead, he paints an attractive picture of monogamous family life and the way its utility and satisfactions contribute to the blessed life of individuals and civil societies (*Rep.* 4.3–4). The biological purpose of monogamous marriage is not to satisfy lust but to have children, which is both natural and a civic duty. Plato's collective mode of child-rearing is literally utopian—it is found nowhere in nature—so it cannot offer us a model; we cannot reflect prudentially on the historical outcomes of such an arrangement if it has never existed. Monogamous marriage, on the other hand, is the most natural of all associations, and the larger society of the state is woven together through intermarriage. Marriage has the power to conciliate political enemies, as the union between Julius Caesar's daughter and his rival Pompey shows. For Patrizi, matrimony thus plays the role that virtuous friendship among male citizens plays in Aristotle's theory of political harmony.

Platonic collectivism also violates utility, since history and experience show that what makes marriage attractive is the deep and lasting satisfactions it offers. Marriage provides us with a companion to whom we are indissolubly linked in true friendship and with whom we can build a complete life, in good fortune and bad, in sickness and old age. Human beings are dependent on others, especially at the beginning and end of life, and the family is our main source of mutual help. A husband and wife raise children whom they care for in childhood and who will care for them in old age; the married couple are thus the central link in the chain of life. Marriage is even a kind of *religio*, a sacred bond, not just among Christians, who include matrimony among the sacraments, but among the ancients too (Patrizi invokes etymology and ancient Roman rites of marriage to prove his point). Marriage helps us face the miseries of old age and death, since when we look at our children and grandchildren we can see something of ourselves and our stock (*genus*) surviving into posterity. *Non omnis moriar;* we will live on in their memory of us. History records only a few examples of male friends who sacrificed themselves for one other, like Pylades and Orestes or Damon and Pythias, but innumerable examples of women and men who sacrificed themselves for their spouses.[68] Turning to ancient poetry to illustrate the great power of the affective bond between husband and wife, he quotes an elegy of Propertius (4.3), in which a woman pines for her long-absent soldier husband, and recalls Orpheus's lament for his lost Eurydice.

Patrizi acknowledges that many marriages are burdensome and lack strong affection, and that family life can be a source of trouble. But on the whole, and from society's point of view especially, it is better than the alternative. He quotes the Roman statesman Q. Caecilius Metellus Numidicus's dictum, "Nature teaches us that we can't live in full satisfaction with wives but without them we can't live at all." Many Romans were tempted to shirk the burdens of marriage, but Metellus in his role as censor, in charge of Roman mores, exhorted the Romans "for the sake of the republic" to embrace matrimony, while discouraging malcontents from speaking ill of the married state, "lest a few rude and refractory men and women prove an obstacle to the rest in taking up the married state."[69] Patrizi concludes that "since almost nothing in all of human life can be found that is entirely unconditional and perfect, we can take it as confirmed experience that no form of friendship is more stable and more enhanced by piety and a sense of duty than matrimony."

Patrizi reviews in some detail the marriage customs of the ancients, beginning with Athens and Sparta. Both had unacceptable customs that violated the principle of monogamous marriage. The Athenians allowed one man to marry two women at the same time, and the Spartans permitted women to have more than one sexual partner, especially if her first partner was a prominent man away on military service. Even Socrates yielded to the force of custom in Athens by having two wives, though Patrizi claims, with a rare touch of dry humor, that he did so in order better to train himself in patience. Patrizi is ashamed to refute the decrees of these two cities, "the most famous not only in all of Greece but in the entire world," but "I daresay nothing seems to me more uncivil and more deserving of condemnation and mockery than these two laws." Both laws undermined the bond of trust that should hold a true marriage together. So too with other corrupt marriage customs in antiquity: those of the Egyptians (reported by Strabo), the British (as described in Caesar's *Commentaries*), the Parthians (as in Justinus), the Armenians (Strabo again), the Lydians (in Herodotus), and the Babylonians (in Curtius Rufus). All of these nations corruptly compromised the principle of monogamy or sexual exclusivity in various ways, leading to a vicious promiscuity and the weakening of parents' sense of duty toward their offspring.

The point of this review of ancient customs, says Patrizi, is "so that everyone might know that the Romans had the holiest customs regarding matrimony, and if they were lacking in anything, that gap has been filled in the best possible way by the canon law of the popes, so that nothing more could be added to that capstone."[70] Patrizi's point is not that the Romans were the best of ancient peoples whose customs and laws should be imitated in every respect. They were perhaps the best overall model (*De republica* 1.2), and certainly had the best marriage customs, but other nations excelled them in other respects. The Romans' use of chattel slavery, for example, is not a model that can be followed by modern Christian states (*De republica* 4.2, 6.4). Roman custom was what best agreed with the mores of Christian marriage in modern Italian cities, and the reputation of

87

the Romans for virtue and durable empire should reassure us moderns that the Roman form of marriage, as perfected by Christian doctrine, was the strongest basis for a polity.

Patrizi's argument for monogamous matrimony illustrates most of the features of his historico-prudential method. It aims, first of all, to be persuasive rather than demonstrative. It does not provide a systematic list of correct teachings backed by philosophical argument in the manner of Giles, but a vision of a better society, together with wise counsels as to how such a society might be achieved. Though he often quotes poetry and cites the opinion of moral philosophers, his primary resource for finding, testing, and proving his political counsels is history. Unlike Machiavelli, however, Patrizi does not try to elicit laws of history. He explicitly rejects, for example, the idea that constitutional changes fall into regular cyclical patterns, as we shall see in Chapter 3. What history does for him and for his readers is to open a vast theater of human actions, counsels, and measures that have been tried in past societies and whose outcomes, practical and moral, we can often judge, enriching our own political prudence. If, as Cicero wrote (*Orator* 34.120), to be ignorant of history is to remain forever a child, familiarity with history can give us a kind of supercharged wisdom, far beyond the ken of any one person, no matter how old and experienced. The proud excitement that bubbles beneath the surface of Patrizi's treatises is the conviction that he has placed at the service of his contemporaries, and for the first time since antiquity, a vast store of experience to which his knowledge of Greek has given him an access closed off to earlier generations.

The multiplication of sources implies a degree of leveling among authorities: no one authority can give us reliable advice in every matter. We have to make our own choices, exercise our own prudential judgment. Plato and Aristotle are particularly valuable—Patrizi advises us to commit their political texts to memory—but as Pliny taught us, no book is so bad that it does not contain something of value. On the other hand, not everything written by the ancients is worthy of imitation. Human mores are in constant flux and those of the past will not always suit the present, nor are the mores of the present to be taken as unchangeable and unimprovable.

It is not true, as most people persuade themselves, that nothing is right except what agrees with our own mores, or that nothing is wrong except what is repellent to those mores. The judgments of human beings are free (*libera sunt hominum iudicia*), and everyone is stirred to embrace those pursuits that are praised by the custom of his country.

We the educated, however, must keep an open mind. The Greeks expected noblemen to perform on musical instruments, but the Romans thought it shameful. "Socrates in Plato thought music so important that a change in music imperiled the state, as though their citizens' fortunes depended on the fiddle"; the Romans took no such view. The Athenians allowed marriage to a sister from the same father; but the Romans thought this was unspeakably wicked. The Spartans allowed maidens to wrestle naked in the palaestra and widows to act on stage for money. Who could bear such behavior in Roman times, or in ours? Yet some of our customs would not be approved by the Greeks, like allowing women to attend dinner parties. We allow our women to go out in crowds; the Greeks kept them indoors. In short, we find many useful counsels in ancient sources but we are not bound to follow their example. What is *honestum* or honorable can best be judged by its outcome.[71]

A good example of this prudent eclecticism is provided by Patrizi's use of Plato. In *On Kingship* (2.2) he praises Plato for his religious and pious wisdom, his recognition that God was the highest good; and elsewhere he relies on Plato's theory of Forms to theorize his own ideal king (ibid., 2.3–4).[72] But he also makes clear in both treatises that Plato was quite often mistaken, particularly about politics. He was wrong to believe that reliance on the written word damaged the mind (*De republica* 2.1), wrong to expel poets from his ideal state (ibid., 2.6), wrong to prohibit his guardians from possessing private property (ibid., 3.6, 6.3), and, as we have seen, wrong to oppose the traditional family. Similarly, the most prestigious states—Rome, Athens, Sparta, and the Persia of Cyrus I—are to be respected and studied for their achievements but are not necessarily to be imitated in every respect. In fact, and rather surprisingly, Patrizi repeatedly cites the ancient Graeco-Roman city of Massilia (Marseilles) as the best ancient model for his modern *optimus status reipublicae*.[73]

Prudence counseled that statesmen who wished to found or reform the best possible states in modern times could not do so by simply elaborating a perfect, abstract ideal, then embodying it in legislation. Politics was not a science. Necessity constrained choice but did not and need not replace it. The prudence of statesmen must negotiate between the limits and possibilities of their own situation and the treasury of past historical experience, using it to stimulate their powers of invention, helping them to adapt measures and customs in the best way possible to the problems of their own times. They would need to take account of the physical situation and climate of their city, its history and political traditions (making a careful estimate of how devoted it was to liberty, for example), the moral character of its people, its civilizational achievements, its relations with its neighbors, and the great moral teachings of the Christian religion. Sometimes long custom has established practices contrary to justice and fairness, and sometimes these have to be tolerated in the interests of stability (*Rep.* 1.2). There was no one best political regime suitable for all republics. As Aristotle had said, the regime should be adapted to the people, not the people to the regime (*Rep.* 1.5). There are better and worse regimes, but the best should not be enemy of the good; improvements need to be made gradually. Though the situations of different states varied, the one invariant was human nature, and the best statesmen would have to have an excellent grasp of how people behaved as individuals and in groups—of political psychology, in other words. Patrizi himself demonstrated his own psychological insight on many occasions, such as in his treatment of political equality.[74]

Patrizi often manifests a reluctance to cite Aristotle, even when he is adopting the Stagyrite's opinions, possibly in order to avoid giving the impression that he was a dogmatic Aristotelian, possibly to highlight his own achievement in reconstructing ancient political wisdom from an unprecedentedly large dossier of sources.[75] But in his historico-prudential method he comes much closer to a genuinely Aristotelian method of practical reasoning than had Giles and other scholastic writers of the late Middle Ages. Patrizi has few outright moral prohibitions among his political counsels—prohibitions against abortion, bigamy, and enslaving fellow Christians are three examples—and these obviously take their force from Christian teaching rather than arising simply from judgments of prudence. But even in these cases Patrizi corroborates moral absolutes with prudential arguments, showing why Christian teachings are also backed by experience and history.

THREE

# Principles of Republican Government

## The Defense of Republics

Though Patrizi was an "optimist" in the sense described in Chapter 2, he was nevertheless a man of his time; he was no missionary for republicanism. As Gabriele Pedullà has well said,

> During the Renaissance Italian republics could prosper and ex-
> tend their dominion over new provinces and cities, but republican
> rule was not seen as a model to be emulated by non-republican
> countries. In short, self-government had no ideologically expansive
> power, and this attitude would not change for centuries. . . . In
> fifteenth century Europe there was no place for any sort of ex-
> pansive republicanism, capable of confronting the monarchies
> on their level. . . . What one finds in the Italian communes is
> therefore a republicanism ready at most to defend the acquired
> rights of the communes and to exalt the efficiency of self-
> government (for example, in favoring virtue through positive
> competition), but reluctant to doubt the legitimacy of other po-
> litical regimes.[1]

Patrizi certainly believed that successful self-ruling cities were a rare phenomenon, however valuable. Most *populi* were not capable of liberty. Since most governments were monarchical—in heaven, in nature, in the church, and in the family—republics were necessarily "ideologically defensive," to use Pedullà's expression.[2]

For a political philosopher like Patrizi, the challenge of defending the value and viability of free cities was especially acute. Italian city-republics had had their defenders since the thirteenth century, but such defenses were generally to be found in the oratory of republican propagandists like Leonardo Bruni or in technical treatises by jurists such as Bartolus of Sassoferrato. Giles of Rome's *De regimine principum*—as we have seen, the most prestigious and popular work of political theory in Patrizi's time—argued powerfully for hereditary monarchy as the best form of government.[3] Many contemporaries thought of popular republics in particular as tawdry, unstable places—rent by violence, unreliable in alliances, manipulated by commercial interests, and therefore deficient in honor and religious devotion. A Portuguese visitor to Siena, for example, was fined in 1451 for insulting the city; he had declared that it was ruled by "grocers, tanners, shoemakers and rustics," who constituted *un reggimento di merda,* a shitty regime.[4] That attitude was widespread.[5] Furthermore, it was clear to the learned that most republics—including the Roman republic, the greatest of them all—were unstable and ended eventually in monarchy, like a tempest-tossed ship coming into a safe port.[6] Most of the hundreds of popular communes that had come into existence in thirteenth-century Italy had been absorbed into principalities and regional states by the fifteenth. The trend of history seemed to favor one-man rule. How much longer could the four remaining independent republics of Italy last?

Patrizi's *De republica* as a whole might be seen as a vigorous response to the dismal reputation of republics in the quattrocento. He takes the issue head-on in the first chapter of his treatise, entitled "Which is better, obeying the just commands of a prince, or dwelling in a free city founded on the best laws and mores?" This was an old quarrel, says Patrizi, about which the Greek philosophers disagreed. Plato had preferred an aristocratic republic, whereas Xenophon—like Plato an Athenian and a disciple of Socrates—took the monarchy of Cyrus the Persian as the best model of civil order. In human history we see that the empires of the nations have been ruled by kings and princes: it seemed best to them to be ruled by a single just and legitimate man rather than by a few or by a multitude of generally ignorant men. It is hard, Patrizi writes, for those of us who look down on day laborers and delivery boys as individuals to revere them when they are combined together in government. Homer, the greatest of poets, rejected government by the many, and both God in heaven and Nature in the animal kingdom seemed to endorse monarchy.

The example of monarchy in the animal kingdom was perhaps why the first men who formed themselves into communities accepted the arbitrary government of a single wise and eloquent man. But afterward everything went into decline as power corrupted men and made arrogant and impudent the princes who at first seemed gentle and mild. In the end they became wicked and cruel and tyrannized their peoples. That was when peoples began to think of liberty, to replace the will of a king with laws, and to ordain magistrates who were capable of obeying as well as commanding.[7]

Against theorists like Giles who claimed that unstable republics inevitably ended in one-man rule, Patrizi here argued the opposite: the tendency of monarchs to moral corruption led peoples to defend themselves with laws and institutions. "I think it is not therefore to be wondered that peoples drove out their princes and kings and consulted their own interests, since it rarely happens that a prince will rule in the same spirit in which he began his reign." His examples are the Roman emperors: of all the Roman emperors only Vespasian changed for the better, "as Tacitus relates."[8] This is not surprising: no animal is harder to rule than man; no other animal is seditious against its herdsman, or tries to mount revolutions against those set over them. (Patrizi, as we shall see in Chapter 6, holds that citizens even of kingdoms bear responsibility for how they are ruled, and can improve their rulers by being good citizens.)

Nevertheless, Patrizi continues, he does not mean to suggest that all republics are just and all princes unjust. Sometimes there arise factious citizens, driven by lust and avarice, who ruin the regime of the best citizens and so taunt them with cruel savagery that no blood will satiate them. This is the way practically all republics end: they survive only so long as their citizens keep violent hands off each other. On the other hand, we read that there were princes who ruled for their whole lives with a favorable reputation among the people, men like Cyrus of Persia (if what Xenophon writes about him is true, Patrizi adds) and Marcus Aurelius, the Stoic philosopher, the best of the Roman emperors. If we had princes like that, there would be no need to talk about republics. What could be better than to live a private life under a just king and prince, untroubled by lawlessness and popular ambition?

That said, nature does not give us immortal and immutable princes, and their descendants, brought up in luxury, surrounded by flatterers, are often worse. That is why, says Patrizi, life is safer in a republic with good mores than under any prince. The republic is lasting and almost immortal; the prince will shortly become old and die. No one prince can have all the virtues. Zeuxis the painter combined the features of five beautiful women to paint the perfect Helen; individual princes may have the virtues of courage or liberality or justice but are unlikely to have them all. But a republic is made up of many people, and every individual will have some part of virtue and prudence. These can be combined so as to make, as it were, a single man of versatile intelligence and vast memory, who is able to see with many eyes, work with many hands, and stride with almost numberless feet.[9] As that most acute of philosophers, Aristotle, said, individuals may know this or that, but everyone collectively can judge of everything. That is why I have undertaken the labor of writing my treatise, Patrizi concludes. I was born in a free city and will be more than satisfied if my scholarly labors can do anything to improve it.

Patrizi's defense of the longevity and collective virtue of republics in comparison with kingships ultimately broadens out into a new sort of idealism about republics that in some respects exceeded that of any philosopher of antiquity.[10] By the time he was writing books

5 and 6 of *De republica,* Patrizi had arrived at the belief that a republic built on virtue could even be perpetual and avoid the cycles of decline that Plato, Aristotle, Polybius, and other classical philosophers had deemed inevitable. Even the most politically idealist text of antiquity, Plato's *Republic,* argued in book 8 that all human polities inevitably decline through a series of regimes, from the best regime, aristocracy, through timocracy (regimes based on honorable ambition and wealth), oligarchy (regimes based on wealth alone), democracy (regimes based on equality and license), and tyranny. In the *De republica,* by contrast, Patrizi declares that Plato was wrong to say all constitutions inevitably decline owing to the ineradicable moral weakness of humanity. Plato is wrong to be so pessimistic, says Patrizi, because:

if it can somehow be brought to pass that citizens act well in perpetuity, follow what is honorable, and flee what is shameful, then the republic will be perpetual, provided that its leaders [*principes*] strengthen their unstable peoples. For just as the whole city is corrupted by their vices and lusts, so it is emended and corrected by their own self-control—virtue being what can keep a constitution stable and lasting. The possession of the best morals as well as the best enactments on the part of those in charge of the people's business [*rem populi*] not only preserves but marvelously augments their status and power. This is a state which the same Xenophon shows by example when he writes of the Spartan republic. For he says that Sparta, despite its small size and thin population, had nevertheless grown in resources, power, population, prestige, and empire in a short time, which aroused in him no small admiration. But when he contemplated Lycurgus's laws and holy institutions, he ceased to marvel.[11]

The implication here, not spelled out explicitly by Patrizi, is that humanistic education in virtue can succeed where Platonic philosophy fails: in perpetuating virtue in the ruling class. Plato's model fails in part because of the faux-scientific nature of its prudence.[12] It assumes, for example, that there is a single pattern of decline that all polities must necessarily replicate; a political philosopher who understands the natural causes of decline can arrest but not ultimately prevent the dissolution of a regime.[13] Patrizi's humane prudence, by contrast, is conditional. It recognizes that decline *may* occur but does not believe that such a decline *must* occur, so long as political elites are vigilant in maintaining their own virtue and in curbing the vicious desires of the citizenry. The moral excellence of their rule can be corroborated by the "best enactments" (*optimae constitutiones*), instituted by legislators who imitate the wisdom of Lycurgus or the founders of Venice.

Human beings are thus in control of their own human destiny in this life, for good or ill. Such a view does not entail a denial of Divine Providence; it denies only that human beings can discern any inevitable laws of history.[14] Because human beings cannot predict the future, they can only act prudently in light of their own experience and historical precedents, guided by the moral principles that are disclosed by reason and by divine counsels (*divina consilia*). Nature's promise is that their undertakings will be prosperous so long as virtue remains the guiding principle of political life.

## Republican Values: The Rule of Law

Patrizi shares with other humanists of his time a disdain for the contemporary practice of law. The deep-rooted rivalry between the literary and legal tribes of Italy stretched far back into the Middle Ages, and contemporary lawyers and jurists were the constant butt of criticism from leading humanists such as Petrarch, Boccaccio, Francesco Filelfo, Poggio, and others. Legal education was regarded by many Italian humanists as a training in pettifoggery and organized greed, withering the soul. It benefited only the rich, who could afford to pay for the best legal advice. At the same time, most humanists revered Roman law, like other products of antiquity, as a golden treasury of practical reasoning as well as of historical information about how ancient society worked. Biondo Flavio, the greatest antiquarian scholar of the fifteenth century, praised the rule of law in ancient Rome, particularly its principle that every Roman, no matter how powerful, wealthy, or well-deserving of the state, was subject to its authority. As he wrote in his masterpiece, *Rome in Triumph,* "The true excellence of Rome lies in the fact that no one could be exempted from a trial."[15] According to Biondo, the rule of law guaranteed an equal freedom—freedom under the laws—to all Roman citizens, whether belonging to the senatorial or equestrian class or to the common people, so that each was contented in its proper status and protected from abuse by powerful persons.

Humanists also pointed to a deeper problem with contemporary attitudes to law. As Petrarch complained, the social system of Christendom in his day was too dependent on an impoverished notion of legality, on mere observance of rules. It was a mistake to believe that law all by itself, backed by the coercive powers of government, was enough to bring order and justice to society. The laws might be good in themselves, but they were all too easily abused by wicked men, who were always greater in number than the good, just as gold and iron are good in themselves, but might be abused by the greedy and the cruel. Laws could also be bad, written by tyrants and oligarchs determined to put their own interests ahead of the common good. Even a good legal system could not function well unless it was run by men of virtue and wisdom. Humanists would have agreed with the ancient Confucian philosopher Xunzi, who wrote that "rules do not create order, people do." Justice is not just a matter of obedience to rules; it is also a virtue that needs to live in the hearts of all citizens.

Patrizi very much belongs to the humanist tradition of hostility to "legalism" (as I have called it elsewhere), exclusive reliance on law and its enforcement for ordering a society.[16] In his discussion of eloquence at 2.4, he attacks the lawyers of his time as ignorant dealers in manufactured obscurity, men who chatter in legalese for gain. His particular concern is their effect on political life. "They generate quarrels that last forever, a thing pernicious in city-states, giving birth to discord, enmities and hatreds among citizens." Much of this turbulence could be avoided if the motivation of monetary gain were removed, and this leads Patrizi to make one of his more striking proposals for reform: to take money and influence out of the legal system entirely. (This proposal will be discussed in more detail in Chapter 4.)

For Patrizi, the main purpose of law in a good republic is to protect citizens from the arbitrary will of magistrates, who can easily become corrupt or arrogant.[17] In a good republic, magistrates obey the law and the people obey the magistrates.[18] That is what distinguishes republics from monarchies, where the king's authority is not bound by laws because it authorizes the laws. But law also, necessarily, plays a role in optimizing a republic's political institutions. Without rule by the right laws, stability, equality, and the rule of the best are all impossible. For example, when the laws permit ambitious persons to seize power (and ambition is almost always a negative passion in Patrizi's lexicon), partisanship is the inevitable result, and the best citizens will be kept out of government. The wrong laws allow citizen wealth to become unequal to the point where political equality is lost. Oppressive laws take away liberty and inhibit the happiness of the people. Laws need to support virtue and learning, or the state will be misgoverned.

A primary consideration for Patrizi in establishing good laws is the need to have them backed by a consensus of the whole people. This requires, first of all, transparency: laws must not be kept secret among the ruling class, as in the early Roman state, but promulgated to the people. Furthermore, though laws should be formulated by the wise, they must also be approved by the people. The Roman practice was to allow an eighteen-day period for proposed laws to be discussed among the people, and bills could not become law without being approved in popular assemblies. Patrizi endorses this Roman practice for use in modern republics.

Popular approval of the laws is not here meant to serve as a proof of their legitimacy, as in the scholastic legal tradition and in early modern political thought. At issue is not the question of popular sovereignty or legal personality: whether the people can act legitimately as a legal corporation, or whether they have the right to require oaths and command actions, or whether they can own or assert actionable rights over individual citizens and negotiate with other states.[19] Rather, Patrizi's advocacy of sanctioning laws in popular assemblies is, once again, prudential. He is supplying one answer to a practical question of governance: What conditions would have to be met to secure the people's willing obedience to magistrates, and especially the obedience of powerful individuals in the state?

> Although a law should be laid down by men of practical wisdom on mature consideration, it should be promulgated, I say, as the Romans used to do. It used to be proposed to the Roman people [for a set period of public discussion regarding] whether the future law is advantageous for the republic. Then, when the people had accepted it, the magistrates would see to its enforcement. Enforcement is much easier when the whole plebs is cognizant of it than if it is drawn up by a few in secret. The people's consensus makes the laws stronger and renders the powerful readier to obey. For we can more easily safeguard what is guarded by many persons, and the authority of the multitude is of no little weight. . . . The best laws are of little moment unless the multitude agrees to observe them.

Patrizi describes the consensus of the people as a *sponsio* or solemn covenant, taking a word from the Roman private law of obligation. "The jurisconsult Pomponius called law the common covenant of the people." It is an obligation that the people impose on themselves.

Patrizi goes on to cite several cases in antiquity where lawgivers—Minyas, king of the Egyptians; Minos, ruler of Crete; Zalmoxis of the Getae; Lycurgus in Sparta; and the second Roman king, Numa Pompilius—claimed their laws were backed by the authority of gods and divine beings. The suggestion, not made explicitly, is that the solemn covenant made by the people with itself will be stronger if the people are told that the laws have a divine sanction. Again, the claim is not that the city's laws *have* a divine source (as, for example, was claimed by Justinian when promulgating the *Corpus of Civil Law*) but that laws are more likely to be obeyed when the people regard them as in some way holy. Later, in book 6, he would recommend that religious rituals should be enacted before the senate issued any new decrees.[20]

In a remarkable parallel passage, the preface to book 5—addressed to Pope Sixtus IV!—Patrizi discusses the instrumental use of religious fear in founding laws. The passage belongs to a wider account of how humanity transitioned from the state of nature to civil life.[21] This required rulers to persuade hard men who roamed about on their own and were accustomed to living by plunder and theft, seeking only their immediate gratification and ease, to take up a new type of life (*novum genus vitae*) involving self-control and justice—a life of virtue that would cost them labor and sweat. "That is why there was need of fictions or fables to impress religious fear upon those who acted unjustly and to raise in them a hope that those who lived justly and kept their hands off the goods of others would enjoy future goods." These deceptive stories were spread with the help of poets, the original *sapientes* or wise men, men like Musaeus and Hesiod, who used *figmenta* to convince wild, uncivilized men to take up toilsome agriculture and engage in beekeeping and in the cultivation of wine, fruit, and olives. Once civil societies were firmly established, such fables were regarded as trifling or absurd.

Patrizi uses this precedent to excuse the philosophers for some of their outlandish pronouncements: Plato's approval of marital communism in the *Republic,* for example, and Aristotle's tolerance of abortion in the *Politics.* These wisest of men permitted depraved customs that they could not eradicate in order to promote many better practices. Aristotle knew that abortion was inhuman but winked at the practice in order to remove economic obstacles to a far greater good, that of maintaining a family. "In our times, however," Patrizi concludes, possibly with a touch of irony, "every citizen knows how to prescribe for himself what he needs to do, so all things can be measured by the standard of virtue, and nothing must be permitted that might seem even in the smallest degree to depart from the finest behavior."

The passage underlines that for Patrizi, the art of making laws was governed by prudence, which must take account of times and places as well as other circumstances such as the current moral strengths or weaknesses of a people and the behavior of neighboring states. In politics, there are no such things as universal laws that apply everywhere and at all times. "One must first of all recognize that law should be adapted to the republic, not the republic to the law.[22] Thus, it is false what some say, that all laws are suited to all states (*civitates*). A lawgiver must be guided by nature and reason; reason is "the seedbed [*seminarium*] of good mores and laws." But Nature does not present its lessons in propositional form, as the Stoics would have it. It does not prescribe particular laws. Nature tells us instead what the goals of political life are: "the well-being of citizens, the preservation of human society, the protection of the city from enemies, and a quiet and blessed life for individuals." It is up to the lawgiver and other statesmen to do their best to achieve those goals by well-designed legislation.

Hence, one should not condemn ancient lawgivers for measures that modern Christians find repellent, but try to understand what their purpose was, what they had to work with, and the broader circumstances of the time. The legislation of Lycurgus prescribed numerous eyebrow-raising customs, like allowing women to exercise naked in the palaestra or encouraging boys to learn how to steal. But if one understands that his overriding purpose was to make strong warriors who could resist the armies of powerful neighbors, one can still admire Lycurgus's wisdom and make use of such measures as may be adaptable to our own times. "One must therefore consider the people and the city in which laws are to be prescribed, if we would give good advice to the best republic." The mild measures of Solon, for example, will be better suited to modern, urbanized, Christian societies than would be the harsh code of Draco.

To be adaptable to different times and places, laws must also be flexible and subject to change. "The vicissitudes of the times mean that laws may not all be stable in perpetuity, but must sometimes be amended or repealed." If the city becomes depopulated from plague, one may have to relax laws restricting citizenship, for example. Often changes occur in the customs of the people, and these too require a response from statesmen. "A change in mores generally seems to require a change in the laws." But this needs to be done in a conservative way. The laws we possess from the Romans and the popes (i.e., canon law), says Patrizi, generally make good models, but moral decay may require additional legislation as a remedy.[23] In ancient Rome, so long as magistrates acted with virtue and regard for the common good, there was no need for the institution of *provocatio ad populum*, final appeal to the people, a populist measure. It was not an institution appropriate to the best republic, but it was necessary at the time.[24] It adds to the flexibility of the laws if magistrates have discretion. The general (Aristotelian) principle is that "the magistrate is the law speaking, the law is a mute magistrate," but magistrates need to be able to apply the law to particular cases. Too many specific laws and prescribed penalties can hobble the exercise of the magistrate's prudence. (Patrizi's emphasis on magisterial discretion is, as will be obvious, characteristic of political meritocracies in general.)

The legislator should never forget that the laws do not bring justice on their own. Only justice in the hearts of men can do that. Justice is a virtue. It is a moral capacity we are born with but that needs to be fostered in the young before the virtue can shine out in their adult lives. Piety toward God is the first duty of justice, and the "little fires" of piety warm our devotion to family, country, and the deity, growing the seeds of the virtues in our hearts. The legislator, however, also has the responsibility to pass laws that correct the citizens' vices, recommend the virtues, and permit a *disciplina vivendi*, a well-ordered way of life, to be educed from them:[25]

> He should imitate nature, which supplies a pattern of virtue and honest utility, and look to what is fair and good, and consult the utility of all citizens, if possible, or at least the great majority. . . .

Let him defend and protect the good, punish the bad, but always on the principle that he prefers not to persecute citizens but to correct their faults.

## Republican Values: Equality

Unlike Plato and Aristotle, however, Patrizi does not think it is the end or purpose of earthly city-states to perfect human nature or actualize its highest potentialities. That, in Christian times, is assumed to be the role of grace and the Church. Patrizi does not say this explicitly, nor does he need to. From the perspective of an immortal soul, destined for life beyond the grave, following the path of virtue as a citizen in the earthly city can at most prepare him for his eternal home.[26] Nevertheless, unlike St. Augustine, Patrizi's goal for the city of man is more ambitious than merely enforcing a semblance of just order in a fragile and fallen world. For him, human society was founded for "its benefits and convenient living . . . and for greater freedom in living, for a safer and happier way of spending our lives."[27] In other words, he embraces a moderate perfectionism.[28] Human virtue and reason, acting on political communities, can optimize, if not perfect, our earthly existence. Guided by antiquity and well-formed human prudence, it is possible for a city-state under the right conditions to achieve certain concrete excellences: it can be stable, lasting, and safe from predatory neighbors. It can be well-ordered by wise and virtuous rulers. It can be physically beautiful and able to secure prosperous, honorable, and culturally rich lives for its citizens and their families. If the city-state is a republic, it must try to do all these things while simultaneously preserving equality and permitting liberty. But it needs to have a good understanding of both values, which are mutually reinforcing.

In the *De republica* Patrizi devoted a long chapter (1.6) to civil equality, with the evident purpose of reforming practices in the city republics of his time. In the popular communes of Italy since the thirteenth century, efforts to impose a form of civil equality had led to a great deal of turbulence and factional strife. Popular remedies for inequality included laws—like the Florentine Ordinances of Justice of 1293/1295 or Siena's anti-magnate act of 1277—which permanently excluded certain noble lineages from holding office. Families that were too wealthy or powerful always threatened to dominate middle-class magistrates chosen by lot from the whole citizenry. Other exclusionary measures inhibited members of political parties (such as Guelfs or Ghibellines) from participation in politics. In Siena during the quattrocento, as we saw in Chapter 1, there were five hereditary political groupings or *monti:* the nobles (*Gentiluomini*), the Nine (*Noveschi*), the Twelve (*Dodici*), the Reformers (*Riformatori*), and the *monte* of the People. Each *monte* consisted of families and *consorterie* that had held power at earlier periods of the city's history. Two of these groups, the Gentiluomini and the Dodici, were excluded from holding the most powerful offices during the whole period when Patrizi lived in Siena. Hatreds between these groups could be intense. When Pius II tried in 1460 to induce the ruling popular party to include members of the Dodici (which included many bankers) on the electoral lists, the citizens came to the pope and begged him to change his mind, saying "they would rather eat their own children than admit the seditious, troublemaking, bloodthirsty Dodici to the *reggimento*."[29]

The exclusion of otherwise qualified citizens from office was justified on the grounds that such groups were by tradition or even genetically incapable of supporting peace and order on a basis of equality. Some exclusionary laws instituted differential standards of evidence in criminal trials, making it (in principle) procedurally easier to convict persons of noble blood than commoners (even if commoners were wealthier and more powerful, as in some cases they were). Sometimes governments even sanctioned forms of intimidation and character assassination, such as the *ammonizioni* of supposed Ghibellines by Florence's Guelf Party.[30] Fines could be doubled and taxes higher for citizens belonging to disfavored lineages. Communal governments became in effect partisan institutions that sacrificed equality under the law and due process in order to protect the rights of favored groups while disadvantaging others. The resulting civil dissensions were exacerbated by the attitude of many citizens that officeholding was principally to be valued as an opportunity for peculation.

Patrizi was highly critical of these practices and attitudes. Inspired by his study of Aristotle and Cicero, he championed a different approach to equality, one designed to secure harmony, liberty, and civic virtue. For him the overriding purpose of civil equality was to maintain concord, a condition necessary to keep the republic strong and stable.[31] Without internal concord, no amount of military power or wealth could save a state from destruction. Without equality, there could be no liberty.[32] To secure equality, citizens should live *aequali iure*—with a sense of equal right—and treat each other justly, "directing all their acts to virtue, being content with what they have and not desiring what belongs to others." The republic, Patrizi states repeatedly, should not be treated as a source of gain for its citizens.[33] The praise of one's fellow citizens should be enough for those who want to hold office. Nothing is more invidious than seeing one's fellow citizens enriching themselves in a short time from communal resources, especially when public funds are in short supply. Magistrates should be few and they should take turns holding office; all magistracies should be limited in time and no one should hold more than one office at a time. The principles governing prosecutions and punishments should be the same for all. Everyone should participate in public duties of some kind, with due account taken of age, ability (*virtus*), sex, and social status. Excluding selected families permanently from office ("which certain cities of our time do," Patrizi says) is not a praiseworthy idea, even if some very learned men defend the practice.[34]

Equality can also be construed as an interior disposition or habit of character, a praiseworthy way of treating fellow citizens—in other words, as a civil virtue. A man with the virtue of equality will recognize the equal right of other citizens to participate in government and obey them when they hold office. One of the lessons Patrizi took from Aristotle and other ancient sources is that a citizen, like a soldier, must learn how to obey before he learns to command. "It is the part of a distinguished citizen to command in the best way possible when he is in charge, and to obey modestly when he is in a subordinate role." This moderate disposition is easier to achieve when public office is sought in a spirit of service and not from ambition to attain high status. When serving in law courts, a rigid impartiality must be maintained; "it causes the greatest discord when some people are seriously punished while others arrested for the same crime get off scot-free." Prudence dictates, however, that a citizen judge with an egalitarian disposition will issue different punishments for the same crime when the harm is greater and affects more people. A ship's pilot who capsizes a ship laden with gold and silver has a greater responsibility than one who pilots a boat filled with pottery, and should be punished accordingly, even though both equally neglected their duty. The disposition for citizens to treat each other equally will be greatly enhanced if everyone does some useful work; that way, useless and envious persons will not try to undermine the position of good citizens, spreading rivalries and hatred.[35]

Patrizi's arguments rely above all on political psychology. Institutions should be designed to maximize concord, participation, and civic virtue. Excluding whole classes and families from power was first of all unjust: those who bore equal burdens (meaning taxes) should have an equal opportunity to win honor (meaning communal offices). Patrizi makes the point, central to virtue politics, that sons of outstanding citizens, like the sons of Brutus, can go bad, while citizens from humble families can rise to become distinguished servants of the state. But even more important, citizens who are permanently excluded from power become *ignavi*, spiritless, resentful, ill-disposed to the city, living always in fear of punishment, without hope of reward. Useless as citizens, they become seditious and inclined to revolution. The man who has no hope of forgiveness will not try to redeem himself by acts of virtue, and the city needs virtue. Only those who have hope of serving in office will work to deserve well of their country. Serving in office is what liberty, in the sense of self-rule, is all about, and everyone wants liberty. The statesman should take advantage of that desire and direct it in positive ways by means of well-thought-out institutions.[36] Allow those who have been excluded to participate in civic functions, if their virtue and the support of their fellow citizens permits it; in this way no one will be afraid that he is suspect to his fellow citizens or think it risky to dwell in a free city. The best father treats all his children equally, as freeborn (*ingenui*). Thus everyone will be zealous for liberty, and one person will not think himself cut off from the *bonum commune* while another person believes he deserves the patronage of the public by some kind of hereditary right. Both attitudes discourage civil virtue.

But isn't civil equality inconsistent with the principle of merit? If all citizens are admitted equally to office, won't that degrade the quality of governance? Patrizi's response, as we shall see in more detail in Chapter 4, is to institute a separate order of magistrates to which access is given on the basis of merit. Wide participation in government promotes equality; legal equality is good; every citizen in assemblies should have an equal voice in approving laws. Nevertheless, magistrates need to be chosen on the basis of virtue, and the good citizen will recognize this fact.

It is not possible that there be equality with respect to individual [magistracies], since it must be stipulated in advance what I have often said, that magistracies are the reward of virtue, not of power or ancestry. . . . Citizens are equal in matters where they can be, so that, when it comes to passing laws, wealth, power, and ancestry should not prevail. . . . But the weak, humble and those without a reputation for virtue should not take it ill that more outstanding citizens are preferred to them in choosing magistrates, so long as they can use what is rightfully theirs and suffer no injury in private matters but are defended by the laws and the magistrates, so that they are preserved without harm, and may acknowledge that they have obtained their due portion from the *respublica*. They ought to confess that they have been dealt with satisfactorily in accordance with their deserts.[37]

Patrizi goes on to warn citizens against the natural tendency to over-rate one's own merits and deserts. Elsewhere (5.7), prescribing rules of civil behavior, he sums up the correct attitude: "Let [the best citizen] be equal to other citizens in liberty, and let him try to be first among them in virtue and glory."

The principle that honors should be proportionate to the capacity of citizens to serve their country was foreign to the practice of popular regimes in late medieval Italy, but central both to Plato's *Laws* and Aristotle's *Politics*. As Plato put it in the *Laws* (6.757a), untranslatably, τοῖς ἀνίσοις τὰ ἴσα ἄνισα: "Equals for unequals are unequal," i.e., unfair. It's unfair to the citizens of the state as a whole when the wicked and incompetent men are given power and the best are not permitted to rule. Aristotle in *Nicomachean Ethics* 5 advocated that citizens be treated with "arithmetical" or equal justice in law and in market transactions but with "geometric" justice in matters of political office: there the best should rule.[38] Patrizi knows both sources well, but chooses to underline his point by citing Pliny the Younger: *nihil est tam inaequale quam aequalitas ipsa:* nothing is so unequal as equality itself.[39] He illustrates the principle of geometric equality with two homely examples (6.1). Citizens all fill their water-jars at the public fountains, but those with larger jars will get more water, and rightly so. Houses have small windows and large windows; they are all open equally to the sun, but the larger window will better illuminate the house.

Thus, when it comes to the exercise of political power, it can be appropriate to treat candidates for office differently on the basis of age, birth, and occupation as well as virtue. The old are to be preferred to the young in general; someone from an old family is more likely to be loyal to the state than an immigrant would be; and a banker may make the best candidate for city treasurer. We shall discuss Patrizi's principles of republican meritocracy in greater detail in Chapter 4; here it is enough to observe that the Sienese humanist sees no contradiction between citizen equality and meritorious governance so long as the merit in question is possessed by the magistrate himself, not his ancestors, and so long as his virtues and learning benefit all citizens.

## Republican Principles: Liberty

Patrizi's understanding of political liberty was inevitably circumscribed by the horizons of his time. Freedom for him was not understood as a right in the modern sense: an imprescriptible claim to engage in certain actions like free speech or the free exercise of religion without interference from others or from the state. Freedom certainly does not denote a universal right to self-government that all men deserve on an equal basis by virtue of their dignity as human beings.[40] Furthermore, liberty in the sense of self-rule, or rule by the will of the whole people, was for him not a criterion of legitimate government, as has already been noted. Like other humanists, Patrizi made virtue a necessary, if not sufficient, condition of legitimate government.

Political liberty for Patrizi was above all a civil status desired and valued by some city-states with deeply rooted popular traditions. It accorded citizens the right to share in the collective rule of their own community. Its opposite was lordship—the default setting of most societies—where powers of command and obligations of obedience were dictated by rigid hierarchies of status and could not be shared with inferiors. Some communities had sufficient virtue or intelligent pride among their citizenry that they simply could not abide such permanent forms of subjection. These communities had developed institutions for sharing power, resources, and responsibility among their citizen body. That, indeed, was the very definition of a *respublica*. True republics loved their freedom so much that they considered *libertas* a kind of *numen* or divinity and were willing to fight and die to defend it.[41] Other peoples were willing to trade freedom for the benefits of lordship, which could be numerous and real.

Sometimes, like the Roman people during the republic, they instituted lords or dictators on a temporary basis to resolve crises.[42] Still other peoples recognized that they lacked the capacity to rule themselves. Patrizi tells the story of the Cappadocians to whom the Romans granted their freedom in recognition of services to Rome. Instead of accepting this priceless gift, the Cappadocians, to the astonishment of the Romans, asked to be given a king, since they had never learned how to use liberty or live with equality among themselves. In contrast, the Athenians were so attached to their democracy that Philip of Macedon and Alexander the Great, after conquering the city, decided to leave their institutions of self-government in place rather than risk instability by attempting to rule over them directly as lords.[43]

Liberty is not and cannot be a universal goal for all states, in other words, and is not desirable under all conditions. Prudence, as always, must be applied. As we have already seen in Chapter 1, Patrizi himself stated that, as far as he was concerned, the best way to live was as a private citizen under a just and virtuous prince. Free states were a second-best, a prudent hedge against the likelihood that princes will grow corrupt over time and be succeeded by heirs who will be even worse. Republics too can become corrupted by violent factionalism, but there is hope that good soulcraft and statecraft can impart to them a permanent, if always conditional, felicity. The condition is that all citizens, and especially the more elite ones, must educate themselves in virtue and be willing tirelessly to commit themselves to the tasks of government. Republican citizenship requires constant effort. Citizens of a free state must develop the virtues that enable civil life. Freedom is the reward of republican government, not a right. Citizens must sometimes be willing to let the law infringe on their private freedoms for the sake of the greater good (1.5). For example, they must accept limits on their personal wealth in order not to compromise the ability to live on a basis of equality with their fellow citizens.[44]

Patrizi's praise of political freedom is thus considerably more measured and qualified than that of some other republican writers of his time. Unlike Leonardo Bruni and Poggio Bracciolini, he has no whiggish historical theory that associates periods of political liberty with cultural flourishing. Unlike Bruni, Machiavelli, and other Florentine writers, he does not link free political institutions and a free way of life with military strength and imperial expansion. As we shall see, Patrizi is hostile to imperialism and believes that an orientation to offensive war can compete with a city's cultural flourishing and ruin its character. A city can be famous and live on in human memory without having an empire. He is thus reluctant to impute any causal link between liberty and the capacity to extend a republic's rule over other states. For him, Rome became great because of its climate and the physical and mental gifts of its people, including virtue, learning, and piety—not its free institutions. Rome remained great long after it had ceased to be a republic, showing that its greatness and its republican constitution were independent variables. In any case, the Roman republic was in every way exceptional.[45] Like most other premodern thinkers, Patrizi assumed that, in general, republican government was possible only in small city-states, and the principal foreign policy goal of a small state will necessarily be the defense of its own territory against predatory foreign powers.

Authors like Bartolus of Sassoferrato or Baldus de Ubaldis in the late medieval juristic tradition regarded the political freedom of city-states, their rights to self-government, as a privilege or concession granted to certain communities by the pope or the Holy Roman Emperor within the larger juridical order of Christendom. For them, city-state liberty was compatible with subjection to higher powers. Patrizi does not think in such terms. He never treats Siena or other republics as communities belonging to an imperial system or sharing a juridical order with other states. His perspective on liberty is more Aristotelian. Like the Stagyrite, he believed that there were certain limits to the capacity for self-rule given by Nature herself. For Aristotle, self-ruling communities like democracies are not artificial constructs of human ingenuity so much as naturally occurring phenomena. They appear in certain parts of the world that have the right climate and that produce human beings who are more intelligent and capable of cooperation. Other regions such as Asia produced populations that needed a sovereign and lacked the virtue necessary for self-rule.[46] Aristotle believed Greece was the part of the world most conducive to self-rule, but it is no surprise that, for Patrizi, history showed that Italy, as the center of the Roman empire, better deserved that honor. (A century later Jean Bodin, also on Aristotelian principles, would come to the same conclusion about France.) The Greek astrologers who calculated that Greece's glory would be eternal were deluded, Patrizi notes, as they themselves would have had to admit, had they lived to see the collapse of Greek power.[47] The longevity of the Roman republic and the spread of its civic norms to peoples throughout its empire demonstrated the superior capacity of Italians to live in freedom and model a free way of life for others (1.2).

## Ranking Constitutions

Patrizi's less than full-throated praise of liberty might in part be explained by the requirements of the literary genre he is using. Unlike Leonardo Bruni's famous orations on Florentine government, he is writing, not panegyric, but a work of political philosophy. On Ciceronian principles, philosophical writing requires calmer and more measured language. But Patrizi's discussion of constitutions and the rule of law in 1.4–5, and his later presentation of the best regime in books 3 and 6, reveal his misgivings about the type of regime whose principal aim is liberty rather than virtue; namely, the popular regime. In popular regimes—as Patrizi's own political experience had taught him—the name of liberty was too easily exploited by unscrupulous persons in order to seize power for themselves and attack the good.[48] Patrizi's own preference is for a mixed regime led by men of virtue and ordered by good laws and a proper understanding of what true liberty is.[49]

Patrizi's discussion of constitutions in 1.4 begins by excluding kingship and tyranny from consideration; these he will later treat in his work on monarchy, the *De regno*. The remaining types of constitutions are polyarchic—constitutions where power is shared among a few or among many. Three are "valued by Socrates and some other philosophers": they are the popular regime, the optimate (pure meritocratic) regime, and the oligarchy of the wealthy.[50] Patrizi then proceeds to distinguish two inferior species of polyarchic constitution: rule by a lower-class mob and rule by an aristocratic junta. Finally, he introduces his best constitution: a mixed regime of free and equal citizens ruled by virtuous magistrates. Strikingly, his analysis is conducted entirely in moral and prudential terms and does not allude to any natural cycles of regime change, unlike Plato, Aristotle, or Polybius.[51]

What is most noteworthy about Patrizi's typology, however, is its originality. It does not do what Giles of Rome and most other late medieval and humanist theorists do—that is, take its bearings from the famous typology of regimes in Aristotle's *Politics*, book 3:[52]

### CONSTITUTIONAL TYPOLOGY IN ARISTOTLE, *POLITICS* 3

|  | Good Constitutions | Corrupt Constitutions |
|---|---|---|
| One | Kingship | Tyranny |
| Few | Aristocracy | Oligarchy |
| Many | "Polity" | Democracy |

In *Politics* 3 Aristotle takes the common good as the criterion for distinguishing good and bad regimes: if those who rule aim at the good of the whole polity, the regime is good; if they rule in their own interest only, the regime is corrupt or bad. Patrizi's judgment of regimes involves a more complex algorithm. He noticeably avoids the tired language of the common good, for centuries invoked by partisans to justify their corrupt actions.[53] He wants the philosophical statesman to consider prudentially, as potentially valid, the aims of the several regimes: the popular regime's love of freedom and equality, the optimate regime's prizing of virtue, and even the value that oligarchs put on wealth. They should weigh the relative stability of regimes, their orientation to war or peace, and the kind of character their rulers display and imprint upon their citizens. A key consideration is how rulers treat the ruled: Do they deal with them fairly, as free and equal citizens, or do they reduce them to tools of their own desires, or, worse, treat them with contempt and cruelty? The ideal regime will be one that balances best the claims of freedom, equality, virtue, and stability, while providing material security and enabling its citizens' full humanity to flourish.

### PATRIZI'S TYPOLOGY OF (POLYARCHIC) REGIMES FROM BEST TO WORST

1. Mixed regime of free and equal citizens ruled by virtuous magistrates (best)
2. Optimate (aristocratic) regime (valued by philosophers, ordered to virtue)
3. Popular regime, self-ruled by its citizens (valued by philosophers, ordered to freedom)
4. Rule of the wealthy (valued by philosophers, but unfree, dishonorable, ordered to wealth)
5. Rule by a *junta* of nobles (imprudent, warlike, unstable, unfree, ordered to honor)
6. Mob rule by the lower classes (unstable, dishonorable, hostile to learning and virtue)

Thus, as Patrizi presents them, the two best "pure" (unmixed) constitutions are the popular regime (*popularis respublica*) and the regime of optimates (or aristocracy).[54] Both of these are described in terms drawn explicitly from Herodotus's account of the debate on regimes between Otanes and Megabyzus at the Persian court (3.80–81).[55] This would seem to be the first discussion of this famous passage in the Latin West since antiquity. (Aristotle is again in the background, since Patrizi, without mentioning or citing him, alludes to Aristotle's judgment that the end of the popular regime is freedom, whereas that of the optimate regime is virtue.)[56] Otanes praises the popular regime, as can be seen, says Patrizi, from his use of the word *isonomia* to describe it, meaning *aequalitas iuris* or equality of right, "since in a republic in which the multitude rules, all things are measured out among everyone in terms of equal right." The other features of a popular regime, according to Otanes, are choosing magistrates by lot, holding magistrates to account after their terms of office (*euthuna*, though Patrizi does not use the Greek word in his summary), and taking counsel about everything in common. The end or purpose of this constitutional order is liberty. Liberty in this context Patrizi defines not as self-rule but as what would, in the early modern period, be called civil liberty (akin to "negative liberty" in modern political theory): "The popular multitude desires nothing more than having the power of living as it wishes [*potestatem vivendi habere ut vult*], which Cicero affirms to be liberty. The [ancient Roman] jurisconsult Florentinus says liberty is the natural faculty of doing that which it pleases each person to do, unless prohibited by law or force."[57] Patrizi does not raise the question whether the multitude is capable of liberty in its higher sense of self-rule, which would require each citizen to be in command of himself, to control his passions and appetites through reason—in other words, to possess virtue.

But there is another kind of constitution, also good, that is praised highly by Megabyzus in Herodotus, where only the virtuous administer the state. The virtuous are a kind of third element in the state, who rely neither on popular favor nor on riches and nobility: "high moral character [*honestas*] alone raises them to rank and magistracy."[58] Megabyzus says that "everything should be entrusted to virtuous men, who give the best counsels and from whom nothing is ever to be feared." Megabyzus's opinion, says Patrizi, seems to be endorsed by Dio Chrysostom and Homer.[59] This is what Cicero called the rule of the optimates, "who are guided in all things by virtue, a habit of mind consistent with reason and the measure of Nature."[60] According to the same author this is the most characteristically human of governments, because of all the animals only humans have virtue and reason.

Patrizi here does not render any judgment about the relative worth of popular versus optimate government. They are both considered good constitutions. But then Patrizi moves down a step and discusses the rule of the wealthy, what Aristotle called oligarchy. This regime, which Patrizi says is close to tyranny, aims at wealth. He admits wealth can be useful to states; quoting Cicero he says that riches provide the sinews of war and the ornaments of peace.[61] However, this kind of regime has grave moral defects: it enriches the few and takes away the freedom of the plebs, reducing them to the status of servants. (Patrizi is careful to specify *famuli,* not the ambiguous word *servi,* which could mean either slaves or servants.) Furthermore, it is a perilous regime to adopt because it does not value virtue or produce great men. In support of this statement Patrizi cites a letter to the tyrant Periander from Thrasybulus, preserved in Diogenes Laertius.[62] Thrasybulus states that bad rulers always need to cut down the virtuous like overgrown ears of corn; virtuous men just get in the way of those who would exploit others.

Patrizi then goes down yet another notch to two regimes that are even more morally defective. They not only exclude whole portions of the populace from the regime, but they treat the excluded portions even worse than wealthy oligarchs do. The wealthy merely make the poor their servants, but these two regimes are actively cruel and abusive toward the excluded.

The first of the two bad governments is rule by a plebeian mob, rule in the name of the lowest classes—day laborers, artisans, and farmworkers—who persecute and rob the nobles and hold the virtuous and the learned in contempt. A plebeian regime like this might be able to last a short while, but it will ultimately be brought down by its own ignorance, inexperience, and meanness of spirit. Patrizi is probably thinking of some episode such as the rule of the Ciompi in Florence (1378). The second bad oligarchy is the rule of a junta. This too will be abusive and cruel. Patrizi's primary example here is the rule of Appius Claudius Crassus and the decemvirs (451–449 BC), which he knows from both Livy and Dionysius of Halicarnassus. A junta is made up of noblemen who use arbitrary violence against the plebs—Patrizi cites the example of Appius's rape of Verginia— and their aggressive spirit, unregulated by virtue, leads them into military adventurism. Sometimes, says Patrizi, this can lead to enlarging the state, but more often it leads to its collapse. Patrizi cites from Dionysius of Halicarnassus the example of the Spartans at Leuctra and the fate of Thebes and Athens when under the control of aristocratic juntas that lacked popular support.[63]

Having dealt with these five pure forms of polyarchic regime, Patrizi now reflects on the principle of inclusion and how it can be reconciled with the humanist preference for virtuous rulership. It seems unjust, he says, entirely to exclude from political power farmers and merchants. Civil society (*civilis societas*) can't survive without them, but their economic roles make them poor rulers; they don't have the leisure to devote to study or politics. But in order that the weaker not appear to be entirely abandoned by the great, they should be included on less important civic committees.[64] He then, alluding to Cicero's discussion in the *De legibus*, speaks approvingly of the Roman plebeian tribunes and commends Marcus Menenius Agrippa for defending the principle that the Senate and the People were one body, *unum corpus*, a speech he knows from Livy (2.33). For Patrizi, the reason that noble *juntas* and mob rule are disastrous is that they pull the community apart, making concord impossible.

After invoking this organic principle that the best republic needs to act in concert like a single body, Patrizi alludes to the Aristotelian idea (again without mentioning Aristotle) that the middle class (the *mediocres*) are the class likeliest to rule *modestius*—in a more restrained, less self-serving way.[65] But if one must choose between the rule of the plebs and the rule of the nobles, the nobles are better, because they don't want to disgrace their ancestors, whereas the plebs are more ready to take risks with their reputation. The nobles in addition will have certain virtues, whether inborn or acquired under the persuasion of their elders. He is careful to add, citing the example of the Decii in Livy, that there are certainly some plebeians, even rustics and men of obscure origins, who have served the state well.

The potential for virtue in all social classes had been a standard humanist political meme since the time of Petrarch and Boccaccio.[66] Here Patrizi uses it to introduce his conclusion, that the best polyarchic regime was one that mixed together popular and aristocratic elements. "I number myself with those who say the best polity is that which is mixed of every type of human being."[67] In proof of this contention he cites two of his favorite texts, Plutarch's lives of Solon and Lycurgus. Solon advised including the *multitudo* in voting and the choosing of magistrates (*in suffragia electionesque magistratuum*) and also in *magna concilia,* presumably meaning something like the Athenian assembly. He then repeats Aristotle's argument (once again Aristotle is not named) in defense of democracy, that it can benefit from the pooling of knowledge in popular assemblies.[68] Just as the hive mind understands the arts better than individuals (here Patrizi adds painting to Aristotle's examples of music and poetry), so too in politics. Thus, while the wise man is he who is aware of how much he doesn't know, the many jointly will be ignorant of fewer things (*coniuncti plures pauciora ignorabunt*). Patrizi's final position on polyarchic regimes is the same as Aristotle's: that the best practical regime is a mixture of popular government and government by the few. But he attributes this judgment not to Aristotle but to Lycurgus, whose constitutional arrangements he knows from Xenophon and Plutarch. Lycurgus made his state great, powerful, and enduring by blending the *paucorum potentia* with the *popularis status.* "He desired to constitute a society from the many to make it better and more stable."

The total effect of Patrizi's analysis is to build a case for popular government, or rather for the inclusion of a popular element in a constitution that also values true nobility, wealth, learning, and virtue. The state will be more harmonious and stable if farmers, merchants, and tradesmen are included in the regime in prudent ways; it will also do justice to their contributions to the republic. The virtue argument for including the people in government is thus based on prudence and a sense of justice rather than on legalistic principles of legitimacy or right derived from popular consent.[69] A good republican regime is organic, recognizing the contributions of all classes to its welfare, and shows its humanity by treating all members of society with fairness, properly understood, and fellow citizens with a spirit of equality.

## Practical Wisdom in Warfare

Prudential statecraft is nowhere more necessary than in preparation for war, in the conduct of war, and above all in the decision to go to war in the first place. A declaration of war is the most consequential decision any ruler or regime can make, and it requires careful analysis as well as a true moral compass. *Martem belli est communem:* Mars doesn't take sides in war. Either side can always win. Wars can make a republic great or they can destroy it.

Though Patrizi does not, like Bruni and Machiavelli, make republican government the best engine of empire—he knows too much history to believe that—he is well aware that many republics past and present have successfully extended their power over their neighbors and won fame in doing so. In classical times, Sparta and Athens vied for hegemonic control over hundreds of Greek city-states, and the Romans established their empire over most of the Mediterranean during the middle republic. In Patrizi's own time, Venice—the contemporary republic he most admired—had extended its far-flung commercial empire down the Adriatic Sea and into the eastern Mediterranean and was expanding its *terrafirma* into northeastern Italy, challenging the Duchy of Milan. Even the smaller Italian republics of Florence, Lucca, and Siena in the fourteenth century had extended their control over many neighboring towns and had created small territorial empires, which they governed from their public palaces. Florence, the self-styled "daughter of Rome," even had dreams of renewing the empire of ancient Rome. Patrizi knew that the longing for empire and glory was strong among republics as well as in principalities. But he believed that to engage in war for the sake of empire was both wrong and imprudent.

In book 9 of the *De republica*, devoted entirely to military affairs, Patrizi accepts as a bedrock principle the rule stated by Cicero in the *De officiis:* one should never engage in war except for the sake of peace. Unlike writers in the scholastic legal tradition, however, he does not immediately proceed to set out and debate the conditions for just war. Once again, his approach is prudential.

According to Patrizi, there are basically three kinds of war. The first is defensive war, which requires no justification. Self-defense and the defense of your family and property are always legitimate, as is taught by nature, reason, and necessity. "Nature commands the animals, reason persuades the learned, and necessity compels the unlearned to protect themselves and their property and to repel all violence against their bodies, their lives, and their fortunes using all resources and any measures." Prudence, however, teaches that we should not wait to be attacked before preparing for defensive war. There are *vagi homines,* wandering men—Patrizi is probably thinking of the notorious "companies of adventure" made up of unemployed mercenaries—who will attack us and plunder our property if we are defenseless.[70] That is why we need a well-trained, permanent citizen force sufficient to defend us in peacetime. We also need careful plans of defense against more organized threats from other polities. Having plans and an effective defensive force prevents panic in case of sudden attack and gives rustics time and protection to bring their animals and farm implements inside the city gates.

Offensive war, however, is a different matter. It is "a more uncertain (*angustus*) affair and requires more prudent deliberation." There are two kinds of offensive war. One is war to avenge injuries and settle disputes with other states—wars of prestige or honor. The other is war for empire.

In the case of the first, the justice of our cause cannot be the only consideration when deciding to go to war. We also have to ask whether we can win the war. Patrizi addresses the citizen magistrates:

It is not enough to consider whether we could fight for the sake of just restitution and declare a just war. We must also consider our own strength and that of our adversaries, the quality of our soldiers, our allies, our supplies, our level of zeal and courage, and how the war is going to be paid for. It's odious to level imposts on private citizens and instantly leads to ill-will. One must also estimate how strong the city's defense works are, how plentiful its supplies of food, how strongly the towns and castles of our territory are held, and whether we have enough machines of war. These and many similar things must be passed in review, and they are most likely to come to your attention when the gates are shut and the enemy needs to be driven back from the walls with slings, arrows, and trebuchets.[71]

Even so, the outcome will always be uncertain, and the city's wise men should keep in mind the famous saying of Hannibal: "Outcomes never correspond to facts less than in wartime, and thus a sure peace is always better and safer than a hoped-for victory."[72]

Aside from these general considerations, prudent leaders must also take into account that republics have intrinsic weaknesses when it comes to offensive war. Offensive war in republics requires the support of the common people, who are fickle and will turn on you the moment the fortunes of war go against you.[73] When a war goes wrong, the senate will be divided and will not support you either, "since, as Plato writes in the Laws, truth is a splendid thing, but persuading people of it is not easy." You will make yourself unpopular with the wealthy too, because you will have to raise taxes, inevitably a source of dissension. Taxes are necessary because offensive war requires you to hire mercenaries and gamble your liberty on "a mixed jumble of men of various national origins who are constrained by no pietas toward your country, no fear of God, no religious awe, but are attracted only by wages." Offensive war also entails risks of political instability, because citizens with large armies under their control can become dangerous. Furthermore, offensive war is bad for the moral health of city, as those who promote it must stir up passions of hatred and revenge, as happened among the warlords of the late Roman republic.[74]

Offensive wars for honor and prestige are imprudent, but the third kind of war, offensive war for empire, is both wrong and likely to be ruinous. Patrizi acknowledges the views of those who say that aggressive war is the only way to enlarge one's territory and empire and achieve glory. Those who argue this way are following the authority of Euripides (quoted via Cicero's De officiis):

If justice must be violated for sake of rule
Let it be so; you may preserve piety in other matters.[75]

In other words, they (like Machiavelli) are willing abandon the splendid reputation of a just and pious man in order to rule, a violation of right that Patrizi regards as base and unthinkable. Such men seem to be praising the Spartans, whose laws (he says) were designed for empire. The proponents of wars for empire give examples of cities that have escaped from imperialistic adventures unscathed and have added to their empires and glory. A nation that seeks glory, they say, should be eager to engage in fighting; otherwise, warlike virtue becomes rusty and the name of your city will die in base obscurity.

Patrizi's response to the champions of empire is to point out that many wealthy cities have been destroyed by war, and many preserved by peace. Furthermore, "the arts of peace are more worthy of admiration than those of war: it is in peacetime that humanistic studies (*bonarum artium disciplinae*) and true virtues find their theater of praise, while in war madness rules, and triumph issues from blood and slaughter." Patrizi admits that glory is not to be despised, that Rome, mistress of the world, earned greater praise than Athens, the mother of all disciplines.

> Yet neither lacked the other's glory entirely. Rome was distinguished for all liberal studies too, and Athens did not lack glory in war; both cities venerated Minerva both armed and unarmed. We however follow more the arts of peace, and we want our citizens to be trained most of all in those arts, since they lead more securely to tranquillity of soul, and we [in this treatise] are describing the republic that follows the path of felicity. Therefore let us be content with our own borders and not engage in war without necessity, or if we ever get into such wars, let us immediately set a limit on our lust for rule.[76]

The phrase "lust for rule" (*imperandi cupiditas*) is reminiscent of Augustine's rebuke of the Romans' *libido dominandi,* and hints also at Patrizi's attitude to Roman imperialists, who (like the British in the nineteenth century) often acquired empire while ostensibly fighting to defend themselves or their allies against injuries. For Patrizi, by contrast, the desire for conquest is morally indefensible. It issues from a character disordered by blind lust for praise and power. Quoting a famous speech of Scythian legates to Alexander the Great, Patrizi declares that the thirst for conquest is unquenchable and leads in the end to utter insanity.[77] It must be kept under control; it must recognize the inherent limits of the human condition: "O wretched condition of mankind, O deceitful hope of mortals, with what vehement desires are we seized, despite knowing that all our futile projects are transitory and that virtue should be our only desire!"

A republic that aims at happiness and virtue will thus be content to remain within its current borders and will refuse to make war without necessity. Its military establishment should reflect these principles. That is why Patrizi calls for republics to maintain small standing armies—not a militia in the Renaissance sense—recruited from its citizenry and farming population.[78] In book 6 Patrizi specifies that up to a third of the city's agricultural resources should be devoted to maintaining this force.[79] This permanent army should be placed under the authority of a civil magistrate. That magistrate (the second consul in charge of military affairs according to Patrizi's optimal constitution) will recruit the bravest youths, who will dedicate themselves full time to military service.[80] He will train them in arms in peacetime as well as in time of war. The magistrate in charge of war should thus be competent in the *ars militaris*. He should establish an early-warning system against invasion, using beacon fires by night and smoke signals by day. Some shrewd and perceptive men, *sagaces aliqui viri,* should also be sent to other countries to seek information about the intentions of foreign peoples and potentates. One should not trust overmuch in their reports, but they can improve the quality of deliberation in the senate if their reports seem to be well founded.

Good leadership is the key to success in military affairs, but in wartime a city should consider who is the best man to lead its troops.

It should find one great captain, an Alexander, to lead the city's troops, and not imitate the Athenians, who elected ten new ones each year. If no citizen is up to the job, the most prudent course is to hire a foreign captain. In looking for such a figure one should apply the four criteria set out by Cicero in his speech *Pro lege Manilia,* a passage often cited in humanist literature on warfare.[81] The perfect captain will have knowledge of warfare; virtue (courage, foresight, vigor); personal authority (reputation); and "prosperity; that is, good luck." Knowledge, moral excellence, and personal authority are closely connected: together they impart the charismatic qualities a commander needs to win love, respect, and obedience from his troops.

His virtue will be amplified by his speaking ability. The leader of great virtue makes men want to obey him and fear being disobedient. Patrizi gives a long list of generals and military leaders famous for their eloquence: Pisistratus, Themistocles, Pericles, Alcibiades, and nearly all the great Roman generals, especially Caesar. This leads Patrizi into a long digression on the need for commanders to have a humanistic education suited to their special tasks and the type of training, but we shall not follow him there.[82] In Chapter 5 we shall return to the role of humanistic education in forming good citizens, magistrates, and war leaders.

# FOUR

# Meritocracy and the Optimal Republic

## Meritocracy and the Best Regime

The best republican regime not only includes all citizens in its political life, but also keeps real political power in the hands of the best
citizens—in other words, it constitutes what today would be called
a political meritocracy. Humanists since Petrarch had promoted the
ideal of a state led by its best educated and most virtuous citizens
(categories often elided in the humanist mind), but Patrizi's *De republica* represents the most sustained attempt of the Italian Renaissance to translate humanist virtue politics—a species of political
meritocracy—into a viable institutional design.

To this end, Patrizi proposes a surprising model: the ancient Greek
city-state of Massilia, located on the site of modern Marseilles. Massilia (or Massalia) was a colony founded by the Phocaeans, Ionian
Greeks from Asia Minor, around 600 BC, and reached the height of
its power in the Hellenistic period, far outstripping its mother city
in importance. It was the capital city of a thassalocracy or seaborne
trading empire that dominated the northwestern Mediterranean and
challenged Carthaginian power, allying itself with Rome during the
Second Punic War. In time it civilized the Gaulish peoples around it,
such that the region became known as "Gallograecia." During
Rome's civil wars it allied itself with the Pompeians and thus lost its
independence when Caesar conquered the city in 49 BC. The Cae-
sareans, however, wisely allowed it autonomy in domestic affairs and

it retained its Hellenic flavor. Under the umbrella of Roman power, the Massilians and the Hellenized Gauls under their sway turned from warfare to cultural pursuits and farming.[1]

Patrizi learned about Massilia principally from his beloved Strabo (4.1.5) and Valerius Maximus (2.6.7) and absorbed positive assessments of its mode of government from Aristotle (*Politics* 6.7, 1321a30) and various passages in Cicero. In his oration *Pro Flacco* (25.63), Cicero, apostrophizing the city, writes:

> Nor do I pass over you, Massilia, . . . whose gravity and civic order I may rightly say should be preferred not only to the peoples of Greece but to those of all peoples—you who, though isolated from other Greek regions, their language and culture, and washed by the waters of barbarism, surrounded by the far distant peoples of the Gauls, are yet governed by the counsels of the best men [*optimates*], so that all nations might more easily praise than emulate your civil order [*instituta*].

Other ancient sources praised the city's physical beauty and rich cultural life. Tacitus (*Agricola* 4.2), for example, praised its culture as "a mixture and happy combination of Greek refinement and provincial simplicity." According to Strabo, Massilia's educated class cultivated the arts of speaking and philosophy, so much so that it became a rival to Athens as a school for Romans eager to acquire Greek learning. It hired famous visiting lecturers at public expense as well as private. Strabo and Valerius Maximus also praised the severe morals of the people. Massilia limited dowries, instituted strict sumptuary legislation to enforce frugality, and preserved intact the mores of its ancestors.

Given its ancient reputation, it is easier to comprehend how Massilia became Patrizi's favorite ancient republic, just as Venice was his most admired modern one. He repeatedly holds up the example of Massilia throughout the *De republica*, praising its severe yet cultivated mores, as shown by its prohibition on the performance of comedy (2.6), its law forbidding women to drink wine (4.6), its fine architecture (7.Pr.), and its vigilance in protecting its city walls in peace and war (9.3). At 6.6 he praises it for its conservatism: how it preserved its mores and institutions even in times of great necessity. He describes how the Massilians kept a sword, used from the founding of the city to execute the guilty, until it was too rusty to use, "so dangerous was it thought to depart from antique custom." "An anecdote like that requires no authority to back it up," he adds.

In books 3 and 6, Patrizi examines Massilia's institutions in more detail. In book 3—a book devoted to laying down the various magistracies and principles of governance in the best republic—he explains that a republic should not have too many magistrates. A model might be the Massilian republic, he remarks, preferred by ancient writers to all others for its order and fairness (*ordo* and *aequitas*). That republic had six hundred senators, of whom fifteen each year held the chief magistracy. To that extent, its government might seem to resemble that of Siena, with its executive Concistoro and its Council of the People, consisting of former magistrates. But Patrizi is more interested in the differences between Siena's and Massilia's institutions than in their likenesses.

At 6.6, applying more than a touch of historical imagination, Patrizi makes Massilia the model for his political meritocracy. That chapter is devoted to explaining how magistrates should be selected in such a way as to prefer the most virtuous and block the merely ambitious and greedy. Patrizi describes Massilia's principles of political selection as follows:

> Among the famous maxims of the Massilians, Aristotle seems to commend this one in particular: that they hold a public tribunal [*iudicium publicum*] every few years in which individual citizens would put forward their names. On the basis of this list it would then be decided who should be admitted to public offices and who should be excluded. The successful candidates would then be appointed to minor magistracies by lot. The more important magistrates would be selected by the senators, six hundred in number,

after much ritual celebration, ceremonies and auspices, as though God were participating in the choice. They did this mindful of Homer's view, maintaining that only good men accepted from God the scepter and command of peoples.

This mode of selection among citizens seems the best one to me. For those who are admitted to public duties as men approved in life and mores do not depart from virtue but even perfect it; if they start to abandon it in any respect they are shortly expelled as men who have become worse. Those who are rejected on account of their lack of self-control or probity or as deficient in other civil virtues, unless they are completely corrupt, are generally led back to a better way of life, so that they may someday be enrolled alongside their contemporaries. Ambition and the thirst for honors, one's mental attitude and mores quite often change, for no one can bear it calmly when they are held up to contempt and mockery, and many young men are roused to action by the spur of envy.

Patrizi then goes on to give three historical examples of great men who were unimpressive as adolescents but later, when challenged by circumstances, acquired great virtue: Manlius Torquatus, Fabius Maximus, and Themistocles. As always, Patrizi attends to the psychological effects of political experiences, how they improve or worsen the character of citizens and statesmen. He then compares the admirable selection procedures of the Massilians with those of "a certain famous republic of our time," transparently his native city of Siena.

These results were achieved by the Massilians. I hold to be less commendable the practice of a certain famous republic of our time. In that republic, as soon as boys are born and have received their baptismal names, they are put down for office in the republic, provided they are the sons of freeborn parents who have held some small role in the state, even via a distant relation. Hence, the names of one-year olds, two-year-olds, three- or at most four-year olds are mingled together with innumerable others in enormous urns, from which, when the time for an assembly approaches, they are drawn by lot; and so long as they have reached the legal age of nineteen years, they are put in charge of magistracies. If they are younger than nineteen, their names are stamped and thrown back in the urn. Yet it often happens by chance that, thanks to the large number of names, those of certain highly meritorious citizens [*dignissimi cives*] lie hidden until they are creaking with age, while other names swim to the surface of persons who ought to be passed over as lazy and base, and these persons discharge public office at the earliest possible age.[2]

It seems to me that a custom like this should be abolished. Public office should not be left to chance, and one should wait at least until the qualities and gifts of young men can be discerned. Thanks to bad luck it can happen that some are fools and (as sometimes happens) mentally disturbed or even scoundrels. The latter, if removed from office, brand their whole families with dishonor, and if they stay in office, bring themselves into mockery and contempt and the republic to ruin.

Hence it is far better to delay [the selection process] for a time and approve a man in accordance with the judgment of many persons. Account should also be taken of age, so that (other things being equal), older men are preferred. The minimum age should be twenty-four. No one becomes incensed that he is not made a magistrate before this age, if the same rule is applied to everyone. Furthermore, no one becomes incensed that an older man is preferred to himself, both because envy is mostly confined to one's peers, and because everyone may hope that he will achieve the same position when he grows older.[3]

In this passage Patrizi has elaborated considerably on his sources, illustrating how easily humanists could turn the ancients into the mouthpieces of their own views.[4] Were he not so eager to hide behind the authority of antiquity, it might be easier to recognize the Sienese thinker for what he was: the inventor of an original and remarkable meritocratic procedure for selecting officials on the basis of virtue and good reputation—a rare Western parallel to Chinese imperial system of examination and merit promotion which (albeit on an immeasurably larger scale) sought to "elevate the worthy" and reduce the influence of social class and wealth in forming a political elite.[5]

Patrizi seems here to be proposing a two-stage process of election. In the first stage, citizens propose themselves for office before a body that is probably some sort of popular assembly (see below). Once the assembly has approved them as persons of good character and general fitness for office, they would be assigned to minor citizen committees by lot.[6] At a second stage the senate might elect them to major magistracies after deliberation, presumably based on their performance as minor magistrates and their continuing reputation for upright behavior. Persons so elected belong thereafter to the senate and the permanent order of magistrates, and they are rotated in and out of major offices.

Patrizi's proposal, it is worth noting, combines sortition and election. Most humanist writers on republics preferred magistrates to be elected and held sortition to be anti-meritocratic, but Patrizi takes a more nuanced view.[7] The Massilians in his imaginary reconstruction use the lot to assign minor magistracies from the electoral lists approved by their assemblies, whereas the election of magistrates for higher office requires senatorial deliberation and election.

Patrizi's more positive attitude to the lot was no doubt influenced by Venice's use of it as an element in its procedure for selecting magistrates—Venice being in his opinion the best republic of Italy. In 3.3, discussing how to prevent wealthy people from buying political power, he commends the Venetians for combining sortition with election in their practice of choosing magistrates:

The Venetians mix together the lot with election, which is obviously the best procedure by far. While the Senate comes crowding into a large hall, those holding magistracies order a ballot box to be set up on a bronze tripod in an elevated place. In this are a large number of silver balls but only nine golden ones. The senate arises and forms a long line, and each one, while the others are watching, puts his hand into the ballot box and draws out a ball. If it is silver, he returns to his place; if gold, he goes up to a bench that has been made ready for the candidates. He waits for the other candidates to join him, eventually nine in number. No one speaks to them, no one nods to them, no one can pass them a note or a letter. They declare their names to the senate for election to the magistracy, and a vote is taken immediately to prevent bribery. Using these and similar precautions, the senate cheats the ambitious, so much so that the worthier candidates are always chosen, producing great harmony among the citizens.[8]

In this case sortition is not employed as it was in late medieval popular communes, to give non-elite citizens a chance for office equal to that of the rich and powerful—a practice frequently corrupted. It is instead used to weed out ambitious candidates for office who would use money, favors, or influence to advance their own candidacies independently of their merit.[9] Families of great wealth and ancestry have much to contribute to the republic, but they should achieve positions of leadership, not through privilege, but through merit.

Patrizi's ultimate goal, as he states in 3.1, is to create a separate order of men, a small class of lifetime magistrates, separated out from their fellow citizens on the basis of merit. These men will take on the public persona, sit permanently in the senate, and take turns holding the republic's highest offices. Thanks to their high moral character, this senatorial order will prefer the republic's good to their private interests. They must never forget that they bear the republic's *maiestas*, its prestige and grandeur. So long as they follow the laws, they will rule others legitimately (*legitime*). In a good republic, Patrizi repeats, the laws command the magistrates and the magistrates command the people. The people accept being ruled by the city's laws, as we saw in Chapter 2, because they themselves have collectively agreed to them in their assemblies.

The rest of the citizens belong to a second order, that of ordinary citizens, who live on a basis of equal right (*aequali iure*) with their fellows. The citizen class will participate in assemblies and hold minor offices on public committees, but will not be involved in deciding major issues of public policy. They will reckon the senatorial order as superior to themselves and obey it as though its members were princes or kings, "or rather as the godlike will and tutelary spirit of the republic [*numen geniumque reipublicae*]." Thus, disobedience to it will seem impious as well as criminal, and magistrates can count on respect for their office and religious fear to exact obedience from good citizens, precluding any need for coercive measures.

## Which Citizens Should Be Admitted to Political Office?

All political meritocracies require a strict separation between the procedures for entering the order of magistrates and exogenous factors that generate social class, such as wealth, ancestry, or influence. In imperial China, and in the modern West after the introduction of civil service examinations, meritocratic procedures were thus designed (with varying degrees of success) to be neutral with respect to riches, noble blood, or the favor of the powerful. In the Anglophone West in recent times, extreme measures have been advocated, and in part adopted, to root out the influence of privilege in society as a whole, so much so that the ideal of meritocracy—that polities should be ruled by their best-educated and worthiest members, those best able to benefit the social whole—has been compromised. Patrizi, however, is more realistic and does not regard the inherited social order as illegitimate *in se*. Like Aristotle, he accepts that the existence of social hierarchies based on ancestry, wealth, talent, and gender are natural and inevitable. Political equality nevertheless requires participation in government by citizens from all social and occupational groups that in any way contribute to the republic's flourishing. This leads Patrizi to consider the advantages and disadvantages of including members of different social classes in the senatorial order.

In book 6, while discussing social classes in city-states, Patrizi begins with a historical analysis of class in the ancient world, concentrating on the Romans. He states, in an overbold generalization, that Roman society consisted of patricians, knights, and plebeians. Despite the great prestige of Rome, however, Patrizi thinks that the Roman class system cannot be used as a model in all respects by modern societies. Nevertheless, he assumes that most city-states, like Rome, will consist of three classes: the nobility, the middle classes, and the laboring classes.

Membership in the nobility (and it will be remembered that Patrizi himself claims to be of noble Roman descent) is based on past services to the state but should nevertheless be conditional. Patrizi expects that a sound patrician class will be self-policing and will exclude those of its members who have degenerated from the virtue of their ancestors. "They need to understand that it is a great burden to bear the good name of their ancestors." If they fail to maintain a noble standard, they should be reduced to the class of plebeians and stripped of their titles. By the same token, lower-class persons, even those from the lowest of the low, *ex infima plebe,* should be raised up and made equal to more noble persons if their virtue and glorious accomplishments merit it. The social elite, in other words, should be open to merit, ready to welcome new men into its ranks, as the ancient Romans admitted the equestrian Cicero into its senatorial class. Noblemen desire honor above all things and it is in their interest to make sure that the best men in the state are included in their ranks.[10]

Having made his bow to humanist orthodoxy, Patrizi turns to reality. The reality is that men of ancient lineage (such as himself) make safer leaders in a republic than those who are but newly summoned to public life. He makes use of an agricultural analogy: just as it is better to distribute land to native farmers who best understand the local climate and soil, so it is better, other things being equal, to leave political power in the hands of old families. Moreover, the common people will more readily accept the authority of those from established families than that of new men:

> For it seems reasonable that those who have had parents, grand-parents, and ancestors honored in public office would accept oversight of the republic as though by a kind of hereditary right, and would stretch every nerve, as it were, to make it greater. For just as land is best entrusted to native farmers who have the best understanding of the climate and soil, so those who have arisen from the senatorial class have learned to fill public duties as though by paternal and ancestral teaching. The whole people tolerates their rule far more readily, nor does it seem to them unfitting that a son holds a magistracy when they remember that his ancestors discharged the same office.[11]

Patrizi next turns to the middle classes, men of means who occupy a position between the nobles and the plebs. Such men too can be safely entrusted with major offices, and with excellent results, so long as they are modest and virtuous, distinguished for learning, or have made themselves useful in some honorable line of work. Aristotle, says Patrizi, thought the state should rely principally on such men because all citizens will welcome them owing to their middling status: they lack the arrogance of men from great families yet do not share in the baseness and servility of the plebs. Patrizi adds his own gloss on Aristotle:

> For great riches and power conjoined with good family will sometimes persuade magistrates to do things that are not useful to civil society and dangerous to the republic, while on the other hand the base mind of the plebs, soothed by no riches and with no examples of fine conduct among their ancestors, will destroy the republic's power and diminish the weight and dignity of public office. The middle classes will be useful in a republic if they so conduct themselves among patricians and plebeians that they are welcome to both and do not seem to fear the one nor pursue

excessive favor from the other, but like sailors steer a course between Scylla and Charybdis.[12]

Finally, Patrizi comes to the plebs. They include a diverse multitude of farmers, stablekeepers, fishermen, shopkeepers, and craftsmen
in the minor arts. (As we shall see in Chapter 5, Patrizi believes that
great artists should rank in the middle classes.) They are persons engaged in sordid gain, therefore not *liberi homines* by Cicero's definition, and include even porters and day laborers who sell their labor, not
the products of their labor—*opera, non artes*. Patrizi distances himself from Cicero's snobbery (in particular his view that "no gentleman
can run a shop"). He recognizes, but rejects as overly perfectionist,
the views of Socrates, Aristotle, and Crates the Cynic, as well as
Roman and Theban customs, that exclude merchants and craftsmen
from political power. Yet the problem remains: How can persons
of such low condition safely participate in the tasks of ruling their
fellow citizens?

Though extremely rare, it is possible, says Patrizi, to find virtue
among such persons. That being so, very few persons of this class
should be admitted to the senatorial order. "Those who are should
be chosen for virtue so outstanding that the obscurity of their origins is illuminated by the splendor of their lives." While his fellow
humanists from the time of Petrarch have been right to draw attention to historical examples of lowborn individuals who became
distinguished statesmen and generals, that circumstance cannot govern
the regular practice of states. Respect must ordinarily be paid to
family origins (*genus*).

Although it sometimes will happen [that lower-class persons distinguish themselves], it will rarely have a good outcome. On this
account ancestry should be respected, and public affairs must only
rarely be entrusted to foreigners, new men, or men of obscure origins, and this only in cases where it has been verified that they
far excel in virtue and experience all their competitors.

Those chosen as magistrates should not be absolutely penniless (*proletarii*),

> lest through penury they be compelled to do something regret-
> table. They should have sufficient means to support their children
> and families in a liberal and honest way from their own profits
> and industry. It is nevertheless in accordance with the republic's
> interests that a few men from this class enter government, and it
> is more to their own advantage that they not leave behind what-
> ever craft they practice. It's shaming for them to return from a
> magistracy and public office back to their shops, where [after-
> ward] they will scarcely deign to pick up again the tools of their
> trade.

In a parallel passage from 1.8, Patrizi further stipulates that merchants can be admitted to public office so long as they do not engage in usury, deceit, perjury, or fraud. Craftsmen engaged in more
honorable forms of gain can be included too, but not day laborers
or delivery boys or ministers of pleasures and lusts. The standard is
that they must contribute somehow to the necessities of city life or
increase its beauty.[13]

By this standard peasants should have the right to participate, but
Patrizi regards this as undesirable. In antiquity, he shrewdly remarks,
farmers were worthy individuals who fought well in war, were fully
involved in city life, and therefore deserved to participate in assemblies. But in modern times agriculturalists are mere peasants, base
persons having little connection with the life of the city, just as we
soft city folk (regrettably, in Patrizi's view) now flee from rustic pursuits. Given the difficulty of changing our present way of life, peasants should be encouraged to be content with their farming duties
and stay away from the city.

Lowborn people, who tend to be more passionate and ignorant,
are potentially a danger to good government. Nevertheless, the
prudent statesman with a sense of right will not exclude plebeians

entirely from office, for two reasons. First, because justice demands it. Account must be taken of the essential contributions the lowborn make to the city. "One must consider that they are one's fellow citizens, and without them civil society could by no means be maintained. The old story is not inapt that teaches how the members of the body could not perform their function without the belly, though it resides in the more sordid part of the body" (1.4). They should not be treated in such a way as to make them repent of the work they do for the republic. Even if they are not admitted to the first rank of citizens, they should nevertheless have some place of honor. "For it seems both just and well suited to preserve concord among the citizens if those without whom the city can scarcely exist and who share its burdens are accorded also some share in its honors" (1.8).

The second reason that the lower class should be included in government is prudence. When choosing magistrates, the statesman needs to consider social stability and solidarity as well as competence and good character. "Some account must taken of the multitude, which becomes seditious and turbulent when excluded from public profit and honor." That is often the way revolutions start. Complete exclusion of the people from all offices and public emoluments breeds envy and distrust and ultimately turns the plebs against the government. The presence of plebeians on civic committees reminds their betters of their responsibilities to the whole community, and nobles can give examples of fine behavior to the plebs, while mixing with them on a basis of formal equality and even forming friendships with them.

It is for prudential reasons, too, that offices should be distributed on an equal basis through all regions of the city (3.2). If most of the offices are distributed to those living in the wealthiest part of the city, the poorer parts of the city will lack honor and offices, and the magistrates will lack intelligence concerning what the whole populace is thinking. If the only consideration in choosing magistrates were virtue, it would make more sense to choose them disproportionately from the best districts in town, which will inevitably include the best

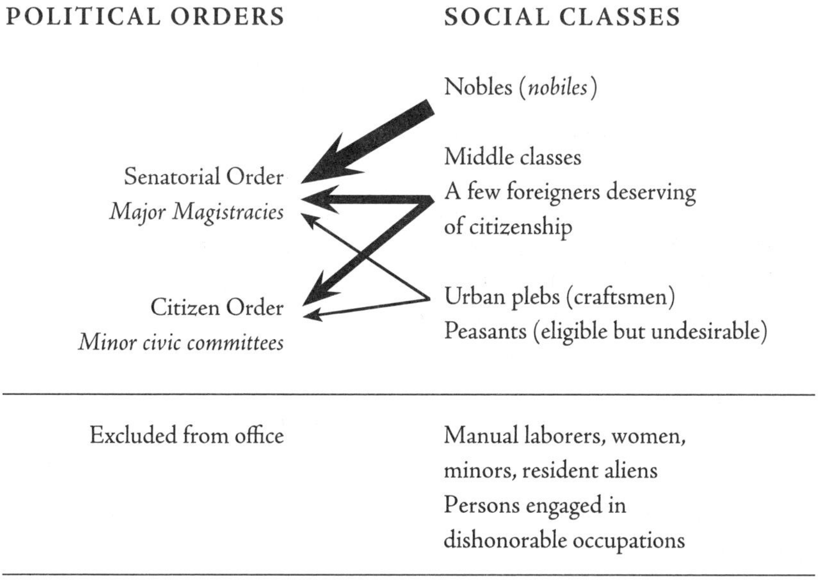

| POLITICAL ORDERS | SOCIAL CLASSES |
|---|---|

Figure 1. Political and social hierarchies in Patrizi's optimal republic.

educated and (therefore) the most virtuous. But maximizing the virtue of magistrates is not the only consideration.

Magistrates are best elected when the city [*civitas*] is so apportioned that the whole city [*urbs*] seems graced with honor, and each region or neighborhood of the city may seem to have its patron or advocate. . . . For to choose magistrates indiscriminately from the whole people, though it may seem desirable in that the greater number of men will contain [more of] the best men, is nevertheless odious and not without peril. For it is possible that at some time the full complement of magistrates may come from a small neighborhood of the city, and then the rest of the city is defrauded of honorable rank [*dignitas*] and will seem destitute of public officeholders. Moreover, those who hold magistracies are like guardians or look-outs of the whole city: they hear many things and see many things which can be useful to the republic. On this account it is preferable for them to be sprinkled among many different places of the city rather than being confined within a small area, so that they may hear more people and speak more freely to them, person-to-person, reinforced by friendship, long familiarity, and family and neighborhood connections—all relationships produced by proximity. Very many cities have been apportioned on this model, even in our times, as in our country of Siena, which still preserves many Roman customs and allots its magistrates by thirds [or by tribes: *tribus*] according to the same order.[14]

## How to Keep the Best Men in Charge

Even with very few members of the lower classes being admitted to magistracies, the real danger remains that the order of magistrates will be influenced by plebeian opinion. In questions of war, for example, the plebs will be all in favor of aggressive attacks on neighboring states in order to acquire more land, which they believe will profit themselves, yet they will resist paying the taxes needed for offensive war and at the first setback will rebel against their magistrates, shifting the blame onto them.[15] As a class they are fickle, ill-informed, and lacking in resolve.[16]

Patrizi's solution to the problem of how to include the people in government without according undue weight to popular opinion is graded participation: members of the citizen order should be kept from public roles that involve them in important decisions requiring prudence and deliberative skill.

Those whose employments are recognized as necessary to the republic should not be refused public office, but honored with those public tasks which they can easily conduct, or allowed to help out on committees. Their participation on these can be regulated in such a way that the city derives little disadvantage, and [thus] the weaker may not seem to be entirely deserted by the more important people.

Italian Renaissance cities had many public committees or *collegia* to maintain defense works and bridges, build and decorate churches, improve sanitation, keep watch on city walls and gates, organize public festivities, and the like. Patrizi is doubtless thinking of such lesser forms of political participation.[17] (A modern analogy might be service on juries.)

The principle of graded participation excludes some Roman precedents. Patrizi does not recommend that the common people have their own dedicated magistrates, like the Roman *tribuni plebis*. He expresses considerable sympathy with the Roman plebs during the Struggle of the Orders, as described by Livy, and he understands that it was the arrogant behavior of the patricians that led the plebs, justly, to demand that a powerful magistracy, the plebeian tribunes, be established to defend their liberties. Nevertheless, the institution of plebeian tribunes was a symptom of class dissensions, not a cure for them.[18] In the best city, a well-educated and virtuous senatorial order would not act like haughty Roman patricians, and Patrizi does not include any plebeian officials in book 3, where he lists the magistracies to be established in the best city.

Patrizi does envision that in his optimal republic there would be popular assemblies, probably to be chosen in the usual way of the time: by lot from approved electoral lists. A citizen assembly might perform certain limited functions such as excluding persons of low reputation from magistracies, as discussed above. It is not entirely clear, however, what sort of deliberative functions Patrizi would ideally like such assemblies to have. At 1.5, Patrizi says that laws should be formulated by the prudent after a deliberative process, but then need to be approved by the people before taking effect.[19] He endorses the Roman practice of rogation, presenting a bill to the people in their tribal assemblies for eighteen days of discussion and approval. He then comments:

For the consensus of the people makes laws stronger and renders the powerful readier to obey them. We can more easily protect what has been approved by many, and the authority of the multitude is of no small weight. . . . Indeed, writing the best laws is of small importance unless the multitude unites in their observance.

Moreover, in 1.4, after endorsing the mixed constitution, he discusses with apparent approval the *ratio Solonis:* Solon's ordering of Athens's assemblies in a way that opened them to the many, not just the few. Solon thought there should be some minimal criteria of merit for inclusion, even in the larger citizen assemblies, but, in principle, all those admitted should have the power of reviewing what was done in peace and war (what the Greeks called accountability or *euthuna*), voting for magistrates, "and much else." Here too, Patrizi mentions the advantages of pooling the knowledge of many people rather than relying on the wisdom of the few.

In this passage Patrizi presents popular participation in politics and popular deliberation in a favorable light, in seeming contrast with his more meritocratic views found in the later books of *De republica*. As was hypothesized in Chapter 1, it may be that Patrizi's ideas evolved after the composition of book 1, and he may have found less reason to praise popular government after his encounter with the fury of the common people in 1464, the year Foligno rose up against him in his role as papal governor. Another possibility is that he regarded Solon's *ratio* as appropriate for its time and place but not the best *ratio* for Italy in his own time. After describing Solon's democratic reforms, he goes on to mention popular elements in Lycurgus's mixed regime:

Nor is the constitution of Lycurgus to be rejected, which raised the small state of the Spartans to empire and high prestige. He divided the city's offices among nearly everyone and combined a popular constitution with an oligarchy, making an ideal blend, and he wished to base his constitution on the many to make it better and more stable. *Yet different times, the differing mores of*

*mankind and the diversity of religions prescribes a variety of in-*
*stitutions. On this account I shall treat hereafter of the republic*
*I deem the more commendable.* (emphasis added)

Here Patrizi seems to be signaling that his commendation of Solon's popular assemblies was a tactical move to defend the idea of
collective deliberation against monarchist criticism, not necessarily
an endorsement of popular deliberation as such.[20] The passage does
not prove that he thinks the counsels of the common people should
be weighted equally with those of the wise. In fact, at 1.8, a chapter
on the inclusion of merchants and tradesmen in government, he stipulates that voting rights, *suffragia,* should be graded in accordance
with merit.

> But in bestowing voting rights, account must first be taken of
> honor and virtue; second of the liberal disciplines, which bear rich
> fruit in a city; third, of nobility—for the children and descendants
> of glorious and illustrious ancestors should not be neglected, ex-
> cept in the case of those who have obscured the renown of their
> ancestors by their own baseness. Fourthly, account should be
> taken of those who benefit their fellow citizens by means of mer-
> cantile activity, artistic skill and industry, and render the city more
> opulent and splendid.

Patrizi does not explain by what devices a meritocratic principle
could be introduced into a republic's voting procedures, but his proposal at least indicates his scale of values and his ambition to accord to the virtuous and well-educated the principal voice in directing
the best republic's affairs. Another possibility is that by *suffragium*
he means merely the expression or endorsement of an opinion (a secondary meaning of the term). In this case the statement above could
be meant as advice to magistrates in charge of public debates. It
might simply refer to the order in which a presiding magistrate should
call upon counselors, as described in the next section.

## *Deliberation and the Virtue of Free Speech*

Whatever the explanation for Patrizi's seeming approval of deliberation in popular assemblies in book 1, by the time he was writing book 3 his primary concern was how to prevent ignorant, greedy, and ambitious persons from influencing the conduct of public affairs. His proposals for managing public debates constitute yet another strategy of meritocratic governance. They articulate reasons the best republic should be committed to free political speech, while recognizing that some counsels are wiser than others.[21]

Patrizi's attention to reconciling the claims of merit and free speech is no real surprise, given the rich experience of public deliberation he must have acquired in his own Sienese republic, particularly the practice of the *proposta generale*. The *proposta generale* was a meeting called several times a year by a magistrate in which members of the Council of the People were allowed to bring forward proposals for reform on any subject (in principle) touching the general welfare of the republic. These could be more trivial matters such as proposals to improve the food supply in the city or repair city gates, but they could also ascend to issues requiring debate on fundamental principles. Meetings could sometimes be stormy and could even lead to the formation of new factions. Practical skills of debate management were required to prevent such an outcome.[22] Patrizi must have witnessed many tumultuous meetings in his years as a magistrate and council member and has clearly given thought to how such meetings should be conducted.

Patrizi presents his proposals for managing public deliberation in book 3—the book devoted to magistracies in the best state—in the course of discussing the role of the senate in 3.3. As we have seen, in the first book of *De republica* Patrizi had praised collective deliberation in the popular assemblies of ancient Greece; here he praises collective deliberation in the senate using a similar argument and similar language.[23]

> Let them come together in a single body, which can see with many eyes and work with many hands; this is why a republic is far

better governed than a monarchy. Whatever a monarch can see, he sees as an individual; he cannot measure everything by [his own] counsel and reason. No one mortal can profess to know everything, and that man who is ignorant of the least number of things is held to be the wisest. But when many learned, serious and wise persons are assembled together, they see everything and foresee everything; nothing can seem dark to them, nothing un- expected, nothing new, nothing unheard-of, and nothing too great.

Given the sort of behavior he ascribes to senators in the passage quoted just below, his proposals in 3.3 for controlling debate in the senate must refer to a non-ideal state. Because the optimal state's senate in principle includes only the wise and the good, it would pre- sumably not require special procedures to control foolish, passionate, and corrupt members. But sound meritocratic procedures can improve even ordinary states.

Meritocratic deliberation should be arranged in such a way as to give the greatest weight to the wisest and most virtuous men in the senate. The senate should be summoned by the chief magistrates, who control the agenda and decide which senators get to speak, and in what order. Debate should be strictly confined to public matters and not involve private interests. Discussion should be free and unconstrained by political alliances, without hatred, jealousy, or envy.

Patrizi then raises the question of how the opinion of the best and wisest senators can be canvassed without giving the presiding mag- istrate too much control over the outcome of debate.

Those who write about politics are of two minds whether to allow individuals to give their opinion [freely] or whether to allow only those summoned [by the magistrate] to ascend the rostrum. It often happens that the magistrates in charge, when they want to extort some outcome, will request the views only of those who agree with them or can be frightened or bribed to say what they're told to say. Then, if others are not allowed to refute their views and bring to light the truth using rational arguments, the city will not get good advice. On the other hand, if everyone can freely speak his mind, the rashness of the majority generally wins, and the more insolent and unruly sort get up and assert plain falsehoods, accusing people, yelling at them, attacking them—so much so that they are likely to impose silence on the more modest and serious citizens. That's how things are sometimes decided that turn out to be less than salutary for the republic.

My advice is to compromise. Let those who have been called upon speak their piece first, and let the magistrates take great care to call upon those who are outstanding for their age, rank, learning, and experience of affairs. Let them afterward give the floor to other senators to speak only on the matters under consideration. It will perhaps be useful to prescribe a limit to the number of speakers. In this way those who have been summoned [to speak by the magistrates] can give their views, and others will be able to debate freely, so the magistrates will not mislead or deceive the senate, while the insolent will not be able to impose silence on the more serious men through their brash behavior.

Free speech in this passage is valued as necessary in political debate to bring out the truth, especially when a magistrate might be trying to conceal it by calling only on those senators who support his own policies or interests. The assumption seems to be that the *rogati,* the few called upon by the presiding official to speak, might not always have the independence to defy a corrupt or scheming magistrate, but that it would be difficult for such a magistrate to control the entire senate. In this case free speech is a hedge against corruption as well as a condition of wise counsel.[24]

But good rules of deliberation are not enough. To speak out against powerful and corrupt individuals requires courage, even when a magistrate lacks direct means to control opinion. In the chapter following, Patrizi tells the famous story, recorded in Plutarch's *Lives,* of how Philip of Macedon tried to isolate Athens's democracy from its few virtuous leaders. These were men who had been opposing his hegemony in Greece, advanced *sub praetextu libertatis,* on the pretext of liberating the country. Philip told the Athenians he would not take away their liberty if they turned over to him ten men only, including the orator Demosthenes, who had always opposed and maligned him in their senate. Many people in the senate sided with Philip, arguing that the interests of the many should be preferred to those of the few. Nine of the men whose punishment Philip demanded were afraid to speak, lest they seem to prefer their own lives to the peace and liberty of the whole state. Only Demosthenes had the courage to speak out. With great wit and presence of mind he told the Aesopian fable of the wolf and the shepherds. The wolf offered the shepherds his friendship and a guarantee of peace if the shepherds would simply turn over to him their guard dogs, who had offended him by their hostility. The shepherds were foolish enough to do so, whereupon the wolf attacked the sheep and killed the shepherds. The story, Patrizi concludes, taught the Athenians not to give in to plots against men whom they could not equal in virtue. "It is all over for republics when a man is not free to talk about public affairs."

For Patrizi, as for other humanists, free speech in politics is a virtue, the courage to defend oneself and one's principles. The opposite of free speech is fearful silence, and the absence of free speech is the sign of a corrupt republic. But, as we learn in other chapters on citizen virtue (*Rep.* 5.5–6), the virtue of free speech, like other virtues, must be regulated by prudence and a sense of fairness. The good citizen gives faithful counsel, setting aside personal interests, and always tells the truth. He avoids anger at all costs, for only calm discussion leads to truth. Virtuous political speech thus requires modesty. "Let [the virtuous citizen] remonstrate with others in a spirit of moderation, and let him endure rebuttal calmly, that the truth may be more clearly exposed to view." Don't act as though you are possessed of unique wisdom in public affairs or show contempt for others. The opposite vices, flattery and adulation, are equally to be avoided.

Silence is sometimes the best form of speech: "The man who does not know how to be silent does not know how to speak."[25] Prudent silence is not the same as fearful silence. Patrizi advises citizens against open and lonely disagreement with the many. "I think that in council it is better to bypass the opinions of the many than to reject them openly." Don't follow the example of Phocion, who reflexively disagreed with popular opinion. Patrizi retells an anecdote from Plutarch about how Phocion once advised a course of action that was enthusiastically embraced by all the people. Turning to a friend, Phocion said, "Have I said something wrong without realizing it?" Follow, rather, the example of Cicero, who always presented himself as a man of the people. Defer to the magistrates, venerate ancestors, and show respect for learning and for the Senate, "as the Spartans did." One may conclude that for Patrizi, sincerity is not the same as truth.[26]

It will be obvious that Patrizi's advice about meritocratic deliberation and free speech, to be at all effective, relies on the goodwill and fairness of presiding magistrates, or at least on the social pressure applied to them by their fellow magistrates to present an appearance of goodwill and fairness. It equally relies on citizens possessing the virtues of speech. Once again, we can see why Patrizi and his fellow humanists placed so much emphasis on the need for the rulers of a state to be men of the highest character. Deliberative bodies will never work well unless they are administered by men who possess the virtues of speech and care about their own reputation.[27]

## Preventing Corruption and Revolution

Patrizi also stresses the need for good character in his prescriptions for avoiding revolution, which, following ancient tradition, he links tightly with moral corruption. As we saw in Chapter 2, the Sienese thinker believed that a republic could remain in an optimal state in perpetuity so long as the leadership of the republic remained virtuous and restrained the vices of the common people by good laws and good example. Virtue brings stability. At *De republica* 6.5 he supplies a more detailed analysis of various ways to prevent a republic from falling into sedition and revolution, but here he places less emphasis on limiting the vices of the people and more on correcting mistakes made by the republic's magistrates and the senatorial class. Much of the chapter is devoted to the problem of restraining powerful persons who are out to increase their own status or wealth. This is the second longest chapter in the entire *De republica,* an indication of the importance Patrizi attached to the issues it addresses.

Aristotle had dealt with the same set of issues in *Politics* 5–6, and his treatment offers a contrast with the approach taken by Patrizi. Aristotle in these books is discussing non-ideal states, and especially how to stabilize and improve his "best practical regime for most states." The latter is the type of mixed regime he calls "polity"—a constitutional government based in the middle classes and restrained by law; it is a blend of the best institutions of democracy and oligarchy. In *Politics* 7–8 he lays out his absolutely best regime, an aristocracy where citizenship is confined to the virtuous.[28] In the "best practical regime," however, Aristotle begins from the assumption that such a govenment cannot be led by the best men, because in the vast majority of states (he means Greek oligarchies and democracies) "you would not find as many as a hundred men of good birth and merit" (5.1, 1302a). In any case, well-born men of great virtue are not the sort to lead revolutions and seize power for themselves. The best practical state will inevitably be led by men of ordinary capacities with conventional ideas about equality. The conceptions of equality characteristic of democracies and oligarchies are partial and tendentious, and therefore inadequate. Democrats see equality in "arithmetical" terms: every citizen should have the same share of honor (meaning offices and political influence) as every other citizen, whereas oligarchs take a "geometric" view and believe that political influence should reflect the size of one's contributions, financial and otherwise, to the state. The democratic conception is safer, says Aristotle, more conducive to stability, and less exposed to sedition.

In the best practical regime, the most a prudent philosopher can hope for is that merit will be considered somehow or other in choosing magistrates, preferably via elections. Aristotle's analysis thus proceeds by diagnosing the causes of sedition and revolution in book 5, then proposes in *Politics* 6 a series of technical fixes to increase stability in each of the principal kinds of constitution. His treatment is directed to his students, budding experts in the art of politics, and other philosophers capable of understanding his intricate reasoning.

Patrizi in his book 6, by contrast, is discussing his optimal constitution, which is founded on the ideal of proportional (or geometric) merit. Leadership in the community should be proportional to individual merit, measured by educational attainments and a record of proven service to the state. Patrizi aims to create via education and culture a critical mass of virtuous men, a separate order of magistrates numerous and authoritative enough to lead a city-state. As we have seen, this order will, by a careful process of selection, be kept distinct from the pyramid of social status based on ancestry and wealth. Herein lies an important difference from Aristotle's approach: Aristotle tends to blur the distinction between good birth, wealth and virtue, while the humanist tradition insists that the springs of virtue are to be found in all classes. Humanists defend "equality in the capacity for virtue," or virtue egalitarianism, a notion foreign to Aristotle.[29]

Patrizi explicitly addresses his counsels about instability and revolution, not to experts in politics or scholars, but to the republic's rulers, persons who might be of "a denser Minerva"—a bit thick, in other words.

> The republic will last just so long as it is ruled by the civil virtues and the best laws. There are no powers that can demolish a harmonious and well conducted city-state. Banish ambition, banish greed, banish pride, banish the plunderer of riches, banish luxury and other foul beasts, and your republic will be stable and enduring. Counsels like these remind us that we would like to teach a thing or two to those in charge of the republic, so that they might understand what is to be avoided and what things should be respected in order to protect the constitution from corruption and revolution.

If we had to do only with men of learning and wisdom, I imagine it would be enough to say that virtue alone makes a republic flourish and vices alone weaken and destroy it. But since our business is with the multitude and our form of speech ought to be entirely popular [*popularis*], I think it will be worthwhile to set out in advance a few principles that can be grasped by the mental and spiritual capacities belonging to individuals of a "denser Minerva," as the saying goes. It isn't enough to have said that justice and equality are the two virtues that preserve civil society and that without them no city-state can endure in peace, unless we touch on certain common errors committed by magistrates and others who want to look powerful in a republic.

Patrizi's advice about stabilizing republics and preventing revolution thus takes the form of a long series of counsels, illustrated by historical examples, designed to inform the prudence of republican leaders. Among Patrizi's prescriptions we may list the following:

1. City governments should never engage in tricks or deceit, in regard either to foreigners or to their own people. In book 9 on military affairs Patrizi allows a legitimate role for *ruses de guerre*, but any behavior that would undermine trust toward the city's government is going to be counter-productive. Republics are poor at keeping secrets, and acts of fraud will always be found out. Lysander of Sparta, although a man of great ability, did not succeed in covering his crimes despite (as he used to say) donning the skin of a fox when a lion's skin would not cover him.[30]

2. Magistrates can and should use severe measures when needed, but to use violence or cruelty against innocent fellow citizens is absolutely wrong. In times of the greatest necessity it may be necessary to cut off limbs, like an experienced surgeon in a case of life or death, but a principle of justice must always be invoked. Never condemn many people at the same time in a summary fashion; to do so is a sure way of causing sedition.

3. Proscribing citizens, confiscating their goods, and driving them into exile is always odious and dangerous. Their friends will sow discord in the city, and though there can never be any just reason to take up arms against one's own country, exiles will nevertheless claim that they do so justly because they were wrongly expelled. It is equally dangerous to restore exiles to their country. If they are restored when their enemies are unwilling, one side or the other will be tempted into tyranny. (Here Patrizi truncates his usual list of illustrations on the grounds that he has already discussed the matter in his poem "De exilio," in the fourth book of his *Poemata*.)[31]

4. One should instead give pardon and absolution for disloyalty to the regime where it can serve a public purpose. (One may remember that Patrizi was himself pardoned in part on the grounds that his poetic gifts were an ornament to the state.) As an authority for the success of amnesty as a policy, Patrizi describes Thrasybulus's amnesty for the oligarchic party of the Thirty Tyrants in Athens after their expulsion.[32] In the case of a general insurrection it is better to punish the leaders and grant a general amnesty to their followers, Patrizi concludes. As Gabriele Pedullà notes, previous humanists had not given much attention to the role of amnesty in pacifying factional strife; Patrizi might be the first political thinker of the Renaissance to recommend such a policy.[33]

5. Oligarchy, rule by the wealthy, is almost as bad as tyranny. It is fueled by ambition and leads to factionalism. Factions have to reward their supporters, and when they do so, it leads to magistracies being conferred on unworthy men. Patrizi gives here a pen-portrait of the oligarch, a man whose blind pursuit of wealth has made him insensitive to the needs of other people, even his own family. Oligarchs, being few, must always live in fear of the many. To protect themselves from the wrath of the people, oligarchs try to take away the citizens' arms and buy the services of foreign mercenaries to protect themselves. Oligarchs reduce the people to penury and engross all wealth

for themselves. This leads the people, in desperation, to call for a champion, who can easily turn into a tyrant. This is one reason that statesmen should favor the presence of the middle classes in government: to dilute the political power of oligarchs. (As we will see in Chapter 5, Patrizi also calls for limits on wealth to prevent the rule of an oligarchy.)

6. Never change old laws and excellent customs. If new laws need to be introduced to deal with new diseases of the body politic, they should be introduced gradually.

7. Magistrates should seek to preserve equality and limit envy, and to this end should institute strict sumptuary laws. Frugality should be encouraged and luxury avoided. All citizens should be encouraged to work; unemployment is the seedbed of sedition.

8. Free political speech on matters touching government policies must be preserved, but calumny and slander should not be permitted. Patrizi does not say whether he approves of laws, typical of Renaissance republics, that restrict free political speech to public spaces.

9. Never permit political magistrates to profit in any way from their offices. (As we will see below, however, Patrizi recommends that public defenders be paid from public funds when necessary.) Magistrates should not accept large financial rewards from their fellow citizens, even in return for fine public actions, and they should not live in a luxurious way, undermining civic equality. This will only arouse envy, that truculent beast, the pestilence that ravages republics. Here and elsewhere in the *De republica* he advises cities to adopt measures that would prevent the improper use of public office for private gain. He is perhaps the first major political thinker in the civic humanist tradition since Cicero to stress how jobbery and other forms of venality can undermine public trust and solidarity.[34]

10. Never increase the power of magistrates too much. To do so creates envy—that ferocious beast—and invites tyranny. Among many historical proofs he recounts the episode of the

Roman decemvirs in 451/450 BC, described by Livy and Dionysius of Halicarnassus, who were given great power to codify the laws but soon abused their civil authority. They tried to accomplish their aims by violence and were ejected from office only after sedition and slaughter. Two other examples of persons to whom cities foolishly granted excess authority were the oligarchy of the Thirty in Athens and Lysander in Sparta. Citing Aristotle, Patrizi states that it is safer to restrict than to increase a magistrate's power, because the more controlled power is, the longer it lasts. That is why the Spartan king Theopompus subjected his own royal power to the ephors, and why Caesar refused to be made a king and kept the name of dictator, and why the tyrant Cleisthenes of Sicyon chose to exercise his absolute power with moderation.

11. If some person does manage to achieve more power in a republic than is fair or prudent, civic leaders should not try to take it away from him all at once, but do so gradually, until he is reduced again to equality with other citizens.

12. The political system in the best republic should be arranged so that individuals may not seek offices for themselves and are blocked from doing so if they do seek them. *Ambitio,* in the primary Roman sense of canvassing for office, is thus prohibited. The word and the practice it signified had a strongly negative sense in classical Latin (*ambitus* in its political sense means "bribery"), but standing for election was seen by Cicero and others as a necessary, if undignified, procedure for achieving public office. Patrizi, however, thinks the practice is inconsistent with meritocracy and permits the wrong people to seek office.

## Magistracies in the Best Republic: General Principles, the Senate, Consuls

Patrizi's counsels on how to avoid civil tumult and revolution help us better to understand his exposition in book 3 of how to arrange the republic's magistracies. These, he says, are to be modeled on

Roman precedents, not Greek, but with certain differences. As we have already seen, he does not recommend the creation of plebeian tribunes on the grounds that they might threaten the authority of the best men, who constitute the senatorial order. Patrizi's fear of granting extraordinary powers to magistrates presumably accounts for his similar bias against dictators, despite their sanction by Roman republican tradition.[35] Both plebeian tribunes and dictators were created in Rome in response to extreme factionalism. They were symptoms of constitutional failure. This parlous condition of the republic Patrizi hopes to avoid by instituting meritocratic soulcraft and statecraft.

Patrizi begins book 3 by invoking (and simplifying) Aristotle's definitions of a republic as "the ordering of a state with respect to its magistracies and public honors" (*Politics* 3.6, 1278b, 4.1, 1289a). "State" here tranlates πολιτεία, *politeia,* in the sense of "constitution." Cities must be ruled by magistrates as a ship is ruled by its pilot or an army by its general. These examples, commonly used to illustrate the superiority of monarchy to republican government, Patrizi uses to explain why magistrates must be few in number.

Patrizi then turns to establishing the moral principles that should govern magistrates in their conduct of civic life.[36] Quoting the Platonic philosopher Crantor, he ranks the four ends of human life, in order, as virtue, good health, honorable pleasure, and riches.[37] Liberal studies are key to acquiring virtue, but they are also valuable in themselves as a source of honest pleasure. Against the Stoic view that the possession of riches does not belong among human goods, he prefers the position of Aristotle that riches are necessary, because there can be no virtue without some wealth. Human beings need food, clothing, and shelter; therefore, some amount of wealth must be necessary, and even the wise need to support themselves. (At this point Patrizi tells some piteous stories about wise men reduced to penury, perhaps remembering his own experiences in exile.) Families and the state need wealth, too, in order to flourish. But the search for wealth cannot be allowed to trump or compete with the other goods of human life, above all virtue. The most important goal for the magistrates who rule the republic remains acquisition of the civil virtues. The principal virtues of magistrates are, in order, justice (which includes *fides,* trustworthiness, and *pietas,* devotion to duty), courage, prudence, moderation and self-control, constancy (*constantia*), and gratitude. Magistrates should also love the present state of the commonwealth, respect the way of their ancestors, and never, ever plot coups or revolutions, which always do more harm than good.

After a chapter on how to choose magistrates, discussed above, Patrizi finishes the book by devoting a chapter each to all the principal magistracies in the best republic. These are treated in order from the highest and most powerful magistrates to the lowest officials with the least authority. He begins with the senate.

Administration (*cura*) of the republic should fall principally upon the senate, a body to be modeled on the Roman Senate, but with consideration of Greek precedents as well. It should consist, by preference, of older citizens, who by nature are less passionate and therefore more capable of rational debate. Deliberation on the constitution and other great matters of state is best left in their hands. "The whole order of the republic and all counsel in doubtful and adverse matters should flow from the senators." They should be respected as the fathers of the people. They should be given responsibility for electing the principal magistrates after due deliberation. They should be the guardians of the laws, and in the rare cases when new legislation is needed, it should be drawn up by a commission of senators learned in the law. They should as a body form the highest court of appeal. Patrizi does not approve the Roman republican practice of *provocatio ad populum,* the citizen's right of appeal in capital cases to a body consisting of the whole people, including senators and patricians.[38] The practice is often cited by historians as the most democratic element in the Roman constitution. For Patrizi, such cases should be kept within the senate. The senate should also be the body that reviews the conduct in office of magistrates and generals. Given the enormous constitutional powers they wield—in theory, greater even than those of Roman senators—Patrizi's senators need all to be persons of the highest moral character, and the example they set for other citizens is key to maintaining order in the state. For this reason they should not be allowed to engage in commerce, apart from the economic activities conducted on their estates. Profit-seeking is unbecoming in a senator.

Patrizi's treatment of the other principal magistracies then follows.[39] Chapter 5 is devoted to the consuls, two in number. Unlike Roman consuls, who by the middle republic shared functions and could check each other, Patrizi's consuls are assigned different functions, a device that increases their executive powers (and makes dictatorships and emergency war commissions unnecessary, though Patrizi does not say that). The first consul administers the city (he has the *urbanam curam*) and supervises the other magistrates, consulting constantly with the senate. The second consul is in charge of military affairs (he takes on the *militaris cura*) and has powers similar to those of *pro tempore* war commissioners in medieval Tuscan communes: he appoints commanders, recruits soldiers, and sees to it that they are well equipped and paid.[40] He has primary responsibility in peacetime for maintaining order in the countryside and keeping watch in the city. In peacetime the first consul is the principal magistrate of the city; in wartime the second consul takes the lead. In wartime the second consul is in charge of defenses within the walls, while the general appointed to take charge of the city's troops (who may, exceptionally, be a foreigner) is in command outside the city walls.

Patrizi gives us frustratingly little explanation of his thinking about executive power, which was notoriously weak in Tuscan republics, with their ingrained fear of tyranny and ceremonial heads of state. But it appears that his division of the consulship by function, when taken together with his Roman understanding of political space-time as divided into domestic and military affairs, *domi et militiae*, is designed to reinforce and unify the power of the executive. The first consul has a supervisory role over other executive officials, making him in effect a chief executive. He presides over the senate, has the power to summon it, and can control its agenda. The second consul, with command of republic's forces in peacetime, and in wartime the power to appoint commanders and pay for supplementary forces, maintains civilian control of military affairs. He is able to act with speed and secrecy. The inability to do so was a notorious failing of Renaissance republics.[41]

In the end, Patrizi's conception of the best republic's executive, at least on paper, is closer to an American presidential system than it is to the mature Roman practice of mutually limiting consuls and relatively independent magistracies. The term of both consuls is one year, the same term as consuls in the ancient Roman republic, but it is much longer than, say, that of the nominal Florentine head of state, the Standard-Bearer of Justice, who held office for only two months. Yet Patrizi does not go to the opposite extreme. Despite his admiration for Venice, he does not follow its model of doges elected for life, as the Florentines were to do in the early sixteenth century. The reason, probably, is Patrizi's conviction that long-held power too often corrupts. Even with terms limited to a year, a consul may acquire the arrogance of power. Hence, Patrizi calls for consuls who abuse their power over citizens to be subject to *provocatio* or appeal to the senate. To obtain "energy in the executive," in Alexander Hamilton's phrase, he is not willing to sacrifice the republican principle that all officials need to be regularly accountable to their fellow citizens.

## The Legal System

The chief legal magistrates, called *praetores*—the usual Latin name for legal officials in Renaissance Italy as well as in ancient Rome— are treated in 3.5. Praetors should be three in number "in our city" (here probably referring to a reformed Siena), one for each *terzo*. They should be men of integrity, learned in the law and familiar with the city's customs. They should have jurisdiction over both public and private law. They should be assisted by a college of nine citizens, three from each third, which should divide into smaller courts of the first instance in the *terzi*. From those courts appeal can be made to the full college, and thence to the praetor himself, an appellate procedure that Patrizi claims will prevent corruption. "In this way the college of nine cannot deceive the praetor, and the praetor cannot force them to commit an injustice." Here the point seems to be that the college meets separately from the praetor, in contrast with the usual practice in Renaissance podestal courts, where the praetor presides over his assembled counselors. In general, court procedures should be designed to prevent wealthy and powerful people from exercising undue influence. Hence, a further appeals process is necessary that will take cases out of the *terzo* or city neighborhod. "I think an appeal process (*provocatio*) from [the praetors'] judgment is necessary, both to make them judge carefully, and also, if they do anything wrong out of injustice or fraud, to have that judgment straightened out, so that justice may be served." For this reason Patrizi recommends another, superior court of three praetors, supported by another college of nine men, to act as a final court of appeal.[42]

Patrizi raises the question whether the city should follow the pattern of many Italian city-states, including Siena, and bring in foreign judges to try certain types of case, especially criminal cases. Since the thirteenth century, Italy had developed a countrywide system of circuit judges called *podestà*, men with university doctorates in law, who would set up their court in a given town for set periods, usually six months or a year, before going on to their next appointment. These police magistrates in principle could never be citizens of the town where they served as judges. The idea was to insulate the courts from local feuds and political passions and to try cases under impartial judges who would apply professional standards of scientific jurisprudence. Patrizi, like many other humanists, is absolutely opposed to this practice. It was unexampled, says Patrizi, in the best ancient republics: the Romans, Carthaginians, Athenians, Spartans, and many other ancient peoples, he writes, always had native magistrates rule over them, never foreigners. This ancient practice is followed by the best of the modern republics, Venice, which has its own system of courts presided over by native Venetian officials.

In the *De republica* Patrizi states that his prohibition against the use of foreign officials in the best republic does not require much argument, such is the weight of ancient authority. But it is easy to infer other reasons for his dislike of the practice. Having foreign magistrates run a city-state's system of justice violates the organic principles of humanistic political philosophy.[43] These call for all governing bodies and military forces to be subject to the prince or supreme civic council. Humanist political thinkers also stress the need for quasi-familial bonds of love and mutual care between rulers and ruled. For example, in his early treatise *De gerendo magistratu*, Patrizi advises the new magistrate to

> labor on behalf of everyone, so that all may understand that their children, wives, fame, and fortune are of no less concern to you than your own affairs, as they would be to the best paterfamilias. Let them have easy access to you. Hear all their cases and petitions calmly. Open your ears to the complaints of the miserable and the suffering, and let no filth or ugliness or misfortune or poverty or isolation stand in the way of hearing everyone equally in an accessible way and responding to their needs. The man who rules over many people must necessarily hear many requests, and you should let no one's complaint tire or depress you.[44]

Patrizi goes on to underline the importance of the judge's human qualities in getting contending parties to accept his judgment and preserving social harmony.

> The man whose case is heard in a humane and affable way seems to receive some partial benefit if what he seeks is denied him in a just way. The man who seeks what is unjust must not be allowed it, but there should be no contention with him involving curses or abuse, but the man should be persuaded, if possible, that what he asks is either impossible or not worthwhile or against the public interest or against his own interest or against the principle of fairness or against the highest moral standards. That way

you can dismiss anyone at all from your presence without any bitterness.[45]

Familiarity with local conditions and neighborly relationships are vital for judgments to be fair and for punishments to be prudently adapted to persons. Always the magistrate needs to value his own virtue above all, for "it is impossible to create a stable and strong regime in which the virtues are not highly honored."

The need for citizen virtue supplies another reason to prohibit the use of foreign judges in the best republic. The practice of outsourcing justice could well lead to atrophy of the virtue of justice among the citizens. "Cato [the Censor] used often to repeat that those who denied the reward of honor [i.e., office] to the virtuous robbed them of virtue." Like many other humanists, Patrizi was attracted by the supposed Persian practice, described in Xenophon's *Cyropaedia*, of educating adolescent boys in the art of judging among litigants in a dispute. Such a practice would be otiose under the system of international *podestà*. For Patrizi, the cold scientific judgments of a foreign expert do not reinforce but instead undermine social harmony.

But the use of native judges makes it all the more necessary for citizens to have confidence in the system of justice. In a later chapter (3.8) Patrizi proposes a special court to deal with the most important and politically explosive cases: those involving capital punishment. In one of many suggestive parallels with Thomas More's *Utopia*, Patrizi deplores the spread of capital punishment in his contemporary world, such that even thieves and other minor criminals are made subject to it.[46] Patrizi has a horror of capital punishment inflicted on rational souls, a punishment for which no compensation can be made if the judgment is passed in error. He gives historical examples of famous men in antiquity, including Julius Caesar, Alexander the Great, and Sabaco the Ethiopian, king of the Egyptians, who shared his hatred of judicial cruelty.[47] The Romans, Patrizi admits, did on rare occasions impose capital punishment on citizens, but only in the most serious cases, mostly in cases of murder, and they were extremely careful not to inflict the death sentence without demonstrating the guilt of the accused.

From a political point of view, Patrizi's chief worry about capital judgments is that they will lead to civil unrest when imposed in arbitrary fashion by magistrates. Such cases are often politicized and partisan. "Civic hatreds and hidden plots can often rush headlong toward revenge when men with the power to inflict death are in command." Summary capital punishment by magistrates, moreover, is sometimes inflicted on subordinates whose guilt is not evident to the people. The people, if convinced of a condemned man's innocence, become outraged when he is executed and will embrace conspiracy theories. There arises a general feeling of insecurity, suspicion, and fear, and the lives of magistrates are put in danger. Widespread belief in a condemned man's innocence, backed by the force of conscience, give great impetus to popular discontent.

The solution to this problem, says Patrizi, is to revive the old Roman magistracy of the *tresviri capitales,* a three-man board of inquisitors who investigated capital cases. Patrizi's account of this board's procedures seems to be largely his own invention.[48] According to the learned Sienese thinker, the board employed a full *quaestio* process, a formal trial where evidence was carefully gathered, testimony taken, and arguments heard on both sides before judgment was handed down. The accused had the right to face his accusers, and defendants too poor to hire an advocate had one appointed for them by the praetors. "The Romans thought it unjust that a man have his life taken, or even given some lesser penalty, without being defended." Extreme care was taken, Patrizi claims, to secure fair judges. The inquisitors put a number of judges' names in an urn, and defendants and accusers would pick out names at random, *fortuita sortitione.* Either party could veto the names of judges whom they believed to be partial or otherwise unsuitable, and other names would be extracted until agreement was reached. The judges selected would then pass judgment, but their judgment could be appealed to other judges, likewise chosen by sortition. Patrizi's fictionalized account of the *tresviri capitales* is then supported by a quotation from Vergil (*Aeneid* 6.431–433), ingeniously interpreted to reveal that Minos, the judge of the underworld, used a similar procedure.

Patrizi never calls formally for an independent judiciary, and indeed legal historians ordinarily trace this concept back only as far as the eighteenth century.[49] But in this passage we can see that the Sienese philosopher, like some of his scholastic predecessors, has considered how the processes of justice can best be insulated from political corruption. The same concern leads him to make one of his boldest proposals for reform in the *De republica:* his proposal at the end of 3.6 to take wealth and personal influence out of the justice system entirely. He sees two ways that this might be done.

The first way is to substitute honor for profit as the main incentive for barristers and advocates in law. *Patroni* who take up cases for plaintiffs or defendants should be prohibited ("if possible") from taking money or gifts from their clients, and instead treasure as their reward the good opinion of their fellow citizens.

> Let orators plead cases as a voluntary service [*officii gratia*], to deserve well of their fellow citizens, and let their reward be universal respect. They should not be allowed, if possible, to accept money or gifts, as was prohibited by Lex Cincia. It is shameful indeed and inhuman to sell your tongue to men when trying cases.

Patrizi traces the dubious practice of advocates in law taking money directly from defendants or plaintiffs back to Antiphon of Rhamnus, a leader of the Athenian oligarchy in the late fifth century BC. The practice continued for centuries.[50] He says it was only the Romans, "from whom all examples of probity and virtue should be taken," who put a limit on the avarice of orators. This happened as a result of the Lex Cincia, a plebiscite passed in the time of the tribune M. Cincius Alimentus (204 BC).[51] Afterward the law was relaxed because it was feared that young men would not try cases carefully if they were not paid. In a parallel passage

(*Rep.* 2.4) Patrizi writes that this was done to prevent the art of eloquence from dying out.[52]

Advocates, like magistrates, must of course be men of the highest character who meet Quintilian's standard of "good men skilled in speaking."[53] Honesty is of the highest importance; perjury by advocates should be severely punished. Corrupt barristers should be censured by the consuls themselves or handed over to the senate for censure. Patrizi has particularly harsh words for *praevaricatores,* sham accusers or defenders who will defend either side in a case for money. They abandon the finest service one can do among mortals, that of defending another in court, and put justice up for sale. They swindle now the plaintiff, now the defendant, and in the end deceive both.

Such behavior implies an abuse of rhetorical skill. Like all humanists Patrizi admires the true eloquence of serious, moral men, but in court there is great danger that the barrister's tongue can be corrupted by avarice. Humanist eloquence of the Renaissance in fact was rarely employed in law courts; most surviving examples of humanist oratory are epideictic, not judicial. Two such ceremonial speeches by Patrizi himself survive.[54] Despite the positive example of Cicero's numerous court speeches, however, Patrizi regards judicial rhetoric as a potential threat to justice. That is perhaps why he repeatedly turns to Cicero himself as an authority when decrying the abuse of oratorical skill. From Ammianus Marcellinus (30.4.10), for example, he cites Cicero as saying, "To me the man does far more evil who corrupts a judge with speech than with money, because no one can corrupt a prudent judge with money, but he can through speech."

The danger of corrupting judges using an advocate's oratorical skills leads Patrizi to make an even bolder suggestion: the art of speaking, rhetoric, might be taken entirely out of legal processes. This idea was prompted by his reading of the historian Diodorus Siculus's account of legal processes in ancient Egypt. According to Patrizi (and here his summary sticks close to his Greek source), the ancient Egyptians used to put in charge of their courts thirty excellent men chosen from the most famous cities, presided over by a magnificent figure who bore a golden seal called "Truth." Before this court defendants and plaintiffs laid written accusations and defenses with proposals for indemnification. The defendant could respond in writing to the plaintiff's written accusation, and the plaintiff to the defendant's response. Once the judges felt they had a good handle on the controversy, the golden seal of Truth was extended toward the party on whose behalf the "reason of the law" was to be adjudged and sentence passed. "The whole case was tried without pleaders, as the Egyptians reckoned that the truth could more easily be elicited in disputes between defendant and plaintiff when they were tried in written form, so that the courts would not be perverted by ingenuity, art, cunning, or audacity."

Patrizi concludes—"so that we look like we've taken something from the Egyptians"—by advising magistrates to decree that public monies, not private, should be shared out to prevent legal judgments from becoming venal, "a thing that is dangerous in every people and often makes regimes unstable." Though not elaborated, Patrizi's advice here and throughout the *De republica* points to a system of justice where legal expenses, both for defendant and plaintiff, would be borne by the public in general. Such a system would prevent the wealthy and influential from possessing undue advantages at law by hiring the best legal counsel. Barristers would be expected to argue cases on a voluntary basis, for honor and to serve their fellow citizens. Or oral arguments might be dispensed with entirely in favor of written briefs, where rhetorical trickery would be less at a premium.

## Censors, Quaestors, Overseers of Provisions, Aediles

Sandwiched between his discussion of praetors at 3.6 and the *tresviri capitales* in 3.8, Patrizi devotes a long chapter to the office of censor, a senior magistrate who plays an indispensable role in the best republic. Here Patrizi again follows ancient Roman precedent selectively. As in the Roman case, Patrizi's censor has the job of keeping track of citizen numbers and making a census of their goods and wealth. This should be done every five years, so that fair tax assessments can be made on citizens in times of need. There should be one censor for each *terzo,* unlike the Roman censors who were two in number and whose responsibilities were not limited to particular parts of the city. Again unlike his Roman model, Patrizi's censors are not concerned with establishing formal social classes on the basis of wealth, as would hardly be appropriate in a meritocracy, where political rank is supposed to depend on virtue.

For Patrizi, the censors' most important role by far is as teachers and superintendents of public morals. His primary exemplar for the office is Rome's most famous censor, Cato the Elder, known for his severe standards of behavior. "Teachers [*magistri*] of decency and restraint are so necessary in a republic that, without them, other magistracies are worthless. For nothing is more useful than a well-mannered people." He distinguishes two senses of the word for manners, *mos:* custom (including civic rites) and good behavior. Both are the censors' responsibility. The censor's *nota* or censure conferred instant infamy, and a person so censured could be deprived of office and would lose social prestige. Patrizi expects his censors to restrain the luxury of the rich and punish wastrels, the idle, the celibate, and those who have allowed their patrimonies to fall into disrepair. They will also take action against moneylenders who practice usury and have by so doing exacerbated conditions of indebtedness among the people.

We can deal with Patrizi's other proposed officials more briefly. They all have ancient Roman equivalents, whose historical origins and etymologies Patrizi discusses. In each case he lays emphasis on their moral functions and qualities.

Quaestors are in charge of collecting and storing tax revenues and keeping public accounts. They must practice good judgment in imposing charges and prevent the odious tribe of tax collectors from committing extortion; by keeping good accounts they can prevent peculation. They should not debase the coinage.

Aediles are the officials in charge of public buildings. Their first duty is taking care of the temples and churches of God, and Patrizi may well have in mind existing public institutions like the Opera del Duomo (Cathedral Building Authority) in Siena and other Italian cities. Although Patrizi discusses the public games of ancient Rome in some detail in book 2, he says nothing there about the role of Roman aediles in sponsoring them. Their main responsibility in the best republic should be the convenience and attractiveness of the urban fabric. They are in charge of aqueducts, fountains, and drains as well as repairing bridges, and they should see to it that streets are clean, level, and laid out in useful and beautiful ways. They will have to work closely with architects and urban planners, as we shall see in Chapter 5.

The *praefecti annonae* or overseers of provisioning are in charge of maintaining supplies of food in case of dearth and preventing price gouging.

Finally, there should be officers in charge of keeping watch by day and by night, for there can be no good defenses without good watchmen.

All of these magistrates will presumably be chosen on the basis of merit, following the mixed procedure of sortition and election outlined above, and all will have terms fixed by law. The city will therefore need a large body of persons of outstanding character and intelligence with many kinds of expertise, especially in law, finance, and engineering. How such an elite might be produced we shall see in Chapter 5.

## Summary: The Patrizian Republic

Before turning to Patrizi's proposals for educational, economic, and ecclesiastical reform, it is worth summing up the distinctive features of the Patrizian republic. One must insist on the adjective "Patrizian" as indicating a coherent ideal of good government distinct from both his sources and from contemporary practice in Renaissance republics. It would be a great mistake to dismiss Patrizi as an eclectic, a scholarly hobbyist rearranging information culled from classical authors in order to fill out some sort of encyclopedia of political thought. He was no more an eclectic than was Aristotle, whose modeling of a best practical regime and an optimal regime in the *Politics* was based on an extensive dossier of political thought and experience. Like any political thinker who is historically literate, Patrizi aimed to reform contemporary political institutions and practices through reflection on the experience of past societies. His access to new Greek sources, however, took him far beyond the usual humanist approach that favored ancient Rome as the model for customs and institutions and Aristotle as the principal guide to political analysis.[55]

Rome and Aristotle remained fundamental for Patrizi, of course, as this chapter and Chapter 3 have shown well enough. But his search for the best political institutions in history and the ones most applicable to contemporary republics took him much farther afield, to Athens and Sparta, to the Persia of Cyrus the Great, to ancient Egypt and India, as well as to the modern republic of Venice. Perhaps the best way to gauge how his thinking was shaped by exploring the new world of politics opened up for him by previously unavailable Greek sources is to consider how the Patrizian republic differs from the Roman, and where it departs from Aristotle's best practical and ideal polities.

Patrizi evidently believed that a humanistic education in virtue, combined with well-designed institutions, could avert much of the turbulence experienced by the Roman republic during its long history and by the city-states of Greece that Aristotle sought to stabilize and improve.[56] Like other quattrocento humanists he rejected the belief of ancient Greek philosophers in inevitable cycles of constitutional decline, substituting an optimistic faith, characteristic of the early Renaissance, in the transformative power of human virtue. With the virtuous in charge of the city, there will be no need for institutional fixes such as dictators to provide stability in emergencies or plebeian tribunes to prevent the oppression of the people by self-interested elites. Good judicial institutions like Patrizi's reinvented *tresviri capitales,* when staffed by morally good and learned judges, will create no need for *provocatio ad populum,* the old Roman right of appeal to popular assemblies on behalf of persons believed to be unjustly condemned to death. A substantial public investment in a small, professional, citizen army and good defense-works will inhibit any tendencies to bellicosity and imperial adventures. Avoidance of imperialism makes unnecessary the maintenance of large, land-hungry armies in the field, led by ambitious proconsuls—a principal source of instability in the late Roman republic. A senate consisting only of former magistrates rather than a hereditary political class will prevent the tendency to identify the interests of the rich and powerful with the common good. A separate order of magistrates with fixed terms of office, chosen for their good character and meritorious service, will develop its own standards of noble conduct resistant to the corruptions of wealth and power. A two-man consulate designed for each consul, not to check the other, but to exercise distinct, primary functions in peace and war, will enhance energy in the executive and lessen the need for a monarch to act as final decision-maker.

Though Patrizi's political prudence was greatly enriched by his reading of Aristotle, and one can find in Patrizi dozens of allusions, acknowledged and unacknowledged, to the *Politics,* the Sienese philosopher nevertheless rejects Aristotle's primary solutions to the problem of political instability. In his best practical state, outlined in books 4–6 of the *Politics,* Aristotle aimed to neutralize political conflict by balancing and blending oligarchic and democratic institutions. His optimal mixed constitution or "polity" would enjoy a common pool of virtue not fully instantiated in any of the individual citizens who filled its councils, assemblies, and boards. Virtue would be generated artificially by a species of moderation and prudence stamped on the citizenry via customs, laws and institutions. No one valued virtue more than Aristotle, but unlike Plato he did not see, in the case of most existing cities, any great prospect for transforming them into ideal states through the power of philosophical wisdom. Aristocracies were empirically possible, but rare and short-lived. At most, in the best cases, a philosopher-statesman might introduce, via elections, a principle of merit into the selection of magistrates. In the case of his ideal state in *Politics* 7–8, Aristotle excluded non-elites entirely from the citizen body and had no use for any wisdom or virtue that might emanate from the laboring classes, nor any interest in using the state to satisfy their disordered wants. They were degraded specimens of humanity deformed by mechanical and servile labor, and philosophical education was wasted on them.[57]

Patrizi had no desire to hear the voices of the common people en masse, especially in the counsels of government, but he also thought, following Plutarch's Solon, that worthy members of the lower classes deserved in some measure to participate in their own rule, and that civic solidarity required it. As we will see in Chapter 5, he also believed that all citizens, so far as possible, should be given an education in letters to increase the overall level of virtue in the citizen body. He had far more appreciation for the value of citizen equality than Aristotle (or any Greek political philosopher, for that matter), and he had far more suspicion of the power of wealth in politics. His proposed reform of judicial institutions to limit the power of wealth and influence on legal processes owes more to the civic traditions of the Italian communes than to Aristotle or ancient Roman law, as does his advice about how to manage public deliberation so as to favor the prudent and wise. His counsels on the conduct of public officials also reflect personal experience, enriched by his reading of Plutarch's essay "Precepts of Statecraft" from the *Moralia*. So too, his advice to magistrates on how to curb the power of over-mighty citizens, manage political turbulence, and attract the loyalty of the common people, reveal close study not only of Livy and Cicero but of Plutarch's *Lives* and Dionysius of Halicarnassus's account of the Roman republic.[58] Perhaps his most original contribution to political philosophy, to my knowledge unexampled in the West before the Renaissance, was his proposal to select via institutional devices a distinct political class that would constitute a separate order of the well-educated and virtuous—a proposal that resembles in certain respects the governing ideals of the Confucian mandarinate in imperial China.[59]

Still, the most ambitious parts of Patrizi's reform agenda—the parts where his debt to ancient Greek literature is most evident—are not found among his proposals to revise the structure of republican political institutions. His real radicalism—the part of his legacy that points most strongly to Thomas More's *Utopia*—is found in his vision of how the city-state might reform and restructure its educational practices, its social and economic system, its built environment, and its relationship to religious authorities. To that part of Patrizi's legacy we now turn.

FIVE

# The Virtuous Society

## Educating the Virtuous Citizen

A principal concern of Italian humanists and the Renaissance movement in general was how best to educate children and young adults
for their future roles in society. Between the time of Petrarch in the
mid-Trecento and the decades when Patrizi was writing, the humanist
movement had considerable success transforming educational practice in the republics and monarchies of Italy. Scholastic education
in medieval universities had been oriented to training professional
lawyers, doctors, and theologians. Humanist education, presenting
itself as an education for *ingenui*—which one might translate as "free
men" or "gentlemen"—was an education directed at social elites, including some women as well as a few promising "scholarship boys"
from the middle classes. As such it emphasized the arts of elegant
speech and gentlemanly comportment. The great court schools of
northeastern Italy—above all those of the Gonzaga in Mantua,
founded by Vittorino da Feltre in 1423, and of the Este in Ferrara,
headed by Guarino of Verona from 1429—put the study of classical
literature in both Greek and Latin at the heart of the curriculum. In
the Tuscan republics of Florence and Siena, humanistic education was
often conducted privately in the palaces of the wealthy. All these
schools set a tone of moral seriousness and piety and insisted on high
character in teachers and pupils. In addition, both princes and republican elites promoted public lectures on humane authors in local

universities and appointed distinguished humanists to teach rhetoric and Greek literature.[1]

As we saw illustrated in Chapter 1 in the case of Patrizi's academic speech *De philosophia*, a regular theme of humanist educational writings was the utility of humane studies to the state. The study of classical literature improved the character of the republic's future leaders and gave them the practical knowledge—above all, through the study of rhetoric and history—that they needed to conduct its affairs. The cultivation of eloquence was of particular value because the best kind of leadership in a state worked through persuasion rather than force. The power of eloquence was multiplied many times when the speaker was a person of good character who could appeal convincingly to shared moral values. A city that perverted its legal system in the interests of the powerful and was constantly ratcheting up its use of surveillance, spies, police, regulations, and cruel punishments—especially when such measures were used against its own citizens—revealed itself as a failed polity. In antiquity, only tyrants employed such measures.

The best states of antiquity, the humanists believed, had not required such brutal forms of control. Humanist literati advocated immersive study of the most successful societies of the classical world—Sparta, Athens, the Persia of Xenophon's *Cyropaedia,* and Rome above all. Such study would set before future rulers examples, both good and bad, of how their own societies might best be reformed. While good laws and institutions were important, what was of paramount significance was the men who made and interpreted the laws and ran the institutions. If they lacked the virtues, above all practical wisdom, those institutions would fail. As both Plato and Aristotle taught, the best measure of successful rulership was the degree of virtue and (therefore) felicity found among the citizenry. In popular republics, where all citizens might hold office, all citizens needed some portion of education and virtue.

Francesco Patrizi fervently agreed with all these principles, tried to exemplify them, and was an advocate for them throughout his life. It is no surprise, then, that in his *De republica* he foregrounds the need for civic education by devoting an entire book to the subject, placed, significantly, just before his book on institutions. Patrizi was by no means the first humanist to discuss civic education, but his proposal for a humanistic reform of the university curriculum was a new departure for the movement as a whole and a key component of his reforming agenda.

None of the four most famous treatises by humanists on education—those written by Pier Paolo Vergerio (1402/1403), Leonardo Bruni (1422/1426), Patrizi's patron Enea Silvio Piccolomini (1450), and Battista Guarino (1459)—had addressed the question of how citizens and magistrates in free republics should be educated.[2] Vergerio's and Guarino's works had been written with princely schools in mind; Piccolomini's was written for a German king; Bruni's for the daughter of a condottiere prince. The longest fifteenth-century treatise on education, Maffeo Vegio's *Six Books on the Education of Children and Their Fine Deportment* (1444), was addressed to religious parents. It modeled the education of children on the formation of St. Augustine of Hippo. However, the earliest humanist writers on princely republics—Uberto Decembrio (1422) and Tito Livio Frulovisi (1435)—had both emphasized the prince's responsibility to promote a literate citizenry and to support the liberal arts, legal studies, and the advanced humanistic disciplines of oratory, poetry, history, and moral philosophy. In the aristocratic republic designed by the Venetian Lauro Quirini (*De republica*, 1449), literacy and moral education are recommended for all citizens, and the *studia humanitatis*—above all history—for patricians. Quirini, however, satisfies himself with laying out general principles and does not go into much detail about the curriculum. As mentioned in Chapter 2, all three of these works survive today in only one or two manuscripts, and it is unlikely that Patrizi knew them. They have been printed only in modern times.[3]

By contrast, Patrizi's discussion of the ideal curriculum for free cities was the most extensive and learned treatment of civic education in the quattrocento. It has never been the object of sustained study, though it surely merits close attention from historians of political thought.[4] While many humanist writings stress the benefits of liberal education to the state, Patrizi was the only author of the fifteenth century to design a curriculum expressly to form citizens and magistrates. He is the first humanist theorist to recommend that citizenship should be conditional on literacy. He is the first republican writer to advocate the regular teaching of humanistic disciplines at public expense. Perhaps inspired by the examples of the library of San Marco in Florence (1444) and the Biblioteca Malatestiana in Cesena (founded 1454), Patrizi was also the first republican theorist to call for the establishment of public libraries in order to nurture citizens and future magistrates in the *optimae artes,* the liberal arts and humanities.[5]

Like earlier humanist writers, but with greater conceptual clarity, Patrizi approaches the problem of civic education on two levels: that of the family and that of the republic. His treatment of how to nurture future citizens and magistrates is thus split between book 4, on household management, which contains a virtual treatise-within-a-treatise (4.6) on how to raise children, and book 2, which discusses the formal education, to be supported by the state, of citizens and magistrates in the liberal disciplines. In his educational theory Patrizi draws on the usual ancient sources popular with humanists: Quintilian's *Institutes of Oratory* and Cicero's *De oratore* above all, combined with (pseudo) Plutarch's essay *On the Education of Children,* translated into Latin by Guarino of Verona, and St. Basil of Caesarea's *Letter to Young Men,* translated by Leonardo Bruni. Patrizi gives more attention than usual to Vitruvius, a favorite author, excerpting several of the Roman author's remarks about how an architect should be educated. Though Patrizi himself wrote a compendium of Quintilian that had some success as a tool of pedagogy, and his patron Enea Silvio Piccolomini had relied on Quintilian almost to a fault in his own treatise on education, Patrizi's theory escapes the professional narrowness of the Roman educator's approach. As ever, Patrizi is alive to the psychological and moral effects of learning various subjects and of using various pedagogical methods. Like other humanists he wants children to learn willingly, without the use of severe punishments, and he believes that the best education comes from teachers who set a fine example and who judiciously employ praise and blame to motivate their charges. The governance of the schoolroom is thus a model for the state.

## The Roles of Wife and Husband

Since the best education is motivated by love and not fear, it is appropriate that the earliest formation of children should be the responsibility of the mother.[6] After a chapter on the duties of the wife, stressing her special authority in all that goes on within the walls of the home, Patrizi inserts the longest chapter in the entire De republica, "On the Duty of Parents in Raising and Educating Children." Its disproportionate length raises the suspicion that it may have originally been intended for separate publication. Many authors have written on childhood education, says Patrizi, especially among the Greeks, but since the family is the seedbed (seminarium) of republics, and my book is on republics, heads of households should recognize that they do nothing more important for the state than to raise and educate children. But responsibility should be divided among husband and wife. The wife is responsible for vivere, the husband for bene vivere. The distinction between mere life and the good life, drawn silently from Aristotle's Politics, means in this context that early education, involving the child's health, speech patterns, and general moral orientation, is the wife's duty, whereas when the child reaches about the age of seven the husband should take on increased responsibility and oversee the training of a boy's mind and character through study of the appropriate disciplines.

Maternal devotion is shown by breast-feeding one's own children (a subject Patrizi discusses at great length, citing Homer, Vergil, and Cicero) rather than putting them out to nurse; an inferior source of milk can lead to moral degeneration, he opines.[7] Mothers should take great care that children learn to speak their vernacular language correctly. Mothers should not let their children listen too much to

servants and others who speak the language badly. She should not
let her children associate with persons of poor character. A woman
who is educated, however, can contribute more than this to childhood development. Sadly, educated women are few. "Our wives
these days are so torpid with laziness that it seems a kind of miracle
if any of them have the least acquaintance with literature." Husbands these days are also at fault: they choose wives for their beauty
and their dowries. They would do much better to follow the advice
of Lycurgus and make it a practice to prefer virtue to large dowries;
such a practice would have the effect of making women more zealous
for learning. Women are capable of great distinction in the disciplines, as the presence of two female members in Plato's academy
showed, not to mention the examples of the poetess Sappho and the
highly cultivated mother of the Gracchi, Cornelia. If you are fortunate
enough to have a learned wife (Patrizi addresses the paterfamilias),
you need not wait until the canonical age of seven recommended by
Hesiod for beginning a child's formal education: your wife can begin to educate the children in Latin letters even earlier than that.
She should begin with educational toys, like flashcards or wooden
blocks with the letters of the alphabet carved on them (as recommended by Quintilian). She should go slowly: give them sips of learning,
not full cups.

If they learn letters from their mother in their tender years, they
will be readier for more challenging studies when the father takes
charge of their education. Children should always show gratitude
to their parents, but they should be as grateful to their fathers for
their education as for their geniture. It is the father's responsibility to
discover where his son's abilities lie. It was a humanist principle
that sons should not be forced into a profession, especially their
father's profession, but should be allowed to develop their gifts whatever they might be. Patrizi gives the paterfamilias detailed advice on
how to observe his children's moral and intellectual development and
to foster their native virtues. *Generosa aemulatio*, noble rivalry between youths, competition for prizes in worthwhile accomplishments,

are vital. Non-voluntary virtues like memory and quickness of intellect should be noted, but the true virtues, the greater virtues, are the
voluntary ones formed by habit and effort. These deserve greater
praise because they spring from our own efforts: virtues like courage,
justice, and the like. "Some add a third genus of virtues, the intellectual virtues, like science, learning, and wisdom." If a father sees
that his children have the potential for intellectual virtues—a *rei
discendae sensus,* a capacity for learning—he should seek out for
them the best teachers of the liberal arts. If they do not, he should
put them to learn some honorable trade.

But if they have any capacity at all, by no means should a father
defraud his children of the chance to learn, and he should view with
equanimity the possibility that his children might excel him in their
mastery of the liberal arts. An education in the liberal arts is the most
valuable thing a parent can give a child.

> They are called liberal because they make human beings [*ho-
> mines*] free from all shameful and sordid forms of gain [*quaestus*],
> and from all sensual pleasure and baseness. They lead us to
> wisdom, than which there can be nothing more excellent for mor-
> tals, and by which we are marked out to join ourselves com-
> pletely with Best and Greatest God. Virtue by itself is sufficient
> reward for such studies, if no other were to be offered to mortal
> men, but virtue always brings honor along with it like a body
> brings its shadow.[8] Indeed, it is an observable fact that not only
> all the best men, but even the worst and most depraved of thieves,
> give honor and praise to the virtuous.

Virtue is charismatic and imparts a kind of invulnerable majesty to
those who possess it in abundance, like Scipio Africanus.[9] Another
model is Ulysses, who through all his perils, labors, and shipwrecks
was accompanied by Minerva, the goddess of wisdom, who restored
to him his fatherland, parents, wife, and children, "so that Homer
might show us that Ulysses overcame all perils through learning and
wisdom."

## *The Role of the State*

Not all fathers will have the resources to educate future citizens. But a state where all citizens participate to some extent in governance needs them to be well-educated men of good character. Ergo, the state needs to make some provision for universal citizen education. Book 2 of *De republica* discusses where responsibility lies for producing an educated citizenry, both basic literacy and more advanced education in the liberal arts.

Basic literacy is the province of the paterfamilias. It is the civic duty of heads of families to make sure that their male children can read, which, given the context, must mean the ability to read Latin. Otherwise, they cannot act well as citizens.

If possible, everyone should learn their letters. . . . Not only should letters be learned, but I hardly think, in a free city, that anyone merits the title of a freeborn citizen (*ingenuus civis*) who is illiterate. For without letters, how can we master or preserve even the least of the arts, to say nothing of the liberal disciplines? Neither mercantile nor agricultural activities may be kept sound without letters. Letters preserve historical memory, instruct posterity, link the past with the future, and compel us always to take account of our lives as a whole. For this reason it is best to imbue youth with letters before setting them to other studies if we wish at some point to turn them into men and count them as citizens. It will therefore be the duty of the best paterfamilias to see with the utmost care to the education of his sons, or at least to their basic literacy. The old Greek proverb says that a man without letters is like a tree that yields no fruit. Then let them go on to practice whatever arts they seem most suited for.[10]

Patrizi here claims that literacy will make even ordinary craftsmen and farmers better and more productive citizens. Being able to read will also give them a deeper sense of community by linking them, via historical memory, to their city's past. It will make them more reflective about their lives. Because citizenship is in part based on merit, and merit is based on learning, no one can be a citizen who is not literate.[11] Literacy is thus a precondition of civic virtue.

But what of higher studies? "But when they have mastered their first elements, it will not be amiss for them to address each of the liberal arts." Does that mean that all citizens should take courses in the liberal arts? Not quite. Patrizi admits that some boys will not have the aptitude for study, and they should be set to mastering some honorable task like trade, navigation, or a craft. The cleverer sort, however, should be encouraged to undertake higher studies.

> Let those who govern the state [*respublica*], therefore, undertake this task before all others: that the city's youth follow [one of two paths in life]. Either they should give themselves up to the study of the best arts [*studia bonarum artium*]—everyone in a free city should have a particular commitment to the disciplines, for Plato says that states become blessed that are ruled by wise and learned men—or if not, since not everyone is cut out for learning, they should practice trade, navigation, or other arts useful to civil society. Each person ought to work on his own account so as to be useful to himself, his family, and his fellow citizens. . . . Leisured [*otiosi*] and low-spirited youths are the poison of the state. They are prone to lust, envious of the good, grasp after others' property, and in the end turn out to be so seditious and turbulent that they threaten the state. Thus, they should not be admitted to public office . . . but forced into frugality, or if that is not possible, fined heavily or exiled.[12]

Not all parents can afford the cost of liberal education for their children, so the republic needs to supplement parental resources and provide public teachers of the liberal arts and their crown, the humanities. The city should also build a public library to provide books, as did King Ptolemy of Alexandria, for those who cannot afford a library of their own.[13] The ancient kings also gave out prizes for poets and orators, an admirable practice that modern cities should imitate. In short—at least in the best republic—ensuring excellence in the liberal disciplines is the responsibility of the whole community. It is also, surely, in the whole community's interest, since the young men being educated in the liberal disciplines will soon be holding public offices.[14]

> For if we want to write about the ideal republic [*de optima respublica*], it will be our responsibility to say in which disciplines we would educate our citizen—the man whom we would make a member of our city. The city's leadership will see to it that each of the disciplines will have the best teachers who will teach publicly, at public expense. For not all private citizens can both feed their children and afford the expense of teachers.[15]

This is perhaps Patrizi's most remarkable proposal in the sphere of education: that all citizens should be literate, and that the ideal city should appoint professors to teach all the liberal disciplines, so that any citizen who wished to learn them could do so, free of charge. One can find calls for universal citizen literacy before Patrizi's time: Plato made one in the *Laws* (810a–b) and the great Neo-Confucian scholar Zhu Xi made a similar proposal in twelfth-century China.[16] But Patrizi was the first modern Western author to propose what is today considered a basic precondition of good democratic governance.

Patrizi's call for an educated citizenry was an inescapable consequence of the logic of virtue politics. Since (1) in republics citizens rule themselves, and (2) virtue politics conditions a state's moral legitimacy, and therefore its concord and happiness, on the virtue of those who rule it, and (3) there can be no virtue without education, it follows (4) that no republic will enjoy moral legitimacy if its citizens are not educated in virtue. It is no surprise that book 2 of *De republica* is entirely devoted to education and precedes book 3's discussion of institutions, just as Aristotle's *Nicomachean Ethics* is propaedeutic to his *Politics*. A statesman cannot lead his citizens to virtue unless he understands and acts with virtue himself. Institutions cannot function well unless the citizen body is educated in the disciplines that lead to virtue and wisdom.

## A Scheme of Public Education

Today the liberal arts are commonly regarded as luxuries rather than public goods. For most parents, the bread-and-butter studies are those believed to offer their children the best opportunities for gainful employment—studies like economics, business, communications, or computer science. For the state the most useful disciplines are deemed to be those that make it more competitive economically or militarily with other states, especially mathematics, the sciences, and engineering. Why did Patrizi—and most Renaissance humanists along with him—take so different a view? Why did they believe that the liberal arts were not only desirable for their own sake but vital to the health of the state? Patrizi explains why in the scheme of public education he lays out in book 2. What the Sienese philosopher offers here is not just the usual trite list of the arts to be included in an *enkyklios paideia,* the traditional list of liberal subjects based on classical authorities. Instead we get an ordered scheme of disciplines, each of which is justified in terms of its public usefulness.

Needless to say, Patrizi does not grade the public usefulness of a discipline in terms of its contribution to the gross domestic product. For a Renaissance humanist, to define public utility only in terms of wealth would be depraved. In Aristotelian terms it would mean placing "external goods" (wealth and status) above the goods of the soul. For a humanist a good education is one that allows all citizens to live the best kind of life they can live. That means a life that includes moral and intellectual excellence, contributing to the common good, and religious devotion.

Patrizi's scheme of public education (Figure 2) begins with a distinction between body and mind. The state should encourage its citizens to train their bodies, which fosters intellectual health, industriousness, and resolution. The gold standard for physical training in antiquity was set by the Spartans, later imitated by the Athenians,

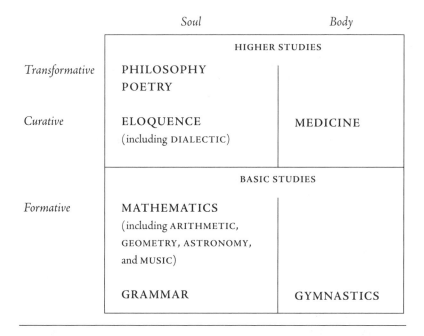

Figure 2. Patrizi's scheme of civic education.

who established public gymnasia and prizes for athletic contests. Bodily exercises should not be overdone, and the young need to engage in the right kind of exercise.[17] Noble youths, who are the boys most likely to serve in the military, should be placed in the houses of knights to learn riding, skill at arms, swimming, leaping, and spear-throwing. The example of antiquity needs to be followed judiciously, however. We should certainly not imitate the Spartan practice of exercising men and women together in gymnasia. Women should be kept soft and at home, as nature intended. Above all, we should not imitate the Roman practice of gladiatorial games in which men were killed to entertain the crowd. This was a repulsive custom that taught cruelty and contempt for human life. "Our city, and all well-ordered republics, will not have such things, if it will heed my advice."[18]

Gymnastics will provide basic training for the body. The basic disciplines for training the mind are grammar and mathematics.

Grammar was invented by the Egyptians and perfected in Greece, but given civic purpose by the Romans, who established grammar schools everywhere at public expense. Grammar is the basis of all other disciplines: without the capacity to read with full comprehension and to write correctly, one can learn nothing else. Patrizi does not say so explicitly, but grammar here must include some exposure to the classical canon of *auctores*, as was usual in the Renaissance classroom.

Another basic study is mathematics. Under this name Patrizi includes the four disciplines of the old quadrivium: arithmetic, geometry, astrology, and music, the disciplines requiring calculation and measurement. He begins his chapter on mathematics by setting out a straightforwardly Platonic view of the reality of essences (which, however, he attributes to Pythagoras). Behind what appears to our senses, which record mutable things, are intelligible things, which are capable of mathematical expression; by learning arithmetic and geometry, children gain access to a world of certainty and reality beyond the realm of the senses. In a more practical vein, measurement is a necessary skill for almost all the plastic arts. Public deliberation requires measurement, too: we must be able to calculate dates and times in order to convoke assemblies and conduct diplomacy.[19]

The state also needs astrology. "We can sanction public astrology in every republic by many arguments and examples." Astrology (which Patrizi does not distinguish from astronomy) is needed in agriculture to predict the weather and the growing season, and experienced astrologers can save the republic from many dangers. Ancient examples include Anaximander, who predicted an earthquake, and Hippocrates, who warned of an impending pestilence. Pericles was able to explain an eclipse to the Athenian army, thus calming its irrational fear of bad omens, while it was Nicias's ignorance of astronomy that led to the Athenian military disaster in Sicily during the Peloponnesian War.

In accordance with ancient tradition, Patrizi includes music under the mathematical sciences. Music is a noble science that educated people should study.[20] It is valued by citizens because it provides delight and relaxation from labor, but it can also serve public functions. It has the power to change moods, so it can be used to fire up soldiers for battle, as the Romans did with their war trumpets and the Spartans with their bagpipes. The right kind of music can suppress lust in youth. Gaius Gracchus controlled the Roman mob by having a servant play the panpipes in the background while he spoke to them, altering the crowd's mood to harmonize with the themes of his oratory. Music has medical uses as well: doctors have used it to heal the sick and cure the insane. In a free city the relaxation and pleasure offered by music are sufficient to justify its study, but "reason and example have taught us that music is useful to the civil man, not only for its delightfulness but to foster the intelligence and to make men readier and more eager not only for military service but for undertaking the highest enterprises."[21]

In chapters 3 and 4, Patrizi links medicine and eloquence together as disciplines that restore health of body and mind, respectively, in the citizenry. A healthy body is a precondition of a peaceful life; and medicine, a most ancient discipline, is a divine gift. "Those in charge of the republic will take care that medicine is learned with the greatest care, and doctors are honored, both because of the discipline's intrinsic excellence and its utility." Eloquence, on the other hand, is medicine for the soul, and thus even more necessary. It heals diseases of soul, no fewer than those of the body, such as anger, avarice, fear, and excessive transports of joy. Thanks to its healing power, eloquence is the mistress of public affairs, and a state that wants harmony and willing obedience from its citizens cannot do without it.

And if we would judge rightly, of all the disciplines none is more suited to the state [civitas] than public speaking [oratoria]. [The "demonstrative" genus of oratory concerned with persuasion] is entirely political, for all public deliberation in a republic requires persuasion and dissuasion in order to dig out the truth. On this account the orator—the good man skilled in speaking, as Cato defined him—will argue for beneficial policies, lest the people slip into false beliefs and approve policies which, after sorrowful experience, they will soon be forced to undo.[22]

Because the orator must advocate what is good, he must know how to find the good: he must therefore link *eloquentia* with *sapientia*. As Cicero taught, eloquence without wisdom is empty and rudderless, worthy of mockery, but philosophy without the flame of eloquence is weak and leaves human affections untouched. "We [civic leaders] will therefore see to it that in our republic many youths who are intelligent and hardworking will study the humanities." Eloquence here is represented as coterminous with the humanities, probably because, in Italian universities, professors of rhetoric were ordinarily the ones who taught classical literature.[23]

Dialectic, on the other hand, discussed in the next chapter (2.5), is presented as a study that is useless except as a mental exercise that sharpens the mind for "certain other disciplines." It acquires civic purpose only as a tool of eloquence. Eloquence needs dialectic in order to make more powerful arguments: "Rhetoric without dialectic is unfit for war, while dialectic without rhetoric is raw and inarticulate." Logic studied in isolation from rhetoric can be pernicious. Though logicians may briefly compel the mind by force of argument, they fail to convince the heart and alter conduct; that is why dialectic needs to be combined with and subject to eloquence.[24]

Both medicine and eloquence are presented as curative arts, disciplines that are instrumental to civic health, bringing into harmony discordant humors in the body and passions in the body politic. The two highest and best of Patrizi's liberal disciplines, poetry and philosophy, by contrast, are transformative. They teach truths that are valuable in themselves, but they are of supreme usefulness to the city thanks to their power to shape character. Poetry and philosophy are therefore the highest of the humanistic disciplines.

As transformative studies, poetry and philosophy are potential rivals of religious teaching, hence their study in Christian societies could be controversial. The chapter on poetry (2.6), the longest in book 2, begins with Plato's famous exclusion of poets from the state in the *Republic*. For well over a century religious critics of the humanities had used this *auctoritas* against the study of pagan poetry in schools.[25] If the greatest ancient philosopher of antiquity, the philosopher whom St. Augustine regarded as coming closest to Christian truth, thought Homer and Hesiod dangerous to public morals as purveyors of noxious myths about the gods, surely Christian educators should stay far from them?

Patrizi's reply, up to a point, follows well-worn paths of humanist apologetic. Philistine critics of pagan poetry simply do not understand how to read either Plato or the poets. Drawing on Plato's *Seventh Letter* (nowadays considered pseudonymous), Patrizi affirms that the Greek philosopher never stated any positive doctrines, so his prohibition of Homer could not be taken literally. Furthermore, Plato in the *Phaedrus* claimed that poetic inspiration was one of the four divine forms of madness, a doctrine Plato advanced to show that poets were holy men and "were engaged in something divine, beyond human powers."[26] Finally, as Patrizi learned from Diogenes Laertius, Plato himself had been a poet in his youth and had written love poetry and tragedy. His teacher Socrates had also written hymns at the end of his life.[27] Philosophy was not the enemy of poetry.

Furthermore, the critics of poetry misunderstood the poets' theology. The ancient bards, when talking about the gods, expected their readers to understand that the "gods" talked about in their poetry had often been bad men raised to the stars through political influence. Poetic descriptions of the follies of the gods were in reality veiled criticisms of evil rulers, like Jove, who before his stellification had a been an evil king in Crete.[28] The best poets of antiquity had been holy seers who transmitted theological truths in the form of poetic myths. Their real purpose was to mock worship of the pagan gods, not to endorse it. Rightly understood, their poetic descriptions of the behavior of the gods revealed the latter as all too human, undeserving of divine honors. In any case, if the anti-humanistic argument is that poets could not have known the truth of Christ before his birth, the same argument applies equally to philosophers. If critics admit that we should read the pagan philosophers because they recognized the truth of monotheism, the same could be said of the early poets, like Orpheus (for example), who wrote eleven centuries before the Trojan War. Poetry was in fact the earliest form of philosophy.

The best city will therefore not drive poets into exile any more than it would philosophers. In a rare personal comment, Patrizi explains at the end of the chapter why he should be the last person to exclude poets from an ideal city:

> We have written enough and more than enough about the poets, but the sweetness of their language and the tender memories I have of them made me go on too long. Indeed, it seemed to me wrong not to protect them as much as possible, as I have enjoyed their company greatly my entire life and have written my own *Poemata* in four books. As a poet myself I couldn't bear to see poets excluded from the city I have been founding, and especially because it has been dear to my heart to hand down precepts of the blessed republic if I could.

Pagan poetry is a rich source of truth and goodness, therefore, and as such must be read in schools. Grammarians would have no learning without the poets, no models of elegant language. The fables of the poets are really moral tales, rendered far more memorable by their mythic garb and beautiful rhymed speech. The edifying myths associated with the Labors of Hercules are enough to show how poetry can teach virtue. The most valuable genre is the heroic poetry of Homer and Vergil, which should be studied and memorized. "They have left to us images of the bravest men to gaze upon and imitate, which make us readier to seek every kind of virtue and praise." Achilles was the standard of bravery for Alexander the Great, for example. Heroic poetry should on rare occasions, perhaps after great victories, be recited publicly at games or theatrical festivals. Satire, elegy, and lyric poetry also contain much to admire and imitate.

Distinctions, however, must be made and a degree of censorship exercised. First of all, only learned poets are to be studied in the best republic. Sometimes the satirists (Patrizi is doubtless thinking of Juvenal and Martial) are a little too frank about the vices they excoriate, but the few offensive bits can be shaved off, leaving them the most holy of poets. In other cases whole genres are to be avoided in public instruction. Patrizi has serious misgivings about the propriety of reading and performing Roman theater, despite the revival of public performances of ancient drama occurring elsewhere in Italy during his lifetime.[29] For Patrizi, tragedy is too violent (he is probably thinking of the gory tragedies of the younger Seneca), too mixed with despair; the tragedians spend too much time illustrating corrupt mores; their language is turgid and inhumane. They make the stupid insane and the volatile angry. "Nearly all tragedy is to be excluded from the best city." Ancient comedy also should not studied in public schools or performed in theaters. It corrupts morals and makes citizens effeminate, lustful, and ripe for luxurious excess. Their subject matter is all about adultery and rape. Quoting Scipio Africanus in in Cicero's *Republic,* Patrizi claims the Romans themselves would never have countenanced its performance had not custom sanctioned it. But the moral gravity of the Romans led them to hold actors in low esteem.[30]

To be sure, Patrizi does not intend to prohibit absolutely the study of Roman drama. He carefully distinguishes between the public culture of the city, with its schools and theaters, and the private studies of learned men. Grave scholars should feel free to study morally dubious authors in private for the sake of improving Latin expression: "Comedy should therefore be driven from theaters, but learned and well-educated men may read it inside their private dwellings if they like, paying attention to its words rather than its sense. Comedy has great elegance, and its speech is pure, polished, and fit for daily use." Patrizi recommends Menander, Eupolis, Aristophanes, Plautus, and Terence. Cicero endorsed Terence as a model of speech, and Varro said that if the Muses were to speak Latin, they would use the language of Plautus. But citizens in general should not devote themselves to comedy. One black mark against the Athenians, Patrizi says, was they spent more of their money staging comedies than fighting wars.

The highest of the civil disciplines in Patrizi's ranking is philosophy, discussed in his seventh chapter. It stands highest because philosophy teaches what virtue is. "We say the best republic is that in which citizens dwell in peace and quiet and are able to do all those things that lead to happiness. Therefore, knowledge of virtue will be the principal necessity for the civil man, and virtue is what philosophy, the pursuit of wisdom, offers us." Philosophy is called the science of all things human and divine, but moral philosophy is what is most useful to citizens.[31] Moral philosophy brings self-knowledge, here defined as awareness of virtue's power to control ugly passions such as fear, elation, lust, and anger. Philosophy pulls these perturbations out by the roots, which is why "every excellent citizen who wishes to benefit not only himself but his household and his country should devote effort to philosophy." From moral philosophy we learn what courage is, a virtue necessary to defend the state in battle, and what justice is, the foundation of the household as well as of civil society.

Patrizi takes his reader on a tour of the history of philosophy, borrowed mostly from Diogenes Laertius, showing particular interest in the achievements of non-Greek philosophers in Egypt (who claimed to have invented philosophy), India, Phoenicia, Scythia, and Persia. He then describes the various schools of Greek philosophy. He culls the occasional saying or wise teaching, such as the excellent rule of India's gymnosophists that astrologers who make false predictions must spend the rest of their lives in silence.

Several pressing questions arise when we consider Patrizi's civic curriculum. First, why does he not prescribe the study of history? Later, in the *De regno*, he ranked history with poetry as the subject that kings and princes most needed to study for examples of magnanimous action and to inform their practical wisdom.[32] In the *De republica* the subject is hardly mentioned. Since the whole treatise is built on deep historical research, one is tempted to say that Patrizi doesn't mention history because he doesn't notice it, the way fish do not notice the water in which they swim. But the most likely explanation is that Patrizi, like Cicero, regards history as a branch of rhetoric. In most Italian universities of the day the ancient historians were ordinarily taught by professors of rhetoric, along with works of poetry and philosophy, and that may be what Patrizi had in mind. History only began to be recognized as a distinct *ars* in the *Actius* of Giovanni Pontano, first published in 1507.[33] There is another possibility too: Patrizi may have felt that the subject needed no special support from the state, as history was already one of the most popular genres of literature in the Renaissance.

The largest and most glaring omission from Patrizi's curriculum of higher studies, however, is any provision for the formal study of law.[34] Law was by far the most prestigious discipline in the civic universities of Renaissance Italy, and its professors by far the most highly remunerated, so Patrizi's omission of legal studies has to be deliberate, perhaps deliberately provocative. The humanist movement, going back to Petrarch and Boccaccio in the Trecento, was bitterly critical of legal education, which it saw as intellectually and spiritually desiccated.[35] The young Lorenzo Valla had been arrested in 1433 at the University of Pavia for disrupting a doctoral defense in law; he had attacked the candidate for teaching barbarism.[36] Humanists saw law as an *ars nummaria,* a money-making skill, not a liberal art. The law schools also had a pernicious effect on civic harmony, humanists charged, encouraging venality and litigiousness, and advantaging the wealthy over average citizens. As we saw in Chapter 4, Patrizi thought that the best republic should take concrete steps to prevent the legal system of the best city from being corrupted by wealth and privilege. There is abundant evidence that humanists throughout the Renaissance were jealous of the high salaries paid to law professors and the great efforts made to recruit distinguished jurists by the citizen committees that managed Italian universities.[37]

Excessively high salaries for jurists made it that much harder for cash-poor cities to fund professorships in other subjects. Throughout the fifteenth century, as Paul Grendler has shown, Italian humanists were involved in pressure campaigns to introduce humane studies into public universities.[38] In many places, and especially at the universities of Bologna, Padua, Ferrara, Rome, and Florence, they had considerable success. In the University of Florence in 1451, the rhetoric and poetry professors absorbed a larger percentage of the budget for professorial salaries than that allotted for canon law and medicine, an unprecedented situation that discloses the high cultural prestige enjoyed by humanism in that city.[39] In 1473 Lorenzo de'Medici sponsored a major reform of Florence's Studio, hiving off the pre-professional study of law and medicine to a secondary university center in Pisa, while reserving the center stage in Florence for humanistic studies.[40] At other Italian universities of the period, one of which was the University of Siena, humanists had relatively little success in dislodging law from its dominant place in the university.

Seen in this context, Patrizi's program of civic education in *De republica* is a visionary project. It implied a major reform of the university as inherited from the Middle Ages. In Italy the *studio* was always a civic institution regulated by citizen boards. These supported, above all, the professional study of law and medicine. Excellent teachers in law and medicine were a considerable source of cultural prestige for a city-state, and the study of other arts was seen as propaedeutic to these highest of professions. Patrizi's project was aimed at changing all that, thus revealing what is surely the fullest expression of humanist ambitions for higher education in the free republics of the Renaissance.

Of course, in the end, Patrizi's vision was never realized outside the pages of More's *Utopia*. Universities are conservative institutions, after all; law and medicine continued to hold their place at the apex of the Italian educational system well into the modern period. But the humanities nevertheless succeeded in making a place for themselves at the base of the pyramid, providing a broad foundation of general knowledge upon which more specialized, professional studies could be built. The early humanists had insisted that all those aspiring to the class of gentlemen had to be educated in the classics, but by the end of the quattrocento it came to be expected that lawyers, doctors, high civic officials, military leaders, and churchmen too would need solid preparation in classical literature and philosophy. Without it they could not discharge the duties of their several professions with humanity and due respect for religion and the norms of civil society. The old quarrel between the humanities and the professions stirred up in the letters and invectives of Petrarch, Coluccio Salutati, and other early humanists would eventually be composed, and a new, more fruitful system of preparing the young for their roles in society established.

## The Moral Economy: The Household, Unfree Labor, and Marriage

The household for Patrizi is the *seminarium reipublicae*, the seedbed of the state, in that it begins the work of educating citizens to live full lives of virtue, civility, and honest industry in the best republic. It also, ideally, trains its members in mild forms of rule and loving obedience, and provides for the needs of the whole family in honorable ways. Households should subordinate their private ends to the greater ends of the political community, but the political community also has an obligation to foster households and to provide stable conditions for them to flourish. The best way to ensure such an identity of interests between city and household is for the senate to be made up exclusively of heads of families.

> Public order and the order of a household agree in many respects. For just as in civil society there are few who rule and many who are obligated to obey, so in domestic affairs there is one person in charge—the oldest—and all the rest who must obey him. And just as in a city one must tolerate with equanimity the just rule of some over others, so we are accustomed to rule the family with gracious indulgence. Magistrates know that they are subject to the laws, and those in charge of families imitate the standard

[*norma*] of the best paterfamilias. It is therefore a fine practice in
certain cities to accept no one into the senate who does not have
responsibility for a family.[41]

In book 4 Patrizi sets out just such a "standard of the best paterfamilias." To do this he draws not only on the usual humanist authorities on "economics" (i.e., household management)—ps. Aristotle's
*Economics* and Xenophon's *Oeconomicus*—but dozens of other historical, poetical, and philosophical sources in Greek and Latin.[42] As
an overall theme, he insists that the rule of the paterfamilias must
combine great solicitude for those under his authority with affection
and understanding. He should not command things that are extremely difficult to perform; he should remember that he too once
had to obey; he should correct others with words, not blows. He
should rule with loving severity rather than savagery, mindful that
zeal, not fear, provides the best motivation. He should concern himself only with the most important functions of family life, and should
be careful to do nothing shameful, lest he set a bad example.

Patrizi then divides household management into two parts: care
of persons and procurement of things. Persons are divided into the
freeborn (*ingenuae*)—husband, wife, children, and other relations,
in other words—and servants. Servants (*servi*) are further divided
into indentured servants (or bondsmen, *addicti*) and chattel slaves
(*mancipia*). The paterfamilias needs to develop discernment in managing all these relationships.

In early Renaissance Italy there was a small trade in household
slaves, mostly non-Christian females imported from the Black Sea
via Genoa. They were a common sight in Tuscan cities, though more
in Florence than Siena. They were often given Christian names after
pro-forma baptismal ceremonies uttered in a language they could not
understand. Naples after 1460 participated to some extent in the
trade in black African slaves, who were commonly used for agricultural purposes. These enslaved persons, usually males, were purchased
from Portuguese slave markets or from Muslim slavers in the southern Mediterranean.[43] High-status families, particularly in Genoa and

Florence, often acquired slaves as luxury conveniences and to display their wealth.

Patrizi, however, was hostile to the use of slaves, on both compassionate and prudential grounds. Even though the Church's canon law did not prohibit the enslavement of non-Christians, he wrote, to have such persons in one's household was inconsistent with the bonds of affection and willing service that should prevail there.

> The condition of slaves is a miserable one, for vile persons serve as slaves, and particularly in our times, when because of the Christian religion a baptized person may not be a slave, and rightly so. It is unjust for that man to be enslaved to [another] man whom, washed in the sacred font, we have consecrated to God. Among the ancients, however, there were great numbers of slaves, so much so that they drove out the freemen from some cities and sometimes challenged their returning lords in battle.

Patrizi's prohibition here echoes the uncompromising antagonism to the slave trade of his patron, Pius II, who in 1462 "condemned black slavery as a *magnum scelus* [a great crime], and ordered bishops to impose ecclesiastical penalties on those who practiced it."[44] By the standards of the time, the position of Pius and Patrizi must count as a humane one. Their older contemporary Antoninus, the Dominican archbishop of Florence, accounted a holy man, decreed that it was licit to keep slaves in servitude after they had been baptized, so long as they had been purchased while still infidels, "since slavery was instituted by divine law and confirmed by the law of nations [*ius gentium*] and canon law." Franco Sacchetti, the novelist and Florentine statesman, declared that baptisms of slaves were invalid because they could not receive them of their own free will: "to baptize such persons is like baptizing oxen." There could be no religious bar to enslaving such people.[45]

Patrizi's discussion of chattel slavery goes on to describe the terrible problems created for the Romans by their use of agricultural slaves in large numbers—perhaps with an eye to discouraging contemporary African slavery in the Kingdom. He relates the horrors of the Servile Wars and the rebellion of Spartacus, which began in Capua, a town about 40 kilometers from Naples. Elsewhere he writes that agricultural slavery was introduced to Rome just before the time of the Gracchi, when corrupt aristocrats began to monopolize public lands for themselves and to oppress the small-holding class.[46] This was an imprudent innovation that undermined social solidarity. Though there existed in literary sources some famous examples of slaves who were loyal to their masters, on the whole it was not prudent to rely on the trustworthiness of slaves. If a paterfamilias did happen to own slaves, he should get rid of the worst ones and offer to give the rest their freedom someday if they make themselves useful to the family.

Indentured servants and bondsmen are a different matter, since their service is in principle voluntary: they chose to become servants, even if they have traded their liberty, temporarily or permanently, in return for material security. The paterfamilias must treat his servants, nonetheless, in accordance with the same principles of humanity that govern his other relationships.

> The free man who commands servants ought first of all to consider that they are men, not beasts, and not to vent his rage against them with beatings and chains. For blows only make them obdurate and unwilling. One should act more mildly toward them by demanding work from them daily, praising their industry not without goodwill, so that they will go about their work with greater alacrity.

We should treat them gently and remember that they are free men, not freedmen (*libertini*, freed slaves), men who may still owe us service once they are free from debt. They should be treated like hired help, given all the respect due to free men, and all agreements made with them should be honored. We should avoid the kind of harsh punishments that can drive them to despair. Patrizi describes a harrowing incident he witnessed personally, when a rebellious servant (*servus*) became so desperate from unrelenting punishment that he seized two of his master's baby boys, ran up a tower, called to his master to come and catch their bodies, smashed their bodies against a wall, and threw them off the tower before jumping off it himself.

While bondsmen dwell in our house they must be well taken care of, with sufficient food, clothing, and shelter.

A famished and shivering servant can offer no service. On this account we ought to remember the kindness and humanity of our ancestors, who desired the name of *patronus*, from the word *pater*, over their chattel slaves rather than the name of lord [*dominus*], a name they rejected as odious. Work should be divided among servants and the stronger ones sent out to do farmwork; the more slender ones and the less strong should be set to practicing those arts for which they seem most apt.

Patrizi is also critical of Roman precedent in his teachings about marriage. The *patria potestas*, the primitive Roman custom that gave the paterfamilias the power of life and death over everyone in his household, including his wife and children, must be rejected. The husband should not tolerate shameful or criminal acts in a wife because they affect the honor of their house, but he should not take justice into his own hands. Husbands who avenge themselves on their wives with the sword are to be condemned as utterly rash and ruinous. They are no better than Nero, who killed his pregnant wife Poppaea Sabina by kicking her in the womb. Cato the Censor said such men are to be regarded as no less despicable than a man who violates divine rites or betrays the republic. Serious criminal wrongdoing by wives should be punished by the law, not by husbands. Persian custom in this case is preferable not only to Roman custom but to the law of Solon that gave the husband a right to kill his wife for adultery (but not vice versa). If a wife commits adultery, the husband should remonstrate with her, appealing to her honor and their common interest in the welfare of the household. But he should never beat, threaten, or insult his wife: such behavior is servile and unworthy of the *familiaris societas*. It will ruin a marriage and undermine the respect a wife should have for her husband. He should nevertheless take steps to prevent unchastity by prohibiting loose and obscene talk and the reading of amorous tales.

Unusually for a Renaissance male—and centuries before Mary Wollstonecraft—Patrizi insists that there should be no double standards. The husband too must abstain from adultery—nothing is worse for "the holy society of matrimony." "The husband's continence will generally keep his wife chaste and win a good reputation for the man himself." Patrizi in this passage (4.4) shows considerable sympathy for wronged women—noting, for example, that the sins of Clytemnestra will seem more tolerable if we consider those committed by Agamemnon. Double standards in adultery violate the Golden Rule as well as the Roman legal principle that anyone who judges another must judge himself by the same law. He approves a law of Julius Caesar that assigned an equal penalty to both men and women taken in adultery. Yet wives will sometimes be called upon to show understanding, especially when husbands must spend long periods away from their wives on campaigns or mercantile ventures. Patrizi praises the wife of Scipio Aemilianus for allowing the great general to keep a concubine, even giving the girl her freedom and a dowry after Scipio's death.

We have already discussed in Chapter 2 Patrizi's view of marriage as a form of friendship, a *societas* based on companionship and mutual love as well as on shared economic interests and procreation. He shows some sympathy for what in the Renaissance was taken as the Greek view of the woman's sphere, first discussed by Leon Battista Alberti in his early dialogue *Della famiglia*.[47] Like Alberti, Patrizi sees the wife's sphere as the home, while the husband is responsible for all that lies outside the home, including money-making and politics. The Sienese moralist is critical, for example, of the Roman practice of allowing wives to attend dinner parties outside the home, preferring the Greek custom of keeping their womenfolk inside, dining only with family members and close neighbors. The woman

has charge of the domestic sphere but Patrizi rejects what he says is
the Egyptian custom, established by Queen Isis, of making the wife
sole mistress of the household, laying down laws that even the husband must obey.[48] Her role is to keep the house in order, preserve
its resources, manage the servants, maintain chastity in herself and
others, and raise children. She should dress decently and well but
not luxuriously.

Should a good wife remarry after her husband's death? This was
a live issue in a society where men were often decades older than
their wives, and where the "merry widow" was a stock figure of
comic tales. Patrizi says that the best matron will be married to only
one man. To remarry is an act of impiety toward her own children,
who will bear on their faces the imprint of her dead husband. If she
has more children, those by her first husband will be at a disadvantage. An older woman who remarries will be charged with a lack of
decency (*pudor*). But remarriage is tolerable if the wife is young and
has no children by her first husband.

Husband and wife are both responsible for the economic welfare
of the household, but the husband takes the leading role. The
household must earn its living in an honorable way. The best and most
natural way to secure an honorable living is through agriculture.[49]
Farming has nothing dishonest about it and does not encourage
avarice. If a man doesn't want to engage in agriculture, there are
honorable alternatives. He can accept a salary as a teacher of the liberal arts. He can engage in commerce, especially overseas trade,
buying and selling but without any dishonesty or deception. He can
practice honorable arts that provide useful and beautiful things
for the city. But usury, breeding wealth from barren money, is
shameful and illiberal.[50] What is earned should be earned by labor.
He quotes a response of Cato the Censor that implied that usury was
as serious a crime as homicide (6.3).[51] Living off rents is also dishonorable, and young people with no occupation are the poison of
the state. Husband and wife should take as much care to preserve
their property as to earn it; otherwise they will be like the Danaïdes,
eternally carrying water in a sieve. They should live frugally, avoiding

luxury, but not squalidly. They should observe the virtuous mean in all things.

Above all—and however the household earns its living—its members should do everything to resist avarice. The avaricious man is nothing but a hungry dog; nothing can be more foreign to humanity than someone consumed with a desire for money. Such a man is not only hateful but destructive to the republic. The main sources of corruption and faction in a republic are avaricious magistrates who engage in peculation, seeking to control public resources in their own and their family's interest. Public monies are never sufficient for all needs, and when citizens see their magistrates enriching themselves during brief terms of office, sedition is the eventual and inevitable result. What drove Pisistratus into tyranny was the resistance of the Athenians to his unbridled thirst to increase his personal wealth from public resources. The praise of one's fellow citizens should be sufficient reward for a magistrate's service.[52]

## The Moral Economy: The City-State

Patrizi's straightforward condemnation of usury and rent-seeking is surprising in a treatise that claims to be adapting ancient wisdom to modern republics. It is particularly surprising in relation to Siena, since many, if not most, of the great Sienese fortunes were made in banking rather than manufacturing.[53] The type of large-scale industrial production found in some Renaissance cities—for example, the wool, silk, and finished cloth industries of Florence—never took off in Florence's neighboring metropolis to the south. In Siena great fortunes made in finance, however, usually ended up in landed wealth in the countryside or in urban property, and the class of wealthy *rentiers* was not small. Moreover, the Catholic Church since the thirteenth century had developed a pastoral theology that, while not formally permitting usury, had elaborated a series of canons to distinguish usury from legitimate return on investments. It aimed to specify licit forms of acquisition and transmission of property, and to instruct consciences in other forms of economic justice and injustice.

The total effect of this scholastic project to regulate the morals of commercial society was to enable a *môyen de vivre* with the emerging capitalist economy of Europe.[54]

In this context it might appear that Patrizi's absolutist position on the evils of usury and rent-seeking was naïve or backward-looking, or perhaps a romantic vision of a never-never land of republican virtue. But it assumes a different aspect when seen in its proper context—the long tradition of humanist reflection on the dangers presented to the commonwealth by wealthy men whose souls had been depraved by avarice. Patrizi's proposals for economic reform in the *De republica* continue this line of thought. But they take the humanist argument against avarice one step further by considering legal and institutional means to restrain it. Indeed, they form perhaps the most radical part of Patrizi's agenda as a political thinker, bringing Italian humanism closer to the kind of thinking about private property found in Thomas More's *Utopia* and, much later, in James Harrington's *Oceana*.[55]

I will not repeat here the sketch of humanist economic thought I presented in *Virtue Politics*.[56] Patrizi endorsed the humanist critique of corrupt wealth in its general lines. He agreed that the insatiable desire for wealth typical of oligarchic cities should be moderated in accordance with some standard of virtue. He believed that an education in classical virtue could be an effective means of limiting the ill effects on civic life of powerful, avaricious men, whose competition to control public resources for private advantage led to factionalism and neglect of the common good. He agreed that the acquisitive impulse was natural and licit if controlled and directed in unselfish ways: to maintain a household or support the republic. Following Sallust, he feared the corrupting effects of luxury on the state and praised the old Roman virtue of frugality. He would surely have agreed with Poggio in his *De avaritia* that Greek philosophy was useful in conceptualizing a harmonious society not diseased by the lust for wealth, though one suspects he would have found Poggio's solution—simply expelling avaricious and greedy men from the state—deficient in practical reasoning.

Where Patrizi parts company with other fifteenth-century humanists is in his proposals in book 6 to alter the economic structures that permitted gross inequalities of wealth, and in his insistence that all good citizens must engage in honest work to support themselves and their families.[57] We saw in Chapter 3 that Patrizi, following Herodotus's "Debate on Constitutions," recognized a tight connection between citizen equality and the laudable desire for political liberty characteristic of popular republics. Vast differences in power and wealth in a city not only made it unstable, as Aristotle had taught, but rendered citizen liberties meaningless. They propelled a republic toward faction, then tyranny.

Usury, which gave rise to debt, was a major source of inequality. "The vortex [of the usurer's greed] drains the patrimony of many households, than which nothing is more destructive in a city," given that sound households form the bricks in the foundation of the state. Debt reduces many households to a state of dependence on the rich; it turns poor citizens into their servants and bondsmen. Inequalities in landed wealth—still the principal source of wealth in the Renaissance—were equally pernicious. When the rich were able to gain control over the vast majority of agricultural lands, as in the middle Roman republic, they proceeded to drive the poor out of their little plots. Then wealthy landowners jacked up the price of grain, making it so expensive that the poor were forced to sell off what little remained of their patrimonies merely to survive.[58] Furthermore, inequality undermined public morals. "An excess of private wealth generally destroys cities, through either the pride and arrogance of the possessing classes, or the rashness and insanity of the needy." Equality of means, on the other hand, made it easier for the law to constrain citizens and made the political device of sortition—whose prudent use Patrizi endorsed—more acceptable.[59]

Patrizi's awareness of the evils caused by economic inequality, when combined with his study of Greek philosophy, brought him to accept the need for the state to exercise some control over the distribution of wealth.[60] He begins by considering the most radical Greek proposal of all, Plato's proposal in the *Republic* for the class of guardians to own all their land in common and to prohibit private patrimonies.[61] Plato's proposal was plausible on its face, says Patrizi, only because he outlawed the family at the same time. People only desire riches for the sake of their families, but if men breed without recognizing their own offspring, as Plato proposes, they will be content with little, especially when the republic provides for them. But for Patrizi, Plato's whole scheme outrages what should be our natural affections toward our children and posterity. Those affections are the basis for our legitimate desire to provide for our family's security and welfare, even after our death; indeed, we should rightly accuse ourselves of sloth if we did not labor to enlarge our patrimonies.

From a civic perspective, it is the legitimate desire to support our families that makes us industrious citizens and makes a city of self-supporting households flourish as a whole. Plato's communism fails because people lack the motivation to labor for the public good alone. Like the Spartan scheme of communal dining for citizens, it would not suit modern societies where citizens work to support families. "There is no people [today] that labors in common or has public dining, without private possessions; rather, most householders [*patresfamilias*] enter society for the sake of utility, that they might live more easily and constitute a civil society [i.e., polity]." Plato's scheme is no more than a pleasant speculation that would be impossible to impose on any existing republic or even on one newly founded. When we consider real cities, writes Patrizi, we will see right away that Plato's words do not match reality, whether historical or present. As a counter-example, he mentions the Spartans, who knew who their wives and children were, yet contributed the greater part of the plunder and booty they won on campaigns to public purposes, while still not neglecting their private estates. Communal ownership of property was therefore not necessary to restrain self-interest in matters of wealth. "Legislators and all magistrates must therefore give careful consideration to individual patrimonies."

Patrizi is much more attracted by two legislative schemes for the equalization of patrimonies mentioned by Aristotle in book 2 of the

*Politics*, those of Phaleas of Carthage and Hippodamus of Miletus. Aristotle is relentlessly critical of both, arguing that the real source of instability in cities is avarice, and that equalizing property will have little effect: "The beginning of reform is not so much to equalize property as to train the nobler sort of natures not to desire more and to prevent the lower from getting more; that is to say, they must be kept down, but not ill-treated."[62] Patrizi—who, as so often, does not mention that Aristotle is his source for both Phaleas's and Hippodamus's schemes—disagrees. Phaleas was the first to recommend that citizens should have private but equal patrimonies,

> an idea that is not unreasonable [says Patrizi]. For everybody agrees that there is nothing that preserves the republic more than equality among citizens, which is seen most of all when there are neither rich nor poor in a city, but when citizens are assessed with equal land and equal patrimonies. As Aristotle affirms, equalizing patrimonies when the city is first founded is not hard to do and brings no small benefit. An allotment of this kind would tend to equality, and human negligence and baseness could easily be restrained by the laws. Many states did not permit patrimonies to be alienated. Solon passed a law to this effect, and [the popular tribune] Voconius among the Romans passed a law preventing private fortunes from being left to female heirs.[63]

Patrizi displays considerably more enthusiasm for distributism here than Aristotle. His positive attitude is striking, given the overwhelming authority in the quattrocento of Aristotle's economic thought and its conservative attitude to property.[64] The only other humanist political thinker to discuss this passage, to my knowledge, was Lauro Quirini, who parrots Aristotle's line that distributist legislation might be viable in a newly founded state but in mature republics was a superficial solution to the deeper moral problem of avarice. This is a way of claiming that moral education, not state intervention in the economy, is the only viable solution to inequalities of wealth. Quirini adds that equalization of property would limit business enterprise and stunt artistic ambition, since there would be no financial motive for individuals to engage in commercial activities and develop artistic excellence.[65]

Even more attractive to Patrizi were the schemes for allocating the city-state's land proposed by Hippodamus of Miletus, which are discussed at length in book 6. Throughout his discussion of Hippodamus the Sienese philosopher reads firmly against the grain of Aristotle's criticism. In 6.1 he tells us that Hippodamus was a man desirous of glory, a famous warrior, with no small learning in the liberal arts. He had led the Milesians in a naval battle against the Athenians and had besieged the Piraeus. None of these details are in the *Politics*, which presents Hippodamus as a oddly dressed eccentric, an amateur philosopher, and a bit of a crank.[66] Hippodamus's first thought in founding the best republic, says Patrizi, was to make a division of the city and its territory. He divided the populace into three classes: artisans, farmers, and defensive warriors (*belli propulsatores*). Each of these groups were allotted an equal number of magistracies by consent of the assembled people. "This division may well have sufficed for the Milesians, who had a small territory and fewer wealthy citizens." Other, larger cities would find it more useful to keep the farmers outside the city, focused on their agricultural tasks, rather than allowing them to become a turbulent element in city government. "This was an excellent idea on Hippodamus's part, and was enough to show the man's genius. Many large cities divided their states along similar lines, following his example." By invoking Hippodamus here, it seems, Patrizi was simply endorsing tripartite class divisions, while (illicitly) enlisting his authority for excluding peasants from political participation.[67]

In chapter 2 we encounter Hippodamus's second tripartite division, this time of landed property, which Patrizi also endorses: "not that we have followed him in every respect, but we have not strayed far from his example; hence it will be relevant to take from this authority the division of the [city's] territory and its lands." According to Hippodamus, the sum of landed property in the city-state should be divided into three parts. One third should go to sacred uses, one third to public use, and the final third should be allotted to private individuals.

The allocation of so large a portion of the city's landed resources for sacred purposes is elaborately justified. As further support, Patrizi cites three other authorities. One is Queen Isis of Egypt, who is said to have handed over a third of Egyptian lands to priests. A second is Aristotle, who advised dividing his ideal polis's land in two, one half for public and one half for private uses; revenue from the public portion would then be shared between public expenses and the needs of divine worship.[68] At the end of the chapter Patrizi adds a third authority, culled from Dionysius Halicarnassus: none other than Romulus, the founder of Rome. Romulus, says Patrizi, reserved part of Rome's land for sacred uses and left another part for public use. What was left over from public uses he divided into thirty equal parts, one each for the private use of individuals belonging to the thirty *curiae* or tribal subdivisions of the Roman people.[69]

As the beneficiary himself of lands appropriated for sacred uses, it is hardly surprising that Bishop Patrizi welcomes the use of public property for religious purposes. Nor was the Hippodamian division an extravagant idea in premodern Italy, where, depending on the region, anywhere between 10 percent and 70 percent of land was already under the control of ecclesiastical corporations.[70] Humanists like Poggio deplored the agrarian wealth thus subtracted from more productive civic uses, but Patrizi defends it.

For religion, ceremonies, mysteries, and divine cult—through which we reconcile and render propitious to ourselves Best and Greatest God—demand holy and innocent men who, imbued with the study of sacred and divine letters, wipe away the clouds of blindness from human eyes. These men need resources so that they can live modestly and preserve and rebuild sacred buildings that have been constructed at enormous expense. They need the fruits of the earth, which rarely or never involve deceit, and require no trafficking, buying, and selling. Hippodamus, Queen Isis, and Aristotle were therefore right to hold that civic leaders should allot a part of the land to religion, lest the divine rites should be conducted in too negligent a manner. Indeed, every good citizen should care deeply about this. We see not only that in our time we who worship the true religion, but in the earliest times too, [the ancients] by decrees of the Senate and by the institutions of princes and peoples with all piety took great pains on behalf of religion, even though their rash superstition was fully deserving of derision.[71]

Poggio, to be sure, was contemplating a situation in the Italy of his day where the lands owned by church institutions were by definition not subject to lay governments, whereas Patrizi is thinking in more organicist terms, in which ecclesiastical institutions would be considered part of the state, though doctrinally independent of it.[72] The second portion of the city's landed property, Patrizi thinks, should be allocated to secular but public uses, principally to support the city's watchmen and its armed forces (*custodes* and *defensores*). Here again he argues for the public usefulness of a standing citizen army.[73] Walls alone do not defend a city; it needs active-duty soldiers to protect its agricultural land, especially at harvest time, as well as its villas and its urban wealth. If the citizen army is supported on the city's land, it will also be able to keep order in the countryside. In less fearful times of prolonged peace, when fewer resources can be expended on defense, some of the earnings from public lands can be placed in the public treasury. This reserve will allow the city to see itself through difficult economic times or sudden military threats without the use of forced loans, which bring hatred upon the republic's leaders and create ill will among those who are required to pay them. Or the city's land can be used to stock public granaries.

Or, if this is unacceptable because of the dangers of storing public monies, the grain collected on public lands can be stored up against times of famine or the distresses of wartime. Columella says that grain can be kept without rotting for up to seven years in strong, underground granaries lined with straw. If this is done carefully and old grain regularly replaced with new, the people can be protected from any siege or famine, rendering it extremely secure and safe from enemies. Arms, indeed, are of little use when the people are starving, and a hungry plebs is always eager for revolution.

It is also better to use public monies than private funds when it comes to building projects like temples, theaters, defensive walls, aqueducts, and other constructions for the use and ornament of the city. Hippodamus held that the third part of public lands should be distributed to private individuals. Patrizi advises that this land should be owned only by farmers. Those who love to live in the city do not need land, and those who enjoy country life are no good at civic concerns. He makes one exception to this rule separating urban from country life. City dwellers, he writes—if they can afford it—should maintain suburban villas planted with kitchen gardens and groves of trees to provide relaxation from the cares of the city. He recommends they furnish their villas with rose gardens, violet beds, fisheries, stockyards, and other things that supply abundant beauty and pleasure. Suburban villas will supplement their proprietor's food supply and require opulence of him rather than effort. A civil man, if he has means to employ others, can indulge himself in these rustic pursuits, and can win praise for them so long as they are conducted in a restrained manner appropriate to a free man, without involving fraud or deceit. A certain number of civil men can so occupy themselves, but if the number becomes very large, both urban and rustic affairs will suffer. On the whole, it is better for city folk and rustics to do what each does best.

Patrizi's overall conception with respect to landed property in republics is for the state to hold the lion's share. "This principle should carefully be observed: that the greater part of the city's domain should belong to the public, while the lesser part should be private." Private citizens should, minimally, have enough to support their families, and even the greatest fortunes should never be so large that they can begin to challenge the republic's authority. In chapter 1 of book 4 he credits this opinion to the Roman consul, plebeian tribune, and military hero Manius Curius Dentatus (d. 270 BC), famous for his frugality and incorruptibility. As a victorious general in the Samnite Wars he had the duty of handing out newly conquered public lands to private individuals, which, laudably, he did on an equal basis, not assigning himself a portion any larger than anyone else. Criticized for reserving the greater part of the land for public uses, he replied, "No one should think his portion of land too small if it suffices to feed himself and his family."[74]

In this passage Patrizi argues for another use of public lands in addition to the purposes laid out in book 6. The republic should be rich in land in part to store grain for challenging times, yes, but also so that it can support needy citizens who cannot buy land on their own. Rather than having them become bondsmen of the rich, Patrizi suggests that the poor should be granted perpetual leases on public land, for which they would pay a tax.[75] The leases would be heritable and could not be revoked except for non-payment of taxes. (Patrizi claimed this system was already in use in Lombardy in his time.) This practice would be of advantage to the state as it would give it a large, regular source of income and thus free it from dependence on unpopular forced loans. Patrizi surely knew, though he does not state this explicitly, that the system of forced loans, often imposed to pay mercenary troops under the immediate threat of war, was a major reason the wealthy had acquired such overwhelming influence in Renaissance republics. The greater the emergency, the higher the rate of interest the rich could charge, so forced loans ended up making the rich richer. If the state had its own soldiers supported on public lands and a tax base making it independent of the wealthy, a virtuous elite would have the means to stand up to the ambitions of would-be oligarchs.

Patrizi takes these anti-oligarchic institutions one step further with another proposal: limiting the size of patrimonies and business profits. As we saw above, Patrizi was attracted by the proposals of Phaleas and Hippodamus to equalize citizen patrimonies, and he recommended them in cases where new cities were being founded. But he recognized that distributist policies such as these could never be imposed *ex post*, in established states where great inequalities of wealth already existed.

> Maintaining agrarian laws is extremely difficult. . . . After a city [*urbs*] is established and the state [*civitas*] has wandered for some time from its founding principles, it is almost impossible to restore equality between patrimonies and agricultural property. The rich will never put up with having their property divided up among the poor without engaging in sedition and slaughter. Furthermore, hard work and laziness are equated if citizens are compelled for a second time to equalize their patrimonies.[76]

In this case practical reasoning, informed by historical study, has to overrule abstract theory. Distributism is an excellent institution for newly founded cities, but redistribution in established cities is imprudent.[77]

In 4.3 Patrizi gives two historical examples of the folly of redistribution, taking property away from the rich and giving it to the poor. The first describes the oligarchic violence set in train by the attempts of the Gracchi to reform Rome's agrarian laws at the end of the second century BC. The Romans for centuries had passed various agrarian laws intended to institute a fair division among the people of lands in Italy and elsewhere won by Roman arms and other territorial acquisitions. But the rich drove ordinary citizens out of their holdings by force and fraud, then used their market power to raise the price of grain, further impoverishing the plebs. The rich got richer and the poor poorer. The plebs responded to this crisis by not having children, which dried up native sources of agricultural labor, so the wealthy brought in slaves and foreigners to take their place. Many of Rome's best men saw that this trend was ruining the republic, but they took no serious steps to reverse it until the time of Tiberius Gracchus. The elder Gracchus as tribune of the people passed a new agrarian law that redistributed land but was otherwise extremely mild and statesmanlike. It didn't punish the senators who opposed the law or demand restitution from those who had illegally occupied land. It even compensated them for their losses before turning the land over to those who needed it. Nevertheless, the rich were so offended that they fought back "as though defending the walls of the city or fighting for freedom." They arranged for Tiberius Gracchus to be cruelly murdered, then granted almost divine honors to his assassin. This terrified the people until Tiberius's brother Gaius was made plebeian tribune in his stead. He tried to carry on the work begun by Tiberius but was driven out of Rome by the faction of the wealthy. Fleeing to a sacred wood, he committed suicide rather than fall into their hands.

Thus even a seemingly prudent action to reform agrarian laws ended in violent death for the reformers, owing to oligarchic resistance. It is noteworthy that Patrizi follows here the sympathetic account of the Gracchi given by Plutarch and Appian rather than the bitterly hostile one found in Latin sources, above all in Cicero. As Eric Nelson has shown, the "Greek tradition" in early modern political thought, unlike the neo-Roman tradition followed by most scholastic jurists and many quattrocento humanists, did not regard the ownership of private property as sacrosanct—as a right derived from natural law via civil law. The ancient Greek authors Nelson foregrounds were far more receptive to state supervision of the private economy.[78] Though Patrizi proposed nothing so radical as Thomas More's utopian communism—for Nelson the first great representative of the early modern "Greek tradition"—Patrizi shared with Greek philosophers like Aristotle (and Plato in the *Laws*) the view that the distribution of private property was a question of civil prudence, not of right (*ius*), and should be made subject to the ends of the whole political community.

Patrizi's other example of the folly of redistribution takes the opposite tack, showing that oligarchs who engross all the wealth of a city-state and do not make prudent provision for the welfare of the people are likely to come to grief. This terrifying story is taken from the Roman imperial historian Justin, who composed an epitome of

Pompeius Trogus's lost history of the kings of Macedonia. The city of Heraclea in Pontus was wracked by sedition owing to a controversy about the division of land between the plebs and the rich (*divites*). A certain Clearchus took advantage of the unrest to make himself champion of the plebs, then imprisoned or drove into exile all the senators. When the exiles mounted a war against him, Clearchus forced their wives and children to marry slaves, and after defeating the exile army, marched the senators through the streets to be mocked by the citizenry as though in a Roman triumph. Then, swollen with pride, he committed many acts of insolent savagery against the citizen body, establishing a tyranny that lasted for generations. All this happened because the citizens of Heraclea had "not known how to take good counsel about dividing the city's land."

Patrizi's own solution to the problem of economic inequality in mature republics is to avoid equalization schemes, but to take other measures to reduce huge disparities in citizen wealth. The republic should impose absolute limits on the size of private agricultural holdings. It should prohibit usury and limit the amount of profit that could be earned in commercial activities. These measures are presented as sound Roman institutions, the original Roman approach to civic equality before the city was corrupted by the rich in the second century BC.[79]

> Those in charge of writing the laws must prescribe a limit on agricultural property, lest the few invade the possessions of the many. Such a measure we see was sanctioned by senatorial decree among the Romans, and long before that by the decemviral laws called the Twelve Tables. In this matter an agricultural plan must be equilibrated with respect to the multitude, so that the produce of the land is supplied to all.
>
> I have discussed this matter at length to instill caution in those who pass agrarian laws. The opulence of the republic is to be left intact, not only for public uses but also for perils in wartime. One should not be afraid that public resources are too great, since

there will be times when both public and private wealth is exhausted. It is sufficient to regulate private wealth so that it is never greater than the laws allow. A limit should also be placed on profit, and there should be oversight to ensure that citizens increase their wealth by honorable labor and industry.

Patrizi does not forget that public officials can misuse public wealth, just as ordinary citizens can abuse their private patrimonies. The dangers of peculation, the abuse of public office for private gain, are repeatedly emphasized in the *De republica*. Any attempt to profit from office must be absolutely forbidden, and to reduce the temptation for self-enrichment is exactly why both the Athenians and the Romans instituted laws limiting officeholding to one year. Patrizi gives several examples of noble Greeks who refused opportunities to profit from office. The virtue of Aristides, who was in charge of the treasury of all Greece, was such that he died without enough money to pay for his own funeral, and his daughters had to be given dowries from the public treasury. The Athenian statesman Phocion was offered a large gift by King Philip of Macedon, whose ambassadors urged him to accept it, if not for himself, then for his sons. He replied, "If my sons are like me, the little field that raised me to high rank will foster them as well; if they are unlike me, I would prefer not to increase their extravagance [*luxuria*] by gifts such as these."[80]

Ideally magistrates should receive no pay at all for public service. As we have seen in Chapter 4, Patrizi would prefer that gifts and emoluments of all kinds be removed even from the legal system, though he allows, under non-ideal conditions, for barristers to be paid small amounts by their clients and for public defenders to be paid by the state to defend the poor in court. As for other offices, the praise of one's fellow citizens should be sufficient reward. Education in virtue is an indispensable tool for inhibiting greed and ambition, but in the end the only effective way for the best city to avoid a descent into oligarchy is vigorous public action to limit economic inequality.

## Republican Architecture and Urban Planning

With family life secured by adequate patrimonies for all households, and with a wealthy state led by men of virtue, conditions will be ideal for creating a physical environment for the best republic: a secure, healthy, and beautiful place that will promote virtue, civic harmony, and religious piety. This aspect of Patrizi's *institutio,* elaborated in books 7 and 8 of the *De republica,* counts among his most original contributions to political thought.

Aristotle, in outlining his ideal polis in book 7 of the *Politics,* had devoted several pages to the city-state's physical site, street plan, and principal monuments. The site should be healthy, he wrote, with good air and an abundant water supply, convenient and defensible. If the polis is a monarchy or an oligarchy it will have an acropolis or a citadel; it will have separate fortifications for noble families, if an aristocracy; a democracy should have no fortified places within the city. Some central places in the city should be laid out using a Hippodamian grid plan for the convenience of urban life, but the city will be more resistant to attack if the "antiquated mode" of jumbled streets and houses is used elsewhere. Cities need to have strong defensive walls and towers adapted to resist "modern" siege methods; they should also be built with an eye to ornament. Temples for religious worship should be built in high places visible to all. Ideally the city should have two agoras or large piazzas, one for the recreation of citizens (Aristotle advises that older men use it for gymnastic exercises), and another nearer the gates for commercial activity. He ends his brief discussion with the dismissive remark, "But it would be a waste of time for us to linger over details like these."[81]

Patrizi, without naming him, challenges Aristotle's view that town planning is not worth the careful attention of a political philosopher. There are some who doubt, he writes, that urban planning is any business of a man who has promised to write about politics (*de civili societate*). But civil teachings are intended to promote the enjoyment of life (*iucunditas vitae*), and architecture plays a great role in creating the conditions for a happy life by constructing delightful public buildings and commodious private dwellings.[82] Well-designed public spaces also promote the best kind of civil conversations in free republics.

> But since the whole tenor of civic teachings is reducible to happiness and tranquil living, *iucunditas vitae* seems to contribute to both. Commodious private dwellings and delightful public buildings bring this about in no small part. Enjoyment of life will be great when we make spaces in piazzas, porticoes, and ambulatories that bring us together with those who share our honorable commercial pursuits, or with those with whom we discuss learned subjects—meditation on which is the nourishment of noble minds—or with whom we consider public affairs, or sometimes when we give or receive faithful counsel with friends about household matters. Sometimes also [enjoyment of life is enhanced] when we take a rest [*otium*] from serious affairs, we make light and amusing conversation our business [*negotium*], and by refreshing our minds, make ourselves readier and more willing to take on serious business.[83]

To supplement Aristotle's rapid sketch, Patrizi composes two whole books that draw not only on Aristotle himself, but also on the Greek and Latin historians and biographers, Homer and the Latin poets, and historical geographers like Strabo. His conception of the physical city is based above all on Vitruvius, the Bible of quattrocento architects and city planners. In book 1, Patrizi had already devoted the entirety of chapter 9 to architecture, defined broadly as *aedificandi ratio,* a building plan or urban design, but this outline is vastly expanded in the later books.

City planning (*urbanistica* in Italian) begins with the choice of a site for the republic, not all sites being equally salubrious for a free way of life. At the beginning of book 7 Patrizi tells us that his previous books have all been about matters pertaining to politics and education. He has discoursed on republican institutions and the studies and virtues appropriate to citizens. In Aristotelian terms, he has dealt with goods of the soul. He now turns to the goods of the body—primarily health—and "external" goods, the means to sustain an honorable human life. "It would do little good to form the best citizen if we did not describe a city [*urbs*] for him in which he might dwell in accordance with civil virtue." It is not enough to have a people educated to live a good and blessed life; you need also to provide an environment conducive to civil tranquillity. Not all plans for the city-state are suited to that end.[84]

Patrizi divides the task of providing a suitable environment for republican life into two parts: finding the best natural environment (book 7) and creating the optimal built environment (book 8). For Plato and Aristotle the choice of the best site for a city was above all a moral one. For example, both philosophers discouraged founding the ideal polis too near a port. Port cities held too much potential for good citizens to be infected with the bad mores inevitably brought in by foreigners in places open to the sea. As centers of commerce they inevitably gave too much prominence to merchants, with their mercenary values. Both recommended inland sites such as Sparta's, a polis both philosophers considered the least morally corrupt of Greek cities. Aristotle was, however, more positive about the advantages of a city having a connection to the sea than Plato, and some of his arguments are repeated by Patrizi.[85]

Patrizi, who valued civic wealth and culture, admired Athens more than Sparta, and knew from history and experience that many impressive republics had flourished by the sea. These included Venice and his idealized Massilia, both of which had lasted for many centuries without suffering moral contamination. Naples and his beloved Gaeta also may not have been far from his mind. For him, the ancient philosophers' worries about the moral contagion of foreigners and merchants were exaggerated, and careful legislators who restricted citizenship on the basis of descent could prevent any ill effects.[86]

> The best site for a city will not be far from the sea or a navigable river, via which excess products can be exported and what the

city lacks can be imported. . . . By these and similar sanctions a republic [*civilis societas*] can be freed of contagion from outsiders and will not lack the conveniences of the sea, through which the embellishments of peace and assistance in war may be supplied. Those who wish to set up a city must therefore choose the advantages offered by ports.[87]

Patrizi's approval of ports as appropriate sites for republics mirrored his relatively positive attitude to mercantile activity. As we have already seen, for Patrizi trade and commerce, though more exposed than farming to the temptations of greed, could both be honorable forms of economic activity. Foreign trade was morally justified (as it had been for the scholastics) when the superfluities of the city-state were exchanged for things it really needed from abroad and not for luxuries. Nevertheless, for Patrizi the best location for a city was within an *ager* or territory sufficiently productive that a city could survive and flourish on its own, without the need to engage in foreign trade. In the preface to book 7 he uses the example of Siena to explain what he means by self-sufficiency.

I can give great thanks to God, Holy Father, that I happened to be born in a country which supplied a sufficiency of all things needed for living well and blessedly, and in which every citizen, even those of average talent and means, could achieve esteem and happiness, so long as he did not fail himself. He will not need external resources to nurture his family with excellence, since there abounds in the Sienese territory [*ager*] everything that Nature is accustomed to give mortals. He will not seek out wisdom from outside or from across the sea, since he has all the Muses as his companions within the city limits, so much so that Siena could seem to rival in every way Alexandria, Tarsus and Athens—three cities that once cultivated literary studies beyond all others in the world. Nor will he fear that his reputation will be kept within the walls of his own house, since the country itself offers him a theater and a stage for all the greatest affairs.[88]

This is patriotic exaggeration, but it shows at least that Patrizi believed cultural goods were as necessary to a happy civic life as material ones. Self-sufficiency, however, should mean just that: enough and not too much. If a territory is too small or unproductive, peasants will not be able to support themselves; they will stop having children or will flee the city's territory for greener fields abroad. On the other hand, city leaders should resist the temptation to acquire large, empty territories (his example is Africa) that are habitats only for dangerous wild beasts and feral men and robbers. Nevertheless, though material self-sufficiency may not be fully attainable, the more a city is able to live on its own, the more it will be able to find happiness.

> It is hard, I think, to find a city that supplies everything belonging to human life and that doesn't to some extent need imported goods. But we give greater approval to those countries that are fed by their own produce and rely less on foreign resources, mindful of Xenophon's saying, "To need nothing is to be one of the gods, to need little is to be near them."[89]

His example of a self-sufficient people, based loosely on a passage in Ammianus Marcellinus (23.6.64–69), is the Chinese (*Seres*, the silk people). The natural abundance of their lands and forests enables the Chinese to live a life of gentle pleasure, at peace with their neighbors. So great is the abundance of their land that they can even supply others with what they do not need themselves.

> For those Seres, whom the cosmographers so much praise and pronounce blessed, abound (as I believe) in all things, notwithstanding they live pleasant lives and enjoy peace with their neighbors. They have the most salubrious of climates and abound in forests, from whose trees they extract the silky down for the use of princes and courtiers. Their land is so fertile that, through the generosity of nature alone, it brings forth grain and fruit without need for digging or sowing. With these the natives can nourish

themselves and even supply their neighbors. But I think even they sometimes desire the resources of outsiders and do not always reject foreign imports.

Patrizi's discussion of city planning, which occupies book 8, begins with praise of architects and the science of architecture.[90] In the preface to the book, addressed like all the others to Sixtus IV, the Sienese philosopher informs the pope that having an excellent plan for public works and a proper distribution of building sites, city walls, and piazzas adds grace and attractiveness to a city.[91] It can sometimes make up for the defects of a site, and furthermore, if errors are made, they can be very hard to correct later on. He gives examples from antiquity of cities improved by good planning and others ruined by the lack of it. Siena is again praised as a place that has been well planned. It is not exposed to noxious winds and is well supplied with water available in beautiful public fountains or delivered directly to the houses of citizens via subterranean pipes.[92] Buildings are constantly being restored there, and the beauty and splendor of the city is increasing daily.

City planning, to be sure, was by no means a rediscovery of the Renaissance. The architectural historian David Friedman estimates that more than a thousand new towns and cities were built in Europe between the early twelfth and mid-fourteenth century.[93] Though the pace of new town building slowed in the fifteenth century, the practices and the patterns of medieval city planning remained familiar from long usage. As we have seen, Patrizi was well aware of Pius II's project to rebuild his native village of Corsignano as Pienza, a so-called "ideal city." What was new in the Renaissance, and what qualified a Renaissance city as "ideal"—those actually built and those merely imagined—was the use of architects trained in classical studies and inspired by the antique.[94] The inspiration that came from the humanist revival of antiquity included not only the classical style in architecture but also the technologies of building, preserved in works like Vitruvius's *Ten Books on Architecture,* Frontinus's work *On Aqueducts,* and Pliny the Elder's *Historia naturalis,* which contained, among much else, descriptions of Greek and Roman technical achievements such as watermills.[95]

In the republics of Tuscany during the later medieval period, new towns and renovations in existing towns were normally overseen by citizen committees making use of mostly nameless *capomaestri*: experienced builders of the artisan classes, familiar with the practical problems of laying out urban spaces and building large-scale monuments. In the Renaissance, the study of Vitruvius, which begins with Petrarch and Boccaccio, gave rise to the more elevated conception of the architect's role that emerges in the mid-quattrocento. Humanist literati appreciated that Vitruvius had presented himself as a man with a liberal education. He had also recommended for architects the study of history, philosophy, mathematics, and medicine as well as more practical techniques of building. Vitruvius became the model for a new kind of architect-engineer, "noble" in the humanist sense of both capable and liberally educated, whose first and most famous exemplar in the Renaissance was Leon Battista Alberti.[96]

Patrizi must have known Alberti either in Mantua or in Rome, and he surely knew other exemplars of the new breed of architect. These included his fellow Sienese, Francesco di Giorgio Martini, as well as Fra Giocondo, the greatest expert on Vitruvius in his time. Both men worked for Patrizi's patron, Alfonso, duke of Calabria, in Naples. From 1476 Martini worked in Urbino for Duke Federico da Montefeltro, a close ally of Patrizi's patrons Pius II and Sixtus IV. Patrizi would have often been in and out of the Sala del Concistoro in Siena's Palazzo Pubblico in the year (1446) when Bernardo Rossellino was designing its elegant, neo-classical portal. Rossellino became a close associate of Alberti, and Patrizi surely met him when the Florentine architect was a member of Pius II's entourage, in charge of building Pienza's cathedral as well as other architectural works sponsored by the Piccolomini clan in Siena. During his ambassadorial mission to Milan in 1465, Patrizi could also easily have met the Florentine artist-architect Antonio Averlino, known as Filarete, who had recently completed his *Libro architettonico*

(1461/1464). An acquaintance with Filarete is even more likely in that the *Libro* was a work written in collaboration with Filarete's close friend and Patrizi's teacher, Francesco Filelfo. This work discussed *inter alia* the founding of two ideal cities, the fortress-city of Sforzinda for the duke of Milan, and Plusiopolis, "city of wealth," a port city in a regional state.[97]

It would be a digression worthy of Patrizi himself to explore in detail his relations with this new culture of Renaissance architecture, centered not only in Florence but also in Siena.[98] In any case, it is surely no surprise that Patrizi begins book 8 by recommending to city planners the use of experts (*periti*) and architects (*architecti*). Near the end of the same book he reiterates his advice to use learned architects, adding the provisos that living architects are better than dead theorists, and the owner of a space who cares about it sometimes outperforms the most learned architect brought in from outside.

> For if those in charge of building will make use of architects, as I said above, they will build everything in a correct way and will not need written precepts, since urban design [*aedificandi ratio*] requires a living instructor rather than a dead theorist [*ratiocinator*]. It is moreover true what is commonly said, that an untrained owner [*dominus*] builds better on his own allotment than the most highly trained architect on another's. The attentiveness and daily deliberation of the owner excels the care and learning of the artist [*artifex*].[99]

We do need, however, to address the question of how Patrizi adapted Vitruvian and contemporary principles of town planning to the needs of republics, with the goal of creating an environment supportive of equality, freedom, and virtuous government. Raising this issue is the more pertinent because the existing historiography tends to regard Renaissance ideal cities as expressions of princely power in states such as Milan, Naples, and Urbino as well as in Pius II's Pienza. Patrizi is our best and almost our only quattrocento example of how neo-classical urbanistics were adapted to the design of republics, in support of a free way of life.[100]

At the end of Chapter 3 we discussed Patrizi's belief that only defensive wars were fully justified. Wise republican magistrates should be extremely cautious about starting a war for honor or prestige, even when it might appear just, and offensive wars for empire were always immoral. That attitude is mirrored in Patrizi's great emphasis, in the first part of book 8, on the city's defensive fortifications, especially moats, walls, turrets, gates, ramparts, and approach roads.[101] Tranquillity, living without fear, is necessary to a healthy civic life because it is sudden terror and insecurity that drives cities into the arms of tyrants. Strong defense works help relieve citizens of their anxieties and prevent panic in case of attack. They give the war consul the breathing room necessary to manage the city's defenses without being forced to call in mercenaries or untrustworthy allies. Properly designed walls, moats, and ramparts can help the city resist even the terrifying new threat of gunpowder artillery.[102]

In chapter 9 of book 8 Patrizi addresses a question that he says has aroused "no small debate among writers on politics: whether to build a citadel in the [capital] city of a free state [*in urbe liberae civitatis*]."[103] His words are carefully chosen. The citadel (*arx*) is defined as an elevated fortification adjacent to the walls, overlooking (*immineat,* which can also mean "threatening") the whole city, and providing a protected entry point for military forces from outside the walls. It is a *praesidium* or stronghold for the whole city, "but no part of the city is safe when the citadel is a place to be feared." Does building a fortified place benefit or harm a free state?

Patrizi cites two authorities. The first is Aristotle. Patrizi often conceals his debts to the Stagyrite, but here the great scholastic authority is wheeled out to warn of the dangers of citadels. Aristotle's cool analytic observation, that citadels are appropriate to tyrannies and oligarchies but not to democracies, is transformed into an admonition that "citadels are useless and dangerous in the best republic and provide an opening for tyranny." "Who can doubt that?" adds Patrizi. "Where citizens dwell together with equal civic rights, they ought to have buildings of equal size. It isn't right for some buildings to loom over and threaten other buildings, while the latter are pressed down and cower beneath the greater ones." The other authority Patrizi cites is the Roman historian Asconius Pedianus, who is quoted with approval for his saying that "a citadel is a tyrant's base."[104]

Aristotle and Pedianus here merely endorse what were commonly held views. In Renaissance Italy popular regimes and republican thinkers generally saw urban citadels as concrete manifestations of tyrannical rule. When Lucca regained its liberty in 1370 from Giovanni dell'Agnello, lord of Pisa, the whole citizenry turned out to pull down the citadel, in a scene reminiscent of the fall of the Berlin Wall in 1989:

> The whole community was made happy when the castle was demolished. . . . Before the hour of Vespers there was not a man or a woman, great or small, who did not mount the walls to destroy the battlements. . . . Many were weeping with happiness, and others seemed crazy and beside themselves. . . . And those who had nothing else, tore down the bricks and mortar with their bare hands, swearing that through them they had been kept down. . . . It is impossible to describe what everyone did, some danced, some sat, some sang . . . others gave orders as if they were lords, some remembered the *signori* who had lived there, some wept for the wrongs that because of [the castle] had taken place, others grieved the death of father or relatives . . . others the dishonor done to their womenfolk . . . so that being there seemed to them a second paradise; others said, "O, now I no longer fear death, since I have seen such liberty!" . . . others felt richer than the emperor himself, and it seemed as if all the citizens were lords.[105]

It is easy to multiply examples of townspeople showing violent hatred of signorial castles built inside cities. When the Venetians freed Brescia from the rule of Filippo Maria Visconti, duke of Milan, in 1426, the townsmen immediately petitioned Venice for permission to tear down the citadel, claiming that their city, "hitherto divided and wretchedly disfigured by the ferocity of tyrants," needed open space so that the citizens who lived inside the walls could have free intercourse with each other (*ad invicem conversari*). The Venetians refused, being doubtful of the Brescians' loyalty, and in 1438, when the city had again been occupied by Filippo Maria's forces, their prudence paid off. The Venetian governor, the well-known humanist Francesco Barbaro, used the citadel to bring in reinforcements and retake the city. As Nicolai Rubinstein sums up in his account of the incident, "To city republics such as Venice, citadels had their usefulness in subject towns, however much they were condemned by republicans as tyrannical in cities ruled by *signori*."[106]

Patrizi reaches his own conclusions about citadels by consulting the pages of history, both Greek and Roman. His discussion cites six cases bearing on the question of citadels. From Plutarch he took the story of Timoleon, who, having destroyed the urban fortress of Dionysius of Syracuse, remarked that "a citadel is hardly ever free from tyranny." Drawing on Plutarch or Xenophon's *Hellenica* (probably via the Latin compendium of Leonardo Bruni), he tells the story of the Spartan general Phoebidas, who in 382 BC took control of the great Theban fortress of Cadmeia, thus initiating an oligarchic revolution against the popular regime.[107] Patrizi's conclusion is that citadels not only encourage tyrants but may also encourage factional strife. Another story from Plutarch, this time from the *Life of Pyrrhus,* relates how the Athenians gave the king of the Epirotes a tour of their citadel. Pyrrhus thanked them politely for their courtesy but advised them never again to let a warrior king see the inside of their fortifications. Two other stories, about citadels in Locri and Tarento, illustrate how careless or corrupt guards had allowed tyrants to take over those cities. His final example provides a nearly perfect parallel to the case of Francesco Barbaro in Brescia: it tells how the Romans delivered Taranto from Hannibal's occupation by getting control of the city's *arx.*

Patrizi's conclusion joins republican hatred of citadels in capital cities with Venetian prudence about the need for them in subject

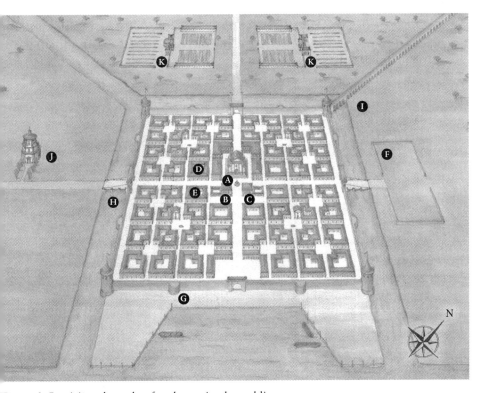

*igure 3*. Patrizi's urban plan for the optimal republic.

| | | |
|---|---|---|
| A  Civic Basilica | E  Odeon and public library | I  Aqueduct |
| 3  Public Palace | F  Campus Martinus | J  Contemplative church |
| C  Episcopal palace | G  Port |    for clergy |
| D  University building | H  Moat | K  Suburban villas |

towns: "From [these examples] we can conclude that a citadel in the capital of a free city is useless, but very necessary in a subject city." Like other republican thinkers of the Renaissance, Patrizi applied different criteria to liberty at home and liberty elsewhere in the dominions of free cities.[108]

The rest of Patrizi's urban plan is similarly supportive of a free society (Figure 3). In a well-known passage of the *Politics*, Aristotle advises tyrants how to maintain control of their cities. Among other measures, the tyrant should suppress what today would be called civil society—private clubs and associations—and outlaw humane education or *paideia*. He should be on his guard against anything that would build trust or reward courage among the political class. Friendships among citizens should be discouraged; "in a word, he should adopt every means for making every subject as much of a stranger as is possible to every other." Everyone in the tyrant's city should be forced to appear at intervals in a large piazza fronting on his fortified palace in order to remind the people who is the boss. "If they are always kept down, they will learn to be humble."[109]

Republican governments of the Renaissance were well aware of these tyrannical tactics. That is why they typically placed a high premium on accessibility to the public of civic buildings, including courts of justice and churches, and created open spaces where citizens could freely assemble. They also tended to be acutely aware of the dangers of too great disparities among citizens in the size of their houses. Many free cities in the quattrocento had fresh memories of coups and partisan disturbances that typically would be headquartered in semi-fortified palaces of powerful citizens who headed factions. Popular governments eventually leveled the high towers that had been built by magnates and *nobili* in the communes of the thirteenth century. Already in that century Florentine popular governments had placed legal limits on the height of houses citizens could build and forced magnates to dismantle their high towers. The Sienese republic was less draconian, but the fifty or sixty towers built by noble families in the city before 1277 had been reduced to a dozen or so by the early sixteenth century. Siena's Piazza del Campo, begun around 1300 under the government of the Nine, is one of the most dramatic examples of architectural leveling in communal Italy. Its semicircle of *palazzi signorili*—their uniform rooflines regulated by law—is dominated by the Palazzo Pubblico and its Torre della Mangia at the base of the shell-like piazza, a clear marker of political hierarchy.[110]

Nevertheless, by the fifteenth century, wealthy and powerful citizens, above all in Florence, were again building vast, highly defensible palaces that made up in depth and length for what legislation had prohibited to them in height. Some of these palace complexes threatened to become alternative city centers. The Medici palace, with its associated church of San Lorenzo and monastery of San Marco, along with nearby houses of family members and associates, provided a neighborhood base for the Medici party. The Piccolomini in Siena, after Enea Silvio Piccolomini became pope in 1458, created for themselves a similar urban enclave, which also, and not coincidently, pioneered a new, more classical style of domestic architecture within the city's late-gothic fabric.[111] The classical style, here as elsewhere, signaled true nobility, love of virtue, and therefore political legitimacy.

Patrizi's advice to urban planners shows in concrete terms his broad alignment with the egalitarian spirit of republican Siena. It may also disclose, perhaps, that *au fond* he was less in sympathy with the signorial projects of his Piccolomini patrons than his cliental relationship to them might lead one to suppose. In any case he recommends for his optimal republic an open, easily traversable city plan with plenty of room for citizens to move about and assemble (8.10). He advises that the *pomerium* or ritual boundary of the city—and hence the city's overall plan—be square rather than round or octagonal. The city should have broad main streets, thirty-four feet wide, leading directly from gates on one side to gates on the other, visible from the gates all along their extent. The streets should be wide enough so that heavily loaded carts will not be impeded in their progress. For a model of good construction, Patrizi recommends that planners study a well-preserved stretch of the Appian Way "not far from Terracina, past Minturno" (directions that seem to reveal a south Italian perspective, as though advising a traveler coming from Naples).

Cross streets should also be laid out so as to lead to other gates, and at the crossroads (*trivia*) there should be "rather broad" piazzas, ideally lined with porticos, in accordance with ancient practice. These porticos should be designed not only to shelter people outdoors in all weathers, but also for cultural purposes. The Romans placed their grammar schools in such crossroad locations ("hence the Latin word for the sciences of the *trivium*," Patrizi remarks), and moderns should establish the teaching of grammar there too, at public expense. Greek philosophers such as the Stoics used porticos like these in ancient Athens for their philosophical discussions. The piazzas should also furnish sites for daily religious devotions.

At crossroads and on street corners it will be helpful to build shrines for the common use of the neighborhood. At these, boys and religious women can perform their devotions. For on holy days set apart for divine matters, everyone ought to come together in the larger temples, but on other days, when we attend to human matters, it will be enough to go to the neighborhood shrines. Hence Propertius's lines,

> I deck shrines with flowers, I wrap crossroad altars round
> with vervain,
> And scented marjoram crackles on ancient hearths.[112]

Patrizi envisages piazzas and porticos as spaces in every neighborhood for families to assemble freely in civil society, associating on matters of mutual interest such as religion and the education of children.

At the beginning of chapter 11 on private dwellings, Patrizi instructs the city planner that "along the streets private houses should be established in a long line, of equal dimensions if possible, so as to embellish the appearance of the city."[113] No house should stick out and obstruct the street. Private dwellings should be built to accommodate the needs of families and not contain useless empty spaces. They should be beautiful, for beauty augments the worth of the man who builds it. This Ciceronian sentiment leads Patrizi to illustrate his idea with two contrasting historical examples. The first was the *novus homo* Lucius Octavius, who was raised to the consulate after the *vulgus* caught sight of his dignified house. On the other hand, the daughter of the great Aemilius Paullus, twice consul and twice triumphator, was not ashamed to live in a small house, together with her husband's numerous relatives and their children, because her husband was a man of virtue despite being almost a pauper.

Patrizi's conclusion, however, comes down more on the side of magnificence than honorable poverty. It is the duty of the citizen to build a beautiful house if he can afford it. For the wealthy to keep their riches locked up in strongboxes for future generations is a mark of avarice. If our ancestors had done that, we would still be living in shepherd's huts. Pomponius Atticus and Scipio Aemilianus, who built nothing, would not have experienced earlier deaths or any diminution of their fame if they had laid themselves out on fine buildings. But the desire to build can go too far, as the odious case of Nero showed, whose pharaonic pile was built on the ashes of his capital city and perverted the natural distinction between city and country. *Rus in urbe* for Patrizi was an abuse of the natural order. In private dwellings a holy mean (*sancta mediocritas*) must be observed, which, as the Peripatetics say, graces everyone in a wondrous way.

Patrizi tells us less about public buildings in his optimal republic. As we saw above, the Sienese philosopher favors a wealthy state, and building magnificent public structures counts among the most laudable uses for its resources. "For temples, forums, theaters, amphitheaters, baths, market places, porticos, and buildings of this kind make a city illustrious and far more remarkable, while funds laid out for a spectacle [*spectaculum*] lasting a short time and soon forgotten are spent uselessly." Well-built structures of solid marble are more lasting and survive for many ages, long after the cities they embellished have crumbled into ruin.

Patrizi recommends that one or more large forums be laid out; one of them should be on the water if the city is a port. They can be built either square in the Greek fashion or oblong in the Roman.[114] He has a long discussion of theaters, including some advice on acoustics drawn from Vitruvius, but finishes by saying that his treatment of theaters is less applicable to modern times, where theatrical performances are at odds with serious Christian morality. This remark accords with his curriculum in book 2, which, as we have seen, counsels against public performances of comedy and tragedy, but calls for occasional public recitations of heroic poetry. Patrizi's advice here contrasts sharply with Alberti's, who (as an author made famous by his comedy *Philodoxeos*) devotes enthusiastic attention to theaters in book 8 of his *De re architectura*.[115]

In general, and unlike Alberti, Patrizi evinces little interest in *spectacula*, buildings like theaters, circuses, and stadiums where the whole populace crowds together to see shows and watch sports. As we saw above, Patrizi's educational program endorses the Greek concept of gymnasia for physical exercise but registers a horror of Roman gladiatorial games. His attitude is not surprising in a philosopher and a bishop, and Patrizi surely knew Seneca's famous letter *On Crowds,* whose theme is the bad effect on character of experiencing humanity in the mass:

> But nothing is so damaging to good character as the habit of lounging at some spectacle [*in aliquo spectaculo*]; for then it is that vice steals subtly upon one through the avenue of pleasure. What do you think I mean? I mean that I come home more greedy, more ambitious, more voluptuous, and even more cruel and inhuman—because I have been among human beings.[116]

As a meritocratic theorist who wants private citizens of the lower classes to participate in public life but not to dominate it, it cannot be an accident that his optimal city contains no *spectacula*. Citizens should be free to assemble in their neighborhoods and other public spaces but not in venues designed to manipulate and inflame their passions.

As though in compensation, Patrizi emphasizes the need for a public library, a building type not treated by Vitruvius and hardly mentioned by Alberti.[117] If a city has gymnasia for bodies, it should have public libraries to exercise the mind. Besides, it needs to raise up learned men who help the city through their teachings and moral example, and who preserve for future generations all things worthy

of memory. The library should be built in a dry, well-lighted location that will preserve the books; it should be paneled and tinted a
green color to help the eyes.[118] Patrizi's humanistic university will
presumably also need lecture halls, but these are not mentioned in
the plans for his optimal republic. Patrizi approves of education in the
home, especially in childhood, but it is clear that he also wants the
liberal disciplines publicly taught at the expense of the republic.
Hence, university buildings of some kind, perhaps resembling the
Casa della Sapienza on the Piazza del Duomo in Siena, may be assumed to be part of his plan for the ideal city.[119]

More surprising is Patrizi's failure to mention the buildings that
often dominate public spaces in Renaissance cities: the palaces of
government like the Palazzo Vecchio in Florence or the public palaces in Arezzo, Lucca, and Siena. Patrizi is also silent about episcopal
palaces such as the one that he himself occupied in Gaeta or the one
built in Pienza next to the cathedral for the town's bishop. We are told
nothing about the appropriate size or location of such buildings. Instead, Patrizi devotes many pages in the final chapter of book 8 to the
design and placement of churches.

Patrizi assumes the city will contain a number of smaller churches
dispersed throughout its fabric, but he counsels the city planner to
provide for two sacred buildings in particular. One is the republic's
principal "temple"—its cathedral church or duomo. This should be
a basilican church established for common use and should be built
not far from the principal forum or adjacent to the most densely
populated neighborhoods. There should be a separate entrance for
boys and women for the sake of decency. The metropolitan bishop
(*civitatis pontifex*) should have charge of the building.[120] All architects agree, Patrizi says, that it should be built on a raised platform
in the middle of the city, so that from it observers can take in the
greatest part of the walls: "For thus the whole city will seem to be
under its protection, and thither all citizens will flow together on
major feasts, as though to a spectacle [*spectaculum*] of that which
is greatest and most divine." The proper *spectaculum* for the people

of an optimal republic is the rites of religion, not theatrical and sporting events.

In addition to this central church for the benefit of all citizens, the city fathers should also plan to furnish a second church, built especially for ordained priests and other servants of religion, to be used as a place for contemplating divine things, where all human concerns may be laid aside. Such a church needs solitude, so should be built in some quiet place, far from the madding crowd. Patrizi recommends that it be erected somewhere in the space between the city walls and pomerium. What he has in mind might be a church such as San Biagio, a lovely Renaissance church set in a grove outside the walls of Montepulciano, designed by Antonio da San Gallo; or Santa Maria della Consolazione, built outside Todi, possibly designed by Bramante. Whether either architect or their patrons knew the writings of Patrizi, directly or indirectly, has not been established.[121]

## Piety and Religion in the Best Republic

Like most humanists of the quattrocento, Patrizi avoids the subject of ecclesiology and has no developed theory of church–state relations. Ecclesiology was at the center of scholastic political thought, in the Middle Ages and afterward, but there is, in general, a loud silence on this subject in humanist political writings. To be sure, humanists often criticize monks, the clergy, and even high prelates for bad behavior. The most famous examples outside Boccaccio's *Decameron* are Poggio's letter on the execution of Jerome of Prague and Bartolomeo Platina's relentless attacks on modern clerical corruption in his *Lives of the Popes*. Humanists like Lorenzo Valla and Marsilio Ficino also developed theologies that flirted with Pelagianism and bypassed the institutional Church as a source of grace and revealed truth. When humanists get close to structural attacks on the contemporary Church, those attacks tend to be anonymous, like Petrarch's *Sine nomine* letters, or scandalous, like Lorenzo Valla's polemical address *On the Donation of Constantine*, written in the interest of King Alfonso of Naples but without his endorsement. Both of these exceptions prove the rule that attacking the legitimacy of the Church as an institution or advocating structural reforms were no-win propositions. After the collapse of conciliarism in the first half of the fifteenth century such behavior was positively self-destructive. Valla himself was quickly brought to heel before the Inquisition in Naples for writing the *Donation* as well as for unorthodox tendencies in his other writings.

The Church's carrots were even more effective than its sticks. A very large number of humanists, beginning with Petrarch, supported themselves on church benefices, and Catholic religious orders boasted many humanist literati among their ranks. It surprised no one that the Valla of the *Donation* quickly learned to control his pen when offered well-remunerated positions in the papal curia and the University of Rome by Popes Nicholas V and Calixtus III. By the time of his speech for the new academic year in 1455, shortly before his death, Valla found himself able to praise the Holy Church for preserving learning after the fall of the Roman Empire and suggested that her cultural mission alone was enough to legitimate her rule.[122] Opposing the institutional Church before the Reformation was analogous to opposing the Communist Party in modern China. While hardly morally equivalent, both institutions created formidable disincentives to those who would make criticisms rising to the level of ideological opposition. In any case, the approach to political reform of most humanists emphasized the moral formation of individual princes and other leaders rather than institutional transformation.

Patrizi had more interest in reshaping institutions than did most humanist political thinkers, but his language, too, became vague on matters related to ecclesiology, and on the numerous live issues of church reform in his time he maintained an eloquent silence. As a beneficed clergyman, a high-ranking prelate, and close ally of Pope Pius II—the man who had saved his life—one might have expected him in his political writings to be a vocal defender of the rights of the Roman church. While acting as papal governor of Foligno, he was certainly energetic in enforcing those rights, and when searching for a dedicatee for his book on republics he ultimately chose Sixtus IV over the city of Siena. But Patrizi hardly mentions the Roman church in either of his political treatises and never defends its claims to temporal or even doctrinal authority.

The reasons for Patrizi's careful silence about relations between sovereign republics and the Roman Church, in the opinion of the present writer, were as much theoretical as personal. There was a fundamental tension between humanist political thought in general and the universal claims of the Church to temporal power. Like most humanists Patrizi took what has been called an organicist view of the state, well described by Guido Cappelli in several recent publications.[123] On this view, service to the *respublica,* or the whole political community, understood as a moral person, was the highest goal of human collective action. The sovereign, whether a republican *signoria* or a single *signore,* ideally should command the highest loyalty of the citizen in the present life. Virtuous leaders served the whole people, and their moral charisma circulated their virtue through the whole body politic, bringing justice, peace, and harmony. Citizens were valued in proportion to their functions in, and service to, the whole community. Well-educated leaders of high character made prudent decisions that served the whole and not just the part. For Cappelli the humanist form of organicism is naturalistic, independent of the juridical hierarchies of the Middle Ages as elaborated by civil and canon lawyers. It was also "in large measure independent of the contingent institutional form of government"— that is, indifferent to the form of the regime, applicable to any. Any passions or outside loyalties that threatened civic concord were illegitimate and dangerous. These could include the avarice of would-be oligarchs, the proud ambition of power-hungry nobles, the selfish greed of condottieri, and the treachery of those whose loyalties were divided or alienated. Such passions the humanists considered to be root causes of factionalism and tyranny, the twin diseases of political life in Renaissance Italy.

Organicist assumptions thus put humanist political thought potentially in conflict with the universalist claims of the papacy and the Roman Church. So long as Church teachings were confined to preparation of the soul for the next life, to be sure, conflict was likely to be minimal. Under normal conditions most Renaissance republics and princes regarded the Church as an ally, a bulwark of peaceful rule that inclined the hearts of the people toward due obedience to their rulers. Nevertheless, the position the Roman church claimed as a juridical and doctrinal authority, placed above merely human authorities, gave rise to many points of friction. Disputes could arise about the appointment of high prelates, ecclesiastical taxes, clerical immunities, marriage law, and other economic interests. The Church claimed final jurisdiction over most of these matters, and the highest court of appeal was the papal curia in Rome. In most cities of Italy, the Church, under the authority of the local bishop, was also the largest individual landowner and an active participant in the urban economy, so that the disposition and use of Church property was a matter of constant concern to civil governments.

Moreover, the Roman Church was itself a major state within the Italian peninsula, claiming direct political authority over a congeries of city-states and territories ranging from the Romagna in the north to the borders of the Kingdom of Naples in the south, and encircling a long arm around Tuscany. Low-level border conflicts and warlordism were common, and occasionally the pope joined one side or another in peninsular wars.[124] During such wars, like Florence's "War of the Eight Saints" (1375–1378) or the war that followed the Pazzi conspiracy (1478–1479), the clergy resident in towns at war with the pope could be regarded as untrustworthy, even as constituting a fifth column. This was especially the case when the pope deployed his spiritual weapons of excommunication and interdict, which the clergy were obliged to enforce. Internal civil conflicts could also arise between citizens with intense Guelf loyalties, who believed that the republic should always fight on the side of Holy Church, and other citizens who preferred a more realistic calculus in determining the state's foreign allegiances.[125]

In his *De republica* Patrizi does not directly address how free states can resolve such tensions with the Roman church. He never discusses the papacy or the Roman church as institutions, and his single mention of canon law simply praises it as a treasury of legal wisdom, ideal for informing the prudence of magistrates (1.5). But his few positive prescriptions imply, minimally, a high degree of deference on the part of clergy toward the lay authorities of the republic in matters of politics.

What little Patrizi has to say about church–state relations in the *De republica* comes in book 3, on magistracies, in a chapter devoted to "divine magistrates." Patrizi distinguishes first between human and divine magistrates. Human magistrates are those who bear the public persona and have charge of the city with the power of command. Some of these have executive power in war and peace, whereas others are in charge of judging legal cases.[126] Divine magistrates "ought to have care over worship services and ceremonies, mysteries, and sacrifices." They are also teachers, "instructing the people in the worship of the true religion and eliminating vain superstition." They should have no formal political power, in other words.

Nevertheless their activities are indispensable to legitimating the acts of the republic.[127] "Laws and ordinances are of very little effect unless they are assisted by sacred teachings and rely on Best and Greatest God." Patrizi then adds a classic "shame-praising" argument (to use Noel Malcolm's fine expression):[128] If the ancients, who were ignorant of the one true God and were led astray by vain superstitions, did nothing pertaining to public life without the bidding of pontiffs, what should we Christians do, who alone worship the true religion and have Christ, the son of God, as authority for our religion?

> Surely we should apply all our zeal and effort to see that nothing is done or placed under consideration without propitiating God with the mysteries and rituals through which we attain eternal life? Sacred actions therefore should always precede human actions. For this reason the senators should be careful to decree nothing in the senate without divine authority. Once God has been propitiated, nothing wrong or unfortunate can happen. Therefore, before undertaking great affairs, the city's bishop

[*antistes*] should be present, whom in the Roman speech we call a pontiff [*pontifex*].

The burden of the rest of the chapter is to insist on the need for close cooperation between divine and human magistrates. In the most ancient times, Patrizi claims, religious and political power were closely allied, if not merged in one person. In an echo of Plato's famous *sententia aurea*—that cities would not be blessed unless philosophers ruled, or rulers became philosophers—he writes:

In the beginning power over human affairs lay with pontiffs; and kings themselves, initiated into sacred matters, had care of both divine and the human things. They could not believe that anyone could rule well without experience of divine matters and commerce with a god. Therefore either priests themselves ruled or princes did nothing except on their command.

Though we follow the true religion, says Patrizi, we should not depart from the example of Romulus, first king of Rome.

Romulus, when founding the city of Rome, called the high priest [*antistes*] of the temples and the sacred rites a "king" [*rex*], and, as though allying his own royal power with his [*quasi socia potestate cum eo regnaret*], wanted him to be the guardian of the laws and ancestral custom.[129] . . . Let us therefore heed with all zeal the dicta of priests, for they are divinely inspired and teach us the precepts of holiness and salvation.

Patrizi assumes in these passages that there will be a basic hierarchy within the priesthood consisting of the high priest, or bishop, and beneath him the diocesan clergy and presumably other persons devoted to the religious life. But he does not establish a hierarchy, either political or spiritual, between the magistrates of the republic and the priesthood. They are rather co-ordinate and mutually reinforcing powers, functionally distinct.[130] We are not told how the "divine magistrates" are to be selected. Does the bishop select them, perhaps in consultation with the senate, or are they chosen by the senate like other magistrates? Patrizi's silence on the issue might even be taken as permitting a role to outside authorities such as the pope, though for a foreign prince to play such a role seems contrary to organicist principles. We are also told nothing about how, precisely, orthodox doctrine is to be established, except that this is a priestly function. Will the divine magistrates of Patrizi's optimal republic defer to the magisterium of the Roman church? Again, we are not told. In any case the chief function of the priesthood and its teachings, from the point of view of politics, is to guide and legitimate the acts of lay rulers. When ancient pagan rulers made use of false religions for this purpose, they were forced to tell useful lies to the people and pretend that their pronouncements were backed by divine authority. But we moderns who have the true religion are not under this necessity.[131]

The priesthood also has a key role to play in fostering piety, construed (following Cicero) as the most important part of the virtue of justice, and a virtue all citizens need to acquire. Statesmen and magistrates for their part should uphold the three civil duties of *pietas:* to maintain divine worship and ceremonies; to encourage a sense of obligation to our country, under God; and to show zeal and gratitude not only to parents, children, and spouses but also to our fellow citizens, "whom we should treat with wondrous goodwill." But it is the clergy who by precept and example will explain the duties of piety to the people. Patrizi's emphasis here, as ever, is on teaching. He says nothing about the usual means employed by the late medieval church to stimulate piety: the pilgrimages, processions, liturgies, devotions, and sacraments, the cult of saints and martyrs, and the like. Nor does he make any mention of institutions like hospitals, orphanages, and confraternities where religious persons cared for and instructed laymen.

Patrizi's silences here should not, I think, be construed as dissent or as an educated contempt for superstition.[132] But his wider position on how the clergy should be supported economically in the optimal state seems to disclose a more radical challenge to the Church's economic power. As we saw above, Patrizi endorses, for newly founded states, a Hippodamian division of the city-state's lands, such that one third of its agrarian territory is assigned to support men of religion. The sacred third is not divided up into individual proprietorships, as in the case of the third of state lands allotted to private citizens. The city would retain ownership of the land, and income from permanent leases would pay for the upkeep of churches and provide a modest, non-heritable living for priests. Presumably, sharecroppers would support the priests by payments to them in kind or in specie, either directly or via the state treasury.[133] In other words, state control of the agricultural property used to support religion would go well beyond the *ius patronatus* allowed to the lay patrons by canon law. Canon law restricted lay founders of churches, even princes, to the *ius providendi et consulendi et sacerdotem inveniendi* (the right to look after the church, to give advice or be consulted, and to find or provide a priest). They did not have the *ius vendendi vel donandi vel utendi tamquam propriis* (the right of selling or giving or using as their own).[134]

What Patrizi seems to have in mind here would bring to an end the regime of ecclesiastical lordship established by the Gregorian reform of the eleventh century and codified by Gratian and later canon lawyers who interpreted the Roman church's evolving body of law. Patrizi's scheme of agrarian reform seems on its face incompatible with the Gregorian position, as stated in the First Lateran Council of 1123, that declares attempts by laymen to claim *dispositio* or *dominatio* of ecclesiastical possessions to be sacrilegious. He also seems to reject the canons prohibiting laymen, including lay rulers, from having property (*dominium*) in churches, exercising *dominativa potestas,* the power of ownership or lordship. It is possible that Patrizi believed that blurring the lines between sacred and political authority in his optimal state absolved him of any charge of contumacy, but it seems unlikely that a canon lawyer would have seen his reform proposals in the same light. His organicist solution to the problem of church–state conflict, in fact, resembles his solution to the problem of oligarchy, and is every bit as radical. By limiting the amount of private wealth that they could command, he would greatly reduce the ability of any rivals to the republic's authority to check or nullify it.

Patrizi's strategy for ending the debilitating conflict between the Church and lay authorities that had done so much to divide, weaken, and corrupt Christendom for the preceding three centuries thus differed both from Petrarch's solution in the fourteenth century and the solutions of Machiavelli and the Protestant reformers of the sixteenth. Petrarch wanted a return to pre-Constantinian Christianity, before religion had been corrupted by the Caesars and before the popes had laid claim to the kingdoms of this world. Machiavelli in the *Discorsi* wanted the opposite, a republic that would refashion the Christian Church and its teachings into a tool of statecraft, greatly enhancing thereby the power of the state.[135] Many Protestant reformers wanted an Erastian church settlement where churches could own property but the state could limit and override their property rights—appropriating monastic lands, for example—and where the civil magistrate was and should be the ultimate and exclusive source of valid religious law. Patrizi by contrast envisaged a cooperative relationship between city magistrates and the clergy, the latter headed by a bishop. The loyalty of the clergy to the civil magistrates would be guaranteed by their economic dependence on the city, but the city would not attempt to interfere with church teachings. Since—thanks to the altered property regime—there would be little tension between the interests of church and republic, the temptation to instrumentalize church doctrines as ideological tools of political interests would in any case be small.

The closest parallel to Patrizi's implicit ecclesiology is to be found in More's *Utopia,* where a simple hierarchy of a pontiff and subordinate priests is imagined, and where clergy are considered to be public magistrates but to have no political power, only religious duties. Like Patrizi's clergy, More's have no private control of property that might tempt them to challenge the authority of the lay magistrates.

In short, Patrizi's solution to the centuries-long struggle between spiritual and temporal powers within Christendom was as original as it was radical. It illustrates, I believe, how the classical revival orchestrated by humanist literati in the quattrocento enabled them to overcome the ideological categories and constraints of the medieval past and to imagine alternatives that, precisely because they were believed to have existed in an admired past, could provide models for polities in the future. As so often, the Renaissance, Janus-faced, strode into the future while looking to the past.

# SIX

# Citizenship and the Virtuous Citizen

## Two Models of Citizenship

A citizen may be defined as an individual holding a privileged position within some polity. Citizenship is legal recognition of that privilege.[1] The privileges of a citizen may include, maximally, an entitlement to participate in the governing organs of the polity—active self-government—or minimally, rights that specify preferences and protections distinguishing them from non-citizens. Citizenship also imposes shared burdens such as taxation, military service, jury service, and voting in assemblies or for representatives in legislatures. Premodern citizenship laws typically exclude women, minors, slaves, resident aliens, and the laboring and serving classes.

Such exclusions do not necessarily imply equality among citizens, however. Historically, the idea of citizenship has been compatible with formal, legal hierarchies within the class of citizens. Among Roman citizens in antiquity, for example, there were a number of overlapping hierarchies: between the senatorial and equestrian orders; between voting citizens in the city of Rome and non-voting citizens elsewhere (*civitas sine suffragio*); between patrons and their freedman (*libertini cives*); and, in the later empire, between *honestiores* and *humiliores*, those due more honor and those due less.[2] In the Renaissance, Venetian law distinguished between the *civis originarius* and the *civis novus*, imposing political, social, and legal disabilities on the latter. Full political rights were restricted to a small group of patricians, estimated by historians to be around 8 to 10 percent of the citizen body in 1509.[3] Siena had even more complex differentiations among those who held citizenship status. The Sienese granted an inferior form of citizenship to townsmen in their territory that voluntarily submitted to their rule, and also carefully graded citizenship rights within the urban population.[4] Nevertheless, the broad development of citizenship law from the late Middle Ages to the present has tended to break down formal, legal hierarchies among citizens, equalize citizen status, and extend citizen rights to formerly excluded categories of persons.[5]

Broadly speaking, classical antiquity handed down to the modern West two conceptions of citizenship. One model, which we can call the participatory model, emerged in the Greek city-states during the late archaic period and was meant to define who had access to political power. In the classical period citizens (πολίτης) were defined as free adult males, almost exclusively descended of citizen parents, who were able to participate in sovereign assemblies and law courts and were eligible to hold magistracies as well. The Greek model of citizenship was theorized by both Plato in the *Laws* and Aristotle in the *Politics*. Both philosophers focused on the nature of citizen virtue, the qualities needed to be a good citizen and magistrate, and how to elicit those qualities via customs, laws, and *paideia,* broadly conceived. Participatory citizenship thus possesses a normative dimension, a concern with what makes a good citizen, largely absent from later, more legalistic definitions of citizenship.[6] The participatory citizenship of the Greeks is the ancestor of the "republican," "communitarian," or "civic humanist" conception of the citizen in modern anglophone political theory.

The other model was Roman citizenship, which can be called the status model of the citizen (*civis*). In the early Roman republic, citizenship followed the Greek model in specifying who had access to political power. But over time, Roman citizenship was gradually extended to allies and defeated rivals in Italy and ultimately— following the Antonine Constitution of 212—to all free males in the Roman Empire. With so enormous a citizen body, and lacking as they did any concept of representation in public law, the Romans could not realistically define citizenship as a right to participate in self-rule; it became, increasingly, what Theodor Mommsen labeled "passive citizenship."[7]

By the early empire, citizenship came to be understood as a status that conferred on individuals certain legal rights. Citizens (and their property) were entitled to equal protection under the law; they could serve in the army and act in their own right (*sui iuris*) for themselves and their dependents in law. They had legally defined rights and privileges: for example, freedom from forced labor, or the right to marry a Roman woman. Citizenship also carried obligations such as paying taxes and maintaining loyalty to the state. Roman citizenship under the empire became politically passive. It did not *per se* entitle the citizen to exercise political rights. Even in republican Rome only restricted groups of Roman citizens had had the right to participate in voting assemblies and jury courts and to hold office, and in practice citizen rights were carefully graded in most communities within the larger empire. The Roman status conception of citizenship is the ancestor of the liberal or rights-based model of citizenship in the modern West.[8]

Roman citizenship as a formal legal status died out with the decline of imperial power in the western Mediterranean. The concept of a universal citizen status also fell into desuetude in the Christian empire of the East, where baptism came to stand proxy for membership in the community. Byzantine documents have only vestigial traces of Roman citizenship law, usually in restricted contexts such as the manumission of slaves. Roman citizenship status was not revived in western Christendom either by Charlemagne, the Ottonian emperors, or the Holy Roman Emperors.[9] With the emergence of the popular commune in Italy during the central Middle Ages, however, something like the Greek model of participatory citizenship made a comeback in the West, although from the start it was always blended with considerations of legal status derived from ancient Roman jurisprudence.[10] By the early fourteenth century, almost all free city-states in central and northern Italy had produced statutes defining citizenship. Prominent jurists such as Bartolus and Baldus debated the principles of membership in city-states, applying texts from ancient Roman civil law and sometimes incorporating definitions from Aristotle's moral works.[11] By the end of the Renaissance, citizenship in Italy had become less connected to participation in government and more of a purely juridical concept. This was a natural evolution in a period when many cities were being subsumed into larger regional states and suffering in consequence a relative loss of autonomy.[12]

Citizenship in Italian cities of the Renaissance was a valuable distinction that allowed a person limited participation in self-government, numerous legal rights and protections, as well as the opportunity to be selected for potentially lucrative offices. For most citizens, most of the time, the benefits of citizenship vastly outweighed the burdens of participation and taxation, especially after it became possible to commute service in the army for a cash payment. By the sixteenth century, many Italian cities restricted citizenship to those who could show that their ancestors had held office in the city. For this reason, the question of who should be admitted to citizenship became one of the more hotly debated issues in late medieval and Renaissance Italy, though it did not lead to any extended theoretical treatment of citizenship as such among jurists, theologians, or scholastic political philosophers.[13] As legal *consilia* of the time disclose, the desire to acquire citizenship in Italian city-states was motivated less by dignitarian considerations than by the practical value that citizen status offered.

The primary concern of citizens then was not for rights that could allow political participation. To be sure, such participation was positively viewed, but it was considered just a part of a complex personal or family strategy. What the medieval citizen was more concerned with were those benefits of citizenship which advanced his and his family's social status, facilitated his business life, gave him an edge over the resident noncitizen within the walls and which protected him as he maintained banking or commercial operations abroad. Citizenship status might confer some tax benefit, the right to gild membership, the promise of reprisals. It was viewed as something tangible, almost with a market value, price tag attached. It might mean the difference between receiving a bequest or seeing it go into the hands of a monastery as the alternate beneficiary. It might mean retention of a dowry or not. Patriotism did flourish, surely, but it was not of the romantic, idealistic variety that a number of moralists have been able to envision in the past two centuries.[14]

The practical benefits of citizenship did not vary significantly between republics and princely states in Renaissance Italy. In both forms of government real political power was held by small groups of oligarchs or by the prince and the ruling group he empowered; in both forms the emoluments accruing from office, in principle shared equally among citizens, were commonly diverted to favor the interests of the prince's courtiers or clients of the oligarchy.[15]

Despite this convergence in practice, when it came to theory, and despite his own emphasis on the shared principles of republic and royal government, Patrizi developed two distinctive understandings of citizenship. The earlier was presented in the *De republica* and so concerns citizenship in a city republic. Laid out principally in book 5, it constitutes the first sustained analysis of the concept of citizenship in the Western political thought since Aristotle's *Politics*. The other understanding may be called "royal citizenship."[16] It was elaborated in book 9 of the *De regno*. It is perhaps even more original than Patrizi's theory of republican citizenship.

In the early modern era, with the emergence of royal states, those aspects of citizenship drawn from the Roman "status" model began to displace the participatory ideals of late medieval and Renaissance city-states. The new conception of royal citizenship emerged to define membership in a regional state headed by a monarch.[17] This development was in large part motivated by the desire of kings to find a new moral/affective basis for loyalty to the crown. In an age of confessional warfare, Christianity had become less useful as a social glue and was often more of an explosive than an adhesive. The old feudal ties of loyalty and service that sustained medieval monarchs were increasingly complicated by the struggle, characteristic of the early modern period, to acquire and retain privileges and prerogatives.[18] Inspired by Renaissance humanism, monarchs and their counselors looked back to ancient Rome and rediscovered citizenship as a tool of government and a way of centralizing and unifying the bonds of loyalty within expanding sovereign states. Royal citizenship offered kings a new way of conceptualizing the mutual obligations between monarchs and their subjects, allowing them to supplement or by-pass existing ties with "intermediate, subordinate, and dependent powers" such as parlements, city governments, and the hereditary nobility with their *privatae leges* or privileges.[19] Unlike the traditional system of feudal and corporate obligations inherited from the past, citizenship had the potential to unite the inhabitants of large kingdoms living under "a diversity of laws, languages, customs, religions and races."[20] Not well studied in historical literature, royal citizenship formed a transitional phase between the Roman status concept of citizenship and modern (so-called) liberal conceptions that define a citizen's rights and obligations with respect to the unified, sovereign power of the state.

## Who Should Be a Citizen in a Republic?

Patrizi's model of republican citizenship, by contrast, is a hybrid, blended from both Greek and Roman lineages of thought and practice. What is immediately striking about his conception of republican citizenship is how inclusive it is by comparison with Aristotle's. Patrizi has many obvious debts to the Greek philosopher, beginning with his functional definition of the citizen as a person capable of performing a citizen's duties. Yet in accordance with his usual practice, he hardly ever acknowledges Aristotle as his source.[21] His failure to cite Aristotle may simply reflect the prejudice of some humanists in the Petrarchan tradition against what they took to be the exaggerated reliance on Aristotle characteristic of scholastic writers. As was noted in Chapter 2, the popular scholastic text against which Patrizi measured himself, Giles of Rome's *De regimine principum*, is based almost entirely on Aristotle. And as we saw in Chapter 1, Patrizi prided himself on enriching the political prudence of the West with hitherto unknown Greek sources. But there may also be at work, in this context, a distaste for Aristotle's less egalitarian conception of citizenship.

Patrizi's preliminary definition of the citizen in book 1 of *De re-publica* announces immediately his departure from Aristotelian authority. "The citizen," he writes,

> must be a native of the place and a child of freeborn parents, or someone who has been given citizenship by the magistrates or laws. I would have him possess the capacity to participate in public office, and I hold that otherwise he ought not to be regarded as a citizen. Nor should he be called a citizen by marriage or by vicinity.[22]

Patrizi here combines principles drawn from late medieval communal law with an Aristotelian emphasis on the capacity to rule, or civic virtue. He also invokes the core principle of virtue politics when he insists that citizen status should be conditioned on virtue. But his definition also relies heavily on the criterion of *ius sanguinis*, freeborn descent from a citizen parent or parents, making only a few exceptions for naturalized citizens.

He would disallow citizenship granted on the basis of *vicinitas*, which here probably means citizenship granted to immigrants from a city's rural territories. It was a common practice in Patrizi's native city of Siena to admit such men to a limited form of citizenship in order to bind their home communities more closely to the mother city and to encourage them to resist encroachment from imperialistic neighbors like Florence or the Papal State. As a rule, aristocratic parties in Tuscan republics tended to be more restrictionist in their immigration policies; popular parties were more welcoming. So Patrizi's opposition to citizenship for *gente nuova* may reflect to some extent his personal allegiances in the context of Sienese communal politics. But he has a reasoned argument for nativism as well, to be examined below.

Patrizi also rejects the idea that a man who marries a native woman or vice versa should be automatically granted citizenship, a common practice in modern democratic states. On the other hand, as we shall see, a man who marries a non-citizen woman does not thereby deprive his own male children of citizen rights.

Patrizi elaborates further on his definition of citizenship at the beginning of book 5, "On the obligations of the best citizen and civic education." He begins, "We must first examine who we think should be considered a citizen in this state of ours, and say whether all the riffraff enclosed within the one set of city walls deserves the name of citizen."[23] One opinion, which Patrizi ascribes to Homer, held that only those able to exercise citizen offices should be citizens. This is a virtue requirement, albeit a rather minimal one, specifying only basic competence. Others, he writes, would allow only those who come from respectable, freeborn (*ingenui*) citizen parents to be enrolled as citizens. Still others think it is enough to be descended of one citizen parent. Patrizi does not immediately take a position on the last two alternatives.

Patrizi then considers precedents in two particular cases: (1) where a city has become depopulated, a situation frequently faced by Renaissance cities after long wars, plagues, or famines; or (2) where citizens living abroad have children born abroad. The second case was often a contentious issue in the commercial cities of the Renaissance, where family members might live for long periods in trading colonies or *fondaci* in foreign cities, and where the political exile of whole families, sometimes for generations, was a common experience.

There were those who, owing to depopulation, gave citizenship to aliens [*peregrini*] so long as they built a house inside the city and practiced a craft [*ars*] or married into a citizen family, notwithstanding [the fact that] the Roman jurisconsults said origin alone makes one a citizen. Relatedly, a son who was born in one city and has a father born in another is said to be a citizen of his real country [*germana patria*], not of the country in which he was born or domiciled. Cicero in the *De legibus* affirms that he had two countries [*patriae*], a real one [*germana*] where he was raised and another by right [*iure*], in which he was born and educated and where he was called to political life [*civilis societas*].[24] He claims the same principle obtained in the case of Marcus Cato [the Younger], who, though a native of Tusculum, acquired Roman citizenship, so was considered Tusculan by origin and a Roman by right.[25]

Patrizi then comes to his conclusion:

> Therefore we shall call the citizen of our [optimal] state [*civitas*] a man of this kind, who has a father among his indigenous ancestors [*inter maiores indigenas*].[26] (One must pay less attention to the mother's ancestry so long as she is freeborn.) We think anyone is fitted to undertake citizen tasks by nature [i.e. heredity] if his virtues allow it. For as we said above, employment in a magistracy is to be alloted as a reward of virtues, not of ancestry or influence.[27]

The linkage of heredity with virtue finds a parallel in Patrizi's position on the legitimacy of hereditary princes in his *De regno*. In the latter text both legitimate birth *and* virtue are jointly the necessary conditions of legitimacy but neither one is sufficient on its own.[28] Patrizi applies the same principle to citizens of republics, though the standard of virtue is much lower: political competence rather than magnificent kingly virtues.

## Inclusion of Workers among the Citizenry in a Republic

Aside from the virtue requirement, Patrizi's criteria for citizenship are similar to those found in numerous Italian cities of his time. But compared with Aristotle, his position with respect to social class is less restrictive. Aristotle too insisted on a minimal level of competence for any kind of democratic citizenship, but in his best practical regime of "polity" in the middle books of the *Politics,* and *a fortiori* in the "polis of our prayers" outlined in books 7 and 8, his standard is much higher. In these two constitutions he rejects hereditary citizenship outright and wants to make the possession of moral excellence the unique standard of legitimate citizen status.[29] Political participation is legitimated by the possession of virtue, and this criterion entails that city dwellers who work for a living in agriculture or in the trades must be excluded from citizenship. Why is that?

Aristotle's argument that virtue constitutes the unique entitlement to rule is a teleological one. The state exists to realize the higher potentialities of human nature—the nature of the political animal—so only those capable of exercising political functions can be full members of a polis. The citizen is defined by his function, which in a non-monarchical polity is to rule himself and others. The corollary is that the city cannot be happy and good, it cannot achieve its purpose, unless it is ruled by men who possess the virtues that allow them to rule and be ruled in turn. In order to possess these political virtues, Aristotle believed, a citizen must have leisure and education. For him this meant that *banausoi*—men who worked full time for their livings, farm workers and "mechanics," a class that included simple craftsmen (*technites*) and day workers (*thetes*)—should not be citizens. Citizen status implied the leisure to sit in the assembly and on juries and to debate political issues at length. In other words, the majority of native adult males in most poleis, on Aristotle's principles, should be excluded from citizenship and office. Aristotle thus uses the principle of virtue to discredit a bedrock principle of Athenian democracy, that all adult males descended from native parents deserve to rule themselves.[30]

Patrizi's criteria of citizenship, by comparison, are much closer than Aristotle's to the standards of Italian city-republics in his time.

Furthermore, it seems unfair [*iniquum*]—for the city cannot be constituted of nobles alone when the mass of the people is far more numerous—for the nobles alone to rule and all the rest to be their servants. For agriculture supplies us with bodily nourishment, and mercantile activity with the rest of our necessities. Hence, insofar as civil society could not exist without farmers and businessmen, those persons should not be kept from public offices whose utility to the republic is seen to be necessary. They should be honored with the kind of offices that can easily be conducted by themselves, for instance helping out on citizen committees. Their participation on these may be controlled in such a way that the city not suffer damage, and the less wealthy citizens may not seem to have been entirely forsaken by the great.[31]

Patrizi here appeals to two principles in defending the inclusion of working men in the tasks of self-government. One is sheer numbers: the aristocratic tail cannot wag the popular dog. Patrizi does not express, but may feel, the force of Aristotle's fear that excluding too many citizens, even unworthy ones, would create instability.[32] What he does express is the need for solidarity in a city: the wealthy and powerful should not ignore the people and their needs.[33] The other principle is the closely related one of fairness, understood in organicist terms. Those who contribute to the welfare of the republic in material terms cannot be excluded from participation in its governance. This is a principle for which Aristotle has little sympathy, indeed directly contradicts: "The truth is that not everyone without whom there would not be a city is to be regarded as a citizen."[34] For Aristotle in his ideal constitutions the principle of virtue simply trumps the principle of fairness. Not all who contribute to the wellbeing of the state deserve to rule in the state.

The difference between the two theorists might be explained contextually. Aristotle lived in a slave society, whereas Patrizi lived in the Christian and commercialized society of the Renaissance. Aristotle was a foreign-born philosopher with a sharp critical stance toward corrupt democratic societies; Patrizi was a loyal citizen of Siena living in exile, a former magistrate, a former provincial governor, and a bishop. But Patrizi's commitment to including working men—

farmers and craftsmen—in the citizen body was also a theoretical *prise de position* related to the broader humanist embrace of the organic or biological model of the state, as we have argued several times already in this study. In the same chapter (*Rep.* 1.4), Patrizi enunciates this commitment explicitly: "I am in the number of those who say that the best republic is the one that is commingled of every class of men."[35] He goes on to praise Lycurgus for establishing a mixed constitution for Sparta. Patrizi himself claims to be following Solon's model (the *ratio Solonis*), the aristocratic form of democracy founded by Athens's ancestral legislator in the sixth century BC at the very beginning of Athens's classical period.

> [Solon taught] that it was better to have more rather than fewer [citizens], although he believed that, to be admitted to the many [*multitudo*], they should be the best and provided with virtue and account taken of their deeds in peace and war. So, too, he held that they should take part in choosing magistrates and in many other matters in which the greater councils are going to take part.[36]

Solon here is presented as a proponent of what the Florentines called *governo largo* (as opposed to *governo stretto*)—inclusive rather than restrictive government. But instead of requiring guild membership to participate in government, as the Florentines did, or possessing hereditary political rights like the Sienese and Venetians, Patrizi's Solon applied some sort of merit test for admission to political rights.

Patrizi even defends the idea, also mooted by Aristotle, that collective and non-expert judgment in some circumstances—art criticism, for example—could prove superior to the judgment of individual wise men.

> [Solon] said the same thing occurred in political regimes as in music, painting, and poetry. In those arts not only the learned but sometimes also the unlearned may offer a commendable opinion. And rightly so, for no one can be found, even among teachers of

wisdom, who would reckon that he knows everything. That man comes closer to wisdom who discerns many things and is ignorant of fewer. For some people know something naturally or through experience that can escape the majority. On that account the many jointly will be ignorant of fewer things.[37]

Patrizi is moved by Roman as well as by Greek examples, citing from Livy the damage done to Rome when the plebs seceded from the city in the early republic and left it defenseless. He is less enthusiastic about rule by men from the middle classes than were Aristotle and earlier humanist republican thinkers such as Leonardo Bruni. Aristotle and Bruni believed that men from the middle classes made the best rulers; Patrizi thought that, realistically, the best rulers were likeliest to come from old, established, and noble families.[38] But there were valid arguments for selecting the best of the middle classes for inclusion in the meritocratic order of magistrates: "Men of the middle ranks, surely, who are neither subservient nor run riot with the affluence of the nobility govern with far greater restraint."[39]

Patrizi differed most strikingly from Aristotle, then, in two respects: his inclusion of some full-time workers in the citizen body and his embrace of the *ius sanguinis*. Aristotle in his empirical analysis of the citizen in the first part of *Politics* 3 treats the presence of banausics in citizen bodies as a regrettable consequence of the misguided popular prejudice in favor of birthright citizenship. In his "best practical" Greek polity, presented in the more prescriptive books 4–6, he tries to neutralize the vices of popular government by balancing them with those of oligarchy and champions meritocratic principles in the selection of magistrates. In his unfinished account of an ideal polity in book 7, perhaps intended for a Greek colony in Asia Minor that would have a non-Greek subject population, citizenship is restricted to a well-educated, virtuous elite, entirely closed off from the working classes and to those without leisure for philosophical reflection.

Patrizi, as we have seen, in general places a high value on work and believes the function of leisure is to provide rest and diversion so as to return refreshed to one's proper work. His attitude to leisure reflects that of Cicero, who classified intellectual work in the various disciplines not as pure contemplative or literary leisure—entailing selfish withdrawal from public life—but as a vital service to the state.[40]

Patrizi attacks in particular leisured (*otiosi*) and lazy youths who have no definite employment, a passage, surely, echoing Cicero's criticism of Catiline and his followers; but it also anticipates in this respect Machiavelli's contempt for *oziosi*.[41] Both Patrizi and Machiavelli shared an admiration for working citizens and a contempt for citizens who lived off the work of others, the *scioperati*. This was a deep and long-standing prejudice in Renaissance republics, going back to the popular *comuni* of thirteenth-century Italy. Patrizi's views here also reflect, however, the general humanist championship of an organic society where the level of public virtue is such that everyone serves his fellow citizens as well as himself and his family, and the rulers of the state take the happiness of all citizens as their first duty. In a city-state where all those who work, whether with mind or body, can and should behave with virtue—a virtue shown, above all, by commitment to their fellow citizens—there can be little justification for denying citizenship to any man, so long as he is engaged in an honorable way of life.

In the background here, too, is the tradition of virtue politics that insists on the capacity of all human beings, whatever their class or sex, to acquire virtue.[42] For Patrizi, including freeborn working men in the citizen body does not and should not necessarily compromise the city's commitment to governance by a meritorious elite. But instead of guaranteeing meritocracy by excluding banausics formally from city offices, as Aristotle recommended, Patrizi expects ordinary citizens to have enough public spirit to recognize their own strengths and weaknesses and to defer to those of greater abilities. Older and wiser members of the community in the senate should select popularly approved candidates to fill the most important offices. The implied obverse is that meritocracy cannot be preserved unless the order of magistrates protects the rights of ordinary citizens and sees that they come to no harm.[43]

## Admitting Foreigners to Citizenship

Nevertheless, membership in the citizen body must be limited somehow, and Patrizi's principle of exclusion relies on *ius sanguinis*, hereditary citizenship, the most important criterion used to determine political rights in the Italian city-states of his time. While some humanists took the same negative view of hereditary citizenship taken by Aristotle, Patrizi argued that restricting citizenship for the most part to the children of citizens had a positive moral and prudential purpose.[44] We can best understand what this purpose is by considering Patrizi's position on the question whether citizenship should ever be conferred on non-native persons.

Patrizi expresses strong approval of the idea of merit citizenship for foreigners in the first chapter of book 5. After discussing the criteria for citizenship in the case of native-born citizens, he continues:

> There will also be a second genus of citizen consisting of foreigners who have rendered our city some outstanding service and are well deserving of citizenship on that account. Those who are [in this way] granted citizenship should also be honored with public office, a favor and kindness the Romans often practiced, following the example of their founder Romulus, who in the strength of his great wisdom would consider the same peoples on the same day both enemies and citizens.[45]

Patrizi relies here on at least two key sources. One is Cicero's *Pro Archia,* a speech in which the Roman orator argued that the poet Archias deserved Roman citizenship for his contributions to Latin literature. The second is a famous speech reported in Tacitus's *Annals* (11.24–26), in which the emperor Claudius argued that Gauls should be allowed to become senators of Rome. These sources credited the Romans with strengthening their state by granting citizen rights to certain meritorious non-Romans who had served Rome well. Such grants of citizenship should not be merely honorary; Patrizi thought merit citizens should participate fully in public offices in their adopted city. "It would be inhumane," he wrote, "to label as foreigners men who deserved well of the state and had placed the country under obligations to them."[46]

But Patrizi also thought that his optimal city-state should be careful not to grant citizenship, or even permanent residence, to too many foreigners. Other humanists, especially those associated with the papal court, like Biondo Flavio and George of Trebizond, had praised the cosmopolitan values of the ancient Romans and even credited Rome's imperial success in large measure to its generosity in opening the ranks of its citizen body to talented foreigners from all over its empire.[47] Patrizi took a different view.

In book 6 of *De republica,* on the civil order of his optimal city, he asks in chapter 4 what moral obligations his citizens owe to foreigners and which of them should be given citizenship. In general, he writes, foreigners and immigrants should be welcomed when they come to the city for honorable purposes. Such purposes include trade and commerce: activities that make our citizens more opulent and supply things the city lacks. Of these, however, only a few should be given citizenship, and those few on the basis of merit; merit citizens should be allowed to buy houses in town and agricultural property.

A multitude of resident aliens [*incolae*], however, is dangerous in every populace, for the plebs is rarely unified when composed of a diverse rabble of men. There can scarcely be concord between men of different nations. Nor is it to be believed that foreigners can be constrained by the same zeal and *pietas* in a brief period of time as natives who derive a nursery of patriotic sentiment from their parents and ancestors and suck down love of their fellow citizens with their mother's milk.[48]

New citizens, he says, should be treated the way would-be seducers are treated by honest women: they will naturally mistrust a man who has made love before to another woman and then forgotten her.

Thus nature has impressed upon us a love of country, and we can never altogether forsake her, no matter the interval of time or distance, no matter the insult or injury we may have received. Thus we should act cautiously with newcomers. Aristotle says that all peoples who take in too many foreigners are beset with sedition and discord for long periods.[49]

Patrizi goes on to repeat some of the historical examples cited by Aristotle, then advises against the Roman practice of extending citizen rights indiscriminately to foreigners.

The Romans, however, gave citizenship to many, especially from among peoples they had subdued with virtue and arms. But even though they had subjected the whole world to their empire and were victorious among nations, nevertheless they suffered an outrage against their welcoming attitude when Crixus and Spartacus, breaking open the workhouses, formed a conspiracy with the slaves and rose up against the Roman empire. Thus, if we would advise the city to its advantage, the laws should not permit foreigners to own agricultural property or a house [in the city] except by a special decree of the Senate, a practice we see observed in our time by the best republics of Italy.[50]

For Patrizi, successful political life in a city-state requires a high degree of loyalty, mutual trust, and sympathetic understanding. Citizens need to love and care for each other and to work for each other's benefit. The city cannot achieve a high degree of concord—harmonious cooperation among citizens and their magistrates, the supreme civic value—when it permits into its community too many resident aliens and makes too many new citizens.[51]

## The Virtues of a Good Citizen

Patrizi's defense of nativism reflects the indispensable role in his optimal state played by correct moral attitudes and good character. Those attitudes and that character can best be instilled in the citizenry by the family and by a liberal education, ideally the one that Patrizi himself designed in book 2 of *De republica* to promote citizen virtue. But cultivating the liberal disciplines is only the beginning. In book 5 Patrizi goes further and lays out the special social virtues and patterns of behavior that a good citizen should cultivate once he is of an age to hold office.

These include, first, *urbanitas* of speech and behavior, acquired from a habit of associating freely on a basis of equality with men outside one's household and from frequenting the company of learned men. Urbanity includes wit, cleverness, and humor: an urbane sophistication whose supreme literary expression is the epigram. Patrizi relies silently on Quintilian, who defined *urbanitas* is "a virtue of language concentrated in a brief saying, and adapted to delight men and move them to any kind of emotion." Quintilian quotes Cato as saying, "a man will be urbane who utters many good sayings and replies, and who speaks amusingly and with appropriateness in conversation, social gatherings, and dinners, and also in public meetings: in a word, on every occasion."[52] Urbanity is especially suited to managing social situations, so that you can challenge those with whom you disagree without fractiousness or defer to them without servility. As such it is a virtue closely allied to *astutia*, adroitness, cleverness in managing others. Its opposite is rusticity, the awkwardness of country folk unused to city ways and ignorant of how to act with people unlike themselves. The rustic manners of peasants count as one reason they should be discouraged from participation in urban magistracies.[53]

But more weighty civic virtues are also needed. Patrizi lists over two dozen virtues, including magnanimity, trustworthiness, constancy, patience, temperance, and above all a disposition to treat others justly. All these virtues will lead to concord in the city, but they must first be planted in the souls of citizens. Patrizi invokes from Plato and the Pythagoreans the idea of a harmonious soul that controls its appetites and passions, especially greed and anger, via reason. Blending concepts from Plato's *Phaedo* and the *Republic* as well as the metaphor of the charioteer in the *Phaedrus,* he emphasizes the social utility of possessing concord in the soul. Peace (*tranquillitas*) is the goal of civic life, and it cannot be achieved if citizens do not have peace in their souls. The duty of prudence is to direct all things by the norm of reason: practical reason needs to dictate priorities (*gerendorum ordo*), apportion time, connect the present with the past, and try to divine the future.

The citizen should realize that his own happiness in civil life depends on the cooperation of others and on everyone contributing to the welfare of all, like sailors in a ship. Nothing makes the city more opulent than citizens working together harmoniously to serve it well; and no power and wealth are sufficient to preserve a city when its citizens split into factions. The republic is an immortal animal and the only way it can die is if it kills itself, as the Roman republic did in the time of Cinna, Marius, and Sulla, or Athens did during the Peloponnesian War.

Concord and peace require us to prefer the public good over our private interests, or rather to see that our private interests are best served by putting the republic first. We owe the republic our resources, our counsel, and our help (*opes, consilium, auxilium*). The bare minimum that we owe to others—what is called the "harm principle" in classical liberalism—is not to injure each other either by deeds or by violent words. The good citizen will do no harm to anyone even if it is to his personal benefit and is perfectly legal. To act this way will make him loved by his fellow citizens and dear to his country. As Cicero truly said, it is glorious to be praised, loved, and respected, but to be feared and hated makes one hateful, contemptible, weak, and a failure. A good citizen should be hedged around by the love and goodwill of his fellow citizens, not by wealth and arms. Only the crafty and weak-minded are kept from vices merely by fear of the laws. *Studium virtutis est quod bonum civem facit.* Zeal for virtue is what makes a good citizen. He will obey the laws even when he could get away with breaking them. He will have integrity and always act in the same way whatever his company, whatever the situation. Patrizi cites the "Speech of the Laws" in Plato's *Crito* as a noble expression of this ideal.

The man of civic virtue will seek excellence in many arts, not out of vanity but so as to be useful to his city. He will raise a family, exercise an honest trade, and live a good life without luxury. If a city has the spirit of frugality, it will not need sumptuary legislation: a man who tries to outdo his fellow citizens in lavish expenses will only disturb public order and impoverish his city. (Patrizi worries in particular about lavish funeral monuments.) He will nevertheless be liberal, and at the same time he will be mindful of what he owes others, so he will be careful to return favors. The good citizen will never lie, he will always keep oaths, he will be modest in speech and prefer silence to loquacity. "A man who does not know how to be silent does not know how to speak." He will give good advice in the senate and not try to corrupt public policy for his private benefit. Hypocrisy undermines the trust of civil conversation, and it is the sign of an evil mind to say one thing and think another. Flattery and obsequiousness are equivalent to fraud and deceit. To flatter the people is as bad as flattering a tyrant. Flatterers can make a prince into a tyrant, "but in a free city, in order to court popularity, they often advocate policies that are against the interests of the republic and sometimes turn the foolish multitude insane."[54]

Virtuous citizens will inevitably compete as well as cooperate, but their rivalries should be noble, about the right things. They should want to win the prize for virtue, not for wealth or status. As Patrizi writes in the *De regno:*

> Citizens should compete among themselves in virtue. Those of more distinguished birth should make every effort to prove themselves the more excellent, lest they be bested by those of more obscure origin. Those who are recommended by no merits of their

ancestors ought to rely on their own virtue so that they outstrip the more noble. The more humble their birth, the more they ought to make themselves illustrious through a greater splendor of virtue. It is not a beautiful thing when citizens compete among themselves for riches and property.[55]

What is truly beautiful is competition in virtue. Patrizi goes on to tell a story, drawn from Plutarch's *Life of Aristides* (25.3–6), that compares the Athenian political figures Callias and Aristides. Callias, the richest man in Athens, was hauled before a court and challenged to a kind of contest with Aristides, a poor man known for his just dealings with others. Aristides defended himself, saying that he thought it right to boast more of his poverty than Callias of his enormous wealth. Many men could be found who made the worst use of their riches, few who used them well. He himself had fewer temptations to the greedy misuse of wealth, being the sort of man who bore poverty with equanimity. Poverty should not be regarded as unlovely in any man except in someone who was poor unwillingly or had become poor through prodigality. Patrizi remarks that the greatness of Aristides was made evident to him by the fact that, after a long and distinguished political career, he remained so poor that he could not afford the expenses of his own funeral and the state had to pay for his daughters' dowries.

The moral of the story is that the highest honor in any state should go, not to those who devote their efforts to making themselves rich, but to those who make their country and its citizens prosperous, increase the prestige of their republic, ensure the safety of its people, and bring glory on themselves through their own moral worth.

## Royal Citizenship

The few histories of citizenship that mention the royal variety trace the concept back to the sixteenth century: to the writings of the Protestant Reformers or to Jean Bodin. They universally ignore the substantial earlier treatment of the concept in book 9 of Patrizi's *De regno*. The *De regno* may well have been one of Bodin's sources, although the French theorist's debts to Patrizi and those of later writers such as Samuel Pufendorf have yet to be explored. But Patrizi's conception of royal citizenship deserves study in its own right as an illustration of how virtue politics could be applied to the problem of loyalty and obedience in princely government.

As in the *De republica*, Patrizi in the *De regno* is no mere compiler, but ventures into new territory when discussing the concept of citizenship. He emphasizes the moral duties of a citizen to the state, personified in the king, in this respect anticipating Samuel Pufendorf's *De officio hominis et civis* in the seventeenth century.[56] Patrizi's discussion of citizenship in the *De regno*, however, departs from both the participatory model of the Greeks and the status model of the Romans. Adult males are considered citizens precisely because they are the king's subjects. Unlike in the legal literature of late medieval Italy, where the *cives* of a city-state within a kingdom are a subset of the king's *subditi* or subjects, along with other *incolae* or *habitatores* of his kingdom, in the *De regno* the term "subject" is used interchangeably with "citizen."[57] A scholastic logician might say that the terms have the same extension, covering numerically the same objects. The *De regno* takes no interest in the legal status, rights, or privileges of citizens. As one would expect in a treatise on monarchy, Patrizi also makes no use of Aristotle's participatory definition of citizenship.[58] Instead, book 9—the last book in the work, largely devoted to the subject of good citizenship—presents in effect an extended argument as to why it is to a private person's benefit to obey his sovereign and cultivate the virtues of the good citizen.

One premise of this argument continues a set of proofs that runs throughout the *De regno*: that monarchy is by far the best form of government, provided the ruler is virtuous. (These arguments will be discussed in more detail in Chapter 7.) A citizen should therefore prefer to be ruled by a virtuous king rather than share power with others as a citizen of a republic, notionally on an equal footing with his fellow citizens. Any rational person will prefer to be ruled by a good king if he wants to live in a peaceful, flourishing, and happy state. To achieve this desire, however, requires a proper disposition on his part—the mental attitude and virtues of a good citizen. Kingly virtues cannot be effective without citizen virtues. Chief among these are a spirit of obedience and goodwill toward the sovereign. Patrizi argues for a symbiotic relationship between the virtues of a king and those of a citizen. Both sets of virtues require a humane education.[59] He quotes the Spartan king Theopompus, who, when praised for his generalship, replied that Spartan kings knew how to command because Spartan citizens knew how to obey.[60]

Both forms of excellence are necessary in a state, but they are interdependent. The prince needs to take the lead. "The obedience of the subject ought to follow from the prudence and erudition [*doctrina*] of the prince." The good horseman knows how to keep his horse from spitting out the bit and throwing off the reins; in a similar way, it is the art of a prince to make his people obey willingly and overcome their recalcitrance by showing them favor, goodwill, fairness, and kindliness (*gratia, benevolentia, aequalitas, benignitas*). If he does so, they will become eager of their own free will to obey him. He should treat them like a father and not like a lord, and rule for the common good and not his own (*Reg.* 9.2). He should reward good behavior and punish bad. His citizens should think of his government as a kind of "theater of virtue, in which everyone's virtues are put on show and their vices hooted off the stage." When their own virtues are put on display on the royal stage, citizens will be motivated to act well their part so as to win the king's applause, the man who is the single fountain of all honor in the state.[61]

By the same token, private citizens play a key role in making their prince good. Prudence—self-interest rightly understood, as Tocqueville might say—dictates that they not abuse his fatherly and easygoing nature. In fact, citizens bear great responsibility for keeping their king from lapsing into vice and becoming a tyrant, and this too should motivate them to act always as good citizens. Obedient, law-abiding citizens who are well disposed to a monarch help him to remain a virtuous, paternal ruler, while disobedient, perverse, and abusive citizens will turn their king into a tyrant. When a prince has to worry that wicked citizens are resisting his commands, disloyally plotting behind his back, he will forget clemency and mercy and use force and cruel punishments to secure his own authority. When the king is a kind and generous father, when his people are obedient and show him goodwill, the kingdom will be harmonious and the king's rule moderate and easily borne.

Patrizi tells the story of Alexander the Great who, as a young man educated by Aristotle, had been extremely gentle and mild but was turned into a cruel and bloody prince thanks to wicked actions by his noble followers. According to Patrizi, once Alexander had defeated Darius and acquired for himself the title "the Great," the childless king became excessively generous and thus raised hope in his subordinates that they might become king in his place. There followed all sorts of conspiracies and nocturnal plots, whisperings and defamatory reports, which had the effect of ruining Alexander's character and turning him into a paranoid, intemperate, and sanguinary tyrant. This was "not so much his as their fault, who had abused their status as his companions and his overly generous nature."

Patrizi goes on to give the citizens of a monarchy further advice on how the virtuous citizen will behave so as to secure the felicity of their kingdom. To be a virtuous monarch does not imply that a king is morally perfect, and citizens should teach themselves to be tolerant of a prince's foibles and personal defects. They should not lose a great good because of a small evil (*Reg.* 9.13). They should respect the king's choice of ministers and counselors, recognizing that it is hard and potentially dangerous to serve a king. Patrizi quotes a saying of Lacydes of Cyrene, the founder of the New Academy, to help him make the point. When King Attalus asked him to enter royal service, Lacydes refused, saying that philosophers, like pictures or statues, are best seen from the middle distance rather than at close range.[62] The moral is that citizens should not envy the king's servants or tear them down, but be grateful for their service, "not roll their eyes as they usually do."

They should respect the king's choice even when it falls on a man of low origins. It was a central teaching of virtue politics that the virtuous should be given power whatever their origins, and the truly noble—those ennobled by virtue and education—should be raised up over corrupt and ignorant members of the hereditary aristocracy. In illustration of this point, Patrizi tells the story of Alexander the Great's actions after conquering the Phoenician port city of Sidon. The king of Sidonia had died without leaving an heir, so Alexander interviewed the leading men of the kingdom to decide who among them should take his place. He passed over many high noblemen of royal blood—men of wealth, power, and military skill—to choose a certain Abactonius, a poor man who worked his own garden and, literally, carried his own water. Alexander's choice was a brilliant success, as Abactonius was "a grave man of high integrity, learned in the humanities, outstanding in every virtue, of mature years and impressive in his appearance." He reigned for many years with justice and equity and his line continued for many generations thereafter. Alexander had recognized that "wisdom may dwell beneath a ragged cloak." Citizens too need to learn this lesson and not question the king's judgment when he elevates the worthy from among those of lesser social origins.[63]

Another lesson citizens should learn from history is not to seek political change. They should neglect neither their own family duties nor those of the state; but they should also not take public duties upon themselves without authorization from the prince.

It goes worst of all with those citizens who do not love the ruler of the city [*civitatis rector*] and are not content with the present state of affairs, but are always seeking change. Nor does it go well with [the opposite sort], those who are seduced too much by the delights of family life. They neglect everything else and are considered useless both by the republic and by their friends and connections. They deserve still more odium who take care of the affairs of others while neglecting their own. After people like this are left without resources through their idleness and sloth, they then carp at the men who undertake public duties, or they undertake them when they are not bidden to do so, and either have to be brought within bounds by the prince or are driven out when they flee the prince's commands.[64]

This passage alludes to a distinctive aspect of Patrizi's theory of royal citizenship (an emphasis also echoed in his parallel account of republican citizenship in the *De republica*): that citizens should not give themselves over to idleness and selfish leisure but should work at some useful activity. In wartime they should be ready to defend their country and willingly pay taxes for its defense. In peacetime they should engage in useful arts of peace: "literary study, agriculture, mercantile activity, commerce that brings in crafts [from abroad], and services." This should be real, remunerated work "by which they can modestly support themselves and their families, and in times of need stand by their prince and the republic." The lazy set a bad example and inject the poison of slackness into the body politic. Men who are idle, given to luxury and dissipation, should be cast out of the community of citizens, as unsound limbs are cut off by doctors lest they infect the rest of the body.[65] Citizens should be industrious and cultivate skills; they should be frugal and work hard at an honorable calling. Here Patrizi seems to be finding his inspiration not only in Cicero but in the contemporary norms of Italian civic life. His attitude stands in contrast to the aristocratic outlook of classical antiquity that imputed great value to honorable leisure (*otium*) or to the philosophical ideal of the contemplative life.[66]

From a wider historical perspective, the most remarkable thing about Patrizi's discussion of royal citizenship is what he does *not* discuss. Patrizi is completely uninterested in elaborating principles of citizenship based on legal or theological reasoning. He lays down no criteria for distinguishing royal citizens from non-citizens. He does not discuss any political rights or legal privileges citizens might have, nor does he distinguish ranks among citizens. His citizens are never said to have a right to resist their sovereign when he acts unjustly. They possess no constitutional means to constrain his power. Patrizi also does not discuss issues in feudal law such as conflicting loyalties, the validity of oaths, and inherited obligations of service, or the correct application of *dominium,* a concept that refers, with significant ambiguity, both to the ownership of property and to lordship.[67] Unlike later writers on royal citizenship Patrizi does not list the duties of citizens, whether derived from natural law or Christian revelation. Nor does he attempt to justify the right of a sovereign to command his citizens.

Indeed, Patrizi does not mention any Christian sources at all, even the famous passages in the New Testament, such as Romans 13:1–5, that require Christians passively to obey their rulers without resistance, and that declare earthly rule to be ordained of God and accountable to Him alone. As we shall see in Chapter 7, Patrizi's king does not rule by the grace of God; he performs no priestly roles and has no thaumaturgical powers. The legitimacy of Patrizi's king does not rely in any way on divine authority or right. In fact, Patrizi explicitly criticizes Alexander the Great for attempting to create a ruler-cult around himself; following this false counsel of prudence, he remarks, was one reason Alexander's dynasty did not outlast him. Patrizi instead praises the Persians in the time of King Cyrus (as described in Xenophon's *Cyropaedia*) for resisting the temptation to divinize their ruler. Kings should be venerated and given respect out of a sense of piety but not worshipped or paid divine honors (*Reg.* 9.5). Citizens do not have a duty to obey their king that issues from a specific divine command.

What Patrizi does give us is something like a pure virtue argument for good citizenship. To my knowledge it is unprecedented in the Western tradition, though details may be taken from Plato's *Laws* and the Cyprian orations of Isocrates.[68] His argument is prudential rather than demonstrative. A formal restatement of it might run like this:

1. Kingship is the best form of government.
2. Prudent citizens will prefer to live under the best form of government, and therefore will prefer royal citizenship to republican citizenship.
3. Kingship cannot be prevented from declining into tyranny without a virtuous citizenry.
4. Therefore, citizens should act with the virtues appropriate to royal citizens, principally the virtue of obedience, and cultivate goodwill toward the sovereign. They should teach themselves to have a correct moral attitude to their king: respect him, love him, show him honor and loyalty, tolerate his failings. By so doing they will prevent him from becoming a tyrant.
5. Humanist absolute monarchy has no formal constitutional constraints, but history teaches that if the king acts unjustly, he will lose the support of his citizens and his rule will come to an end. If citizens lack the virtues, they will turn their prince into a tyrant and they will trade the best form of government for the worst.

The argument requires both king and citizen to consider not what is right and wrong but what is better and worse. An exaggerated sense of justice is the enemy of the tolerably good. Citizens therefore need to cultivate practical wisdom, a sense of when evils should be tolerated and goods should be preserved. They need to be conservatives in the best sense: men who understand that good things are easier to destroy than to preserve, and hard to recover once they have been lost.

Hence, the study of history is indispensable to Patrizi's sort of political prudence, for two reasons. Practical wisdom in Aristotle's understanding is by definition a reflection on experience and memory, and history vastly extends the natural memory of individuals. The old are wiser than the young because they are better able to assess the outcome of actions in the present that are similar to those in the past; hence, students of history will acquire a kind of vicarious life experience, making them prudent far beyond their years.

Second, history is important because all practical judgment is comparative, and without an awareness of how well or badly actions can turn out, citizens will fail to appreciate, and feel gratitude for, what they have. They will overestimate the vices of their rulers as well as the shortcomings and injustices of the present moment. They will rush frivolously into ill-considered projects of reformation, lacking the ability to judge their likely consequences. Unlike Plato (but not unlike Aristotle), a prudential approach to politics does not try to adjudicate epistemic claims about the good but assumes that ordinary citizens are able to make sound moral judgments about matters affecting themselves.[69] The goal of political education is not to provide an elite with scientific knowledge of the Good, as in Plato's *Republic.* It is rather to inspire citizens with a love of higher and nobler goods, and above all to encourage them to put the good of the kingdom ahead of their private goods. It teaches them to strive for goals higher than the base and selfish objectives of personal wealth and status that ordinarily absorb human energies.

Patrizi's approach to royal citizenship assumes that the power of a king is a fact and not a claim to be debated by lawyers. This is only to be expected, given his desire to influence the *Regno* of southern Italy ruled by the House of Aragon. The Aragonese dynasty's claim to rule was challenged throughout the quattrocento both internally, by the old barons, and from abroad, by the House of Anjou. It ultimately rested on military conquest and the threat of armed force. From the time Alfonso the Magnanimous established his rule in Naples in 1443, a large proportion of the king's subjects and his foreign rivals regarded his rule as illegitimate.[70] If willing obedience was ever to replace brute force as the basis of royal governance, the king would have to embrace the new avenue to legitimacy opened a century before by humanists in the Petrarchan tradition: the moral legitimacy that comes from virtuous rule. He could do so only with the prudent cooperation of morally excellent citizens who would accept his rule in their own higher interest. Such an approach to legitimacy did not and could not enjoy corroboration from the mystifications of the law or religious tradition. Patrizi taught that it would remain contingent on good character, both that of the king and that of his citizens. Human beings, in other words, would have to create justice and social harmony on their own, by embracing virtue. They needed to understand that their own moral self-cultivation was also a public good.

# SEVEN

# Virtuous Absolutism

## PATRIZI'S DE REGNO

### Rethinking Monarchy: The View from Gaeta

When Patrizi published his treatise *On Kingship and the Education of a King* a dozen years or so after allowing his work on republics to circulate, he knew that some critical eyebrows would be raised, especially in Siena. Those who regarded republics and principalities as conflicting forms of government (*pugnantia*) would charge him with inconstancy, while others would sneer that being an authority on republics did not make you one on kingdoms. So he devoted the first chapter of his new work to explaining why he was justified in writing on both regimes. His strategy was to emphasize that the differences in statecraft between the two kinds of rule were, practically speaking, rather small. He paraphrased a passage from book 4 of Plato's *Republic* to this effect. The Athenian philosopher, he said, classified under the genus *respublica* both rule by one person and rule by a plurality of persons.[1] Patrizi then gave examples of several ancient writers, including Aristotle, Plato, and Xenophon, who wrote on different kinds of regime. He concluded that men's judgments are free (*libera hominum esse iudicia*), and it is no vice to praise one form of government without vituperating another, or, if you like, to praise all legitimate forms of government. The things that matter most in governing others are common to all kinds of regime. It doesn't necessitate a departure from either reason or virtue to give counsel both to a monarch and to a republican regime. Patrizi thus distinguishes himself from state propagandists like Leonardo Bruni and Pier Candido Decembrio, whose panegyrics of their own regime types involved denigrating the regimes of other states.[2]

Patrizi's more historical and prudential approach leads him to dismiss such ideological posturing as superficial. A real political philosopher will take account of the deep-rooted political cultures that shape various peoples, the *varia gentium consuetudo.* Some peoples are used to obeying princes, others are used to obeying magistrates with short terms of office, ruling and being ruled in turn, and civil equality. Each kind of *populus,* being content with its own civil order, spurns that of the other, and even hates it. He repeats from the *De republica* the story of the Cappadocians, who were so accustomed to obeying a prince that they refused republican liberty even when the Romans offered it to them. Some individuals, like Solon, simply could not live under any form of government other than the one they were raised in; others found it possible to transfer their affections, like the great democratic statesman Themistocles, who after being ill-treated by an ungrateful Athens, sought succor from Athens's great enemy Xerxes.[3] A free political culture matters to many of those who enjoy it, but not to everyone. In any case, writes Patrizi, fair critics will allow his choice to write on both regime types. Unfair critics are of no concern, as their names will soon be forgotten.

It is nevertheless reasonable to ask whether Patrizi's own private views on the relative merits of republics and kingdoms shifted after moving to the Kingdom of Naples and taking up residence in Gaeta. Chapter 1 of this book quoted an epigram from the late 1460s where Patrizi ponders what his life might have been like if he could have again the choices available to a young man. His fantasy then was to live under a just king, who would listen to his advice and reward him with a modest property and a magnificent library.[4] During the years just before Patrizi finished the *De regno,* in 1483 / 1484, Siena was convulsed by a popular uprising that led to the execution and exile of many distinguished citizens belonging to the Nove. Patrizi must have known most of these men, as he wrote bitter epitaphs for several of them, taking to task his city, now addressed as "Babylon," for its lawless folly and violence. In a series of ten epigrams (146–155) he bewails the insanity of the common people (*vulgus*), turning on itself, brother on brother. They are utterly ungrateful for their legacy of good government:

> You proscribe the fathers of your country and the holy senate who gave you laws of freedom for so many centuries, who surrounded you with walls and furnished you both with laws and the arts of Pallas, who gathered uncounted wealth and snatched you from so many wars and dangers, causing you to enjoy great benefits instead.[5]

He wakes up at night sweating from a dream in which he had seen Siena's walls falling down, her fortresses crumbling and her churches on fire, the people falling upon senators with bloody knives, polluting holy things. "God grant that these dreams be vain!"[6] The Sienese people have descended to tyrannical acts that even Phalaris or Nero could not have imagined. "You proscribe and condemn innocent men, strip them of their goods, you murder the virtuous. May the gods punish you and send you all to hell!"[7]

Did these events change Patrizi's views on the viability of republican regimes? As we saw in Chapter 1, he had had direct experience of political violence in Siena a quarter century before but had still found himself able to celebrate republican values in the *De republica*. But by the time the *De regno* was finished, he had enjoyed a peaceful life in the Kingdom of Naples for almost two decades. Did his attitude toward kingship change as a result? It was his own patron, Alfonso of Calabria, after all, who had brought an army into Tuscany during the war following the Pazzi conspiracy (1478–1480) and had used his influence in Siena to strengthen the position of the Nove against populist elements in the government; it was Alfonso's departure for the crusade of Otranto in 1481 that had made possible the popular uprising against the "best men," an uprising Patrizi deplored. Alfonso's armed presence had illustrated dramatically one way a good regime could be stabilized: by obtaining support from a friendly king.

Placed just before the series of biting epigrams written against the popular government in Siena is another poem, epigram 144, which offers an indication of how Patrizi's thinking about regimes had been changing.[8] In its title he asks Polymnia, the muse of sacred poetry and eloquence: Which is the more excellent regime, a kingdom or a republic?

Who carries off the doubtful palm, dear Polymnia?
Tell me, shall the duty of rule fall to a king or a people?
"It will belong to a king, for thus the Sisters have decreed,
Thus sings Apollo, and Pallas herself so teaches."
Yet what king may be found to whom all things are known,    5
Who wants to be a disciple of great Jove?
"Well then, tell me who has ever seen a harmonious people?
Power makes patricians lose their minds, the people are foolish.
The former let loose with cruel rods and axes,
The latter flee and return when reconciled with words.    10
If ever the people get hold of the unguarded reins of power
You can give up now, Laestrygones: they will beat you for
    savagery.
*The best republic is that which royal power sustains*
*But which the people administer with moral zeal.*"[9]

The poetic language used here lacks the formality that would allow us to draw firm conclusions, but one plausible hypothesis is the following. Patrizi now believes that the best prospect for peace and harmony in a republic is when a free city comes under the aegis of monarch who allows it to preserve its best republican traditions. This was what happened when the Antigonid kings of Macedon in the Hellenistic period and later the Romans took away Athens's independence but allowed the city to retain its traditional democratic form of government. By so doing they guaranteed the city's internal stability, while denying it an independent foreign policy. The Romans called this *patrocinium* (protection) or *clientela* (clientela). The same principle was observed in the "dyarchies," or provincial governments of Renaissance Italian states; Patrizi himself had served as governor of an unstable dyarchy in Foligno.[10] Popular revolutions in Siena (as in other Tuscan republics) tended to be triggered by major shifts of allegiance in foreign relations, which suggested that permanent submission of a self-governing city to a single monarchy might provide greater stability. Patrizi may well have seen the advantages of accepting the protection of a king for his kind of republic, whose highest goods were peace, moral flourishing, and self-government. A king who incorporated a free city into his realm but did not try to exercise direct control over its internal civic affairs might provide the best compromise between both systems, royal and republican.[11]

The *De regno* also discloses here and there a new skepticism about republican values such as liberty and equality, and a new appreciation of kingship as a vehicle of meritocracy. Toward the end of the treatise (9.2–3), for example, Patrizi writes that, in republics, "nothing is so unequal as the very thing that seems to be equality." The commitment of republics to equality in practice generates nothing but envy and the desire to tear others down. It leads the best citizens to be treated badly by the vicious multitude, like the ancient Athenians who used ostracism to drive out their most deserving citizens. Republican *populi* fear and envy those with practical wisdom, but absolute kings, because of their untrammeled authority, fear and envy no one. They are therefore secure enough to choose outstanding individuals as their ministers.

Patrizi here reverses a traditional argument of republicans against monarchs: that they cannot abide competition from talented men, so they cut down the most outstanding men to guarantee their own primacy. To the contrary, Patrizi writes, it is easier for the virtuous man to acquire a magistracy from a king than from a multitude, since the multitude does not know how to estimate a man's value. The king and his counselors can choose qualified judges, but the multitude is not a good judge of anything. To lead the multitude in a republic requires *ambitio*, seeking its favor before elections, debasing yourself before the unworthy "like a slave offered for sale." Kings make better leaders in wartime because they guarantee unity in the chain of command, and troops perform better when in sight of their king, who can most amply reward their virtue. The Athenians, by contrast, fearing the political influence of great military leaders, entrusted their wars to a board of ten generals, leading to disastrous disagreements about the conduct of wars. Republics are ungrateful to their best citizens; a good king rewards them. Only unified rule under a king can repress factionalism. The monarchical form of rule is authorized by many analogies with natural rule in the cosmos: for example, the way a single rational will rules the body or the way God rules the universe.[12]

More indicators of Patrizi's changing attitude to republics come in the third chapter of book 1, where he produces a new typology of constitutions with significant changes in terminology. In the typology of the *De republica,* Patrizi began by eliminating kingship and tyranny on the grounds that his treatise dealt only with republics.[13] This required him to replace the standard Aristotelian paradigm of six constitutions with a more complex analysis, limited to polyarchic regimes that made use of power-sharing arrangements ("political" regimes, in Aristotle's lexicon). In Patrizi's typology there were six of these, differentiated by their moral character and their treatment of those outside the ruling group. Instead of a binary division of good and bad regimes, following Aristotle's artificial distinction between ruling on behalf of the whole as opposed to the part, Patrizi ranked polyarchic regimes using multiple criteria. The optimal regime in principle was the mixed regime of free and equal citizens ruled by virtuous magistrates, but aristocratic or popular republics might be preferred in view of local traditions or contingencies such as the relative distribution of virtue among social classes.

In the *De regno* Patrizi reverts to what, at first sight, looks like the Aristotelian paradigm of six constitutions as famously laid out in *Politics* 3. This decision was enforced by the focus on kingship of Patrizi's treatise, but there are important differences from Aristotle's typology. Indeed, despite its obvious Aristotelian paternity, Patrizi claims to be deriving his paradigm from the most ancient political thinkers of Greece—namely, the poets, above all Homer. In the *De republica* Patrizi had interpreted Aristotle as a republican theorist, against the weight of scholastic opinion that saw him as a monarchist. By attributing his new constitutional typology to the archaic poets of Greece, he could place in their mouths a new preference that was now, most likely, his own.[14] Kingship, said the old poets, was superior to the other legitimate forms of government, aristocracy and popular rule.

PATRIZI'S TYPOLOGY OF REGIMES (*POLITIAE*)
in the *DE REGNO* (1.3)

| | |
|---|---|
| *Regnum* (kingship) | *Tyrannus* |
| Paternal authority | |
| *Optimorum civium potestas* | *Paucorum potestas* |
| (aristocracy) | (oligarchy) |
| In Greek, ἀριστοκρατία | In Greek, ὀλιγαρχία |
| Marital authority | |
| *Popularis societas* | *Plebeium dominatum* |
| (democracy) | (rule by the plebs) |
| In Greek, ἰσονομία or | |
| δημοκρατία | |
| Fraternal authority | |

The most striking innovation upon Aristotle's terminology here is that democracy is now identified as a good form of constitution. Aristotle had used the word to denote the corrupt rule of the *demos*, and in this negative construction of the term he was followed by most European political thinkers before the late eighteenth century.[15] Patrizi in the *De republica* had used *respublica* for all polyarchic regimes, excluding monarchy and tyranny, and had used Herodotus's term *isonomia* (written in the Greek alphabet) or *respublica popularis* for the legitimate rule of the people. By so doing he had removed the ambiguity of Aristotle's terminology, which equivocates between *politeia* as constitution in general, and *politeia* understood as a legitimate popular regime (sometimes translated into English as "constitutional government").[16]

In the *De regno* Patrizi accepted into Latin the transliterated word *politiae* to describe constitutions (also called *civiles administrationes*) in general. Instead of *respublica,* he now substituted the expression *civilis societas* for all non-monarchical constitutions (thus providing a humanist equivalent for the scholastic term *regimen politicum*), and ἰσονομία (written in the Greek alphabet) or *popularis societas* to specify a good popular regime. However, Patrizi now felt the need to explain that the word δημοκρατία was another term for popular rule and was a species of government "approved by philosophers." Drawing on a distinction made by the ancient jurist Gaius, he explains that the word *plebs* refers to the people, but excludes the class of "patricians and senators," while *populus* refers to the entire citizen body, including the senatorial class. Thus δημοκρατία should mean rule by the people, not by the plebs, and is a good regime, not mob rule. In other words, one criterion that makes a popular regime good is the inclusion of the senatorial class in the regime. The rule of the plebs alone, a *plebeium dominatum* or *plebeia gubernatio,* is always bad. Thus Patrizi, like Polybius, put δημοκρατία in the class of good regimes, but he did not endorse the use of the word *democratia* in Latin. To transliterate the word as a technical term was for him unnecessary and a solecism, since a correct Latin equivalent already existed.

The suspicion arises that Patrizi might have read book 6 of Polybius, the third-century-BC historian who was the first political philosopher to classify democracy as a good form of government. But on balance this seems unlikely. He surely knew books 1–5 of the *Histories,* probably in the translation of Niccolò Perotti, but book 6 was a *rara avis* before the sixteenth century. Patrizi never makes use of book 6's theory of *anacyclosis,* the idea that all polities went through an inevitable cycle of seven constitutions, from despotism to kingship, tyranny, aristocracy, oligarchy, democracy, and ochlocracy (mob rule). Then the cycle begins again with a new despotism, and the cycle starts over again. He never uses Polybius's rare term *ochlocracy*, mob rule.[17] Patrizi's theory of constitutional degeneration is more Aristotelian: tyranny is a corruption of kingship; oligarchy of aristocracy; rule by the plebs of a sound popular government. Patrizi also rejects the fatalism of Polybius's theory of *anacyclosis*. Each of the "good" constitutions has the potential to be permanent if the rulers are virtuous, and each corruption of a good constitution can be restored if the right people return to power. For Patrizi, no change of regime is inevitable; the fate of a regime depends on our own will and moral character.[18] Patrizi's positive understanding of the term *demokratia* is more likely to come from his reading of Greek historians like Herodotus and Thucydides as well as Isocrates, Demosthenes, and the other Attic orators.

The more interesting departure from Aristotle appears in Patrizi's way of patterning modes of political rule after household relationships.[19] Aristotle identified three natural ways of ruling others, all modeled on the household: the royal (rule of one man in the interests of all), the political (power-sharing among citizens), and the despotic (rule of one man in his own interest). These reflected the kinds of rule found in households: kingly rule was like the rule of parent over child, political rule was like that of husband over wife, and despotic rule modeled the subjection of slave to master. This will not do for Patrizi: he is hostile to slavery and wants to exclude it from Christian households. Moreover, to say that political rule, where equal citizens took turns ruling each other, was like a husband's authority over his wife, was an awkward analogy, given that a good husband should never yield his authority over his wife, nor his care for her. Patrizi therefore reshapes Aristotle's modes of rule in line with the Christian values of Renaissance Italian society. A king is like a father, but political rule should be disaggregated into aristocratic and democratic forms. Aristocratic rule, where a class of citizens holds permanent authority over all others, but in a loving way, is like the rule of husband over wife. A democracy, where citizens take turns ruling others but older men are preferred to younger, is more like the relation of brothers in families, which may be rivalrous but is based on mutual love. In good societies, there is no room at all for slavery.[20]

## The Argument for Monarchy

That absolute kingship was more compatible with meritocratic principles than republican government was a lesson Patrizi had learned from Isocrates.[21] In the second book of *De regno,* alluding to and adapting Isocrates's *Nicocles,* Patrizi praises kings as permanent magistrates who can master the arts of rule over the course of their lives, unlike constitutional magistrates who only have short terms of office to learn their jobs.[22] Republican magistrates carry their private interests with them into office, knowing they will soon return to private life, and this makes it harder for them to serve the common good and practice the virtues of justice and equity. It is wrong for the worse to rule the better, and a wise king will always be better placed than any republican government to make merit the basis of his administration. He can command the resources of the best counselors. Private men are fortunate when they have a few friends of learning and distinction, but the king's munificence will attract the very best scholars and philosophers into his service, even from beyond the borders of his kingdom.[23]

Patrizi's principal argument for monarchy, however, has to do with the relative stability of regimes. It is a matter of constant emphasis in the *De regno* that there should be only one supreme decision-maker in the kingdom, a single individual with final *arbitrium.* The unitary power of decision became known as sovereignty in the early modern period (*summum ius* or *summum imperium*), and theorists like Hobbes alleged that it could reside in collectivities such as the English Parliament or the Venetian Senate as well as in monarchs. In modern times, sovereignty or supreme authority is often said to reside in the people.[24] This abstract way of thinking about sovereignty did not exist within Patrizi's horizon—it required a strong view of the autonomy of law, to which humanist virtue politics was inherently hostile.[25] For Patrizi, as for his Greek sources, the problem to be solved by monarchy was the problem of political discord, leading in extreme cases to factionalism, sedition, tyranny, or civil war. There were ways to keep discord in check in constitutional republics, many of them discovered by the ancients, but to expect more than a transient unity of wills in a state governed by the few or by the many was an expectation that, for Patrizi (at least in *De regno*), could find no support in the pages of history. Those who favored republican government were willing to tolerate a degree of discord for the sake of freedom, and a virtuous citizenry was a safeguard against injustice, the main source of discord. But there would eventually be a reckoning. The study of history revealed that republics didn't last, and monarchy was nature's remedy for the inherent instability of polyarchic rule.

In the *De republica*, Patrizi had taken the view that a republic might continue indefinitely so long as its leaders continued to offer examples of virtue to the people and acted to suppress vice. In *De regno* Patrizi presents all republican or polyarchic government (a *societas civilis* in his new terminology) as inherently unstable. The positions taken in the two treatises, to be sure, are not necessarily incompatible. Within a shorter time scale, the tendency to monarchy may be countered by the underlying disposition some peoples have for freedom. As we have seen, different peoples have different customs, and the *varia gentium consuetudo*, the varied political cultures of nations, may last for centuries. This was why ancient Athens kept reverting to a popular regime throughout its classical period, despite attempts by tyrants and oligarchs to dominate it.[26] Intelligent and virtuous statesmen learned ways to prolong the life of popular government. But eventually Athens, too, in the wider sweep of history, had to yield to the Macedonian monarchy and the empire of the Romans.

The same pattern played out in Roman history, Patrizi's prime example of the inevitability of monarchy. At the end of book 1, after some general considerations showing why any decision made on behalf of many persons requires some unity in the process of political decision-making, Patrizi gives us a potted history of the Roman republic.[27] It began when the corrupt tyranny of Tarquin the Proud made the name of king (*rex*) hateful to the Romans. The Romans tried to rule themselves constitutionally, sharing power between classes; but whenever a crisis arose, they took refuge in the monarchical principle in the form of a dictator.[28] Patrizi admits that Rome conquered the world in its consular period, but in the typical fashion of monarchical theorists he ascribes its success to innate Roman *virtus* rather than to its free constitution.[29] But eventually, in the first century BC, from the time of Sulla onward, the competition for glory among warlords, each aiming at tyranny, led to continual sedition and bloody factional strife, and the people yearned for peace. Finally, it was recognized that peace could come only from the rule of a single person. Even Cicero, "whose continual care was for the best condition of the state [*respublica*]," recognized that it would be better to be "well tyrannized" than to continue in a state of violence and disorder.[30] Thus Roman history showed the necessity of Caesar's unification of power for the continuance of the Roman state. Caesar was killed by misguided tyrannicides, but the imperial system established by Augustus brought Rome lasting peace, concord, prosperity, and good government. If so great and virtuous a people as the Romans had chosen monarchy after a long and unhappy experience with power-sharing arrangements, that could only add to the weight of history's verdict.[31]

Questions of geographical as well as chronological scale also pointed to the need for monarchy.[32] Absent universal empire, a single city did not have the resources to defend itself against predatory neighbors, some of whom could draw on the resources of an entire region. Successful warfare required manpower, and manpower, territory. This showed that a polity, in order adequately to defend itself, must be a territorial state encompassing the resources of many cities and lands. No doubt Patrizi was holding before his mind's eye the territorial kingdom of southern Italy in which he resided and to whose future king his book was dedicated.[33]

In this case, too, there is a shift in emphasis, rather than a contradiction, between the *De republica* and the *De regno*. The earlier treatise had argued that a small professional army could protect a city-state against most enemies, subdue brigandage in its outlying lands, and bring its people peace of mind. In the *De regno* Patrizi claims it is a matter of common sense and experience—perhaps thinking of Alfonso's recent campaigns in Sienese territory—that a city-state cannot resist a determined royal army.

Patrizi here is taking for granted the view of his Greek sources that democracies and oligarchies were governments typical of city-states, and that these by nature were relatively small in scale. Single cities can provide the necessities of life for their peoples, but in the long run they are not big enough to defend themselves from all potential predators or to conduct offensive wars for empire. Only kings can do that. A king, by Aristotle's definition, is not a king unless he is sufficient unto himself, and so excels everyone in all goods that he does not require anyone's help to provide for the welfare of his people. A territorial monarchy, with its greater resources and manpower, will always provide a more effective defense of its region than a city-state, and city-states will lose in any military competition with kingdoms. In the *De republica* Patrizi advised the optimal city-state to aim at self-sufficiency; in the *De regno* he is now of the opinion that only kingdoms can be self-sufficient when it comes to war.

To escape their weakness, city-states sometimes banded themselves together into confederations. Patrizi argues, however, that a confederation of city-states—his example is the Lycian Confederation of twenty-three cities, which later was cited by James Madison as a model for American federalism—will be subject to the same conflicting interests and factions that beset any polyarchic form of government.[34] They are like parts of a body lacking any single mind or heart. Thus, a confederation of city-states will also be unstable and short-lived, and may end in the tyranny of a single city over the rest.[35] Such a confederation of city-states would be better ruled and better defended if they submitted to the rule of a king

who can rule justly and maintain vigilance on behalf of all of them. At that point all of them will be allowed to act in accor-

dance with virtue, the end which seems to be, as it were, the goal
of human society and of an allied multitude of human beings.
For they are uniting not only to remain alive—mere life is something they have in common with the mute animals—but that they
may live well and blessedly, and that it may be permitted them to
find happiness.[36]

Living according to virtue is the end of human society; an "allied
multitude of human beings" must here refer to the kingdom. Life in
a city is mere life; life in a territorial kingdom is the good life. This
claim represents a dramatic revision of Aristotle's famous principle
(*Politics* 1.2, 1253a) that prepolitical life is mere life, whereas a life
lived in a polis enables the good life, the life in which all the highest
capacities of human nature can achieve perfection.

Patrizi's final argument for the superiority of kingship is that, historically, the office of king was of divine origin.[37] God gave primitive
men reason, which led them to form societies for mutual aid and to
develop their powers of speech. But corruption set in; everyone began
to seek their own good and neglect common needs. This prepolitical
society realized that the only way to settle disputes and guide the
human flock toward common purposes was to have a single shepherd.
They chose the man who was most outstanding in virtue, speech,
and courage to rule them and provided him with the resources to
support his life and office so that he would not have to engage in
illiberal, banausic tasks. This figure came to be regarded as divine,
and authorities such as Homer recognized that no one could rule
well without divine power. Patrizi shows that it was common among
ancient peoples from all three continents (no distinction is made
among Greeks, Romans, Persians, and Egyptians in this respect) to
regard their kings as having divine sanction and divine qualities. In
illustration of this point he relates a story from Herodotus describing how Darius had been acclaimed king of the Persians thanks
to a divine sign.[38] (Patrizi's version leaves out the scheming of Darius's
groom to manage the auspices.) In short, Patrizi rejects Aristotle's
developmental model of political institutions, which saw kingship

as primitive and democracy as the inevitable future, given the multiplication of large, wealthy urban centers in Greece.[39] Patrizi shows
the same reverence for the holy, uncorrupted, primeval government
of humanity that his contemporary, Marsilio Ficino, showed toward
the primordial sources of religious knowledge, the ancient theology.[40]
And the primeval government of humankind, founded under divine
auspices, was royal government. Patrizi's argument for the divine
character of the kingly office is thus exquisitely historical; it is a
humanist argument distinct from juristic claims that the rule of individual emperors or kings was rightful owing to divine approval.

## Can Monarchical Power Be Virtuous?

Even if Patrizi's readers were willing to grant that monarchy was of
divine origin and in principle the best form of government—and that
its advantages were worth the sacrifice of city-state liberties—the
question still remained whether the good prince, without whom there
could be no true monarchy, could ever really exist. Patrizi in the
De republica had expressed doubt that princes with absolute power
could be kept from corruption, and throughout the fifteenth century
humanists who favored republics made the same argument. It was
made in its most extreme form by Poggio Bracciolini, a long-serving
papal secretary, later the Chancellor of Florence, who maintained
in his well-known treatise De infelicitate principum (On the misfor-
tune of princes) that political life was inevitably dominated by
men who sought power for the sake of wealth and status. Men of
virtue who wandered into the courts of princes would be ignored,
mocked, or corrupted. If by some fate a good man were allowed
to ride the wild horse of the state, he would soon be thrown from
the saddle. Literature and philosophy had no effect on power-
seeking men, and only privati, private individuals, who did not seek
to control or despoil others could hope to achieve virtue and true
felicity.[41]

Patrizi was well aware of Poggio's arguments, although, in keeping
with his uniform practice of not identifying modern authors, Poggio's

name is never mentioned.[42] By the nature of his response, nested among several chapters of *De regno* book 1, the Sienese humanist seemed to understand that Poggio's critique involved at least four interrelated issues. One was whether political power was compatible with virtue.[43] A second was whether nature had so constituted human society that the retention of political power inevitably required immoral behavior—an assumption Machiavelli would later take as his starting point in *The Prince*. Or in other words, is virtue reliably rewarded and vice punished in the political sphere, in this life? This was a question Plato had answered in the negative at the end of the *Republic*. The third issue was whether the tendency of all human things to undergo moral decay—a tendency of both individuals and states—could be arrested or even reversed by human wisdom and virtue. The fourth was the issue, fundamental to ancient political thought, whether it was possible to produce in political leaders, via education, the degree of virtue and wisdom necessary for benign rule, or at least to instill in them sufficient appreciation for political wisdom that they would be willing to take good advice from the wise.

Patrizi confronts the first issue in a chapter entitled "Whence the pattern of fine living that leads to felicity, and whether a king or a private individual is more fitted to fine and blessed living."[44] He repeats the gist of Poggio's argument, laying out a contrast, taken from Isocrates's *Ad Nicoclem,* between how a private citizen's way of life prevents his doing evil, and how the life of a prince encourages bad morals and tyrannical conduct.[45] Worse, the depraved prince corrupts his own people, who will follow his example more than his words. Few have access to princes and kings, and those few are afraid to speak freely. Instead they flatter and corrupt and make impossible the task of offering a prince wise counsel. But, says Patrizi, there is an answer to such pessimism:

Generally led by such reasoning, the best men think private life is safer and more excellent and far more suited to fine and blessed living than the life of a man who exercises power from his earliest age amid such delights. Such a dilemma, thus simply enunciated, has a solution that is not hard to find. For who has so feeble and dark an understanding that he doesn't prefer to be Socrates and not [the corrupt oligarch] Critias, or Brutus rather than Tarquin, the man who brought down the Roman monarchy by his tyrannical abuse of it? Come, compare Brutus to Numa Pompilius: who then is not going to prefer the royal dignity to private life?[46]

Patrizi then goes on to describe how Numa (in an account derived from Livy and Plutarch) was a wise and holy private citizen called reluctantly to the kingship by the Roman people, who then distinguished himself in that role above all others. By his justice and moderation he led the fierce Roman clans to gentleness and a love of peace; he promoted agriculture rather than the pursuit of riches; he gave the Romans religious fear and taught them to honor the gods.

What the example of Numa Pompilius shows for Patrizi is the possibility of nullifying the noxious moral effects of absolute power by holding out to the prince the greatest reward of all. It is the reward that comes to all who rule justly: "the honor and glory and imperishable fame peoples will bestow upon them in every age." The virtue of a just king gives him a kind of divinity, a power that is more than human to bring blessings to his people. Unjust kings and tyrants, by contrast, are despised in life because of the foul cruelty and injustice they inflict on others; after death they are held in perpetual execration by the living and suffer terrible torments among those below. The tyrant is a repulsive figure, a lump of foul deformity. In between is the virtue of the *privatus*, real but limited in its effects and in the honor it confers. A noble thirst for true fame and glory, a love of the superexcellent goodness that benefits mankind, can be stimulated by a humanistic culture of praise and blame. But Patrizi insists that the thirst for goodness and felicity is rooted in human nature, even if the desire for good must be cultivated and directed:

Nature begets human beings who are neither good nor bad; it renders them fit for goodness yet inclined to what is bad. Reason persuades us of this, intelligence reveals it, experience teaches it, and Aristotle, basing himself on proofs of the Old Academy, bears witness to it. Nature herself has sown in us little celestial fires and seeds, as it were, of the virtues, which if allowed to grow quickly bring forth the finest fruit, as Plato says. From these are born a pattern of acting well and living with rectitude, which represses all turbulent affections, orders the human faculties and strengthens habits of virtue. These paths lead us to felicity, desirable for its own sake, supplying us with everything we need, lacking nothing.[47]

It is harder for a prince to be a good man because of his environment, but the rewards for success are correspondingly greater, and in the end far overbalance the sacrifice of his lower impulses. Nor will divine help be lacking to princes who rule with justice.

In the course of the *De regno* Patrizi offers the king two broad incentives to follow the path of virtue. One is the honor argument outlined above: to be a good king is necessary to his honor, and the felicity or infelicity of his kingdom is an expression of his own moral status, just as the royal regalia are the signs of his legitimate title. Goodness, to be effective, has to be real, not a lie or a fiction. Lies will out, as Cambyses taught his son Cyrus, and their discovery will make a king distrusted by his friends and his people. The worst sort of lie is self-deception. Honor cannot live without truth; the harmony in the king's soul can be maintained only by truthfulness and integrity. It is a sign of tyranny when a king's court is filled with lies, calumny, dissimulation, flattery, adulation, and other forms of dishonesty. The worst dishonesty is when the king inflates his own achievements by boasting, which makes him unlovable. "He who loves himself too much will have no rivals."[48]

It is precisely the dishonesty involved that would foreclose for Patrizi any consideration of the kind of benign tyranny presented in Xenophon's *Hiero*, where a tyrant pretends to act like a good prince in order to achieve his own selfish goals.[49] A prince who has been brought up to care about things like honor and nobility would never, should never, want to do what is right for his people only for his private benefit, concealing his true motive. Cunning is not the mark of a king, as Isocrates taught in the *Agesilaus*.[50] To rule well for no other reason than to cling to power would be a base and shameful idea. It would mean enslaving oneself to a passion. Such an idea could appeal only to someone of corrupt, tyrannical character, and would violate the true prince's sense of self-worth. It would take away the dream of virtue politics, the return to the Golden Age, when power and virtue and wisdom dwelt in the same house, a condominium whose stupendous effects still echoed in human memory as the glory that was Greece and the grandeur that was Rome.

But can a king be confident that his virtue will be rewarded in the sphere of politics, and that his kingdom will be made happy by his virtue? That question leads to the other argument or incentive for royal virtue: the nature argument. Was Nature herself ordered in such a way that acting with virtue would lead to felicity in this life, for states as well as for individuals? To answer in the affirmative, Patrizi understood that he had to clarify the relationship of nature to the human will, which he attempts in *Reg.* 1.12, a chapter on fortune, fate, and chance. It cannot be said that Patrizi's flood of quotations, many from Homer, rises the to level of argument, but his intent is clear enough. He admits that ruling well is the hardest human act, and no amount of virtue will help the king retain popular favor without good fortune. "Not only for barbarians does trust depend on outcomes." Yet Fortune is the companion of the virtues and should not be called a goddess. She is not omnipotent over human affairs. Fortune is merely a sudden and unexpected event whose effects, when malign, can be counteracted by good counsel and the king's perseverance in virtue. Patrizi prefers to think of Fortune in the manner of the Greek tragedians, as Nemesis striking down the proud. Homer was wise to speak of Fate rather than Fortune in his poems. He understood it, "not straying from true theological reason," as the divine will. Even so, fate was not inexorable in the Stoic manner; fate did not govern all human affairs with an iron will. It merely struck down rash mortals who blamed the gods for their adversities, when in fact the true cause lay in their own folly and cowardice. The point of Patrizi's discussion is evidently to carve out a space for human virtue in the world of nature and to combat Poggian fatalism about politics and power. The courts of princes are not impregnable fortresses of corruption that can never be conquered by royal virtue, guided by prudent counselors. *Principes,* political leaders, were not evil of necessity. As Patrizi's contemporary Marsilio Ficino wrote against astrological fatalism, "the wise man shall dominate the stars."

That the cultivation of human excellence could alter what might seem to be fixed patterns of decadence was a bedrock principle of Renaissance culture. But whether it was truly possible to achieve moral goodness through education, culture, and strenuous effort was ultimately a theological question. On this question Patrizi (and one sometimes has to remind oneself that he was a bishop) was a confirmed Pelagian, or perhaps semi-Pelagian. But he was careful to avoid a formal charge of Pelagianism—the claim that a Christian can earn his own salvation through moral effort—by confining his optimism about human nature to the present life. Salvation in the next life is not at issue, but only what humanity can do for itself in this life. Patrizi is careful to specify that he is only discussing *human* felicity, the *finis humanarum rerum,* the end of human affairs in this life, or what Aristotle in the *Ethics* called the specifically human good (*to anthropinon agathon*).[51] The human good is not wealth or status, nor is it eternal felicity beyond the grave—the sphere of religion—but rather virtuous activity in accordance with reason, here and now. We depend on God for salvation in the next life but on our own capacities in this one. To be sure, our capacity for virtue comes from God operating in nature, is helped invisibly by God, and is potentially godlike, returning us to God, but it depends on our free will.[52] Without some commitment to a doctrine of free will, there can be no possibility of virtue politics, of political reform enabled by the explosive power of human virtue.

## The Ideal Prince

It was noted in Chapter 3 that Patrizi was not an "exclusivist" in the sense of regarding one type of regime as the only legitimate form of government. As a follower of Petrarchan humanism he does not espouse the view of any one philosophical school, and the same principle applies to politics. Lack of dogmatism is a general feature of his political writings, which are measured in their judgments and avoid the extremes of panegyric when describing historical figures. Characteristically, he rejects Pliny the Younger's statement that one can only praise the *optimus princeps,* and that it would be arrogant to teach him.[53] Patrizi responds drily that he regards adulation as a far more serious crime than teaching the doctrine of Greek philosophers. He notes that certain men have been criticized for praising qualities that they should have kept silent about, "either because [those qualities] seemed to be too trivial or because they were entirely repellent, almost shameful, and unworthy of a free man."[54]

In any case he is remarkably independent in his judgments about the great monarchs of history. Unlike Petrarch, for instance, his judgment on Augustus (whom he prefers to call Octavian) is frigid. Octavian was a cruel man in his youth, and for Patrizi there was no quality so repellent, impious, and inhuman as cruelty. Octavian's later good fortune veiled the wickedness of his youth, and once he had achieved supreme power he became milder and more forgiving.[55] He is thus, with Vespasian, a rare example of a prince whose character improved after achieving power. Octavian and his more depraved successors were accepted, not because they were virtuous, but only because Rome was sick of civil war. Clearly influenced by his reading of Plutarch's biography, Patrizi found Julius Caesar, on the other hand, worthy of the greatest admiration and imitation: he was the model general, the best in history; he was a man of extraordinary civil virtues; he was an elegant writer and speaker; he was never cruel or tyrannical. Yet he had vices as well, such as prodigality and an unhealthy thirst for popular favor (*ambitio*), and he can never be excused for attacking his own country. His ruling passion (which he shared with Pompey) was for personal domination, a goal to which he subordinated the *salus et dignitas* of the Roman people.[56]

In general, Patrizi's position is that he is describing in his treatise what an ideal prince would do and be. The ideal prince is a mental picture, which he compares to a Platonic Idea, like the ideal image of Jove in the mind of Phidias the sculptor. Patrizi does not expect that any one historical figure or state will provide an adequate model in every respect. That is why an ideal is necessary. Plato did not look to the Athenians or Spartans for a model, but he "devised a new and imaginary perfect city, gazing at that idea I spoke of just now, a city that never was and never shall be."[57] Patrizi's method was expressly modeled on Cicero's *Orator*, an attempt to paint a portrait of the ideal orator, which itself looked to Plato's theory of ideas for inspiration. Patrizi even quotes the following passage from the work:

> "But I am firmly of the opinion that nothing of any kind is so beautiful as not to be excelled in beauty by that of which it is a copy, as a portrait is a copy of a face. This ideal cannot be perceived by any human sense; we grasp it only in mind and thought." *And when a little bit later he talks about Phidias, he says,* "In the mind of that artist there dwelt a surpassing vision of beauty; at this he gazed and, all intent on this, he guided his artist's hand to produce [the god's] likeness."[58]

Quintilian's ideal orator in the *Institutio oratoria*—a work Patrizi had condensed for the use of his pupils during his years in exile—was no doubt in the background.[59] In *The Prince* Machiavelli famously ridiculed previous political theorists who "have imagined republics and principalities that have never been seen or known to exist." The image of an ideal prince for Machiavelli was no more than a blind alley and a distraction from the *verità effettuale*—from what really works for those who want power: "How men live is so different from how they should live, that a ruler who does not do what is generally done, but persists in doing what ought to be done, will undermine his power rather than maintain it."[60] But the paradox of Patrizi's idealism is that it enables a kind of realism, albeit one foreign to Machiavelli's understanding of political reality. The Sienese humanist's mental vision of an ideal prince gave him an independent moral standard to decide which actions of great figures in the past were worthy of emulation and which were not. Using his standard, it was possible for Patrizi to consider figures like Julius Caesar and Augustus and even Xenophon's idealized Cyrus, not as plaster saints of politics, as other humanists too often did, but as real human beings who had accomplished great deeds despite their faults and mistakes and mixed motives. Machiavelli's realism, and the whole basis of his political science, started from the assumption that human beings could be counted on to do the self-interested action, and that appeals to moral principle or religion were either manipulative or delusional. Readers may decide for themselves whether a "realism" that excludes the influence of ideals on rulers and ruled alike provides an adequate account of "how men live."

## The Sources of Royal Legitimacy

Patrizi's idealistic realism can be illustrated by his position on the sources of royal legitimacy. Here he differs somewhat from the standard humanist view, which privileges moral legitimacy above all other kinds. At the beginning of book 2 of *De regno* Patrizi defines the king as "a good man to whom it has been given to rule states [*civitates*] and peoples because of his high birth or through lawful election."[61] He tells us this definition has been modeled on Cato's definition of the orator as *vir bonus dicendi peritus,* a good man skilled in speaking, and Strabo's understanding of what a true poet was, "as though without virtue an orator has no power to speak nor a poet to sing."[62] The force of his definition, in context, is to emphasize that the legitimacy of a king depends not just on ancestry or some constitutional process but on virtue as well. Nevertheless, the need for just title is recognized. Legitimacy comes from two sources, both of them necessary but neither in themselves sufficient: lawfulness and virtue.

Patrizi thus holds a humanist mirror to the criteria of Trecento jurists like Bartolus and Baldus, who had insisted that legitimacy rested both on lawful title and on the lawful exercise of power.[63] Patrizi, however, has detached the question of just title from the web of legal fictions that for late medieval jurists sustained the authority of the Holy Roman Empire and the Papacy. He lived, after all, in an age when European kings were abandoning their traditional deference to pope and empire. So it is no surprise that for Patrizi, just title has nothing to do with the Holy Roman Emperor or the pope. It is either simply inherited like a piece of property or proceeds from an unspecified process of lawful election, which might be anything from popular acclamation to the vote of an aristocratic counsel. Or it might conceivably be a cross between the two, such as the process, used in the glorious days of the Antonines, by which virtuous emperors chose their own successors via adoption.

In place of the jurists' conception of just exercise, usually presented as adherence to law or respect for customary rights and due process, Patrizi substitutes the idea of virtue as a source of legitimacy. An act that proceeds from a just king is *eo ipso* just, and his acting justly is a condition of his legitimacy. Though piety is one of the royal virtues, and the overall guidance of Divine Providence is acknowledged, neither the king's legitimacy nor that of his dynasty is said to come from divine right. Nor is appeal made to the Platonic idea that true legitimacy comes from a scientific (in the sense of certain) knowledge of the Good.[64] Indeed, Patrizi explicitly excludes the study of theoretical subjects from the prince's education, advocating instead a literary curriculum meant to educe moral and civil virtues and also to provide the practical knowledge (like geography or calculation) needed for effective princely rule.[65]

Patrizi gives an example of how to adjust the claims of virtue and lawfulness in his discussion of how the royal succession should be managed.[66] Unlike some humanists (such as Petrarch), he does not declare a preference for elective monarchy. Yet the principle of virtue should not be entirely overlooked. When the king who has lived a life of virtue is old, he should give due thought for who shall succeed him, like a wise father who plans for the good of his family after his death. He will have already seen to it that his sons have had a good education and training in rulership, "so that they may be similar to him not only in appearance but in virtue and mores, that the king may seem not to have departed, but to have been made younger." Nature and custom demand that the oldest son inherit the title.[67] But it might happen that the eldest son is a wicked man, like Commodus, son of the philosopher-emperor Marcus Aurelius. In such a case the king should think of what Alexander the Great said when asked on his deathbed who should succeed him. "The worthiest," was his reply. Heeding this advice, the king should follow the example of great kings who chose someone other than their eldest sons to succeed them. It might also happen that the king's sons are too young to rule, and in this case the king should weigh the example of Phraates, king of the Parthians, who chose his brother Mithridates to occupy the throne after him. A king might also consider the example of the Egyptians, who (according to Diodorus Siculus) in questions of succession treated bastard children on an equal basis with legitimate children, even ones born of slave mothers, thus enlarging the pool of available children from whom to choose the best. (It may be remembered that Ferrante of Aragon, who ruled the Kingdom of Naples in Patrizi's time, was the son of King Alfonso by his mistress.)[68] In short, the stability provided by the usual rules of legitimate succession should be the first consideration, but the king should be prepared to set the rules aside when the virtuous exercise of power might be compromised. "When a successor will be unworthy, the interests of the kingdom must be consulted rather than the order of nature or one's descendants."

Laws of succession such as the Salic Law in France were regarded as fundamental law in most European monarchies, beyond the power of kings alone to abrogate or modify. Patrizi's counsel to set aside the rules of succession when necessary on prudential grounds in the interests of virtuous government thus spotlights another characteristic of his theory of kingship: its thoroughgoing absolutism. Patrizi's king is constrained by no constitutional apparatus of parliaments or noble councils or independent courts. Whom he takes as his counselors is entirely a matter of his own choice. No one has a right to be consulted, and there is no one except God to whom he is accountable.

The standard list of monarchical analogies reinforce the point. Patrizi's teacher Filelfo made such a list in the preface to his translation of Xenophon's *Cyropaedia*. The need for a principle of unity in government is shown, Filelfo wrote, in theology by God's rule over the cosmos, in mathematics by the generation of all number from unity, in physics by the prime mover, in psychology by the hierarchies of soul over body and mind over the other faculties of soul, in ethics by the queenship of Wisdom over the other virtues, in natural philosophy by the V-formations of flying geese, in economics by the authority of the paterfamilias over his family; in ecclesiology by the rule of Christ over his disciples and St. Peter over the Church.[69] For a king's subjects to call him to account over his actions would thus be as unjust and unthinkable as the universe calling its Creator to account, or the body seeking a check on the power the soul, or the passions and appetites exercising a veto over reason.

Given the force of such analogies, Patrizi, like his teacher Filelfo, held it right that "the king contain all magistracies in himself alone, and be considered a law over all persons." This does not make a king's rule unlawful or arbitrary. In *De regno* 8.6 Patrizi discusses "how the king should act with respect to the laws." He should obey good laws himself in order to set an example; it is wrong and undermines justice for him to command others to obey a law he does not himself observe. He should not be like a parent who says, "Do what I say, not what I do." The king has power over all law, but that does not mean he should rush into projects of reform. In fact, he should respect the historical achievements of Roman law. Isocrates taught that the king should repair the laws and make new ones for the sake of concord, for the utility of citizens and to stop incessant lawsuits. This was sound advice in Isocrates's time, says Patrizi, when the world was not so full of vice and greed. But in later times, as morals declined, laws improved. "Good laws arise from bad morals, as the proverb has it."[70] Eventually the Romans brought civil law to a high state of perfection. "As they conquered the world with their arms, they emended it with their laws, with courts of justice, and with good moral conduct." There is no need to look to the Greeks when it comes to law, since "everybody agrees" that the books of our Roman jurisconsults excel those of the Greek philosophers in gravity, eloquence, learning, and wisdom.

This means that kings need not labor to write new laws or reform old ones. They can simply enforce Roman law, the law of the *populus Romanus,* victor over all nations and all kings, which prescribed a legal code of civil wisdom for the whole world, the faithful image of divine and natural law. Roman law is universal and eternal, Patrizi holds—a view that contrasts markedly with his view of communal law (or *ius proprium*) in *De republica.*[71] It has lasted far longer than the laws of Lycurgus, which endured a mere five hundred years. Kings are advised simply to endorse this law and direct their energies to choosing the most virtuous and learned men to interpret it.[72] Magistrates should be required to observe the laws themselves; there should be equality under law; and in every courthouse there should be inscribed the words *Whoever decides what is right for another should adopt the same standard of right for himself.*[73] Innovation is sometimes needed when new crimes and outrages are invented by human wickedness, but in general, Patrizi advises his king, the application of the law is best left to lawyers and jurists.

What should limit a king's power, for Patrizi, is not law or constitutional devices but his own prudent consideration of what functions he can best perform and the practical limits imposed by his own knowledge and energies. For this reason he should leave sacred things and ceremonies to the high priests (*pontifices*) and civil legislation to the senators. He should, however, exercise oversight of the senators to make sure that when they pass laws, they are not opening more avenues to litigation than to justice. They should be discouraged from unnecessary innovation. In matters of law, kings are urged to exercise moral discernment, so that the rigor of the law is not confused with cruelty, or prudence with low cunning. Royal justice should always be high-minded and noble in its ends, marked with mildness, humanity, and clemency.

In general, because the king has no constitutional or legal limits to what he can command, his need for prudence is all the greater. Outcomes always have to be considered, though Patrizi is far from embracing the consequentialist calculus of Machiavelli, in which principles of action are retrofitted to the desired outcomes. Princely prudence should feed on the nourishing bread of history rather than the thin gruel of lawyers. History will teach him which authorities are to be followed, or not followed, in given circumstances. For example, Greek authorities like the legislator Lycurgus and the philosopher Plato prescribed property-sharing schemes for their polities, and even Aristotle taught that healthy cities should take steps to reduce income inequality. Patrizi now in the *De regno* thinks such measures are inadvisable, not only because Roman law protects property, but because history shows they are impractical.

Here again we find a marked revision in Patrizi's views. In the *De republica* he embraced schemes to prevent great inequalities of wealth on the grounds that economic inequality led to the oppression of the poor by the rich and therefore to political instability.[74] In the *De regno* he holds that a just monarch will be able to prevent factionalism and oppression through his unique, overwhelming power. The causes of inequality among households can be traced to the injustice of powerful persons, and a good prince will prevent such injustices from occurring in the first place. Hence, in the *De regno* Patrizi advises against formal measures that would equalize either property or honor. They will run up against natural differences in ability, and so force the legislator who tries to preserve those measures into acts of manifest injustice or malfeasance. In an argument reminiscent of the libertarian theorist Robert Nozick, Patrizi writes that forced redistributions of property have been tried in the past but have always failed because in a short time the industrious became rich again and the lazy poor; at that point it will seem grossly unfair to divide patrimonies a second time, "making the lazy equal to the industrious."[75] The same principle is applied to *isotimia*, the Greek name for the practice of equalizing rewards.[76] A regime where all must have prizes cannot well be preserved by law, since "one person will seem suitable through virtue and industry for any and all offices, while another has to be entirely excluded from all public duties because of carelessness and disgraceful behavior." For a ruler to defy the principle of merit results inevitably in injustice and incompetence.[77]

## How the King May Become Virtuous

God helps those who help themselves, and to help himself the king has to know how to acquire the virtues and to quell the passions that will lead him astray, blackening his honor. That is the task that occupies the bulk of *De regno*. Like all Renaissance literati, Patrizi takes it for granted that the humanities provide an indispensable training in virtue, and he lays out in the second half of book 2 a specialized curriculum for a king. It is stipulated, as in all humanist educational writings, that his teachers must be moral men, and his companions decent and respectable boys. His studies must of course begin with grammar; that is, learning Latin. Grammar is the artisan of speech, the interpreter of poets and historians, the commander and chariot of all other disciplines. He should then go on to read poetry, especially Homer among the Greeks and Vergil from among "our Latin authors." "This heroic reading (*heroica lectio*) is of great use to princes and kings, whose minds will be lifted up by the sublimity of heroic song." It will show them what nobility and virtue look like in action and will motivate them to imitate such actions. He should then go on to the other poets, lyric poets like the Spartan Tyrtaeus, the tragedians Euripides and Sophocles, and the comic poets, too—but selectively, heeding Plato's warnings in the *Republic* to read only poets with a strong moral message. (Patrizi provides an example of selective reading himself by failing here to mention Plato's doubts about the moral value of Homer.)

After the poets he should read history, the school of princely prudence, which Cicero called "the witness of time, the mistress of life, the life of memory, and the messenger of truth." All kings and political leaders and commanders of troops need to read history, for countless examples of virtue are found in its pages. Patrizi introduces an elaborate *paragone* showing why the reading of history is more inspiring for a king than having sculpted images of great men in his palace.

> For if the likenesses of bodies and images made with the hand of artisans are wont to stimulate the minds of youth to the imitation of those whose images they are, how much more will histories and the records of great deeds accomplish this, works that express the mind and soul, not the lineaments of the body and the outward appearance of its form? History excels the image by as much as the mind excels the body.[78]

The "virtuous environment" is useful, but history more useful still. (Patrizi, whose interest in the plastic arts appears frequently in the *De regno*, helpfully recommends that sculptors represent heroes with togas or armor like the Romans, rather than naked like the Greeks, because the hero's mind is more fully expressed in the Roman way.)[79]

The reading of history should be followed by study of the orators, particularly Demosthenes and Cicero, who excelled all others, not just in eloquence but *in morali sapientia*. And as Cicero himself taught us, eloquence is vain without the study of moral philosophy. At the end of book 2 Patrizi describes the virtues of royal speech and recommends that the prince memorize maxims and sayings that are salted with prudence. Socratic irony, however, verges on untruth and should be employed by private men only. The prince should never speak anything but the naked truth.[80]

Beyond these core disciplines of the *studia humanitatis*—Latin grammar, poetry, history, oratory, moral philosophy—there are other liberal disciplines worth studying for their practical utility, such as arithmetic, geometry, music, and astronomy—the traditional *qua-drivium*. These too are surveyed in book 2. Geography and travel literature deserve the king's particular study, Patrizi writes at the end of book 3, and it is recommended that he scrutinize painted pictures of the world, *mappamundi*, especially those parts of it where wars might be conducted. But he should avoid purely theoretical and abstruse studies, instead concentrating on more evident matters that treat of civil life and fine conduct, and studies that perfect his powers of reasoning and speech.[81] These should all be appropriately adapted to royal education. For example, he should seek models, not for the virtue of liberality, which befits private men, but instead for magnificence, which befits a king. Patrizi also provides in book 3 a list of appropriate and useful outdoor activities, such as riding, hunting, fowling, swimming, and playing ball. The study of agriculture is useful for every citizen and paterfamilias, but also for princes, as the examples of Cyrus and Lysander show.

Nevertheless, the best way to spend his leisure is to frequent the company of learned men. This is what Isocrates recommended in the *Ad Nicoclem*, Patrizi notes. The king should avoid flatterers and yes-men (*assentatores*), and also men whose only recommendation is their lively talk and easy ways. He should prefer accomplished, well-mannered men whose writings and counsel will help him perform great deeds. His religious advisers should recommend true religion and worship of the divine and not retail superstitions, foolish fears, and old wives' tales. Quoting Terence, he advises the king to consort with men from whose company he will not depart without having learned something of value.

Above all (and this advice fills the first half of book 4) he should avoid those who speak evil and untrue things, flatterers, adulators, dealers in gossip and calumny. The fable of Ulysses and the Sirens warns us allegorically against the effects of such bad company. Informers (*delatores*) too should be regarded with extreme suspicion, but not entirely disregarded. The ones who lie should be punished by law, but sometimes such men give information that is true and salutary: Caesar should have paid attention to the tale-bearers who warned him about the plan to murder him in the Senate.

In general the king should cultivate an atmosphere where people feel able to criticize him in his presence. *Regium esse bene agere et male audire:* the royal way is to listen to the evil but to do what is good. Following the pattern of Xenophon's Cyrus, he should do his best to become aware of how he is regarded by his people. This will create in him a healthy incentive to avoid even the smallest shameful acts, lest they be bruited about and grow in the telling. It is natural for those who spread evil rumors about kings to be regarded as lovers of the multitude, zealous in the cause of liberty and virtue, while those who praise the king will inevitably be considered flatterers or persons corrupted by promises of profit. But princes need to know what the people are saying about them, to prevent self-deception and self-indulgence. Patrizi recommends the practice of the painter Apelles, who according to Pliny hid himself behind his paintings so he could hear what people said about them.[82] If he does all this, he will solve the "problem of counsel" and not open his ears to evil advice while closing it to the admonitions of the wise and the good.

The rest of book 4 and all of book 5 are consumed with a description of the passions the king should expel or control, such as anger or laziness, and the damage they can do to him and to his kingdom. The order and list of passions track to some extent their treatment in Giles of Rome's *De regimine principum,* revealing the presence of that work on Patrizi's desk.[83] Books 6–8 treat the kingly virtues, beginning with fairness and equanimity, the monarchical analogue to the republican virtue of equality. Plutarch's *Moralia* make a frequent appearance in these pages.[84] Fortitude and justice are singled out for extended treatment.

## Civil Friendship, Humanity, and Piety

Five whole chapters of book 8 are devoted to a treatment of friendship, drawing on Cicero, Plato, Epicurus, and examples culled from Roman history. Still, as ever, they disclose a distinctively Patrizian approach.[85] In general, friendship is a "virtue of reciprocal benevolence, reconciling through a kind of equitable conduct (*aequitas*) persons who are similar in their mores and virtue." Patrizi then explains how friendship enhances consensus: "Friendship ought above all to offer this: that there be a great consensus among friends about desires, loyalties [or goals: *studia*], and opinions. The finest bond of friendship is thought to be wanting and not wanting the same things." There are three kinds of friendship: natural, civil and guest-friendship (*amicitia hospitalis*). Natural friendship is further subdivided into three kinds: *pietas* (devotion to God, rulers, parents, and elders); *indulgentia* (love and kindness toward children, descendants, and those under our authority); and *necessitas* (relations with equals, like relatives and friends). Patrizi attributes the first distinction to Plato, relying silently on a brief passage in Diogenes Laertius's *Life of Plato,* but, as in the case of his discussion of the "Massilian constitution," Patrizi's treatment alters and elaborates extensively on his source.[86]

Given the overall aim of his work, Patrizi's focus quickly turns to civil (or social) friendship. In a civil context friendship is more rightly described as *societas,* a society established for the sake of common utility. If voluntary friendships knit society together, society itself will be in a sense consensual, not coerced and artificial, and bound together by goodwill, not simply law. Patrizi heaps praise on civil friendship, described as a kind of mutual goodwill that is greatly reinforced from rubbing shoulders with one's fellow citizens inside city walls, and sharing a climate, diet, mores, religion, education, physical environment, and speech. The common experience of living in the same society generates a "marvelous kind of charity among citizens." "If anyone should remove this common friendship from the life of human beings, he would seem to have ripped the sun out of the cosmos, as Cicero says."[87]

Patrizi says that this kind of friendship "among many" is more appropriate to a king than the philosophers' preferred form of friendship among the virtuous few. Because of his supereminent position a king can never enjoy the intimacy of a philosophical friendship.

Epicurus, remarkably, is here cited as an authority against Aristotle's privileging of friendship based on virtue. (Aristotle's name is again suppressed.) What is possible for a king is civil friendship. Patrizi compares the royal kind of civil friendship to a paterfamilias's affections, which should extend to the whole family and not just to his wife. Civil friendship requires that the king reward merit with honor, but the needs of the poor should also be included in his benevolence. "In distribution, although he should benefit everyone, he should preserve distinctions of merit [*meritorum discrimen*] and give more honor and responsibility to the more excellent, but more of what is needful to the poor. For the recompense of virtue is honor, of neediness, gain." The prince can support civil friendship by allowing the poor to earn their living and by preventing magistrates from oppressing the people. In other words his role is to prevent too-great inequalities of power from creating oppression and dependency in his kingdom, a concern that is continuous with Patrizi's prescriptions for a healthy republican society. The king should also enforce equality in his personal circle. A king can have friends but not favorites. Through civil friendship he will be able to rely on the goodwill of his citizens; through civil friendship he need fear neither foreign nor domestic arms.

◆        ◆        ◆

Two virtues deserve special comment: *humanitas* and *pietas*.[88]

Among the more interesting inventions of Patrizi's *De regno* is the political function he creates for the virtue of *humanitas*, which challenges Aristotelian, patristic, and scholastic models of sociability. Aristotle in the *Politics* distinguishes good from corrupt constitutions by the criterion of whether the rulers serve their own interests or the common good. He does not, however, explain the affective basis for a commitment to the common good on the part of an individual ruler or ruling part (*politeuma*), beyond a general disposition to the virtues, meaning above all a disposition to be law-abiding (general justice) and a disposition not to take more than one's share and give to everyone what they deserve (particular justice). In the broader context of Aristotelian ethics these dispositions might seem to be mainly actuated by a desire for personal distinction and therefore a form of self-love. In books 8 and 9 of the *Ethics,* however, Aristotle finds the affective basis for political society in his concept of friendship. The kind of true friendship needed to combat the centripetal interests of individuals in politics is built on respect for the virtue of others. Respect for others' virtues, in turn, builds trust—*fides* in Bruni's translation—which allows people to be confident that political leaders will act in other-regarding ways and not be secretly scheming for their own selfish interests.

Christian interpreters since Lactantius saw such moderate dispositions as inadequate to the new Christian age of grace. Pagan virtue could never overcome selfishness and pride; for patristic authorities such as Lactantius, mere friendship among the political elite would never overcome the illimitable egoism of fallen man. But the new Christian age of grace had released an overflowing of the heart with love toward God and one's fellow humans, a new exchange of mercy and forgiveness among all peoples. This could serve to unify political society as never before. The Christian community from apostolic times had believed that obedience to the commands of Christ was cemented by love for Him and for each other.[89] Augustine accordingly revised Cicero's definition of a republic as a people united by law and utility by making love the basis of political association. The people of a state for the great patristic authority was "an assemblage of many reasonable beings united through a harmonious sharing of the things it loves."[90] Augustinian thinkers of the later Middle Ages argued that this Christian love provided a far more effective social glue than pagan virtue and political friendship. The scholastics of the High Middle Ages, interpreting earlier Christian authorities, sometimes appealed to a notion of "love for the common good," explained in terms of Augustine's *ordo caritatis,* an ordered benevolence toward others rooted in the Christian's love of God.[91]

Patrizi, by contrast, in his chapter on *humanitas* finds the affective basis of good rulership (and good citizenship) in natural sympathy between human beings. We possess an *affectio generalis* that inclines the mind to love and benevolence toward mankind (*ad dilectionem benevolentiamque hominum*), even those we do not know. By nature, we rejoice with others in their successes and feel for them in their sufferings. Hence, we offer help to the indigent, water to the thirsty, directions to travelers, all out of a sense of right action toward our own kind instilled in us by natural affection. It is the part of a free or noble man (*ingenuus*) to love his fellow human beings, while narrow and perverse wits hate their own kind. Such men the Greeks called *misanthropes,* identified by their lack of humor. The idea bears some resemblance to David Hume's conceptions of natural sympathy and benevolence in the *Treatise of Human Nature* (1739–1740)— conceptions informed, like Patrizi's, by Cicero's views of the social virtues. In this respect, Patrizi's conception is closer to the moderns than to the medievals.

When strengthened by habit and reflection, Patrizi writes, the general disposition to benevolence becomes the virtue of *humanitas.*[92] This is a virtue we must acquire if we are to be truly human. The man who obeys nature can never harm another man, and indeed nature instructs us that human beings must go further than merely avoiding harming others: we must always do good to each other. When we refrain from harming others, we thereby excel those below us in the order of nature, the animals, and when we benefit each other, we imitate God, the giver of all gifts. The essence of being human is to be humane. Thus, the noble or free man will help others freely; if he demands repayment, he is a mere usurer.[93]

But how is *humanitas* acquired, this virtue so basic to a good polity? Humanity (or *philanthropia,* "an elegant word used by the Greeks") is greatly aided by education ("or *paideia*") and that is why the ancients used *humanitas* to mean instruction and training in the "good arts," and called the liberal disciplines *humaniores literae,* the literature that makes one more fully human.[94] This was appropriate, because this kind of education belongs only to the human species, with its higher rationality and moral sense. And that most pleasant form of companionship, the companionship of humane letters, though appropriate to all mortals, is so in the highest degree to kings and princes, who are the supreme givers of benefits to their citizens, the most godlike of human beings. For Patrizi, the education of *principes* in the humanities is thus a fundamental condition of good government.

The virtue of piety, *pietas,* also had an important role to play as a social glue. Piety for the ancients was the virtue that enabled us to do what is right in relation to our family, friends, benefactors, country, and God. It supported the general virtue of justice because it disposed us to render to each his due. "Piety underlies the virtue of justice," wrote Cicero. "It is that by which we reverence our parents and other elders, our relatives, friends, benefactors, and likewise our country, which is another parent, and likewise God." Piety is based in gratitude for the unearned benefits we have received from our parents, our country, and God. This reverence and regard is closely allied with notions of love, charity, devotion, holiness. Without piety, a civil society will collapse. As Cicero wrote, "In all probability, the disappearance of piety toward the gods will entail the disappearance of loyalty and social union among men as well, and of justice itself, the queen of all the virtues."[95]

Quoting Cicero as well as Aristotle and the Platonists, Patrizi holds that civil piety is rooted in the law of God and in a lively awareness of our obligations to Him and to others. Christian sovereigns are rightly instructed by the supernatural truths of revelation. But all nations, whatever their religion, share a natural knowledge of the divine and therefore a pious recognition of what they owe the gods. That is why the ancients, who often were models of piety, can be our guides in the present, even though they lacked the light of revelation. Their example teaches us, above all, how to be fully human, how we can best develop our potential for human excellence, or virtue. In their exemplary piety we learn that someone who does not know God lacks fundamental self-knowledge and cannot follow the Delphic maxim to "know thyself," γνῶθι σεαυτόν. Without piety, which Lactantius defined as *notio Dei,* intimacy with God, we lose our humanity, sinking to the level of mere animals.

In Patrizi's understanding, *pietas* is thus closely linked to *humanitas*. God's goodness to us requires us to be humane to others, and this fundamental humanity and care for our neighbors is what binds communities together and builds trust and a sense of common purpose. All states, whatever religion they embrace, have an obligation to punish the impious and sacrilegious. Kings and princes who preserve piety and religion will have greater rewards in the afterlife, far above those accorded to private citizens, however pious, as we learn from Cicero's *Dream of Scipio*. Impious rulers, such as Cambyses, king of the Persians—who attacked the fine temples of the Egyptians, filled with beautiful paintings and statuary, with more ferocity than he fought the Egyptian armies—would receive at last the full weight of God's punishment.[96] This remark might easily be read as a veiled condemnation of the fourth-century Christians who destroyed so much of ancient art. The fuller humanity that flows from *pietas* is why we respect the buildings and works of art created by the devotion of our fellow human beings, even if we do not share their religious beliefs. Christian faith perfects the natural virtue of piety, but it should lead us to acknowledge and honor the beauty, truth, and goodness we find in other ages and other cultures, not deride or destroy them.[97]

## Monarchy, Dyarchy, and the Future of Republics

Patrizi, like other humanist political thinkers of the Renaissance, never addressed in any sustained way the problem of how to combine the advantages of monarchy with those of a free city-state. For him, as for Machiavelli, monarchy and republican self-government remained irreconcilable forms of political life. Each had its advantages and disadvantages; each would remain estranged from the other thanks to diverse and deeply rooted political cultures. Free Italian city-states had in practice long made use of *signori* on a temporary and legally limited basis, as both Greek and Roman republics had before them, but the danger that such arrangements would lead to tyranny was obvious.[98] Great power brokers such as the

Medici had exercised informal signories in republican states, but their legitimacy was always in question. In imitation of the Venetian dogeship, Florentines in the early sixteenth century had tried to strengthen the office of Standard-Bearer of Justice (*Gonfaloniere della Giustizia*), hitherto a ceremonial head of state, and make it into a quasi-monarchical magistrate elected for life, but the experiment had not proven successful. Most humanist political thinkers continued to hold that any attempts to introduce monarchical institutions into a free state on a permanent basis was a kind of contradiction in terms. As Machiavelli was later to write, "No firm government can be devised if it is not a true princedom or a true republic, because all the constitutions between these two are defective."[99]

Patrizi learned this lesson, for his part, from reading ancient history and ancient political writers. He was aware from Greek history that simple regimes like democracy and oligarchy were likely to be unstable internally. Externally, in terms of their foreign relations, a city-state culture like ancient Greece was also perilous territory for those who desired to dwell in peace. When Athens and Sparta and their allies acted with common purpose, they could beat even the overwhelming armies and the limitless wealth of the Great King of Persia, as Herodotus's history showed. But absent that external threat they would destroy each other through internecine wars, as Patrizi knew from Thucydides, Plutarch's *Lives,* and Xenophon's *Hellenica.* Eventually they became so weak that they were easily subdued by the Macedonian monarchy. The Roman republic, though a more balanced regime, had also proved unstable in the end. After the Roman people had defeated its last great foreign rivals in the second century BC, it fell apart morally and was torn to pieces by rival warlords. It was only able to bring a halt its to unending civil wars by allowing Augustus to establish a strong monarchy, retaining only the hollow shell of its republican institutions.

Patrizi was also aware that ancient political theorists such as Plato (in the *Laws*), Aristotle, and Isocrates had proposed fixes for instability and moral corruption in non-monarchical states. Isocrates wanted to reinvigorate the Areopagus, restoring the constitutional role it had

had in the sixth century BC; that ancient court, he hoped, might act as a stabilizing force, protecting the interests of the community's middle and upper classes against radical democrats. It is unknown, however, whether Patrizi knew the *Areopagiticus,* the speech in which Isocrates had made this proposal. It also remains a matter of doubt whether he had devoted close study to Plato's *Laws.* He certainly knew Aristotle's proposals to blend and balance oligarchic and democratic institutions, though he rejected them. He also rejected Aristotle's more ideal proposal to create a pure aristocracy.[100]

Patrizi presented his own proposal—for republics to be governed by a distinct meritocratic order based broadly in the citizen community— as, potentially, a permanent solution to the problem of instability. A successful outcome would depend above all on the ability of the city's rulers to maintain virtue in themselves and in the citizen body. But it would seem that in the latter part of his long life he changed his mind about the prospects for stabilizing modern republics. His mature view considered another solution, quite different from the one adopted by Machiavelli.

The conclusions Machiavelli drew from his reading of the ancients reaffirmed for him the possibility of founding a well-governed and powerful republic. Ancient history taught him that a republican regime like Florence could flourish by reviving, insofar as it was possible, the customs and institutions that had made the middle republic of Rome the mistress of the Mediterranean.[101] In taking this position he was inspired principally by Livy and Dionysius of Halicarnassus; but he also pondered the analysis of the Roman constitution made by Polybius in book 6 of his *History,* a text Patrizi probably did not know. During the 1520s Machiavelli tried to convince the Medici (in another of his numerous failed prophecies) that they would never be able to establish a monarchy in Florence because the city's political culture and socio-economic structure made it inalterably republican.[102] Only by improving its republican institutions could it hope to stand up to predatory monarchs such as the kings of France and Spain.

In his *Discourse on the Remodeling of the Government of Florence* (1520), directed to Pope Leo X, the head of the Medici clan,

Machiavelli proposed a way to transition Florence from what was effectively a Medici monarchy to a new republican constitution. His well-ordered republic would leave behind the failures of Florentine governments of the past, replacing party regimes with a government that served the common good. Like Patrizi he proposed to create a permanent governing class of older men, a body of sixty-five magistrates who would hold office for life and take turns governing the republic under the leadership of a Gonfaloniere. Like Florence's traditional Signoria these men would represent the guild community and all three classes in the state—the nobles, the middle classes, and the poor—but membership would be weighted in favor of the two upper classes. A council of Two Hundred, similarly weighted toward the upper classes, would approve legislation. The popular voice would be heard in a much larger council, to meet in the vast Sala del Cinquecento, built under Savonarola and adjacent to the Palazzo Vecchio. This body would oversee the sortition of magistrates. It would not, however, acquire any powers until the current Medici rulers were deceased. As long as they were alive, the Medici would retain a disguised monarchical power that would enable them to protect themselves and their supporters. After their death, their monarchy would wither away and Florence would emerge as a "true republic" for the first time in its history. The Medici would have in effect become figures like the great ancient legislators, Lycurgus and Solon, who fashioned aristocratic and democratic republics respectively and who relinquished their temporary monarchical power once the new constitution they had created was in place.[103]

Patrizi in his late period, it would seem, arrived at a different solution to the problem of instability and moral corruption in republics, one that looked back to Hellenistic monarchies and to Italian regional governments of the more recent past. It was rooted in a more realistic assessment than Machiavelli's of a city-state's potential to defend itself militarily.[104] As we have seen in this chapter, Patrizi came to believe, and with good reason, that in an age of mobile artillery and ever-larger armies, a city-state could never resist for very long the power of a determined royal army, backed by the manpower and financial resources of a regional state. The invasion of Italy in 1494 by Charles VIII of France, with an army larger than the entire adult male population of Florence, demonstrated his foresight. Even a federation of city-states, lacking centralized leadership, would be at a serious disadvantage in any war with a powerful prince. Hence, a republic would have the best chance of achieving felicity if it subordinated itself to virtuous royal power. With strong defenses and a well-trained, professional citizen army a single city-state could make attacks upon itself costly, but full and lasting security would not be possible without foreign support.

The solution toward which Patrizi gestured in the poem quoted earlier was thus to institute a kind of dyarchy, combining the stability and decisive leadership offered by monarchical rule with royal guarantees of local liberties. Stability and protection would compensate cities for the loss of full autonomy. This solution may seem to moderns like a betrayal of the ideal of liberty, a cowardly capitulation to *force majeure,* but it may not have appeared in that light to Patrizi or to many of his contemporaries. Dyarchy, after all, though it has fallen out of favor in our age of nation-states, has been a common political arrangement since ancient times. It may even become a live option once more if China and (less probably) India and the European Union should evolve into what are now termed "civilization states": a mode of government in which a central monarchical power provides military guarantees and a final court of appeal but tolerates under its aegis a plurality of political systems and diverse political cultures.[105]

In the West the system first emerged with the Hellenistic monarchies of the third century, where individual Greek city-states and whole city-state federations submitted to the hegemony of more powerful monarchs like the Antigonids of Macedon or the Ptolemaic kings of Egypt. Under the Romans the Greek city-states became provinces of the empire, lightly governed by Roman promagistrates, but they retained a measure of self-government. Both the medieval Islamic caliphate and the Holy Roman Empire aspired to be civilizational states, bound together by a common religion and legal tradition and a single, supereminent ruler. The British Empire instituted a more formal dyarchic system in India after the 1919 Government of India Act, in which the British retained ultimate power to tax, police, and administer the higher courts, but provincial governments were allowed a large measure of self-government under locally elected ministers. More recently, a form of dyarchy has been proposed for China by modern political Confucians: the central government would allow democracy at a local level, while provincial and national levels of government would be dominated by a meritocratically selected elite.[106]

Patrizi's model looked back to the Hellenistic-Roman dyarchies but was also, surely, informed by contemporary dyarchies established between former city-states and regional states like Florence, the Duchy of Milan, and the Republic of Venice. In these cities a measure of self-government was devolved upon local citizen bodies but foreign relations were controlled by the central government. Patrizian dyarchy would, in other words, be a more successful version of the dyarchy Patrizi himself administered as papal governor of Foligno, corroborated by good institutions and virtue in both the prince and the citizen body. From the point of view of citizens in the city-state, autonomy in foreign affairs and full authority to tax themselves would be sacrificed for the sake of greater internal stability and a more effective defense against predatory foreign states. The success of the arrangement would ultimately depend on the practical wisdom and good sense of the central power in its dealings with localities. A wise king in the humanist mold would be moderate in his rule and allow a considerable measure of personal liberty while encouraging virtue. Patrizi, of course, does not think of protecting citizen liberties by guarantees of individual rights, an invention of the seventeenth century, but he expects that the king's virtues of prudence, moderation, and humanity, when combined with his cultivation of civil friendship, will provide a measure of protection against arbitrary or tyrannical behavior on the part of the sovereign.[107]

Neither Patrizi's nor Machiavelli's solutions to the threats of factionalism and tyranny were, in the end, the ones European states adopted in the early modern period. Small republics in Switzerland, the Netherlands, and the United States in its revolutionary era would organize themselves into confederacies for mutual aid. The path to the large modern nation-state would lie through late medieval constitutionalism, a web of customary, legal, and institutional constraints on monarchical power. These would be imposed by the representative institutions that emerged from medieval parlements. Control of financial resources, in an era of continual and ruinously expensive war, ultimately allowed the people to challenge the sovereignty of monarchs.[108] It was this evolution that made it possible to combine monarchical styles of government, involving hierarchies of command and centralized bureaucracies, with republican ideals of self-government, individual liberty, and the supremacy of law over the magistrate's or the ruler's will. Thus, only in the modern world have republican principles been embraced by large, regional states and embodied in their constitutions, written and unwritten. Before the seventeeth-century British Commonwealth and the American federal republic, it was taken for granted that "it is natural for a republic to have only a small territory."[109]

Nonetheless, modern Western political cultures are infused, to some extent, with the political prudence of Patrizi and Machiavelli. Machiavelli's late constitutionalism foreshadowed what happened in Great Britain when royal power withered away and the king was compelled to take advice from his estates in Parliament, an institution designed to favor the nobility and wealthy commoners. Moreover, as Gabriele Pedullà has recently argued, Machiavelli pioneered a major aspect of political modernity—namely, the ability of modern states to accommodate a plurality of conflicting opinions and interests within their political systems, while not at the same time undermining the sovereign's legitimacy. Modern states do this by accepting as legitimate a moderate degree of non-violent conflict between parties or classes of persons in a state and by adopting (in principle) procedural neutrality toward them. The contrast is with premodern states—like late medieval Florence and Siena—that were ideologically holistic and valued concord, stability, and tranquillity above all other political goods. Such states saw all political conflict as illegitimate. They resorted to tumult and violence only with extreme reluctance, as a last resort, in order to restore lost political virtues. Pedullà traces this positive evaluation of "conflictualism" back to Machiavelli's appreciation in the *Discourses* for the paradoxical ability of Roman republican "tumults" to generate political solidarity in waging war.[110]

Later republican thinkers such as the American Founding Fathers discovered solutions to republican weakness and instability by proposing dyarchic arrangements not wholly dissimilar to those endorsed by Patrizi. This is not, of course, a matter of direct influence. So far as one can tell, neither of Patrizi's major political works had crossed the Atlantic before the early republican period, and in any case Patrizi did not formally propose dyarchic government in any of his published works.[111] Yet James Madison, Alexander Hamilton, James Wilson, and John Jay, the chief architects of the U.S. Constitution of 1787, also faced the question of how to reconcile republican liberty with stability and regional defense. Like Patrizi they rejected the idea of a loose federation of small republics in favor of a dyarchic system, worried that confederations tend to lack a common will, given their diversity of interests, or that they risk coming under the tyranny of their most powerful member. They too believed (risibly, from a contemporary point of view) that national government might lead to greater moderation in governance.[112] It was the Founders' aim to create a strong national government ("federal" in the confusing American usage), a "great republic," and to abolish the weak and failing confederation created during the Revolution among thirteen former colonies, lately independent republics, each with its own political culture and diverse in their economic bases and confessional loyalties.

The dyarchy the Founders created assigned to the federal government an explicitly limited set of enumerated powers, including taxation, regulation of trade, laws of citizenship, diplomacy, declarations of war, and higher courts of appeal. Other powers were meant to be left in the hands of the former thirteen colonies, including local courts, magistrates and legislatures, the police power, schools, most social and economic regulations, and establishments of religion. The Founders tried, moreover, to create a strong executive power—a term-limited elective monarchy—that would be dominant in wartime and in foreign relations. It would provide "energy in the executive," but would be kept from tyrannical behavior in domestic politics by legislative and judicial checks. This form of two-level or dyarchic government was enshrined above all in the Senate, where each state, irrespective of size or population, was assigned an equal number of senators, with a view to protecting the individual interests of the thirteen republics within the federal system.

The dyarchic system devised by the American Founders was obviously far more complex and sophisticated than anything imagined by Patrizi or, for that matter, any other political writer of the early modern period. Since the time of its creation the smaller state-republics have gradually ceded their constitutional spheres of independence to the federal government—an outcome students of Roman imperial history might have predicted.[113] The old republican dyarchy has transitioned into a modern nation-state. But whatever its successes or failures, the wide-ranging debates over the US Constitution show that the generation of the American founders—Federalists, Anti-Federalists, and the large body of educated citizens they addressed—were full participants in the traditions of political reflection founded during the Italian Renaissance.[114] Both Patrizi's historico-prudential method (filtered mainly through Grotius, Pufendorf, and Montesquieu) and Machiavelli's quasi-scientific political realism were very much in evidence during the early American republic.[115] But of the two forms of political reflection, it may well be the Patrizian form that was the more influential.

# Conclusion

## Patrizi and Modern Politics

In the modern imagination, the Italian Renaissance has the reputation of being an age that produced extraordinary artistic masterpieces, fascinating historical characters, and breathtakingly violent and corrupt governments. In popular culture, films and novels revel in their Medicis and Borgias, whose vast wealth and lust for power are matched only by their hypocrisy, cruelty, and sexual excess. From the Medicis and Borgias, whose sins are gleefully exaggerated and whose virtues are forgotten, it is an easy step to find in Niccolò Machiavelli the most characteristic voice of Renaissance politics. Tens of thousands of college lecturers have relished introducing callow undergraduates to his cynical analyses of power in politics, believing that they are revealing through him how the world really works. Machiavelli advises his prince to "learn how not to be good": how, in the right circumstances, committing fraud, exterminating enemies or allies, and manipulating religious superstitions can advance a ruler's interests. What student can fail to hear Old Nick's words, whispered in the ears of young Medici princes, as a revelation of the Renaissance's dark, secret soul?

One would never guess from this popular image, shared also by some scholars who should know better, that the dominant theme of secular literature in Italy, from the second half of the fourteenth century to Machiavelli's own time and beyond, was the pressing need for a revival of classical virtue and wisdom.[1] The need for virtue was felt to be particularly urgent amid the fevered politics of the age, where princes were always in danger of turning into tyrants and republics were always threatening to ruin themselves through bitter partisan strife. The hope of most humanist literati since Petrarch was that the glory of Greece and the grandeur of Rome could be brought to life again and remake the souls of modern men and women. The primary tool for this transformation in their eyes was education, *institutio*—not just study of classical literature in classrooms but modeling one's language and behavior on the noble Greeks and Romans through all of life. Classical *institutio*—a common Latin translation of the Greek *paideia*—could be fortified by modern neo-classical literature and philosophy and by a new, classical inspiration in the plastic arts and the urban environment. In the period covered by this book, humanists also began thinking about reform in terms of *institutio* in its other sense: the laying down of customs, rituals, and forms of governance. These new *institutiones* also looked to the classical past for models.

The obscuring of the Renaissance's classical ideals by its more lurid, Machiavellian image in modern times is one reason that Francesco Patrizi of Siena, the greatest political philosopher of the humanist movement and the most representative voice of its virtue politics, has all but vanished from modern histories of political thought. There are other reasons as well, to be sure. After a century when his great political treatises, in various formats and languages, were printed in editions rivaling in number those of Aristotle and Machiavelli, publishers in the seventeenth century decided that the works of "the great Patrizi" were no longer suited to their readerships. That age was becoming more skeptical about the potential of virtuous princes to transform polities and looked instead for ways to restrain power-hungry rulers from imposing unwanted wars, taxes, and creeds. In more modern times, less comfortable with the heritage of Greece and Rome, it has not helped that Patrizi presented his ideas in two vast treatises written in Latin and studded with thousands of classical quotations and exempla. Moreover, modern political philosophers in the analytic tradition expect, and respect, tight argumentation, elaborated from a limited number of premises, with careful attention to logic and scientific rigor. Patrizi holds firmly to political values like peace, liberty, and equality, but seeks a path to them through prudential reflection on classical history and literature, including poetry. He lacks the *esprit de système*. He has arguments, but they are often hidden in forests of quotation or made obscure to us by our ignorance of their context. Patrizi's arguments have to be reconstructed in ways sometimes resembling the way Confucian statecraft is reconstructed by modern political philosophers.[2] What's more, Patrizi is rarely prescriptive. He counsels but does not presume to legislate. Nor does he provide, like Machiavelli, pseudo-scientific policy nostrums, a bag of political tricks or *modi* that rulers can turn to their profit. Rather, he seeks to inculcate practical wisdom, *phronesis*. He offers moral guidance based on tradition and experience rather than scientistic certainties.[3]

Patrizi's present oblivion is unfortunate, because, as I hope this book has shown, he is a thinker of extraordinary originality, who may also have a message for our time. He offers counsel on the reform of government that is both internally consistent and remarkably independent of the conventional wisdom of his own day—and of ours. It is widely believed today that humanist authors such as Patrizi must be unoriginal because they spend so much time quoting the ancients. Patrizi's case shows the opposite: that knowledge of antiquity (and not just Graeco-Roman antiquity) could be a powerful stimulant to original thought. His meritocratic proposals for choosing magistrates and conducting public deliberation are unexampled in humanist writings of the Renaissance. Equally radical are his proposals to insulate the legal system against the power of wealth and status. His scheme for agrarian reform—one that would free the poor from dependence on the rich and reduce conflict between the Church and lay rulers—was radical in his time and would still be radical today. Patrizi's convictions, based on Aristotelian and Christian sources, concerning the indispensable role of the household and the family in maintaining a healthy state, deserve consideration by legislators in our own time. His hostility to slavery and his commendation of marriages based on mutual love and friendship, with equal standards of faithfulness between men and women, can still win our admiration.

So too his prudent counsel against engaging in offensive wars for empire. Patrizi wants a wealthy state, but the riches of the state would be used to neutralize the influence of wealthy families, not to wage offensive wars. From a classical liberal perspective, he does not take seriously enough the dangers of a wealthy state, but it must be remembered that the Patrizian state is presumptively guided by laws approved by the whole people and administered by magistrates whose entire education and ethic of service is designed to suppress selfish interests. His discussion of how urban planning can support a free civil life has to my knowledge no parallel in Renaissance writing on architecture or politics. His sustained discussion of citizenship—the first by a political theorist since Aristotle—adapts Aristotle's own emphasis on citizen competence and virtue to the legal and social environment of Renaissance cities. His treatment of royal citizenship in the *De regno* is, I believe, the first in the Western tradition, though it would not be the last by any means. His proposals for civic education—particularly his advocacy of universal citizen literacy and public funding for teaching the liberal arts—went well beyond the imaginings of other quattrocento humanists and can still strike a sympathetic chord among educators today.

So much do Patrizi's positions seem applicable to present concerns that the historian has to resist the temptation to tuck him neatly into a "republican tradition" from Aristotle to the American Founding Fathers, or to turn his writings into another golden nugget in the treasury of the Western tradition that we moderns can draw upon at need.[4] To do that would mean losing our awareness of the differences between Patrizi and modern republican thinkers and thus would disable our own practical wisdom, our own sense of what is possible and what most needs to change. We live in an age dominated by human arrogance, proud of its scientific accomplishments, contemptuous of the past, and convinced that we have nothing to learn from history. In political science this arrogance has led to a stale dogmatism about what human beings are, what they want, and what they deserve to demand from each other and the state. Algorithms and equations, surveys and policy documents can be translated easily into legislation, we believe, and the right laws and regulations can solve all our problems and maximize our individual and collective utility. In the present moment we (in the United States) are surprised and mystified when all our science, all our wealth, all our good intentions and aspirations for moral purity, floating free from the reality of human nature, have led us to the brink of social and political collapse. We now know where Utopia lies, its longitude and latitude—why don't we just set course for it and raise our sails? Perhaps only the looming failure of our political systems can break this species of proud ignorance and send us back to the school of history to learn what has gone wrong.

We can make a start by listening to wise men from the past like Francesco Patrizi. That old Sienese statesman understood that we are neither angels nor devils but human beings, ensouled bodies, capable of both good and bad actions. We are not automata driven by self-interest but can be both selfish and selfless. A humane education can make us more human while a merely vocational one will provide us with full coffers and empty souls. Good institutions can improve us, and bad ones will make us worse. A good state is one that makes its citizens better and applies the same moral standards to its relations with other states. We know these things, not from theology or social science research, but from humane studies, reflection on what our finest poets, historians, orators, and philosophers have taught us about the past. Voices like Patrizi's, representing a great age of human achievement, the Renaissance, can make us aware how unnatural our own abstract and mechanical ways of thinking about politics are, especially when it comes to concepts like liberty, equality, and meritocracy. The practical wisdom of the past can awaken us to the absurdity of our own boundless ambitions for politics. It can remind us what our political values meant in concrete terms before they became encrusted with pseudo-scientific theories and neutered by entrenched economic interests.

Liberty, for example. Liberty for Patrizi does not mean a list of rights guaranteed by law or the right to vote for other people to represent us in distant cities. It is a way of living our lives. It means resistance to being treated like a servant by wealthy neighbors down the street. It means being able to speak without fear in assemblies. It means allowing persons whom you might think of as your inferiors— shopkeepers, weavers, bakers—to rule over you when it is their turn to do so. A free state is one whose own citizens can and will defend it from attack by predatory neighbors. It has noble public spaces where its citizens can freely associate, buy and sell without fraud, teach their children, and worship God. It has assemblies and courts that people can rely upon to settle their differences fairly and punish those who deserve punishment. A free state is one that is loved by its own people, who compete with each other to serve it well and to win praise from their fellow citizens.

Political liberty for Patrizi does not involve high-flown declarations of rights and abstract affirmations of respect for the dignity of all persons. Rather, it is understood in the Athenian sense of public decision-making by roughly equal citizens, who protect themselves from the powerful by sharing power, ruling and being ruled in turn. When Patrizi's city goes to war, it will be because the citizens have voted for war in their assemblies, knowing that their sons and brothers will soon be in the field, and that some of them may die. Personal liberty is constrained by law, religion, and custom, and citizens know that preserving their personal liberty depends on not lapsing into license and luxury. Political liberty begins with a desire to prevent tyranny, but becomes precious over time, a way of life, a *numen* or divinity for which citizens are willing to fight and die. It is not an abstract right to which all human beings are entitled, but the jealously guarded possession of those who truly care about it. Most peoples are in fact servile, willing to take orders from lords and masters, and are well ruled by princes. Princely rule, too, can be improved by prudence and humane education, but it is not the same as the shared rule of a free people over itself.

Patrizi learned from his reading of history and Greek philosophy that real liberty could survive only in a society of equals, and that political equality could not be separated from economic equality. Modern liberal political thinkers in the eighteenth century came to believe that the two could be separated, and that liberty could be secured by law and constitutional devices even amidst vast economic inequalities. Socialists in the nineteenth and twentieth century pointed out that liberal politics, when combined with unlimited economic freedom, was a formula for oppression; but they themselves proved willing to sacrifice every human liberty in order to enact their dogmas of communism or redistribution. Patrizi already in the fifteenth century understood from his study of history that communism was unnatural and redistribution impracticable. A fair distribution of private property was possible when founding a new state, but redistribution in established societies would end in injustice and ultimately civil war. Patrizi's more prudent proposal, to limit the amount that individuals could own or the profits they could earn, might be adapted to modern conditions—something similar was promoted by distributists like Hilaire Belloc and G. K. Chesterton in the early twentieth century. On the other hand, Patrizi's advocacy of a wealthy state surely would only work if the state's political leaders could live up to his standard of meritorious leadership—if, in other words, they were well-educated persons of fine character and practical wisdom who shared with each other an ethic of service to the public.

Patrizi's most difficult theoretical problem, indeed, was reconciling the claims of merit, equality, and freedom, a problem that still besets modern liberal democracies. City-state liberty in the Renaissance allowed all qualified citizens to have a voice in government and to participate to some extent in the city's public life. But for Patrizi only the meritorious should hold the highest offices and sit in the senate. Persons lacking ability and good character do not have a right to rule others. For the city to flourish, the voice of the meritorious must predominate in the senate, where the most important decisions affecting everyone are made. This, of course, was easier said than done, given the ideological deformities of both rich and poor, noted already by Aristotle. Hence, Patrizi's scheme of meritocracy was elaborated as a theoretical alternative to both populism and oligarchy.[5] For him there were two great enemies of good government: a passionate, ignorant mob and a ruling elite driven by *ambitio* and *avaritia:* the desire for lordly rule over others and the desire to use public office to enrich oneself and one's family. Some of Patrizi's measures against populism, diseased ambition, and peculation passed into the republican tradition; others would obviously be unworkable in large-scale republics. But the spirit of Patrizian meritocracy still has, I believe, something to offer the present time.

In recent times meritocracy has been understood as a set of principles designed to reshape social hierarchies as a whole—to make the distribution of social, economic, and political rewards match the abilities and effort of individuals, and to check the advantages of privilege. The boundless ambition of modern meritocracy, functioning as informal social policy, has made it controversial and, lately, dysfunctional. In recent times, it has been increasingly criticized from both left and right. Progressives evince concern that the admissions and promotion policies that confer membership in meritocratic elites are still biased toward privileged groups and against historically oppressed communities. Conservatives worry that current meritocratic elites have become missionaries of an alien global culture, hostile to traditional religion and patriotism.

An emerging post-liberal politics believes that modern American meritocracy has run up against what has been called the "Iron Law of Meritocracy."[6] The goal of post–World War II meritocracy in the Anglo-Saxon democracies was to open up a closed elite to intelligent and hardworking members of groups previously excluded from social and political power. The "Iron Law of Meritocracy" states, however, that the inequality produced by the meritocratic system itself will eventually produce a new corrupt elite that barricades itself off from those outside it. Having all the wealth and power, it will use its position to increase inequality still further and block social mobility. It will choose to restrict the rewards of merit to its friends, its classmates, and its children. It will develop its own culture in ways that will require any postulants to elite status to remake themselves in the image of their betters. It may even use its cultural power to impose uniformity of belief on society as a whole, in a way uncomfortably reminiscent of twentieth-century totalitarian states.

Patrizian meritocracy, by contrast, is more limited in scope; it is *political* meritocracy. It separates the problem of good leadership from the wider problem of social and economic justice, assuming that justice ultimately comes from what rulers (including judges) *do*, not from what may be written down on paper. It aims to create a large pool of well-educated citizens. Of these, some can be chosen for lesser offices on the basis of good reputation and academic attainments, then promoted by the senate through an informal *cursus honorum* on the basis of their performance in office. At any given time, therefore, the city will be governed by an order of magistrates and former magistrates distinct from the socio-economic pyramid and rewarded by honor rather than financial inducements. The order of magistrates is designed to attract honor-seeking men whose highest reward is recognition of distinguished service by their fellow citizens.

Meritocratic measures are designed to insulate the process of selecting magistrates from the influence of wealth and lineage, but Patrizi well understands that this will be difficult when wealthy individuals and foreign institutions (like the Roman church) are able to challenge the power of the state. That is why he places such emphasis on the "Hippodamian" tripartite division of the republic's land— land, of course, being the principal source of wealth in the preindustrial world. The Patrizian state controls, in effect, two thirds of the landed wealth of the republic. One third is leased out to support the clergy and religious services, and another third is used to support the city's professional soldiers and to give honorable work to the poor. Only the last third of the republic's land is allotted to citizens as private property. The result of this division is to make the clergy dependent on and therefore loyal to the republic, to reduce inequality between rich and poor, and to keep poor citizens from being debt slaves of the rich. Only when the poor cannot be stampeded into revolution by hunger and desperation, only when the wealthy cannot manipulate government in their private interest, only when public authorities are backed by a wealthy state, can a meritocratic order of magistrates hope to govern successfully.[7]

Patrizian meritocracy thus seeks legitimation in a way different from that of modern American meritocracy. In America, ruling elites believe that they deserve their wealth and positions of power because they have earned them. They are smarter, earned higher marks on examinations, and attended better universities, while those whose services they now command are assumed to be stupid or lazy. If ever members of the elite are honest enough to acknowledge their un-earned advantages and try affirmatively to share those advantages with some of the less fortunate, that merely reinforces their disdain for the vast majority who must still be left behind.

Patrizian meritocracy, by contrast, legitimates itself by an ideal of honorable public service. Human excellence, virtue, does not exist merely to achieve personal distinction, but also to serve (in Plato's celebrated phrase) "our family, our friends, and our country." All citi-zens, if they are rational, should prefer to be governed by the best among them, and that preference is meritocracy's truest and only justification. It is unfair to everyone when the republic is ruled by the vicious and ignorant rather than by its best citizens. Meritoc-racy therefore requires that magistrates do not use their position to enrich themselves or act in lordly ways. Only a strict ethic of service can preserve concord among citizens. The honor-seeking man must learn to act in office in a spirit of equality and service toward his fellow citizens, and citizens outside the order of magistrates must learn to accept the leadership of those whose abilities and proven experience have entitled them to positions of authority.

An ethic of service is one reason that Patrizian meritocracy is easier to justify than the modern American variety. Another reason is the inclusion of good moral character in its idea of merit. Modern Americans show their membership in the elite by their dress and computer skills, by what they eat, where they live, what entertainment they consume, and what they believe. Many think that cost-free adherence to an ever-changing set of political dogmas is sufficient proxy for good character—that "virtue-signaling" is the same as virtue. Patrizi, like all Renaissance humanists, held that membership in the elite needed to be earned by making a serious attempt to be competent and morally good. That required, first of all, sustained study. One should study grammar and rhetoric in order to learn how to speak with precision and power. One should learn from great poetry and oratory to love noble behavior. One should deepen one's insight into good character by reading moral philosophy. And one should acquire practical wisdom from the study of ethnography, biography, and history.

Study was not enough, however. Parents needed to choose teachers who were morally upright as well as competent, and they needed to be vigilant in keeping their children away from bad companions. States needed to establish a structure of incentives that would reward the good and exclude from power those with corrupt motives. One way that states could accomplish this was to honor work and discourage idleness. Even contemplative activities, as Cicero advised, needed to have a civic purpose. The city could not rely solely on laws, surveillance, policing, and punishment to maintain order. Unless it trained virtuous citizens through public education, oriented to civic ends, no amount of force would be sufficient to create the conditions for peace, felicity, and orderly government. Everyone today bewails the scarcity of good leaders, but it is less often appreciated that good leadership in a state also requires good behavior in ordinary citizens, as Patrizi taught in both his *De republica* and *De regno*. It was a humanist belief, which also happens to be true, that persons of high character make good leaders. People will accept the leadership of a good man or woman if they respect that person's character and believe that he or she intends their good and the common good.

Francesco Patrizi, in short, offers those who study him a form of political wisdom that is rapidly disappearing in our time. He is a philosopher steeped in history, a traditionalist who criticizes recent traditions by recovering better, more ancient ones. He not only looks to the wisdom of the Greeks and Romans but seeks also to learn from all the civilizations of the ancient world to which Graeco-Roman literature gave him access: Persian, Phoenician, Egyptian, Indian, even Chinese. Nor does his search for wisdom blind him to the faults of the past. He respects the virtue of the Romans but has deep misgivings about their reliance on slave labor and about the *patria potestas* that gave a father the power of life and death over his family. He finds institutions worth imitating and worth avoiding both under Roman republican consuls and under the emperors; he admires political measures in both Athens and Sparta. He does not provide lawyerly exegeses of rights and wrongs, nor does he pretend to scientific knowledge of the laws of history. He uses the experience of the past to foresee undesirable outcomes, but also to increase the repertory of available solutions to the challenges of his own time. He knows that the practical wisdom of the true leader needs to be informed by history, because without some standard of comparison we cannot see the successes and failures of our own time, its dangers and opportunities, in a realistic perspective. Without a knowledge of the past, we become blind to what is truly valuable in our traditions. In a time when the study of history is disappearing from our schools, replaced by pre-packaged "narratives" designed to promote political messaging, Patrizi can remind us of the priceless value of seeing ourselves and our times through the eyes of historical periods and places other than our own.

# Appendix A

## List of Patrizi's Works

*(Compiled with the assistance of Caroline Engelmayer)*

*Conspectus:*

a. Letters
b. Latin Poetry
c. Grammatical Works
d. Speeches
e. Historical Work
f. Political Treatises

A. Letters

1. *Letters.* De Capua 2014 divides the surviving letters into two groups: (1) the Foligno Corpus (173 letters), written while Patrizi was the governor of Foligno, and (2) the *Lettere sparse* or scattered letters (sixty-three letters from and to Patrizi), collected from various manuscript sources by De Capua. The complete text of the letters was edited in De Capua's unpublished doctoral thesis (De Capua 1991). The letters are quoted extensively in De Capua 2014. See below, 355n63.

B. Latin Poetry

2. *Poematum libri IV.* A collection of forty-two poems in various meters, composed in Patrizi's early career and scribally published in 1461 with a dedication to Pope Pius II. See Chapter 1, 17–19. The collection was never printed but survives in several manuscripts, of which *B,* an early presentation copy (dated 1461), is cited in this

book. A number of the poems also circulated independently. The only poem to become well known was 2.2, "De Christi Natali," which survives in at least eighteen copies and was printed in Padua in 1482 and in later anthologies of Neo-Latin poetry. In some manuscripts it passed falsely under the names of Francesco Filelfo or Tommaso Schifaldo; the latter studied with Patrizi at the University of Siena. In modern times, two poems were published in Altamura 1941 (1.5, 4.4) and three more in Avesani 1968 (3.2, 3.3, 4.5).

3. *Epigrammaton liber.* A collection of 345 epigrams of varying lengths, composed by Patrizi in the latter part of his career and apparently left unpublished at his death. They survive in a single manuscript, G. See Chapter 1, 50–52. Twenty-three of the poems were published by Leslie Smith in various articles cited in the Bibliography.

## C. Grammatical Works

4. *De metris Horatii.* A treatise on Horatian meters, surviving in two manuscripts, probably written between 1441 and 1446. See Chapter 1, 17.

5. Epitome of Quintilian's *Institutes.* Written probably between 1457 and 1460 and dedicated to Patrizi's pupil Francesco Tranchedini. See Chapter 1, 33. It survives in at least fifteen manuscripts and was printed in Paris in 1554, falsely attributed to Pier Paolo Vergerio the Elder. The preface was printed in Bassi 1894, 438.

6. Epitome of Priscian's *Institutes of Grammar.* Probably written between 1457 and 1460. It survives in at least six manuscripts. See J. Black 2001, 142–143; De Capua 2014, 102.

7. Commentary on Petrarch's *Canzoniere.* The work was commissioned by Patrizi's patron, Alfonso, duke of Calabria in 1476 or 1477. It is the only surviving work of Patrizi written in the vernacular, apart from a small number of letters. It survives in at least six manuscripts. See Chapter 1, 53; Paolino 1999, 2000; De Capua 2014, 180–191.

## D. Speeches

8. *Oratio de laudibus philosophiae* (Oration in praise of philosophy), composed for the inauguration of the school year in Siena, 1426; the surviving version was probably revised at a later date. See Chapter 1, 21–22. The work survives in two manuscripts. In the second

manuscript it carries the title *De studiorum artium optimarum laudibus* (In praise of studies of the finest arts). An edition and translation by Caroline Engelmayer and James Hankins is in preparation. See Fioravanti 1979, 134n1; Fioravanti 1993, 199n23; De Capua 2014, 26–27.

9. *Oratio ad Hippolytam Mariam Sfortiam.* Also called *De maritalis coniugii dignitate oratio* (Oration on the worthiness of the marriage union) or *De matrimonio* (On marriage). Delivered in Milan before the court of Duke Francesco Sforza at the wedding of his daughter Ippolita Maria to Alfonso, duke of Calabria, in May 1465. The work survives in at least eight manuscripts and has been printed in modern times in Tateo and Tateo 1990. See D'Elia 2004, 6, 85, 112–113, 171–173; De Capua 2014, 175–180; and Chapter 1, 46.

10. *Oratio ad Innocentium VIII.* Oration delivered as the representative of King Ferrante of Naples to celebrate the crowning of Innocent VIII as pope, 29 December 1484. There are at least three surviving manuscripts, and the work was printed and distributed from three separate bookshops in Rome in 1484. See De Capua 2014, 179n; and below, 357n90.

## E. Historical Work

11. *De origine et antiquitate urbis Senae* (On the origin and ancient history of the city of Siena). The date of composition of this historical essay is uncertain, but it probably falls after 1460. The work survives in twelve manuscripts and remains unpublished. See De Capua 2014, 77.

## F. Political Treatises

12. *De magistratu gerendo.* A letter-treatise directed to Patrizi's pupil Achille Petrucci, written about 1445. Included by De Capua among the *Lettere sparse* (no. 39). See Chapter 1, 27–29. It survives in at least eight manuscripts; M is the codex cited in this volume.

13. *De institutione reipublicae,* datable to 1461/1471, although the presumed dedication copy is dated 1479. For the dating, see Chapter 2. Originally commissioned by Pius II, it was finally dedicated to Pope Sixtus IV and to the city of Siena. It survives in at least eleven manuscripts and many printed editions (see Appendix B).

14. *De regno et regis institutione,* datable to 1481/1484. Dedicated to Alfonso, duke of Calabria, heir to the throne of Naples. It survives in at least six manuscripts and in many printed editions (see Appendix B).

# Appendix B

## Editions, Translations, and Compendia of Patrizi's Political Works, 1518–1702

*(Compiled by Victoria Pipas)*

1518. PARIS: Pierre Vidoue for Galliot du Pré. *De institutione reipublicae libri novem, historiarum sententiarumque varietate refertissimi, hactenus numquam impraessi.* Edited by Jean Savigny. USTC 144871. First edition of the Latin *De republica.*

1519. PARIS: Pierre Vidoue for Galliot du Pré. *Enneas de regno et regis institutione, opus profecto et historiarum varietate et sententiarum gravitate commendandum, hactenus nunquam impressum.* Edited by Jean Savigny. USTC 145052. First edition of the Latin *De regno.*

1520 [1519]. PARIS: Pierre le Brodeur. *Compendiosa seu rerum memorandarum breviuscula, uberrima tamen descriptio, ex immensis Francisci Patricii Senensis De regno Deque regimine reipublicae voluminibus nuperrime deprompta . . . Cui additur aureus codiculus De institutione principis christiani ex libro Erasmi novissime excerptus.* Epitome compiled by Gilles d'Aurigny. USTC 184074. First edition of the Latin epitome of *De regno* and *De republica.* (Print date 24 March 1519 *old style.*) Printed with an epitome of Erasmus's *On the Education of a Christian Prince.*

1520. PARIS: Pierre Vidoue for Galliot du Pré. *Francisci Patricii Senensis pontificis Caietani De institutione reipublicae libri novem, historiarum sententiarumque varietate refertissimi, hactenus numquam impraessi.* Edited by Jean Savigny. Second edition of the Latin *De republica.* Confirmed from the copy held by Bayerische Staatsbibliothek, online reference BSB-ID 918831.

1520. PARIS: Pierre Vidoue for Galliot du Pré. *Livre tres fructueux et utile à toutes personnes de l'institution et administration de la chose publicque.* USTC 11043. First edition of the French translation of the Latin *De republica.*

1531. PARIS: Pierre Vidoue for Galliot du Pré and Jean Petit. *Francisci Patricii Senensis pontificis Caietani. Enneas de regno et regis institutione, opus profecto et historiarum varietate et sententiarum gravitate commendandum, hactenus nunquam impressum.* Edited by Jean Savigny. USTC 138030, 209304. Second edition of the Latin *De regno.*

1534. PARIS: Nicholas Cousteau for Jean de la Garde. *Livre tres fructueux et utile à toutes personnes de l'institution et administration de la chose publicque.* USTC 11073. Second edition of the French translation of the Latin *De republica.*

1534. PARIS: Pierre Vidoue for Galliot du Pré and Jean Petit. *Francisci Patricii Senensis pontificis Caietani De institutione republicae libri novem, historiarum sententiarumque varietate refertissimi cum annotationibus margineis indiceque vocabulorum factorum dictorumque memorabilium copiosissimo.* USTC 138225. Third edition of the Latin *De republica.*

1543. PARIS: Arnoul and Charles L'Angelier. *Compendiosa rerum memorandarum descriptio ex immensis Francisci Patricii Senensis De regno Deque institutione reipublicae voluminibus, deprompta. . . . Cui additur aureus codiculus De institutione principis christiani ex libro Erasmi novissime excerptus.* Epitome compiled by Gilles d'Aurigny. USTC 195363, 195364. Second edition of the Latin epitome of *De republica* and *De regno,* together with an epitome of Erasmus's *Education of a Christian Prince.*

1543. PARIS: Guillaume Thibaut, Jean Foucher, Poncet Le Preux, and Michel de la Guierche. *Compendiosa rerum memorandarum descriptio ex immensis Francisci Patricii Senensis De regno Deque institutione reipublicae voluminibus, deprompta. . . . Cui additur aureus codiculus De institutione principis christiani ex libro Erasmi novissime excerptus.* Epitome compiled by Gilles d'Aurigny. USTC 200230. Third edition of the Latin epitome of *De republica* and *De regno*, printed together with an epitome of Erasmus's *Education of a Christian Prince.*

1544. PARIS: Charles L'Angelier. *Le livre de police humaine, contenant briefve description de plusiers choses dignes de memoire, sicomme du gouvernement d'une royaume et de toute administration de la republique.* Epitome compiled by Gilles d'Aurigny. Translated into French by Jean le Blond. USTC 48126. First edition of the French translation of the Latin epitome of the *De regno* and *De republica.*

1545. VENICE: Aldus Manutius the Younger. *De' discorsi del reverendo monsignor Francesco Patritii Sanese Vescouo Gaiettano, sopra alle cose appartenenti ad una città libera e famiglia nobile.* Translated into Italian by Giovanni Fabrini. USTC 762223. First edition of the Italian translation of the Latin *De republica.*

1546. PARIS: Charles L'Angelier. *Le livre de police humaine, contenant briefve description de plusieurs choses dignes de memoire, sicomme du gouvernement d'une royaume & de toute administration de la republique. . . . Reveu & corrigé avec grand diligence par le dict translateur* [vol. 1]. *La seconde partie du livre de police humaine, contenant succinctement le gouvernement des royaumes & enseignement des princes . . . Ensemble une brief recueil du livre d'Erasme qu'il a composé de l'enseignement du prince chrestien* [vol. 2]. Epitome compiled by Gilles d'Aurigny. Translated into French by Jean le Blond. Two volumes. USTC 1075. Second edition, in two volumes, of the French translations of the Latin epitome of *De republica* and *De regno*, printed with an epitome in French of Erasmus's *Education of a Christian Prince.*

1547. VENICE: Comin da Trino. *Il sacro regno de'l gran' Patritio, de'l vero reggimento e de la vera felicità de'l Principe, e beatitudine humana.* Translated into Italian by Giovanni Fabrini. USTC 762198. First edition of the Italian translation of the Latin *De regno.*

1549. PARIS: Jean Foucher, Vivantius Gaultherot. *Compendiosa rerum memorandarum descriptio, ex immensis Francisci Patricii Senensis de regno deque institutione reipublicae voluminibus deprompta. . . . Cui additur aureus codiculus de institutione principis christiani ex libro Erasmi novissime excerptus.* Epitome compiled by Gilles d'Aurigny. Copy held by the British Library. USTC 154778, 200548. Second edition of the Latin epitome of the *De republica* and the *De regno,* printed with an epitome of Erasmus's *Education of a Christian Prince.*

1549. PARIS: Etienne Groulleau, Oudin Petit. *Le livre de police humaine, contenant brieve description de plusiers choses dignes de memoire. . . . Ensemble un brief recueil du livre d'Erasme qu'il a composé de l'enseigne-ment du prince chrestien. Reveu et corrigé depuis les derniers imprimez.* Epitome compiled by Gilles d'Aurigny. Translated into French by Jean le Blond. USTC 457, 83639. Third edition of the French translation of the Latin epitome of *De republica* and *De regno,* printed with an epitome in French of Erasmus's *Education of a Christian Prince.*

1550 [1549]. PARIS: Charles L'Angelier. *Le livre de police humaine, contenant brieve description de plusiers choses dignes de memoire . . . Ensemble un brief recueil du livre d'Erasme, qu'il a composé de l'en-seignement du prince chrestien. Reveu et corrigé par le dict translateur* [vol. 1, 1550]. *La seconde partie du livre de police humaine, contenant succinctement le gouvernement des royaumes, & enseignement des princes* [vol. 2, 1549/1550; 1549 is the date given in the colophon]. Two volumes. Epitome compiled by Gilles d'Aurigny. Translated into French by Jean le Blond. USTC 461, 75903 [vol. 1]; 75904 [vol. 2]. Fourth edition, in two parts, of French translation of the Latin epitome of *De republica* and *De regno,* printed with an epitome in French of Erasmus's *Education of a Christian Prince.*

1552. PARIS: Pierre Gaultier. *Compendiosa rerum memorandarum de-scriptio ex immensis Francisci Patritii Senensis de regno deque institutione reipublicae voluminibus deprompta. . . . Adiecimus item praeter auream libellum de institutione principis christiani ex libro Erasmi exerptum.* Epitome compiled by Gilles d'Aurigny. USTC 196496. Third edition of the Latin epitome of *De republica* and *De regno,* printed together with an epitome of Erasmus's *Education of a Christian Prince.*

1553. PARIS: Madeleine Boursette, Jean Ruelle, Guillaume Thibaut. *Le livre de police humaine, contenant brieve description de plusiers choses dignes de memoire. . . . Ensemble un brief recueil du livre d'Erasme, qu'il a composé de l'enseignement du prince chrestien. Reveu et corrigé depuis les derniers imprimez.* USTC 16104, 37150, 41037. Second edition of the single-volume edition of the French translations of the Latin epitome of *De republica* and *De regno* (based on Groulleau and Petit), printed with a French epitome of Erasmus's *Education of a Christian Prince.*

1553. VENICE: Aldus Manutius the Younger. *Il sacro regno del gran' Patritio, de'l vero reggimento e de la vera felicità de'l principe e beatitudine humana.* USTC 847036. Second edition of the Italian translation by Giovanni Fabrini of the *De regno.*

1554. PARIS: Guillaume Thibout. *Le livre de police humaine, contenant brieve description de plusiers choses dignes de memoire. . . . Ensemble un brief recueil du livre d'Erasme, qu'il a composé de l'enseignement du prince chrestien. Reveu et corrigé depuis les derniers imprimez.* USTC 20647. Reprint or reissue of the 1553 French translations of the Latin epitome of *De republica* and *De regno*, printed with a French epitome of Erasmus's *Education of a Christian Prince.*

1559. PARIS: Jérôme de Marnef. *Compendiosa epitome commentariorum Francisci Patritii Senensis Episcopi in duas partes secta. . . . Accedit his de institutione principis christiani ex libro Desiderii Erasmi brevis collectio et insuper ex Stobaeo, Quod optima sit monarchia.* Epitome compiled by Gilles d'Aurigny. USTC 152610. Fourth edition of the Latin epitome of the *De republica* and the *De regno*, with an epitome of Erasmus's *Education of a Christian Prince* and an excerpt from Joannes Stobaeus's *Anthology.*

1560. PARIS: Jérôme de Marnef. *Compendiosa epitome commentariorum Francisci Patritii Senensis Episcopi in duas partes secta. . . . Accedit his de institutione principis christiani ex libro Desiderii Erasmi brevis collectio et insuper ex Stobaeo, Quod optima sit monarchia.* Epitome compiled by Gilles d'Aurigny. USTC 152816. Reprint or reissue of the 1559 Latin epitome of the *De republica* and the *De regno* (de Marnef), with an epitome of Erasmus's *Education of a Christian Prince* and an excerpt from Joannes Stobaeus's *Anthology.*

1566. PARIS: Jérôme de Marnef and Guillaume Cavellat. *Compendiosa epitome commentariorum Francisci Patritii Senensis episcopi in duas partes secta. . . . Accedit his de institutione principis christiani ex libro De-*

*siderii Erasmi breuis collectio et insuper ex Stobaeo, Quod optima sit monarchia. Omnia diligentius et accuratius recognita.* Epitome compiled by Gilles d'Aurigny. USTC 156914. Fifth edition of the Latin epitome of the *De republica* and the *De regno*, with an epitome of Erasmus's *Education of a Christian Prince* and an extract from Stobaeus's *Anthology*.

1567. PARIS: Jean Charron for Gilles Gourbin. *De regno et regis institutione libri IX.* With a preface by Denis Lambin. USTC 158227, 158228, 139755. Third edition of the Latin *De regno*.

1569. PARIS: Gilles Gourbin. *De institutione reipublicae libri novem.* USTC 140607. Fourth edition of the Latin *De republica*.

1569. VENICE: Domenico and Giovanni Battista Guerra. *Il sacro regno del vero reggimento, e de la vera felicita del principe.* Translated into Italian by Giovanni Fabrini. USTC 847041. Third edition of the Italian translation of *De regno*.

1570. PARIS: Jérôme de Marnef and Guillaume Cavellat. *Compendiosa epitome commentariorum Francisci Patritii Senensis episcopi in duas partes secta. . . . Accedit his de institutione principis christiani ex libro Desiderii Erasmi brevis collectio, et insuper ex Stobaeo, Quod optima sit monarchia. Omnia diligentius et accuratius recognita.* Epitome compiled by Gilles d'Aurigny. USTC 170004. Sixth edition of the Latin epitome of the *De republica* and the *De regno*, with an epitome of Erasmus's *Education of a Christian Prince* and an extract from Stobaeus's *Anthology*.

1573. MAINZ: Kaspar Behem. *Erster theyl des heÿlige Reichs eines wahren Regentens und gewisse glucksaeligkeyt eines gebiettenten Fuerstens.* Translated by Johannes Christoph Becker. USTC 653805, 2215682. First edition of the German translation based on the Italian *De regno*.

1574. LYONS: Benoît Rigaud. *De l'enseignement, estat et regime de la chose publique.* Translated by Jean le Blond. USTC 14833. Third edition of the French translation of *De republica*.

1574. PARIS: Jérôme de Marnef and Guillaume Cavellat. *Compendiosa epitome commentariorum Francisci Patritii Senensis episcopi in duas partes secta. . . . Accedit his de institutione principis christiani ex libro De-*

*siderii Erasmi brevis collectio et insuper ex Stobaeo, Quod optima sit monarchia. Omnia diligentius et accuratius recognita.* Epitome compiled by Gilles d'Aurigny. USTC 138580 and 170978. Seventh edition of the Latin epitome of the *De republica* and the *De regno*, with an epitome of Erasmus's *Education of a Christian Prince* and an extract from Stobaeus's *Anthology.*

1575. PARIS: Gilles Gourbin. *De institutione reipublicae libri novem.* USTC 170263. Fifth edition of the Latin *De republica*.

1576. LONDON: Thomas Marsh. *A moral methode of civile policie containinge a learned and fruictful discourse of the institution, state and government of a common weale.* Translated by Richard Robinson. USTC 508259. English translation of the Latin epitome of *De republica.*

1577. PARIS: Gilles Beys. *Les escrits tres dignes de mémoire, de . . . François Patrice, evesque de Cayetete. Contenus en neuf livres Latins, traictans du regne ou domination d'un seul, dicte monarchie, et de l'institution d'un bon roy . . . Livre premier.* Translated by Jean Ferey. USTC 56187. First edition of the French translation of book 1 of the Latin *De regno*.

1577. PARIS: Jérôme de Marnef and Guillaume Cavellat. *Compendiosa epitome commentariorum Francisci Patritii Senensis episcopi in duas partes secta. . . . Accedit his de institutione principis christiani ex libro Desiderii Erasmi brevis collectio et insuper ex Stobaeo, Quod optima sit monarchia. Omnia diligentius et acuratius recognita.* Epitome compiled by Gilles d'Aurigny. USTC 171394. Eighth edition of the Latin epitome of the *De republica* and the *De regno*, with an epitome of Erasmus's *Education of a Christian Prince* and an extract from Stobaeus's *Anthology.*

1578. PARIS: Jean de Bordeaux, Jean Hulpeau, Marc Locqueneulx, Michael Julian. *De institutione reipublicae libri novem multo quam antea emendatiores.* Edited by Jean Nicodon. USTC 138791, 138792, 138793, 170425. Sixth edition of the Latin *De republica,* corrected.

1578. PARIS: Jean de Bordeaux, Marc Locqueneulx, Jean Hulpeau, Michel Julian. *De regno et regis institutione libri novem, multo quam antea emendatiores.* Edited by Jean Nicodon. USTC 138794, 138795, 170434. Fourth edition of the Latin *De regno,* corrected.

1582. PARIS: Gilles Gourbin. *De regno et regis institutione libri IX.* USTC 170613. Fifth edition of the Latin *De regno*. Privilege dated 18 September 1583.

1584. PARIS: Claude Micard. *De l'estat et maniement de la chose publique, ensemble du gouvernement des royaumes et instructions de princes. . . . Plus y est adjousté un petit abregé du livre d'Erasme, touchant la doctrine et enseignement du prince chrestiens. Le tout mis en bon ordre, avec une table des matieres principales.* Translated by Jean Le Blond. USTC 75188. Third edition of the French translations of the Latin epitome of *De republica* and *De regno*, with the French epitome of Erasmus's *Education of a Christian Prince*.

1585. PARIS: Gilles Gourbin. *De institutione reipublicae libri novem.* USTC 170765. Seventh edition of the Latin *De republica*.

1589. PARIS: Guillaume Chaudière. *De l'institution de la république.* Translated with a running commentary by Jacques Tigeou. USTC 7236. First edition of a new French translation of the Latin *De republica*, relying heavily on the two prior editions (1534; 1574) of the French translation of the Latin *De republica*.

1590. PARIS: Guillaume Chaudière. *De l'institution de la république.* Translated by Jacques Tigeou. USTC 39189. Reprint or reissue of the 1589 French translation of the Latin *De republica* (Chaudière).

1591. COLOGNE: Johann Gymnich III. *Compendiosa epitome commentariorum Francisci Patritii Senensis in duas partes secta. . . . Accedit his de institutione principis christiani brevis collectio et insuper ex Stobaeo, Quod optima sit monarchia. Omnia diligenter et accurate recognita.* Epitome compiled by compiled by Gilles d'Aurigny. USTC 623833. Ninth edition of the Latin epitome of the *De republica* and the *De regno*, with an epitome of Erasmus's *Education of a Christian Prince* and an extract from Stobaeus's *Anthology*.

1591. MADRID: Luis Sanchéz. *De reyno y de la institucion del que ha de reynar.* Translated by Henrique Garcés. USTC 340893. First Spanish translation of the Latin *De regno*.

1594. MONTBÉLIARD: Lazare Zetzner. *De institutione reipublicae libri IX.* Edited by Lazare Zetzner. USTC 146376. Eighth edition of the Latin *De republica.*

1594. MONTBÉLIARD: Lazare Zetzner. *De regno et regis institutione libri IX.* Edited by Lazare Zetzner. USTC 110230, 658063. Sixth edition of the Latin *De regno.*

1594. STRASBOURG: Lazare Zetzner. *De institutione reipublicae libri IX.* Edited by Lazare Zetzner. USTC 658066. Simultaneous separate issue of the 1594 Latin *De republica.*

1594. STRASBOURG: Lazare Zetzner. *De regno et regis institutione libri IX.* Edited by Lazare Zetzner. USTC 658064. Simultaneous separate issue of the 1594 Latin *De regno.*

1595. STRASBOURG: Lazare Zetzner. *De institutione reipublicae libri IX.* Edited by Lazare Zetzner. USTC 658065. Reprint or reissue of the 1594 Latin *De republica.*

1599. TORGAU: Printer of Friedrich Wilhelm I, Duke of Saxe-Weimar. *De regno et regis institutione libri IX. . . . Eiusdem de institutione reipublicae.* Edited by Johannes Wanckel. USTC 658067. First edition of the Latin *De regno* and the *De republica* together in one volume.

1608. STRASBOURG: Lazare Zetzner. *De institutione reipublicae libri IX.* Edited by Lazare Zetzner. USTC 2105928. Ninth edition of the Latin *De republica,* and second edition containing Zetzner's editorial interventions in the Latin *De republica.*

1608. STRASBOURG: Lazare Zetzner. *De regno et regis institutione libri IX.* Edited by Lazare Zetzner. USTC 2001715. Seventh edition of the Latin *De regno,* and second edition containing Zetzner's editorial interventions in the Latin *De regno.*

1610. PARIS: Nicholas Buon, Robert Foüet. *De l'institution des royaumes et republiques.* USTC 66772, 6025973. Second edition of Jacques Tigeou's French translation of the Latin *De republica.*

1666. HELMSTEDT: Henning Müller. *Franciscus Patricius Lib. IIX. De institutione reipublicae titulus XV.* In *De bibliothecis atque archivis virorum clarissimorum quos aversa monstrat pagina libelli et commentationes,* 35–36. Edited by Joachim Johannes Mader. Copy held by the Bavarian State Library, Munich. Anthologized excerpt of book 8, chapter 15, of the Latin *De republica.*

1702. HELMSTEDT: Georg Wolfgang Hamm. *Franciscus Patricius Lib. IIX. De institutione reipublicae titulus XV.* In *De bibliothecis atque archivis virorvm clarissimorvm libelli et commentationes . . . Secundam editionem,* 35–36. Edited by Joachim Johannes Mader and Joseph Andreas Schmidt. Copy held by the Bavarian State Library, Munich. Anthologized excerpt of book 8, chapter 15, of the Latin *De republica.*

## DOUBTFUL AND GHOST EDITIONS

1514. PRATO. *De institutione reipublicae.* USTC 847035. The copy cited in USTC and other reference works, said to be held in Biblioteca Diocesana B. Lucia Broccadelli, Narni, Italy, has been confirmed by the library to be the 1518 Paris Latin edition of the *De republica,* lacking a title page. "Prato" was likely a misunderstanding of the bookseller's name, du Pré (Pratensis).

1520. PARIS: Pierre Vidoue for Galliot du Pré. *Enneas de regno et regis institutione, opus profecto et historiarum varietate et sententiarum gravitate commendandum, hactenus nunquam impressum.* Edited by Jean Savigny. USTC 145030. The library holdings listed in USTC for this imprint refer in fact to the 1519 Latin *De regno* or to the 1520 Latin *De republica.*

1578. PARIS: Guillaume Julian. *De institutione reipublicae libri novem multo quam antea emendatiores.* Edited by Jean Nicodon. USTC 170426. Doubtful edition: All known copies listed in USTC refer to the 1578 Latin *De republica* (Michael Julian). Guillaume (his brother) was an active publisher-bookseller at the time, so it is possible he also sold this edition, but no copies have been located with his name on the title page or in the colophon.

# Appendix C

## Patrizi's Epigram 14
## "What Would Make Me Happy"

See Chapter 1, 49–50. From G, f. 5r–v.

De optata felicitate

Si mihi nunc redeat numquam speranda iuuenta,
    adnuat et uotis Iupiter ipse meis,
iustum optem regem, facilem qui praebeat aurem,
    sit tutela bonis exitiumque malis.
Sit mihi parua domus, puteus breuis, ⟨h⟩ortus et unde
    luceat assiduo nigra culina foco.
Grex mihi non sterili pinguis pascatur in agro;
    arua quoque et messes et bona uina ferant,
tum mihi Palladia collis densetur oliua
    perpetuumque ignem caedua silua dabit.
Haec parua optanti sint munera: maxima praestet
    aemula Pergameae bibliotheca mihi.
Illic Cecropii primum Latiique poetae
    ordine seruentur* grammaticique simul;
sint quoque rhetoribus mixti magisque patronis
    qui populum eloquio perdomuere suo;
historici memores aeui testesque uirorum
    finitimum teneant e regione locum.
Post radio numeros scribunt qui et puluere metas
    et qui stellarum praedocuere uias

---

\* *Correxi ex* seruentum *ut vid.*

345

quique simul pondus numerumque dedere per artem
uocibus et dulces instituere modos.
Nec procul hinc subeant rerum qui reddere causas
possunt atque animi dicere iura ualent
et qui Chaldaeo praedocti dogmate norunt
ex nihilo magnum cuncta creasse deum.
Sint quoque qui mores hominum uitamque beatam
constituunt positis finibus usque boni.
Hos inter libros Tithoni ac Nestoris annos
Optarim atque Argum uincere luminibus.

# Abbreviations

B        Berlin, Deutsche Staatsbibliothek, MS Hamilton 482, dated 1461, containing Patrizi's *Poematum libri IV.*

BAV      Vatican City, Bibliotheca Apostolica Vaticana.

BNP      *Brill's New Pauly,* Hubert Cancik and Helmuth Schneider, eds. (Leiden: E. J. Brill). Published online, 2006–.

CTC      *Catalogus Translationum et Commentariorum: Medieval and Renaissance Latin Translations and Commentaries: Annotated Lists and Guides,* Paul Oskar Kristeller, F. Edward Cranz, Virginia Brown, and Greti Dinkova-Bruun, eds. 13 vols. to date (Washington, DC: Catholic University of America; Toronto: Pontifical Institute for Mediaeval Studies, 1960–2022).

DBI      *Dizionario biografico degli italiani,* 100 vols. (Rome: Treccani, 1961–2020), cited from the website www.treccani.it/biografico/.

Epg.     *Epigram* from Patrizi's *Epigrammaton liber.* Texts are cited from the one surviving manuscript, G. The MS contains 345 epigrams, of which 23 were edited in three articles by Leslie Smith (see Bibliography), who also assigned numbers to each item in the collection. See also https://projects.iq.harvard.edu/patrizisiena.

F        Florence, Biblioteca Medicea Laurenziana, MS Gaddi 167, partly autograph, containing *Rep.*

G        Phyllis Goodhart Gordan MS 153, deposited at the Rare Books Reading Room, Bryn Mawr College. The unique copy of Patrizi's *Epigrammaton liber.*

ITRL     I Tatti Renaissance Library.

M        New Haven, Yale University, Beinecke Library MS Marston 147, ff. 61r–65r. Contains Patrizi's *De gerendo magistratu.*

Poem.    Patrizi, *Poematum libri IV.* Cited by book and number of the poem within each book. The text in this volume follows *B.* See Appendix A and https://projects.iq.harvard.edu/patrizisiena.

Reg.   *De regno et regis institutione,* cited by book and chapter from the 1518 *editio princeps. Ded.* indicates the prefatory letter of the entire work, directed to Alfonso, duke of Calabria, while *Pr.* indicates the proems of books 2–6 of the work.

Rep.   *De institutione reipublicae,* cited by book and chapter. *Ded.1, Ded.2,* and *Ded.3* indicate the three dedicatory letters prefixed to the entire work (see Chapter 2). *Pr.* indicates the proem of each book. Cited from the *editio princeps* of 1518, collated with the partially autograph *F* and the dedication copy *V.*

USTC   *Universal Short Title Catalogue.* Hosted by the University of St. Andrews. 2011–. Online.

V      Vatican City, Biblioteca Apostolica Vaticana, MS Vat. lat. 3084 (1479), the dedication copy of *Rep.,* viewable online at digi.vatlib.it (DVL).

# Notes

## Introduction

1. Hankins 2019.
2. Lee 2016 provides an overview of this tradition.
3. Lee 2016, 16.
4. On Locke's debt to Christian principles, see Waldron 2002; Pritchard 2014.
5. Copenhaver 2019.
6. Hankins 2019, 206–215.
7. Pedullà 2021a, 115–116 notes: "Writing in the 1460s, Patrizi was the first modern political theorist to take his information mostly straight from the Greek historians. . . . This impressive rise in historical evidence alone suffices to make both the *De institutione reipublicae* and the *De regno* a real turning point in the early modern reception of Athenian democracy. . . . In the 1460s and 70s Patrizi was clearly much more informed about Athenian democracy than anyone before him in the preceding one thousand years."
8. See Appendix B.
9. Battaglia 1936, a dual study of Patrizi and Enea Silvio Piccolomini, devotes seventy-five pages to Patrizi, most of which is given over to the analysis of his two major political treatises. The basic biographical data was first collected in Bassi 1894; Battaglia was able to add some new details by consulting archival materials in Siena.
10. Pedullà 2010; Quintiliani 2014. A pamphlet by Francesca Cristina Nardone on Patrizi (Nardone 1996) is useless, having no source references or bibliography. The only copy I have been able to locate is in the Biblioteca Nazionale Centrale in Rome. (I thank Ornella Rossi for helping me to confirm this.) Owing to pandemic restrictions I have not been able to gain access to the Oxford Ph.D. thesis of P. Benetti Bertoldo (1996), but I thank Francesco Nevola for sharing with me his detailed notes on the thesis.
11. De Capua 2014. De Capua edited all of Patrizi's letters in her doctoral thesis (De Capua 1991), but the thesis has not yet been published.
12. For the far less well documented case of Giannozzo Manetti as a provincial governor, see Connell 2001.
13. Young used the term "meritocracy" as a pejorative term in his dystopian novel, *The Rise of the Meritocracy* (1958). As Gabriele Pedullà informs me, the first person to use the word "meritocracy" in a positive sense was probably the Harvard sociologist Daniel Bell (1972). I am far from the first scholar to apply the term to a Renaissance political thinker; for example, Alison Brown (in Guicciardini 1994, xx–xxi) uses it to describe Guicciardini's philosophy of government.
14. Hankins 2019, esp. 38–40 and passim.

15. Hankins 2019, 495–512.

16. See Chan 2013.

# 1. The Formation of a Political Philosopher

1. See Boschetto 2018 for the effects of Bernardo Machiavelli's illegitimacy on his son Niccolò.

2. The indispensable starting place for all study of Patrizi's life is De Capua 2014, which, being far more than a study of Patrizi's letters, in effect provides a *biografia documentata* of Patrizi's life and works from birth to death.

3. See *Rep.* 6.1, a passage where Patrizi is commenting on social ranks in ancient Rome: "My ancestors were originally derived from this [patrician] order, hence the *cognomen* 'Patrizi' has stuck in perpetuity to our family. We originated in Rome and rose to prominence in Siena, a fact indicated not only by a long line of grandparents and ancestors, but in ancient documents and tokens I have discovered belonging to our house, and inscriptions in very ancient marbles may be seen in many places in Rome down to the present day." Patrizi included further discussion of his family origins in his unpublished historical essay *De origine et antiquitate urbis Senae* (On the origin and ancient history of the city of Siena); see Appendix A. He does not mention that one of his ancestors, also called Francesco Patrizi, was a prominent early member of the Servite order; he was canonized as a saint by Pope Benedict XIV in 1743.

4. On Petrarch as the founder of a new moral discourse centered on virtue, see Quondam 2010, 254–304.

5. See Beccadelli 2010.

6. Marrasio 2016.

7. *Rep.* 2.6. In *Epg.* 5, a poem about his longing to return to Siena, Patrizi invokes the Fonte Gaia as one place that he wants to revisit, a fountain dedicated to Apollo and the Muses (text in L. Smith 1968, 100).

8. Enea Silvio Piccolomini in 1458 described him as a poet unjustly exiled from Siena; see De Capua 2014, 100n, citing Pius II 2001, 225–226: "Francesco Patrizi, of whom many poems (*poemata*) are extant [which] are sought after by the learned."

9. These are contained in *Poem.*, book 3, which is described as comprising lighter poems of entertainment. They include *Poem.* 3.7 (On the difficulty of love affairs), 3.8 (On the insanity of lovers), 3.13. (Naeera to the wind about her love affairs), 3.14 (A rebuke of love, to Synolphus), 3.17 (To Cynthia on the love affairs of Achilles). Patrizi declares here that love poems are morally acceptable "so long as soft lewdness and wanton games are kept far off." It may be the harsh reception of Panormita's *Hermaphrodite* that discouraged Patrizi from similar licentiousness, though his patron Piccolomini, the emperor's court poet, continued to compose erotic poetry, including the bawdy comedy *Chrysis* (1444), until he became a cardinal. Patrizi's few poems on love in book 3 anticipate the discreet and elegant erotic poetry later practiced by humanists like Cristoforo Landino and Pietro Bembo. Patrizi himself continued to write occasionally in the genre in his *Epigrammaton liber.*

10. Patrizi's *De metris Horatii* is dated by De Capua to his years of teaching in Siena (1441–1446), which predates Filelfo's collection of *Odes* (1455 / 1456). See Appendix A and Filelfo 2009.

11. See Grant 1965, 159.

12. Patrizi's commitment to peace in Italy, as so often for humanists, was balanced in at least one poem with a call to join the crusade against the Turk: see "Otia haec" (*Poem.* 1.2, to Pius II). Patrizi's patron Pius II was the most enthusiastic papal proponent of crusade in the quattrocento.

13. For the scant literature on Patrizi's poetry, see Bassi 1894; Altamura 1941; L. Smith 1966–1968, 1968, 1974; and Avesani 1968.

14. His one work in Italian was a *Commento* on Petrarch's *Canzoniere*, which (predictably) is his only work to receive detailed study from modern Italianists; see above, 53–54, and Appendix A.

15. Patrizi's only two works printed in the incunabular period were the *De Christi natali* and a speech for Innocent VIII's coronation; see https://projects.iq.harvard.edu/patrizisiena.

16. See Chapter 2, 79–80.

17. Field 2017, chap. 5. Filelfo's experience of exile and his hostility to Cosimo de'Medici are poured out in his "De exilio": see Filelfo 2014. The latter work displays a deep hatred of political power in the hands of the wealthy, an attitude Filelfo seems to have instilled in his star pupil, Patrizi.

18. See Pertici 1990; De Capua 2014. Petrucci was a bitter enemy of the Medici, even though he was said to harbor ambitions for personal power in Siena similar to Cosimo's.

19. In general, see Ciccolella 2008; Wilson 2017.

20. Dati credited Patrizi's *auctoritas* for his "conversion" to the study of eloquence from philosophy; see De Capua 2014, 39. Regarding Greek studies in Siena, the Florentine Lapo da Castigionchio should also be mentioned: he began his study of Greek under Filelfo in Florence before joining his teacher after the latter's flight to Siena. He and Patrizi became good friends, and their correspondence (De Capua 2014, 335–339), only partly published, is our best source for this period of Patrizi's studies. On Lapo's career and his translations from the Greek, see Riccardo Fubini in *DBI* and Gualdo Rosa 2018.

21. *Epg.* 140, "Ad Pacificum Neapolitanum" (G, 48r).

Οὔνομα σοὶ γλυκὺ, ὦ εἰρηνικὲ παρθενοπαίε,
Γλόσσα δὲ σοὶ πικρή, τ'ἄλλα γε πάντα καλῶς.
Your name is sweet, O irenic Parthenopean,
You have a bitter tongue, but the all the rest is pleasing.

Pacificus is possibly to be identified with the poet Pacifico Massimi from Ascoli, known for his acerbic wit, for whom see the entry of Alessandra Mulas in *DBI* 71 (2008). It is not clear why Patrizi would call him "Parthenopaeus"—i.e., Neapolitan.

22. Not enough work has been done on Patrizi's sources to know the extent to which he relied on contemporary translations from the Greek and what texts he may have read in the original. Since almost all of Patrizi's Greek sources (see Chapter 2, 77–79) had in fact been translated by contemporary humanist scholars, it seems likely that he used them whenever he could; his contacts in Rome, Florence, and Ferrara would have kept him up to date with the latest Latin versions. As further evidence that Patrizi did not rely entirely on translations, the following may be noted. In the *De republica* 9.6 he translates a line of Pindar; in the *De regno* he translates from Hesiod's *Works and Days* (6.10) and from Homer's *Odyssey* (9.19), and he turns a Greek proverb into Latin at 4.1. In *De republica* 8.5 he quotes five lines in Greek from (ps.) Herodotus's *Life of Homer*; these lines are not translated in the dedication copy *V* and are omitted entirely in the *editio princeps* of 1518 and all subsequent editions. Although the pseudo-Herodotean life of Homer had been translated previously by Petrus Parleo, Patrizi says that he does not remember having read the lines anywhere else. Patrizi frequently inserts Greek words and phrases, with their Latin equivalents, in both his major political works.

23. See also Filelfo 2005 for his status as a poetic innovator. Patrizi, along with Enea Silvio Piccolomini, was among the first to use the Sapphic ode for Christian religious subjects. He also included Catullan hendecasyllables in his *Poemata*, a meter that had only begun to be revived in the 1420s; see Gaisser 1993. On the ties of affection and mutual aid

between teacher and pupil, see the many letters to Patrizi in Filelfo 2015: for example, *Epistulae* 6.39 (dated 1448), 8.18 (1451), 9.20 (1451), 14.11–12 (1458, urging Nicodemo Tranchedini to help Patrizi in exile), 25.4 (1465, on a point of Greek etymology), 25.5 (1465, asking Patrizi for a copy of Ammianus Marcellinus), 25.8 and 25.11 (1465, consoling Patrizi for his sufferings from irritated bowels), 25.16 (1465, answering a letter from Patrizi in Siena).

24. Filelfo may also have sparked in his pupil Patrizi an interest in ancient music; see Hankins 2021c for Filelfo's study of ancient Greek music, which shares sources with Patrizi's verse history of music in *Poem.*1.4 and his account of the history of music in *Rep.* 2, discussed below in Chapter 5.

25. Schmitt 1972, 49–51; Schmitt edits the text (= De Capua 2014, 343 [letter B 35]) on pp. 171–177. Material from the letter was later redeployed in *Rep.* 2.7.

26. Grendler 2002, 209–214. Lines 2022, chap. 5, gives a detailed account of the introduction of humanistic studies in Europe's most prestigious university, Bologna. On the revival of the University of Siena in this period see also Denley 1991. For Patrizi's later ideas on the reform of civic education, see Chapter 5.

27. Unpublished; Caroline Engelmayer and I are preparing a critical edition with translation for *Rinascimento*. In the second manuscript, after the title *De studiorum artium optimarum laudibus,* the scribe adds: "facta in aula dominorum Senensium in principio studii" (delivered in the palace of the lords of the Sienese at the beginning of the school year). It may be that the speech was revised after 1426 since it makes use of several sources, such as Diogenes Laertius and Plutarch, that were available in Latin only at a later date.

28. For the Sienese Studio in the quattrocento, see Fioravanti 1981; Ascheri 1991b; Denley 2006, 2007. To treat theology as a genus of philosophy is a striking reversal of medieval scholastic hierarchies. On the understanding of philosophy as *omne scibile,* see Robert Black, "The Philosopher and Renaissance Culture," in Hankins 2007, 13–29.

29. For Patrizi's mature views on civic education, see Chapter 5.

30. See Andreoccio Petrucci's admiring comments on Patrizi's brilliant delivery of the speech, in a letter to the *rimatore* Francesco Tolomei in Pertici 1990, 95–96 (Letter 39, dated 23 October 1426). For Patrizi's father as a close supporter of Andreoccio, see ibid., 125–126 (Letter 60), where Petrucci calls him "amicus et familiaris meus."

31. For the history of Siena in the later Middle Ages and the Renaissance, see Bowsky 1981; Ascheri 1985; Waley 1991; Ascheri 2001, 2021. For the fifteenth century, see esp. Pertici 1990; Shaw 2006 (the latter, despite its title, is mostly about Siena).

32. Bowsky 1962, 379n56; Bowsky 1981, 262. See also Ascheri 2001. The close alliance between the Tolomei, the Piccolomini, and the Patrizi is also shown by their cooperation in establishing a major religious foundation of the fourteenth century, the Abbey of Monteoliveto at Asciano.

33. For Mario Ascheri's misgivings about the term "mercantile oligarchy," see Ascheri 1991a as well as Ascheri and Franco 2020. Patrizi would later recommend curbing the economic power of large landowners as a way to equalize wealth; see Chapter 5.

34. For these ideals, see the letters exchanged between Andreoccio and Pannilini in Pertici 1990, also briefly discussed in Hankins 2019, 58–60.

35. See Appendix A. Eight manuscripts of this text are known at present. I quote from M, which is available online through the Beinecke Library (Yale) website. At *Rep.* 3.1 Patrizi states that he is omitting much that might be said about the conduct of magistrates, having already composed a treatise *De gerendo magistratu* in his youth. In fact, several passages from the *De gerendo* were excerpted verbatim and inserted at various places in *Rep.* For Patrizi's teachings on the proper conduct of magistracies, see also the numerous letters exchanged

with Achille, listed in De Capua 2014, 327–358 (Sezione B); for the disappointing performance of Achille as *podestà* or chief justice of Foligno, see below.

36. See also Chapter 4, 155–156, for further discussion of Patrizi's teachings on the correct comportment of magistrates.

37. According to unpublished research of Mario Ascheri and his équipe (see also the documents cited in De Capua 2014, 359–386), Francesco appears in the *Libri dei leoni* as officially resident in the *terzo* of San Martino and a member of the Nine, holding the office of Prior and representing them in the Concistoro as follows: "Franciscus Iohannis (Nannis) Francini (de Patriciis 1440 May–June; 1447 March–April; 1453 March–April)." He was a counselor of the Capitano del Popolo for the September–October term, 1452, and in this capacity would also have privileged access to meetings of the Concistoro. According to a personal communication from Mario Ascheri, Patrizi was elected chancellor of the city probably sometime in 1446 but resigned it in favor of his pupil Achille Petrucci in the March–April term of 1447, presumably upon his election to the priorate. Denley 2006, 212–213, points out that it was illegal to hold a teaching post at the Studium concurrently with other civil offices. De Capua 2014 notes Patrizi's two appointments as *podestà* in Radicofani (1446) and in Montalcino at an indeterminate date; the evidence for the latter appointment comes from Patrizi's poem "De casu fulminis" (*Poem*. 2.4).

38. See Pertici 1992 for a detailed account of the "conspiracy." On *coniuratio* and Renaissance conspiracy literature, see Celati 2021.

39. See Pius II 2004, 1:151 (1.31.2).

40. See Pius's *Epistolae familiares* (Leuven, 1483), sign. t ii v: "Cometes qui visus hoc anno est opinioni quae de se fuit abunde satisfecit. . . . In plerisque civitatibus seditiones excitavit, maxime apud Senam urbem, unde non parva civium pars exclusa est" (The comet visible in this year satisfied abundantly its reputation. . . . In many cities there were uprisings, most of all in Siena, thanks to which no small part of the citizens were expelled).

41. Though a confession obtained under torture cannot count as evidence for modern historians, it seems unlikely that Patrizi's sympathies were not strongly on Antonio's side. In his later historical work, *De origine et antiquitate urbis Senae*, using the first person, he exculpates Antonio from the charge of tyranny, arguing that Petrucci, being descended from Marcus Petreius, a Catonian and a bitter opponent of Julius Caesar, was presumptively by family tradition a republican opponent of tyranny. See Pertici 1990, 105; De Capua 2014, 77n2.

42. Filelfo 2015, *Epistula* 14.3, to Tranchedini (31 December 1456). Filelfo tries to soften the charges against Patrizi, observing that "a popular regime scarcely ever exists without sedition," and suggests that his friend Francesco's only problem was the envy that always accompanies outstanding men; he begs Tranchedini to help him in his distress.

43. Pius II 1571, 832 (Epistula 358), cited in De Capua 2014, 79n.

44. See De Capua 2014, 80, 387–391, for the documents.

45. On Patrizi's family, see De Capua 2014, passim; L. Smith 1974.

46. On the remarkable figure of Tranchedini, who maintained a pan-Italian network of contacts among humanists, see the entry of Maria Nadia Covini in *DBI* 96 (2019); it may have been at Filelfo's urging (note 42 above) that he added Patrizi to the squadron of humanists educating his son Francesco. His wide literary circle is documented in Florence, Biblioteca Riccardiana, MS Ricc. 834.

47. The work survives in at least sixteen manuscripts and was printed in 1554, falsely attributed to Pier Paolo Vergerio the Elder. Another pedagogical work, an epitome of Priscian, was written about this time, possibly also for Francesco; it too had a considerable circulation in manuscript. For both works, see Appendix A. The latter text is discussed in Bassi 1894, 438, and De Capua 2014, 107.

48. On Rinuccini, see Giustiniani 1965.

49. De Capua 2014, 110. Formerly under the nearby Badia di Passignano, already famous for its wine, the *pieve* was later monopolized by the Medici family, numbering Giulio de'Medici, the future Clement VII, among its *pievani*. In Letter B 33 (1467/1471) Agostino Patrizi conveyed to Francesco a proposal from Leonardo Dati, bishop of Massa, to trade benefices with him, his *pieve* for the church of San Giorgio in Siena; in 1474 Lorenzo de'Medici also asked him to give up the benefice (B 30). Patrizi refused both offers. See De Capua 2014, 197n.

50. *Poem.* 3.3; the text is in Avesani 1968, 63.

51. See Hankins 2019, chaps. 6 and 7. See also the summary above, 49–50, of Patrizi's *Epg.* 14 (*G*, f. 5r–v) from the late 1460s, which expresses a similar sentiment in favor of learned retirement to the country. In *Rep.* 6.2 he makes suburban villas an exception to his general rule that farmers should stay in the country and city dwellers should stay in the city: see Chapter 5, 208.

52. On their relations, see Gualdo Rosa, Nuovo, and Defilippis 1982, 21–26.

53. *Epg.* 56 (*G*, f. 19v). Ognibene taught at Vicenza from 1453 to end of his life. He translated Aesop, Plutarch's *Life of Camillus*, Xenophon's *On Hunting*, and a work of St. Athanasius. In 1469 he gave a course on Quintilian that may be related to Patrizi's *Epitome*. He composed well-known commentaries on Cicero's *De officiis*, Sallust, and Valerius Maximus. Patrizi also wrote an epitaph for Calderini, *Epg.* 169 (*G*, f. 55v), with whom he shared a love of Silver Age Latin poetry.

54. *Poem.* 4.5; my translation. For the date and circumstances, see De Capua 2014, 100; the text is in Avesani 1968, 63. Pius's entry into Siena is described in his own *Commentaries* 2.21.3 (Pius II 2003, 285). For Patrizi's longing to return to Siena, see also the prefaces to the *De republica*, discussed in Chapter 2, and his *Epg.* 5 (ed. L. Smith 1968, 100). He eventually composed, not a chronicle in verse of Siena, but a short historical essay on the ancient origins of Siena. It is still unpublished and unstudied (it survives in at least twelve mss.); see Appendix A.

55. *Poem.* 3.2. The poem commemorates Pius's solemn entry into Mantua but implies that Patrizi himself is not in Mantua. The 116 hexameters celebrate Gonzaga's building projects, such as his defense works, his building of *templa deorum* with bronze doors (possibly a reference to San Sebastiano, designed by Leon Battista Alberti, under construction at the time of the Council), his revival of the arts of sculpture and painting, and his support for the humanities (naming specifically Bartolomeo Platina, who had been tutor to Gonzaga's sons and, Patrizi writes, was currently studying Greek in Florence). It is possible that Pius arranged for the terms of Patrizi's exile in Verona to be changed in December 1459 so that the poet could join him in Mantua (45 kilometers south of Verona) before the close of the Council.

56. For example, the well-known anthology of Neo-Latin poetry, Bottari 1719–1726. The *De Christi natali* (*Poem.* 2.2) is a bucolic dialogue between Lycidas and Menalcus with a *nuncius* and St. Joseph also as speakers. It may well have been one model for Milton's *Lycidas*. Pius II wrote an admiring response to Patrizi's poem, consisting of eleven elegiac couplets, dated 23 March 1460 (Pius II 1994, 201). Patrizi's two Sapphic odes in honor of the Blessed Virgin were possibly written in imitation of Pius himself, who composed a Sapphic ode on the Passion of Christ. See Pius II 1571, 963–964 = Pius II 1883, 365–367, no. 87; see also his Sapphics *De nativitate domini*, ibid., 364, no. 85. Both of Pius's poems were written in the 1440s. Filelfo also included several Sapphic odes in his *Convivia mediolanensia* of 1442/1444, for which see Hankins 2021c.

57. As Avesani 1968, 30, points out, neither the dedication copy to Pius (BAV, MS Chis. J VI 233, which has Pius's papal arms together with Patrizi's, but the latter without a bishop's mitre surmounting his arms), nor the elegant presentation copy (Berlin, Deutsche Staatsbib-

liothek, MS Hamilton 1461, dated 21 September 1461) style Patrizi as bishop of Gaeta, which implies the collection was finished before Patrizi was elected bishop in March of that year.

58. For the themes of the *Epaenetica*, see Avesani 1968, who dates the collection to 1463/1464. See also De Capua 2014, 162–164, who shows that the anthology was organized by Agostino Patrizi Piccolomini (ca. 1435–1495), an amanuensis and protégé of Pius II, later (1484) bishop of Pienza and Montalcino. Agostino was also the pupil (but not a close relative, despite his name) of our Francesco Patrizi and later his most dependable literary collaborator. Agostino appears often in Francesco's correspondence and helped him assemble the sources used in *De republica* (see Chapter 2). For their relationship, see De Capua 2014, 155–172, who provides an extensive supplement to the short account of Agostino in the *DBI* article (2014) by Nelly Mahmoud Helmy.

59. See Hilary 1978, who calculates that 23.5 percent of the 820 appointments made by Pius during his pontificate recorded in the Vatican Archives were nepotistic. Lodrisio Crivelli, in his *Apologeticus adversus calumnias Francisci Philelphi pro Pio II* (21 November 1464, consulted in BAV, MS Ottob. lat. 1199, ff. 24r–31v), says that Pius was blamed for taking small notice of major cultural figures of mid-century Rome such as Biondo Flavio, Cardinal Besssarion, and members of the latter's circle. See also Marsh 2019, 183–187. Even a humanist friendly to the Piccolomini faction in the papal court such as Bartolomeo Platina (*Vita Pii*, 18, cited by Bauer 2006, 45n166) says that "he seemed to love his relatives on his mother and father's side and especially his nephews more than was fitting in a pope."

60. De Capua 2014, 116. My account here relies heavily on her meticulous reconstruction of Patrizi's governorship (chap. 2, 111–172).

61. On Italian-style dyarchy, see Law and Paton 2010, *ad indices*. On the wider problems of papal government and the role of intellectuals in this period, see the rich studies of De Vincentiis 2002a, 2002b. For more on dyarchy as a governing hierarchy in which a superior power agrees to limit its sovereignty over an inferior power, see Chapter 7, 309–317.

62. For the general situation in the Papal States at the time of Pius's accession, and Pius's plans to forge them into a princely territorial state, see O'Brien 2015, 35–41, 170–180.

63. The dossier was edited in De Capua's doctoral thesis (1991) but never published; a list with a summary of the contents of each document is given as Sezione A in De Capua 2014, 251–325; the letters are extensively quoted and discussed in chapter 2 of that study. The collection of letters, the so-called Foligno Corpus, had a certain circulation in manuscript form; De Capua lists seven copies of the collection in literary manuscripts of the later fifteenth century in her discussion of its tradition (De Capua 2014, 223–247).

64. De Capua 2014, 117.

65. De Capua 2014, 117–118.

66. De Capua 2014, 119.

67. De Capua 2014, 286–287 (Foligno Corpus, A 73–75).

68. Jones (1974, 228) writes, "In Pius II [Sigismondo] had chosen an adversary bitter, obdurate and pertinacious, who for the next three years, unmoved by the remonstrances of the other Italian powers, was to pursue him with blind and absorbing rancour." See also D'Elia 2016, esp. chap. 1, on Sigismondo's "black legend," which to a great extent was the creation of Pius's propaganda war against him.

69. See Chapter 2 for further analysis of the genesis and progress of *Rep*.

70. De Capua 2014, 313–315 (Foligno Corpus, A 143).

71. De Capua 2014, 143n3.

72. Ammanati's detailed account in his *Commentarii* is reproduced in De Capua 2014, 146–148; for Patrizi's more summary account, see ibid., 149–150.

73. De Capua 2014, 152n.

74. De Capua 2014, 230–231. An edited and annotated version of the Foligno Corpus, De Capua's codex *V*, copied in the seventeenth century, may have as its source a manuscript in the hands of Olivier's commission.

75. De Capua 2014, 152–153n4.

76. The speech Patrizi gave on this occasion, the *Oratio ad Hippolytam Mariam Sforzam (De matrimonio)* was delivered in Milan on 19 May. On this speech, see D'Elia 2004, ad indicem. The speech includes reflections on matrimony later incorporated into *Rep.*, book 4; see below, Chapter 4. The work survives in at least eight manuscripts and has been printed twice in modern times.

77. Quoted from Bauer 2006, 33, who gives a balanced account of Platina's relations with Paul II.

78. Bauer 2006, 64n247.

79. Hankins 2011, 34–35.

80. *Rep.* 2.Ded.2.

81. No attack on Patrizi is found in Crivelli's *Apologeticus* (BAV, MS Ottob. Lat. 1191, f. 24r–31v), the text to which Filelfo was presumably responding, but Filelfo may well have heard rumors that Crivelli had joined the chorus of slander against his former student.

82. Filelfo 2015, Epistula 26.1; see the accounts in Bauer 2006 and Marsh 2019.

83. Patrizi praises Gaeta's welcoming attitude in the first preface to the *De republica*, where he speaks of "the pleasantness of the city of Gaeta and the kindness of its citizens toward me. They treat me not as foreigner and immigrant but like a native and fellow citizen, embracing me with courtesy and reverence. One may add as well the marvelous fruitfulness of the region and the wonderful healthiness of the climate." This account of Gaeta was excerpted by an unknown hand and inserted into a codex of the *De republica* now at the Abbey of Montecassino (MS Cas. 425, f. 1); the excerpt carries the title *De laudibus civitatis Caietae* (In praise of the city of Gaeta). It is a remarkable statement, given Patrizi's own restrictive attitude to immigrants in the *De republica*: see Chapter 6, 256–258. A number of Patrizi's epigrams deal with Gaeta, including epigrams 130, 172, 180, 259, and 274; in 172 and 180 he speaks in the personified voice of Gaeta, who is styled "the nurse of Aeneas," following an old etymology.

84. *Epg.* 188; text in L. Smith 1968, 125. On Patrizi's Gaeta period, see De Capua 2014, 172–221.

85. Patrizi addressed to him *Epgg.* 248 and 259; 248 is edited in L. Smith 1968, 120. Patrizi probably knew Fra Giocondo already from his Verona days; see Chapter 1, 35. It is possible that the Sienese architect Francesco di Giorgio Martini, who also worked for Alfonso, was involved. On their connection, see further in Chapter 5, 220.

86. Ilarione of Verona 1473, an imprint that also contains an elegy written by Ilarione. The work is summarized and partly edited in Fuiano 1974. The dialogue takes place between Ilarione and the humanist printer Johannes Philippus de Lignamine, another protégé of Sixtus IV. There no mention of Patrizi in the published portions, but for their close relationship going back to Patrizi's time in Verona, see Chapter 1, 35. Ilarione (ca. 1444–1485) composed an epigram in praise of Patrizi's *De republica* (De Capua 2014, 199; see also Chapter 2, 63), and Patrizi wrote a lament (*Epg.* 170) for Ilarione's death by drowning. Ilarione knew Greek well and translated the ancient rhetorician Hermogenes as well as several patristic works. His wide literary, philosophical, and historical interests are attested in the *Dialogus*. The nearby town of Itri on the Appian Way, which Patrizi calls Hydrum Lemurnum, also harbored a friendly grammarian, named Giovanni Andrea, who sent Patrizi truffles and received epigrams in thanks; see *Epgg.* 198 and 278.

87. See Hankins 2019, chap. 6, on Petrarch's refuges. At *Reg.* 9.8 (see Chapter 7, 265), Patrizi quotes the philosopher Lacydes, who, when asked by King Attalus of Pergamon to

enter his service, refused, saying that "philosophers, like pictures or statues, are best seen from the middle distance rather than at close range."

88. Cardinal Ammanati, defending him to the Cardinal of Naples, who had complained of Patrizi's lack of deference, wrote that he was "ineptus ad omne obsequium," no good at subservience (Battaglia 1936, 96n2). His pride in what he believed to be his noble Roman ancestry may have prevented him from displaying the degree of servility requisite for the life of a courtier. It is worth observing that Patrizi does not pull any punches in his *De regno*, addressed to his patron Alfonso of Calabria, heir to the throne: the duke (who was a famous warrior) is advised that justice, not war, is the king's highest calling, and that control of the passions (Alfonso was notorious for his unbridled appetites) was the key to virtue. Unlike in the *De republica*, in the *De regno* there is almost no discussion of military affairs, a subject that might have been thought to appeal to the victorious leader of Christian resistance to the Turks at Otranto.

89. *Epg.* 14 (*G*, 5r–v), probably from the late 1460s, "Men deeply learned in Chaldaean lore" may refer to Homer and Hesiod, who in *Reg.* 8.15 are said to have learned their theology from the Chaldaeans and the Egyptians. The Latin text is given in Appendix C.

90. The mission of 1484 was to congratulate the Genoese prelate Giovanni Battista Cybo on his election as Pope Innocent VIII. Because Ferrante's relations with Genoa were poor, Patrizi may have been chosen because he was not Neapolitan and was only tenuously connected with Ferrante's court. Patrizi's speech on that occasion was the only other work of his printed during his lifetime, apart from the eclogue *On the Nativity of Christ*. The speech survives in three manuscripts and three Roman imprints from 1484; see De Capua 2014, 179, and below, Appendix A. It praises Innocent in stock terms as the bringer of a new golden age and highlights past services of the Aragonese kings to the papacy; Alfonso, duke of Calabria, Patrizi's patron, is singled out for his famous victory over the Turks at Otranto.

91. Capobianco 2000, 2:362–376, who discusses Bishop Patrizi's role in refounding the sanctuary of the Madonna della Civita (1491) above the town of Itri on Monte Fusco, rededicating it to the Immaculate Mary (as recommended by the Council of Basel). Patrizi mentions the sanctuary in an epigram (197) addressed to the town, *Ad Hydrum Lemurnum, oppidum Viae Appiae,* probably from the 1480s. (The sanctuary is now a pilgrimage site visited by half a million devotees every year, according to Wikipedia, a figure difficult to credit.) While still in Foligno, Patrizi had an unhappy experience when his vicar, Fra Lorenzo of Fundi, was accused of peculation (1463)—"that sacrilegious scoundrel Lorenzo," as Patrizi called him. At this point Patrizi's former student Agostino Patrizi Piccolomini stepped in to help him with diocesan affairs until he was able to take up residence himself late in 1464. The experience may well have commended to Patrizi the merits of administering his own diocese.

92. Its provenance and rediscovery is described in L. Smith 1968.

93. In *Epg.* 200 (*G*, 64r), Patrizi begs the muse not to desert him in his old age; after all, "*senectus* is the most perfect of the ages of man." On the *Epigrammata*, see the three articles by Leslie F. Smith listed in the Bibliography. Smith (1968) hypothesizes, based on some indications in the manuscript, that Patrizi intended the collection to be divided into four books. Patrizi wrote a dedicatory epigram (3, *G*, 1v) to Cardinal Francesco Todeschi Piccolomini, later (1503) Pope Pius III, perhaps intending the dedication as compensation for having presented his *De republica* to Sixtus IV instead of to Cardinal Francesco, as the latter had requested (see Chapter 2, 62). That he also planned to present the work to the city of Siena is implied by *Epg.* 6 (*G*, 2r–v). The earliest datable poem is *Epg.* 2, probably from around 1467, and the latest is *Epg.* 196, from 1488 (see below). Smith believed that the epigrams were arranged roughly by date of composition but in some cases had already been repositioned within the codex with a view to an eventual arrangement in four books.

94. Epigram collections of all four poets are available in the I Tatti Renaissance Library. On the history of the genre in the Renaissance, see Ciccolella 2016; see also Beer, Enenkel, and Rijser 2009. In the presentation poem (*Epg.* 6 = G, 2r–v) addressed to Siena, Patrizi urges the city to read his *Epigrammata* and not to point a finger angrily at him, because all the poems contained within it are decent; Pallas will be there to control her sister (Aphrodite), so that she comes dressed decorously in wifely garb.

95. *Epgg.* 336 (On the first invention of epigrams) and 337 (The foreign words used by the man who first transformed the epigram into wicked and impious trifles), discussed by L. Smith 1968, 99, and Prete 1981, 218. See also *Epgg.* 309 (That obscene verses should not be read) and 165 (ed. L. Smith 1968, 117) where he issues a conventional, mock-modest apology for the triviality of his own Camenae. Following Filelfo, Patrizi takes a similar view of the moral decline of music, which has to return to its early Greek modes to recover its original power to inspire civic virtue. For Filelfo's exploration of this historical scheme of rebirth in music, see Hankins 2021c. *Epg.* 311 is addressed to Carlo Valgulio, a follower of Ficino with whom Patrizi also shared an interest in the history of ancient music.

96. Patrizi's relations with Alfonso are illustrated in *Epgg.* 7, 26, 35, 86–87, 180, 191–194, 259–261; these are courtly in character and suggest intermittent contact with Alfonso of Calabria's household, based in the Castel Capuano on the other side of Naples from Ferrante's Castel Nuovo in the harbor. The duke also had a palace in Gaeta, so Patrizi would not necessarily have had to travel to Naples to be in contact with young Alfonso.

97. *Epgg.* 146–155; see also 174 and 204. These were written in the mid-1480s when Siena "came to be governed by one of the most self-consciously popular regimes of any Italian city of the fifteenth century" (Shaw 2006, 57). In the war between Florence, the papacy, and the Kingdom of Naples following the Pazzi conspiracy of 1478, Alfonso of Calabria had based his army in Sienese territory with the willing acquiescence of his ally Siena, entering the city itself in 1479. Like Pius II, the duke used his influence in Siena to restore a number of the exiles and their family members who had been banished from the city in 1456–1458, probably those referred to in *Epg.* 204 (To Sienese exiles returning to their country). It was Alfonso's presence in the city and his open support for the Nove faction against the Riformatori that led to the populist reaction of the mid-1480s (Shaw 2006, 57–61). This seems to have made it impossible for Patrizi to return to Siena, effectively imposing upon him a second exile. See *Epg.* 172, where the city of Gaeta addresses the city of Siena, urging the poet's stepmotherly city to take back a man who does her honor and to restore his property so that he may have modest means to support himself. *Epgg.* 146–155 may have been intended in part to register Patrizi's support for Alfonso of Calabria's policies in Siena, which were also backed by his patrons in the Piccolomini clan. A more positive attitude to his native city is found in Patrizi's *Epg.* 6 (To Siena, his most opulent country), probably written much earlier, perhaps around the time of the dedications to Siena of *Rep.*, ca. 1470.

98. For the epigrams addressed to his family, see L. Smith 1974.

99. See the careful prosopography in Furstenberg-Levi 2016, where Patrizi's name does not appear even in the index. He is similarly absent from Bentley 1987.

100. Hankins 2011; Furstenberg-Levi 2016.

101. The only epistolary contact between Patrizi and Panormita came in 1461, when Beccadelli asked a favor of him in his role as governor of Foligno; see De Capua 2014, 341. In several letters to Patrizi during his Gaeta period (ibid., 177–178, 334–335) Filelfo asked to be commended to Panormita and asked Patrizi's advice about approaching Alfonso's teacher for a post at the Neapolitan court; there are no surviving replies from Patrizi to these requests. There are also no recorded contacts with Pontano, who proudly publicized his role as royal tutor—for example, on the base of his portrait bust by Adriano Fiorentino, where he is styled "Alphonsi Calabriae ducis praecptor" (Tutor to Alfonso, duke of Calabria).

102. *Bessarion's academy.* Patrizi received one letter inquiring about patronage from Bessarion (De Capua 2014, 296–297, dated 1463) while governor of Foligno; he wrote an epigram (*Epg.* 211) addressed to Bessarion's longtime secretary, Niccolò Perotti, about a literary dispute regarding the dedicatee of elder Pliny's *Natural History*. He also wrote an epitaph for Domizio Calderini, whom, like Ilarione, he probably knew already as a student in Verona (see Chapter 1, 35). He seems to have had no connections with Theodore Gaza, the greatest Greek scholar of the humanist movement before the time of Poliziano. *Pomponio Leto's academy:* There is no record of correspondence or other exchanges between Leto himself or Platina or any of the nearly one hundred other authors known to be associated with Leto in the two phases of his academy's existence: see https://www.repertoriumpomponianum.it/ for a list. The only real exception is Giovantonio Campano, to whom Patrizi addressed a short epigram (*Epg.* 173). Campano was close to Pius II and Cardinal Ammanati, and Patrizi would surely have met him while governor of Foligno. Campano himself was a bishop who served as governor of several papal states and a noted epigrammatist, who also wrote a biography of Pius II. Patrizi had a friendly exchange of letters with Marsilio Ficino in 1459 about his epitome of Quintilian, but in the Gaeta years his only known link to Ficino was via Carlo Valgulio (see above, 358n95). For the nature and membership of Ficino's academy, see Hankins 2011.

103. See *Epgg.* 7, 26, 35, 86, 87, 180. Two short Latin speeches by Ippolita have been translated into English in King and Rabil 1983, 44–47. Patrizi wrote five short epigrams (191–195) after the death of Ippolita Maria in 1488, four of them as epitaphs for her marble tomb, the fifth in the voice of the dying wife to her husband. He had been the official orator at their wedding twenty-three years earlier. Patrizi also composed an epigram (196) in the voice of King Ferrante, addressed to his grand-daughter Isabella, the daughter of Alfonso and Ippolita Maria, who was leaving for Milan (1488) to marry Gian Galeazzo Sforza. None of these epigrams have been cited in the scholarship on Ippolita Maria or on Isabella, who like her mother had an interest in good letters. These are the latest datable epigrams in the collection.

104. See Pontano's *Antonius,* in Pontano 2012–2020, for the carnivalesque atmosphere of these semi-public gatherings. Against this view is the report, possibly inflated, that Pontano served as Ippolita Maria's private secretary, see Bryce 2002, 66.

105. For Ippolita Maria Sforza's role in encouraging vernacular literature in the Kingdom of Naples, see Cox 2008, 41. Alfonso's circle also included Iñigo d'Avalos, a noble Aragonese and a great patron of letters and music as well as a noted bibliophile. Many of his books entered the royal collection after his death. His learned daughter Costanza was also a student and proponent of vernacular literature. Despite his humanist teachers and despite his real support for humanist culture, Alfonso was himself preoccupied with war and religion, though he shared with Patrizi a delight in architecture. The date of 1476/1477 for Patrizi's *commento* is De Capua's, but Alfonso's request for a commentary on Petrarch may go back even further than that: see *Epg.* 7 (*G,* 2v), where Patrizi pleads with Alfonso to be freed of the task of interpreting the enigmas of the Tuscan poet, whom he accuses of producing obscure and lovesick nonsense from his burning breast.

106. See *Epgg.* 199 and 202 to Giovanni Albino, on Atalanta and the golden apples, edited by L. Smith 1968, 122–123. Their meaning is obscure, but Patrizi seems to be asking wittily for payment of a hundred gold coins for his "golden apples," which, like those cast before Atalanta by Hippomenes, were keeping the runner from victory.

107. The whole affair is analyzed in detail by De Capua 2014, 179–192. For Patrizi's attitude to Petrarch, see Paolino 1999, 2000. It has not yet been demonstrated whether another commentary, on Petrarch's *Trionfi,* is correctly ascribed to Patrizi; see De Capua's discussion. The *Epigrammaton liber* contains five epigrams entitled *Triumphi* (73–77), which might as easily relate to Porcellio's Latin *Triumphus Alfonsi regis* as to Petrarch's Italian *Trionfi;* see De Capua 2014, 92.

## 2. The Great Political Treatises

1. Flavio 2005, 301–309 (Romagna, 6.25–31).
2. Hankins 2019, 67–69, 257–258.
3. Alberti 1988, 1 (but my translation).
4. Hankins 2019, chap. 11.
5. Hankins 2019, chap. 9.
6. Hankins 2015; for "classic" music, see 246.
7. Hankins 2017.
8. The letter lacks a heading but is convincingly attributed to Patrizi by De Capua 2014, 197–198, who published it for the first time. The last phrase quoted ("since from the beginning . . .") was probably intended to excuse himself to the cardinal, who had offered to sponsor the work himself (see below). Some phrases from the letter were reused in the preface to Sixtus IV of the second book of the *De republica,* evidence that should further cement De Capua's attribution of the letter to Patrizi, if any is needed. It is worth noting that Patrizi refers to his earlier treatise as *De civili societate* in *Reg.* 2.6.
9. *Commentaries* 2.21.9, in Pius II 2004, 289. For Pius's version of Sienese history, where the exclusion of the nobles from the highest offices in 1277 (reaffirmed in the constitution of 1403, hence the phrase "more than fifty years") was a voluntary renunciation by the nobles, see ibid., 2.13. For Patrizi's poetic celebration of the grand entry, see Chapter 1, 35–36. For Pius's views on popular republics and the moral deficiencies of the *plebs,* see Stolf 2012, 343–350.
10. Adams 1989 (quotation on p. 50); C. Smith 1992, 98–129 ("the first ideal city plan to be built in the Renaissance"); and Nevola 2007, for Pius's plans to renovate the urban spaces of Siena.
11. Nevola 2009 was the first architectural historian to link Pius's urbanism with book 8 of the *De republica,* though some excerpts from Patrizi's *Rep.* were made in an appendix in Tönnesman 1990. Pienza's design shows, among other things, a careful reading of Vitruvius, who was an important source for Patrizi's ideas about urban planning in *Rep.* 8; Patrizi's friend Fra Giocondo was later considered the greatest humanist authority on the text.
12. For the documents, see De Capua 2014, 193–212.
13. *Epg.* 2 (ed. L. Smith 1968, 117–118), which states that he has been working on the treatise for six years. If he began the treatise in 1461, this would date the epigram to around 1467.
14. Patrizi seems to have intended his *Epigrammata* to be dedicated to Cardinal Francesco in compensation for giving the *De republica* to Sixtus IV; see the dedicatory poem, *Epg.* 3 (*G,* 1r–v), where he writes that Pythagoras, Plato, Solon, and other ancient political writers have not placed themselves at the cardinal's service, but that he might like the epigrams better, and they might bring him more praise in the end, "for serious works are praised, but humorous ones are read."
15. See Horace, *Ars poetica* 388–389.
16. De Capua 2014, 196.
17. *Epg.* 4 (ed. L. Smith 1968, 118). If one can read the *totidem* in line 15 as referring back to the nine Muses, then we can posit that Patrizi kept the *De republica* with him for nine years, thus dating the epigram to about 1470 and making it roughly contemporaneous with the letter from Agostino Patrizi just quoted.
18. Ilarione wrote that Sixtus had summoned him back to his household twice, and that he had twice been disappointed (*bis revocatus, bis illusus*); see Gualdo Rosa, Nuovo, and Defilippis 1992. He may well have recruited his friend, the scribe Petrus Ursuleus, to

prepare the dedication copy. Ursuleus's beautifully written and decorated work (*V*), however, was only finished in 1479, and it is doubtful whether by that date it could have served as a dedication copy (De Capua 2014, 200, 203). On Ursuleo, see Sciancalepore 2006. Patrizi composed an epigram (44) critical of the illuminator's work (edited by De Capua 2014, 206), which was also copied into *V*.

19. The epigram is published in De Capua 2014, 199; it was appended to the partly autograph copy of the *De republica* in the Laurentian Library (*F*).

20. See Chapter 2, 81–83.

21. Hankins 1990, 1:110–117; Hankins 2019, 97–98. A thorough study and edition of this text has now been made by Paolo Pontù Donato, in Decembrio 2020. Michele Savonarola, *De esse verae republicae* (On the essence of the true republic), surviving in only one manuscript, is currently unavailable for consultation or reproduction at the Biblioteca Estense in Modena. Savonarola, too, advocates a monarchical republic; see Hankins 2019, 89.

22. See Hankins 2019, chap. 3, for the traditional use of the term *respublica* to refer to any legitimate state, including a monarchy. The use of the term *respublica* to mean "non-monarchical government" only became widespread among humanists in the fifteenth century; Patrizi uses the word in the modern sense in the title of his treatise.

23. Cappelli 2020a. The work survives, as far as is known, in only one manuscript of the fifteenth century.

24. At *Rep.* 1.6 Patrizi says "it is now time to discuss the selection of magistrates," a topic, he writes, that must begin with the question of which classes of citizens should be able to hold magistracies; but before addressing that question he needs to discuss whether farmers deserve admission to magistracies because of their material contributions to the welfare of the state (see Chapter 4, 137). The long discussion of which socio-economic groups should participate in government is put off to book 6; the question of how to select magistrates is split between books 3 and 6. The discussion of the role of architecture and town planning in republics is truncated in this book but further elaborated in book 8.

25. Several of the prefaces to individual books, especially books 7 and 8, with their praise of Patrizi's *patria* Siena, look as though they may have originally been intended for Pius II.

26. There is some uncertainty about the distribution of materials between books 4, 5, and 6: the instructions on agriculture in 5.9 might have fit better in 4.4, and the treatment of agrarian policy in 4.1 might have been better included in 6.2. At 3.1 and 3.4 he promises a separate and more detailed treatment of religion later in the treatise, but this is never provided.

27. So, for example, the discussion of whether to admit immigrants to citizen status in 6.4 would go more naturally in book 5, as would the discussion at 6.7 of why and how citizens should give beautiful and dignified names to their children.

28. Elections and the control of ambition are first discussed in 3.3, but Patrizi's ideas are developed in more detail in 6.6. Patrizi's position on private property in book 4 has to be taken together with its elaboration in 6.3. There is also some overlap between Patrizi's long discussion of the education of children (which looks as though it might have been planned as a separate treatise) and the teachings on the education of the political class in book 2.

29. At the end of 5.10, for example, a chapter ostensibly on sumptuary legislation, Patrizi uses his discussion of funeral monuments to launch into a discussion of funerary poetry in the Roman poets. At the end he admits that he is a bit off topic: "I have said more than I intended about graves, but the pleasure of talking about the subject drew me out more than I had hoped." For an example of an insertion that disturbs the order of exposition, see the end of book 2, where after a stirring summary of his educational doctrine and an assertion of

the superiority of mental to physical exercises, he cannot resist adding a series of anecdotes about ancient athletes who overdeveloped their physiques.

30. For Patrizi's conception of their relationship to the earlier books, perhaps somewhat *forzata*, see Chapter 5, 215–216.

31. *Rep.* 1.10. For the "virtuous environment," see Hankins 2019, 51–54. The idea that painting is a near relative to learning reflects the teaching of Leon Battista Alberti's *On Painting* (1436). Patrizi also defends at the end of book 1 the Albertian view that practitioners of architecture and the plastic arts are more than mere *opifices* or workmen and should count as *professores* of humanistic disciplines, so long as they are literate (i.e., read Latin) and their practices are informed by the study of antiquity; see further in Chapter 5, 219–221. Noble youths should study the plastic arts as part of their education, he adds: it is a sign of the worthlessness of modern youth that they care more about making money than the arts. Further remarks on the civil usefulness of the arts occur in *Reg.* 2.10, where he compares the arts with history as a source of moral inspiration: "For if the likenesses of bodies and images made with the hand of artisans are wont to stimulate the minds of youth to the imitation of those whose images they are, how much more will histories accomplish this and the records of great deeds, which express the mind and soul, not the lineaments of the body and the outward appearance of its form? History excels the image by as much as the mind excels the body."

32. Nevola 2007, 2019. For Patrizi this aesthetic appreciation of government, with its visual correlative, might have begun with contemplation of Lorenzetti's *Allegory of Good and Bad Government*, a fresco he could have seen every day while serving as a magistrate in Siena. For Patrizi's relations with town planners and architects like Bernardo Rossellino, Filarete, Fra Giocondo, Alberti, and Francesco di Giorgio Martini, see Chapter 5, 220–221.

33. *Rep.*, Ded.3.

34. See his *Commentaries*, 2.21–22, in Pius II 2004, 284–296; Shaw 2006, 39–56.

35. At the end of *Rep.* 1.1, after praising the institutions of Siena ("which ranks, if not second, at least third among the republics of our time in the general estimate"), he adds: "If I may in any way be of service to her [Siena] and lead younger men to enjoy better success, that outcome for me would be delightful."

36. For example, *Rep.* 3.2, 5.9 (where, addressing the reader, he refers to *Senam, patriam nostram*); for places where his praise and blame of ancient institutions seems silently to be pointed critically at Sienese institutions, see 1.6 (political equality inconsistent with excluding whole classes of citizens from office), 3.2, 6.6 (a sharp criticism of Siena's system of sortition), 5.10 (on the reform of sumptuary legislation). At 3.6, he writes that "our city is divided into three regions"; Siena was divided into *terze*, as Florence was divided into quarters and Rome into fourteen regions.

37. See Chapter 5, 219–220.

38. For more on Patrizi's criticism of the use of foreign officials in a republic, see Chapter 4. The praise of Venice's nativism may be aimed at humanists such as Biondo Flavio, who admired ancient Rome for its readiness to grant foreigners citizen rights and even high office and military commands.

39. The great work on the Greeks' conception of *paideia* remains Jaeger 1986.

40. The work survives in at least two distinct redactions; these remain to be sorted out by a future editor. On the process of composition, see De Capua 2014, 215–219; De Capua believes the work was begun even before the publication of the *De republica*.

41. De Capua 2014, 216. The two epigrams that refer to the *De regno* (144 and 163) give us no clues about the dating of the work. Patrizi wrote prefaces to Sixtus IV for all nine books of the *De republica*, but it is not clear why Patrizi did not compose prefaces for Alfonso

to books 7–9 of the *De regno*. Had something happened to weaken Patrizi's devotion to his prince?

42. For Patrizi and the recovery of Greek monarchical theory, see Hankins 2019, 386–398. For Greek monarchical theory, see now Atack 2020.

43. See Skinner 2002, 136–138. The recent literature in Italian may be accessed through Delle Donne 2015, Cappelli 2016, and Heil 2022. See also the introduction to Pedullà's edition of *The Prince*, xviii–xxviii, where he lists authors of political *trattati,* reviews the historiography, and discusses Machiavelli's innovations with respect to the earlier tradition.

44. For the dates, see Garzoni 2014.

45. For Giles, see further in the next section of this chapter. Giles of Rome's *De regimine principum* survives in more than three hundred Latin manuscripts and was translated into several vernaculars. It was published three times in Latin, twice in Catalan, and once in Spanish during the incunabular period. After that, the next (and the last) edition to appear was published in 1607.

46. A more detailed analysis of the contents of the *De regno* is given in Chapter 7.

47. *Rep.* 2.Pr.: "[In antiquity] every educated person was acquainted with Egyptian learning. As Diodorus Siculus tells us, Orpheus, Musaeus, Melampus, Daedalus, Homer, Lycurgus, Solon, Pythagoras, Plato, Eudoxus, Democritus, Euripides, and many others who illuminated all the disciplines of all the nations went there to acquire that learning."

48. The most egregious embroideries involved Patrizi's account of the ancient city of Massilia, the magistracy of the *tresviri capitales* in Rome, and his biographical account of Hippodamus, the philosopher and town planner (see ad indices).

49. See Grafton 2007.

50. For Patrizi's sources, see the source notes to *Rep.,* available on the website of the Patrizi Project, https://projects.iq.harvard.edu/patrizisiena. I exclude authors Patrizi seems to be citing from intermediate sources (a group that includes Callimachus, Euripides, Musaeus, Sophocles, and Tyrtaeus).

51. *Rep.* 2.6: "But neither the poets nor even the philosophers knew God before the advent of our Savior Jesus Christ, who as the one son of God made the Father known to mankind and founded the true religion through which the dark shadows were removed and all false belief." In this passage Patrizi also reaffirms his skeptical reading of Plato as an author who affirmed no positive doctrines. For Patrizi's early letter advancing a skeptical interpretation of the ancient Academy, see Chapter 1, 20–21.

52. See *Reg.* 2.4. Patrizi also shows familiarity with the Platonic theory of recollection at 1.9. In his account of corporeal and external goods at 2.1, Patrizi rejects the Stoic view that they cannot count as real goods and writes that he follows the Academics and Peripatetics "and Plato before all, who in a wholly religious and pious way said that God was the highest good, and that through virtue alone we get to cleave to the source and end of all human goods, via similitude to God. Plato decided that divine justice was the universal law for everyone, which assigns rewards for the good and punishments for the bad." At 4.11, discussing the passion of love, Patrizi cites Plato's *Phaedrus* and its theory of the four forms of divine madness, probably from Leonardo Bruni's partial translation of that text. At 8.15, discussing piety, he cites Hermes Trismegistus and seems sympathetic to the idea of an ancient theology. At 9.21, discussing the rewards a good king can expect in the afterlife, Patrizi cites the Myth of Er from the end of the *Republic.*

53. Though Ficino's complete translation of Plato's dialogues was not printed until 1484, portions of his translation, especially his translation and commentary on the *Symposium,* were circulating in manuscript form as early as 1469; see Hankins 1990. Patrizi wrote an epigram on what Aristophanes says about hermaphrodites in the *Symposium* (*Epg.* 206, G, 66r),

probably in the late 1470s or early 1480s. Ficino's translation of Hermes, completed in 1463, was circulating already in the later 1460s: see Mercurius 2011.

54. See Chapter 7, 303.

55. Richardson 2021, 205, citing Love 1998.

56. In a preface Pietro Crinito described how he had to force Bartolomeo Scala to allow his *Defense of Florence* to be printed, "since you [Scala] have never been of a mind that any arguments could induce you to have any of your works published." The issue for Scala may have been the inaccuracy of printers, for Crinito promises him to turn the work over to "the kind of typographers who will print it with such care and precision that they will reproduce the archetype exactly." See Scala 2008, 235.

57. R. Black 2013.

58. See my article on Patrizi and More's *Utopia*, forthcoming in *Moreana*. As Appendix B discloses, printings of Patrizi's political treatises were often paired with Erasmus's *Education of a Christian Prince* by sixteenth-century printers.

59. Peltonen 1995, 19, 31–34, 40, 43, 46, 50–58; for the Lambin edition and the Robinson epitome, see Appendix B. Jacques Tigeou added a running commentary to his French translation of *Rep.* (Paris, 1589).

60. "Among the most widely read": Briggs 1999, 19.

61. For Giles's influence in the later Middle Ages, see Hankins 2019, 622n53. On Giles's political philosophy, see Blythe 1992, 60–76; Lambertini 2019.

62. For a survey of Giles's sources, see Briggs 1999, 11.

63. For Giles's hostility to lawyers, see Giles of Rome 1607, 309: "[Jurists], since they do not argue artfully and dialectically, are called by the Philosopher [Aristotle] 'dialectical idiots' [i.e., ignoramuses]. Thus jurists, since they talk in stories (*narrativè*) and without reason about politics, can be called political idiots. Hence it is obvious that those who know politics and moral sciences are more to be honored than those who know laws and rights, since those who know and give the cause are more honorable than those who just talk and don't name the cause." By contrast, Patrizi, like other humanists, had contempt for modern jurists (see 2.4), who "chatter for profit" and cause civil discord, but admired those of ancient Rome, whom he often cites.

64. That Patrizi expects criticisms from scholastics for his method is evident from the first preface of *De republica* to the Sienese: "But perhaps it will be considered a vice— especially by leisured and lazy people who wish to seem clever about other peoples' books and envy those whom they despair of equaling in intellect—that I have translated a great deal from Greek writers and have taken much from the Latins too, which I have turned to my use. To respond to such persons, I think I should generate very little trust in my writings if I should rely entirely on my own authority, especially in political education, which must rely on persuasion by examples rather than extortion via arguments (*argumentis extorquenda*)." In medieval Latin *extorquere* also means "to subject (someone) to torture."

65. See Hankins 2019, 11–14. On the subordination of dialectic to rhetoric in humanist culture, see Nauta 2021. Pius II, Patrizi's learned patron, privileges the habitus of *prudentia* above that of *scientia* on the grounds that *prudentia* makes us good, whereas mere *scientia*— say, mastering the books of Aristotle or legal literature—allows us to distinguish good and bad but doesn't make us love or hate them. See Pius II 1571, 619–622 = *Epistola de differentia inter scientiam et prudentiam et de poetis* (Letter on the distinction between scientific knowledge and prudence, and on poets).

66. See Hankins 1990, passim, for the difficulties these doctrines caused for Christian readers in the quattrocento. My own view is that Plato's discussion in *Republic* 5 represents a form of intellectual play, but *iocari serio*, exploring radical alternatives, while the *Laws* presents his more considered beliefs about how Platonic principles might be embodied in legislation for an actual society; see Annas 2017.

67. Aristotle's arguments are rehearsed extensively, by contrast, by Giles; see Giles of Rome 1607, 416–432 (3.1.7–12).

68. The argument is also made in poetic form in Patrizi's *Epg.* 137 (*G*, 47v), entitled "Marriage is superior to all friendships, proved by the example of Camma who avenged her husband Sinatus in a feigned marriage by slaying Synorix, who had killed him." The poem is based on a story in Plutarch, though Patrizi's knowledge of it more likely comes via Francesco Barbaro's *De re uxoria*, an important intermediate source for Patrizi's teachings on marriage; see Barbaro 2021, 84–86.

69. Patrizi's source is Aulus Gellius 1.6.1–2. See also Patrizi's *Poem.* 3.6, "De incommodiis matrimoniae" (On the inconveniences of marriage). In *Rep.* 1.7 he writes that to remain celibate throughout life and refuse the duty of procreating children is contrary to natural law; male celibacy was even punished by the Roman censors. Religious celibacy was presumably an exception.

70. Biondo Flavio makes same point about Roman religion in his *Roma Triumphans*, books 1–2.

71. I paraphrase a passage in *Rep.* 1.Pr.

72. Discussed in Hankins 2019, 397, 403.

73. See Chapter 4, 126–128.

74. See Chapter 3, 107–108.

75. Hankins 2019, 16. Another more speculative explanation is that Aristotle's *Politics* would have been associated for Renaissance readers with Bruni's popular Latin translation. Bruni, himself a declared Aristotelian in his political thought, sent a copy of the translation to Barnaba Pannalini, the chancellor of Siena, for the use of Sienese statesmen. Patrizi's work might then be seen as containing an element of Florentine–Sienese rivalry, in that Patrizi's *De republica* was an attempt to displace Aristotle's position as the leading authority on politics, incidentally showing the superiority of Sienese to Florentine scholarship.

# 3. Principles of Republican Government

1. Pedullà 2020, 88.

2. See Hankins 2019, 391–392.

3. The difficulty free republics had defending their system of government was dramatized in Brandolini 2009, a Socratic dialogue (dedicated to Lorenzo de'Medici) in which the chief interlocutor, King Mattyas Corvinus of Hungary, systematically dismantles the defense of republican government mounted by the Florentine merchant Domenico Giugni.

4. Shaw 2006, 8.

5. See Trexler 1980, 279, 290–297, for the "honor deficit" of the Florentine republic; Hankins 2019, 382, on Mario Salamonio's defense of popular government against the weight of ancient opinion; and Shaw 2006, 248–249, on the unreliability of republics as allies—*popoli* are described as acting like "hares and rabbits." Pedullà (2020, 59–63) stresses in this connection the survival of chivalric values, which reinforce aristocratic attitudes; Hankins (2019, 374–377) discusses how civic humanism challenges chivalric values.

6. For the ubiquity of this attitude, see Pedullà 2018, 12–14. For Patrizi's later view of the unviability of republics in the longer term, see chap. 7, 274–277.

7. Note that Plato, Aristotle, and Polybius all think of corruption as generational, implying that children will naturally be worse than their parents, whereas Patrizi here worries more about the corruption of individual princes over their lifetimes.

8. Patrizi paraphrases Tacitus, *Histories* 1.50.

9. See also the discussion in chapter 4 of Patrizi's theory of deliberation (*Rep.* 3.3), where the superiority of collective prudence to princely prudence is also stressed.

10. Eric Nelson points out to me that there are hints at various places in Plato's *Laws* (a text Patrizi knew well) concerning the potential longevity of aristocratic polities that might have inspired Patrizi's idealism on this point. The contemporary example of Venice, widely viewed as a more successful republic than any in antiquity, was never far from Patrizi's mind, as will be seen below.

11. *Rep.* 6.5. Patrizi's selective reading of Xenophon to support the possibility of a polity's avoiding corruption is an inference from *The Spartan Republic* 14: Xenophon himself does not claim that republics can be perpetual for as long as they remain virtuous, but Patrizi seems to draw that conclusion from Xenophon's explanation for the lapse of the Lycurgan constitution in his (Xenophon's) lifetime. Patrizi may also be inferring the permanence of the Spartan state from the longevity of its kingship, noted in Xenophon, *Agesilaus* 5. In *Rep.* 5.2 he says, in a clear echo of Sallust's famous dictum on concord (*Bellum Iugurthinum* 10), that it is concord among citizens that makes a republic grow and allows it to enjoy liberty forever. "Hence no conviction in a free republic can be more excellent than this: if individuals are raised to act in harmony, cities will surely grow and enjoy perpetual liberty. . . . That ancient utterance is true which states that a republic will be lasting and an immortal animal that never dies, unless it brings violence on itself and resolves on its own death." The Sallustian dictum is discussed with reference to Patrizi in Pedullà 2018, 15–23.

12. The contrast between Plato's scientism and Patrizi's humanist prudence is evident when one considers *Statesmen* 293c–d, which argues that *basilike* or kingship is a science: "It is, then, a necessary consequence that among forms of government that one is preeminently right and is the only real government, in which the rulers are found to be truly possessed of science [*episteme*], not merely to seem to possess it, whether they rule by law or without law, whether their subjects are willing or unwilling, and whether they themselves are rich or poor— none of these things can be at all taken into account on any right method. . . . All other forms must be considered not as legitimate [*gnesias*] or really existent, but as imitating this; those states which are said to be well governed imitate it better, and the others worse" (Loeb translation). Plato then goes on to say, however, at 294b, that no one type of legislation will work for all states and that there is no *episteme* capable of producing "any simple rule for everything and all times." It is highly unlikely, however, that Patrizi knew the *Statesman* at the time when he was writing the *De republica* in the 1460s.

13. Hankins 2019, 305–317. Humanists familiar with patterns of regime change in the recent history of Italy would have had difficulty validating Plato or Aristotle's (or Polybius's) theories about regular patterns in constitutional change. On the fluidity of Italian republics between signorial and political rule, see Pedullà 2020, 56.

14. On humanist ideas about the laws of history, see R. Black 1987.

15. Hankins 2019, 303–304. Patrizi and Biondo (1392–1463) coincided for a time at the papal court, where Biondo was a papal secretary.

16. Hankins 2019, ad indices.

17. My exposition here generally follows *Rep.* 1.5, with consideration also of passages in 2.4, 3.6, 3.8, and 5.Pr. For Patrizi's reverence for Roman law, see also the parallel discussion in *Reg.* 8.1, where he stresses the universal application of Roman jurisprudence and states that "everybody agrees that the books of our jurisconsults exceed those of the Greek philosophers in gravity, eloquence, learning and wisdom."

18. A principle already stated in the *De gerendo magistratu*.

19. On this tradition, see Lee 2016.

20. See Chapter 5, 236–237.

21. See Gambino Longo 2018.

22. A maxim from Aristotle, *Politics* 4.1, 1289a14, who is not acknowledged; in fact Patrizi's idea of prudent lawmaking is heavily indebted to this whole chapter, with its metaphor

of the lawmaker as a trainer of athletes. It will be noticed that Patrizi's view undermines the Roman idea of a *ius gentium,* a universal law of nations, which in the early modern period became a tool of empire, as it had been for the Romans. Patrizi's attitude is not surprising, given his general dislike of imperialism (see below).

23. See further Chapter 5, 235.

24. See Chapter 5, 169.

25. Patrizi's language follows closely that of Cicero in *De legibus* 1.22.

26. Hankins 2019, 25–30. At *Reg.* 8.15, writing on piety, Patrizi writes that after the coming of Christ, human beings were made *divinorum consiliorum compotes,* sharers in the divine counsel (a humanist way of saying that we received divine revelation), and learned how to live with holy innocence and how we can achieve immortality. At *Reg.* 9.21 he states that we are Christians and do not need Plato's fables of the afterlife, as we have the Son of God to teach us about immortality; and we must take refuge in Christ's teachings if we wish to enjoy felicity and life with the saints. See also *Reg.* 5.21, where Patrizi says that acquisition of the virtues makes us resemble God and makes mortals immortal. It is striking that Patrizi never cites the passage of Cicero's *Somnium Scipionis* (5), so often invoked by humanist proponents of civil religion, where Africanus is made to say, "for all who have preserved their fatherland, furthered it, enriched it, there is in heaven a sure and allotted abode, where they may enjoy an immortality of happiness."

27. *Rep.* 5.2.

28. See Chan 2014.

29. Shaw 2006, 52–53. See Pius II, *Commentaries* 2.13.6, in Pius II 2004, 258–259.

30. For the laws of *ammonizioni* of 1359 that licensed leaders of the Parte Guelfa to "warn" political unreliables not to accept office—which in effect turned into a system of depriving political opponents of office—see Brucker 1962, 170–172.

31. For concord (*homonoia*) as a supreme goal in ancient political thought, see Hahm 2009. Patrizi here may be echoing the political principles of Pius II, who aimed to remove the political disabilities of the nobles and the Dodici; as Antonio Petrucci said of Pius after his death, his aim was to establish the *concordia ordinum,* an ideal of Ciceronian stamp.

32. *Rep.* 6.3.

33. E.g., *Rep.* 3.12 and 4.Pr.

34. One of the learned men alluded to might be Leonardo Bruni: see Hankins 2019, chaps. 8, 10, and 20, for Leonardo Bruni's defense, using virtue arguments, of exclusionary practices. Patrizi, of course, might easily be thinking of various educated men in his own Siena, like Ludovico Petroni (a follower of Bruni), who supported the existing exclusions.

35. Patrizi's view that work is valuable because it contributes to social harmony may be contrasted with the modern dignitarian view; for example, Pope John Paul II's 1981 encyclical, *Laborem Exercens:* "Work is a good thing for man—a good thing for his humanity—because through work man not only transforms nature, adapting it to his own needs, but he also achieves fulfillment as a human being and indeed, in a sense, becomes 'more a human being.'"

36. The need for measures that will motivate ambitious citizens to serve the interests of the state is also a theme in Francesco Guicciardini's later *Dialogues on the Government of Florence,* in Guicciardini 1994, 107–108, 114–115.

37. *Rep.* 6.1.

38. Aristotle, *Politics* 5.3.

39. Pliny the Younger, *Letters* 2.12. Patrizi's awareness of Aristotle's argument is clear from *Rep.* 6.1, where he discusses the need to establish a ratio of virtue among citizens.

40. Pedullà 2020; see also Hankins forthcoming-a.

41. *Rep.* 6.Pr.: "Republican teachings cannot be prescribed for all peoples. It is enough if those heed us who imagine liberty for themselves as a kind of divinity, men who would prefer to die rather than let liberty be weakened in any degree."

42. For the use of lordship in Renaissance Italy as a temporary alternative to republican power-sharing in times of extreme factionalism, see the literature cited in Pedullà 2020, 57. Another possibility, not mentioned by Patrizi, is that former republican regimes under long domination could learn to live as republics again: see Bruni 2001–2006, 2:475–476 (8.83), where after an extended period of rule by tyrants and *signori* the Florentines had to teach Lucca how to be a republic again.

43. *Rep.* 6.Pr. Contrast this with the sentiment of Leonardo Bruni, that all peoples naturally desire liberty but not all are capable of it (Hankins 2019, 228).

44. See further in Chapter 5, 203–213.

45. See *Rep.* 7.2, where he attributes Rome's success at dominating barbarians to its innate capacity for virtue; to wise counsel; to its geographical situation; and to the physical gifts of its warriors, such as endurance. Rome, he says, invented more than all other nations and improved what it received from others; hence, it subdued all other nations in a relatively brief period of time. For Patrizi, empires are controlled and made lasting by virtue, excellence of mind and learning. Thus, in the debate over the sources of Roman greatness between Leonardo Bruni and Biondo Flavio (Hankins 2019, 296–301), Patrizi sides strongly with Biondo. His perspective may have been informed by reading Appian (translated into Latin in 1452/1454 for Pope Nicholas V), who took a similar view of the sources of Roman power.

46. Aristotle, *Politics* 4.1, 4.12.

47. *Rep.* 7.2.

48. In book 6, a passage that may reflect Patrizi's experience in Foligno, he writes: "Republics are corrupted by the fault of those who govern them, for they falsely make a show of liberty's name, and especially when ambition and avarice takes hold of them, so that they forget the good of the public and alter everything to favor their own interests and neglect civil society, seducing peoples with vain rumors, assailing them with lies, spreading false fears, so that power is given them by the people solely for them to take revenge on other citizens who would control their infamous behavior."

49. Note that the present account of Patrizi's constitutional analysis modifies and at certain points corrects the one presented in Hankins 2019, 369–374; the somewhat different analysis in the *De regno* is discussed below in Chapter 7, 277–281. See also the discussion in Pedullà 2021a, 119–123.

50. By mentioning Socrates, Patrizi is signaling, I believe, that he is transcending the standard Aristotelian constitutional analysis by combining it with the regime analysis of Plato in *Republic* 8. "Valued by" [*censentur*] could also be translated "rated by," which might indicate that the first three constitutions discussed in the chapter (popular, optimate, and oligarchic) were ranked and theorized by philosophers, whereas his descriptions of mob rule and rule by a noble junta are taken from historical experience. In fact his description of mob rule is presented as a product of direct observation, a situation familiar to his readers, without citing an ancient authority, whereas his description of a noble junta is taken (perhaps diplomatically) from a single historical source, Livy. I am inclined to favor the translation "valued" since Patrizi elsewhere (*Rep.* 3.1), citing Crantor, includes wealth as the fourth of four legitimate aims for human life, which in ranked order are virtue, good health, honest pleasure, and riches. Admittedly, this interpretation would make Patrizi the first Western political thinker to rate oligarchy among the "good" constitutions, though hardly the last; in the early modern period a polity ordered to wealth and honest pleasure would be rebranded as a "commercial republic" and celebrated by classical liberal theorists like Adam Smith and Benjamin Constant.

51. For cyclical analyses by other Renaissance humanists, see Hankins 2019, chap. 12.

52. There are, to be sure, more nuanced analyses of the various constitutions in the later books of the *Politics;* see Hansen 2013; but the sixfold analysis of book 3 was by far the most familiar to most late medieval and Renaissance writers.

53. Pedullà 2018, 65–69. For George of Trebizond's critique of the idea of a common good, see Hankins 2019, 346–348. Against the view of some scholars that discarding the criterion of the common good was a principal innovation of Machiavelli, see Pedullà 2018, 5. The classic work on the concept in the Middle Ages is Kempshall 1999. Patrizi, in contrast with most medieval theorists, regards serving the common good as an ideal that may have to be compromised for prudential reasons; a magistrate will do his best, but sometimes his actions may only be able to serve "the great majority" and not the whole people.

54. Patrizi does not here use the term *democratia* to mean popular rule. For his terminology of regimes or constitutions, see Hankins 2019, 86–87, 308–309. At *Rep.* 6.Pr he uses *democratia* (transliterated in Roman characters) to describe the Athenian constitution.

55. The terminology follows that of the translation of Herodotus by Lorenzo Valla, whom Patrizi surely knew from his time as Sienese ambassador to the court of Pope Nicholas V. Patrizi may have looked at the Greek text as well, since his name for popular government is ἰσονομία, legal equality, printed in Greek characters in the 1518 edition and written in Greek letters in *V.*

56. Aristotle, *Politics* 4.8, 1294a; 6.2,1217a.

57. *Rep.* 1.4. Patrizi's definition of this kind of liberty looks back to Cicero, *Paradoxa Stoicorum* 33 (Paradoxon 5) and *De officiis* 1.20: "His idem propositum fuit, quod regibus, ut ne qua re egerent, ne cui parerent, libertate uterentur, cuius proprium est *sic vivere, ut velis.*" The definition was taken up by the second century AD jurist Florentinus, quoted in Justinian, *Digest* 1.5.4. The distinction between civil liberty and liberty in the sense of participation in ruling the state goes back at least to Aristotle, *Politics* 6.2, 1317b.

58. On the virtuous as a third force in politics, see Hankins 2019, 242–246.

59. See Dio Chrysostom, *Discourses* 2.21 (*On Kingship*). For Dio Chrysostom's *De regno* (= *Discourses* 1–4) in the Latin translation of Gregorio Tifernate (first printed in Venice, 1471), see Hankins 2019, 392, 394–395; in the *De regno* Dio is cited as an authority on monarchy.

60. Cicero, *De inventione* 2.53.

61. Cicero, *Pro Lege Manilia* 2.

62. Diogenes Laertius 1.7. The *Lives of the Philosophers* had been translated in 1431 by Ambrogio Traversari.

63. Dionysius of Halicarnassus, *Roman Antiquities* 2.17.

64. On the reasons for including the plebs, see further below, Chapter 4, 156–158.

65. *Politics* 4.11.4–11.1295b. For organicism as a principle of humanist political theory, see Cappelli 2012, 2018.

66. Hankins 2019, 40, 202.

67. This would include Aristotle, who is not mentioned, Cicero in the *De legibus,* and Polybius, whose praise of the mixed regime, found in book 6 of his histories, Patrizi probably did not know; see Hankins 2019, chap. 12.

68. *Politics* 3.11, 1281a.

69. See the Introduction, 2–4. One may contrast Patrizi's organicist/prudential defense of popular government with Marsilius of Padua's theory of consent in *Defensor Pacis* 1.13, 1.15. Marsilius rejects the virtue argument, instead combining an Aristotelian theory of collective deliberation with a quasi-physical theory that a polity can only be successfully ruled by its "weightier part." Marsilius distinguishes between discovering the law, which is a

work of prudence, and establishing or authorizing law, which is the business of the whole population (or its "weightier part"). Marsilius of Padua 2005, 65–72, 88–90.

70. An example from his own lifetime were the mercenary troops of Jacopo Piccinino, who came marauding into Sienese territory in 1455–1456, causing political instability in the republic; see Chapter 1, 31.

71. *Rep.* 9.1. In the previous paragraph, the 1518 edition incorrectly reads *augustus* for *angustus*.

72. Livy 30.30.

73. A point made also in *De gerendo magistratu,* where Patrizi likewise discourages offensive warfare as generally imprudent. There he writes that it is usually the younger men who are hot for war, another reason to prefer older men in government.

74. Patrizi's contemporary Diomede Carafa, a humanist advisor and close friend of King Ferrante as well as something of a war hero, took a similarly negative view of offensive warfare, advising his prince to beware of anyone telling him that a war was necessary. He adds to Patrizi's arguments the claim that whoever attacks first in a war will likely be at a disadvantage owing to God's disfavor: "For it is well known from ancient and contemporary experience that the one who is the first to cause discords will be, almost miraculously, the one who is not only defeated in battle, but also suffers the graver losses and the more bitter disasters. This can be considered an evident proof that this type of injustice [causing wars] is unpleasing to the Divine Majesty" (Carafa 1668, 74).

75. *De officiis* 3.82; Cicero quotes Euripides's *Phoenician Women,* ll. 524–525. Those who knew their Cicero would remember that these lines were "always on the lips" of Julius Caesar.

76. *Rep.* 9.1.

77. See Quintus Curtius Rufus's *History of Alexander* 7.12.

78. The idea to maintain a small standing army may possibly come from Demosthenes, Philippic 1, translated by Bruni.

79. *Rep.* 6.2; on the resulting contrast with Machiavelli concerning the importance of fortifications, see Chapter 5, 222–226.

80. For the consulate in Patrizi's republic, see Chapter 4.

81. Hankins 2019, 265–255.

82. Here Patrizi may be following the lead of Roberto Valturio's *De re militari* (ca. 1460), for which see Hankins 2019, 266–270.

# 4. Meritocracy and the Optimal Republic

1. On ancient Massalia, see Yves Lafond, "Massalia," in *BNP.*

2. Perhaps Patrizi's unhappy experience as governor of Foligno in the 1460s with Achille Petrucci as his *podestà* changed his view, expressed in the *De gerendo magistratu* of ca. 1445, that virtue was a sufficient proxy for years; see Chapter 1, 40–41. Patrizi himself first held the Sienese priorate at the age of twenty-seven.

3. Compare Aristotle, *Politics* 7.14, 1332b, for the point that the young do not resent being governed by the old.

4. Patrizi's description of Massilian meritocracy rests on a single sentence of Aristotle, *Politics* 6.4, 1321a30 (Loeb translation): "And the bestowal of a share in the government upon the multitude should either go on the lines stated before, and be made to those who acquire the property-qualification, or as at Thebes, to people after they have abstained for a time from mechanic industries, or as at Marseilles, by making a selection among members of the governing classes and those outside it of persons who deserve inclusion." An earlier refer-

ence to the Massilians (5.5, 1305b) describes the city as an oligarchy made unstable by nobles who had been excluded from the government. In particular there seems to be no evidence for the *iudicium publicum* where young men were chosen for inclusion in the class of magistrates, or for the religious ceremonies Patrizi claimed to have accompanied the choice of magistrates—although in the latter case he may be making a plausible inference based on general ancient practice.

5. For Chinese meritocracy based on Confucian principles, see Bai 2012.

6. This process here amounts to an implicit proposal for reform of the usual communal practice of scrutiny for office (*scruptinio*). This process, invented in the fourteenth century, resulted in the preparation of electoral lists from which names would be chosen by lot for office. Exclusion from the lists ordinarily was made on the basis of minimal formal criteria such as not having paid taxes or having had a family member in the same office within a defined period. Meritocratic criteria such as reputation or learning were rarely, if ever, applied.

7. See Hankins 2019, 58, 62. Patrizi also advises the use of sortition in choosing judges for capital cases; see below, 162. In a draft "Memorandum on the Reform of the Constitution of Florence," written after 1521, of which only 224 words are extant. Machiavelli called for a long-term Gonfalonier of Justice to be chosen by a mixture of sortition, appointment, and election by a Great Council. See R. Black 2022, 171.

8. Compare to the much more elaborate cinquecento account of Contarini 2020, 21–25 (1.4).

9. Alamanno Rinuccini in his *De libertate* approves sortition for a similar reason, to negate the effect of Medici influence over the choice of Florence's magistrates; see Hankins 2019, 548–549n126.

10. In modern sociology this is known as "sponsored mobility," where members of an elite recruit members of the lower classes into a status elite. It is usually applied to educational selection, but can have a broader application to political meritocracy. As a mode of selection, sponsored mobility contrasts with pure sortition, where all citizens have an equal chance at political office, and contest selection or pure meritocracy, where magistrates are selected on the basis of examinations and performance in office. See Turner 1960.

11. *Rep.* 6.1.

12. In *Rep.* 6.5 he advances the further argument that rule by the middle classes is a protection against oligarchy.

13. For Patrizi, the list (*Rep.* 1.8) of acceptable trades includes "Flatores, fusores, statuarii, caelatores, excussores, figuli, vitrarii, sutores, lanarii, vestiarii, coriarii, textores, fabri, tignarii, lapidarii, caementarii, ferrariique, et alii complures" (metal workers, smelters, sculptors, carvers, threshers, potters, glass blowers, tailors, wool workers, leather workers, weavers, craftsmen, carpenters, stoneworkers, masons, smiths, and many others).

14. For electoral purposes Siena was divided into three districts, or *terze*. The principle that different parts of the city should be represented in its government was generally accepted in late medieval and Renaissance city-states.

15. See Chapter 3, 122.

16. Patrizi is capable of praising the virtues of common people; see, for example, *Rep.* 6.5 where he praises the Roman people for their generosity in not despoiling the proscribed even when urged to do so by Marius and Cinna, "so gentle were the minds of the common people (*vulgus*) and respectful of human decency."

17. See Waley 1988, chap. 3.

18. *Rep.* 1.4: the *tribuni plebis* were those *qui libertatem publicam a superbia nobilitatis tuerentur:* who protected public liberty from the arrogance of the nobility. Patrizi's view of them is clearly influenced by the discussion in Cicero's *De legibus* 3.17–25, where Cicero's

brother Quintus rejects the magistracy as imprudent while Cicero himself defends it as a safety valve for popular discontent.

19. *Rep.* 1.4 on the rule of law; see Chapter 3, 99–100.

20. In a parallel passage in *Rep.* 6.1, Patrizi says that Romulus allowed the plebeian class to elect magistrates, to pass laws, and to decide whether to go to war, "although they had no unfettered power to do any of these things unless the senate had first approved it." He gave the vote (*suffragium*) to the whole people—not *viritim* (on a principle of "one man, one vote") but in centuriate assemblies controlled by patricians. But Patrizi follows this description with the statement that today we need to depart from Romulus's ordinances, for example in the conduct of war; what should be retained is the Roman division of the *civitas* into three classes.

21. Patrizi's counsels may be compared with similar practical advice later offered by Guicciardini: see Guicciardini 1994, 118–120.

22. Shaw 2006, 8–11.

23. See Chapter 3, 119.

24. Compare Rinuccini 2002, 82, 85, for freedom of speech as a virtue protecting liberty. See Chapter 1 for Patrizi's contacts with Rinuccini.

25. A paraphrase of a saying by Epicharmus, quoted in Aulus Gellius 1.15.15.

26. In the *De gerendo magistratu* (M, f. 66r), he advises the magistrate to "conceal and don't trust anyone with the *arcana* of the republic or the counsels of your own mind, for everything is done in a twisted or wrong fashion in public business where control (*censura*) of silence [i.e., confidentiality] is neglected. . . . One should also conceal the counsels of the prince, for if these are made public, they necessarily become useless."

27. See Pontano 2019.

28. See Chapter 6, 250–251.

29. See Hankins 2019, 40–41, 296, 499–500.

30. Lipsius 2004, 511, quotes this same example from Plutarch's *Life of Lysander* 7, but recognizes it as a source for Machiavelli's famous advice to be both lion and fox in *The Prince* 18, which Lipsius is inclined to excuse; see Waszink's introduction, 184. More likely Machiavelli is inverting Cicero's equally famous advice at *De officiis* 1.41 to be neither a lion nor a fox but a man.

31. "De exilio ad Gregorium Lollium," unpublished, in Patrizi's *Poem.* 4.7 (*B*, 88v–92v).

32. Patrizi is probably basing himself on Xenophon's *Hellenica* 2.4.39–42, which he may have known through Leonardo Bruni's epitome, *Rerum graecarum commentarius* (1439), perhaps supplemented by Cornelius Nepos, *Thrasybulus* 2–3.

33. Pedullà 2021a, 118.

34. See Knights 2021, 85–89, on the civic humanist tradition and the emerging idea of office as a public trust in seventeenth-century Britain.

35. Pedullà 2018, 114; Pedullà 2020. At *Rep.* 3.5 Patrizi criticizes only the role of Julius Caesar as *dictator perpetuus* but does not condemn outright the limited, emergency dictatorships of the early and middle republic. In *Reg.* 1.13 he regards the existence of dictatorship under the republic as proof that a popular republic cannot really operate without some kind of monarchical principle.

36. In general, Patrizi's principles of practical reason or prudence in politics were nourished by Cicero's *De officiis* and *On Laws* as well as Plutarch's *Moralia,* particularly the essay "Precepts of Statecraft" (*Praecepta gerendae reipublicae*), which was translated into Latin by Niccolò Sagundino before 1464 (but probably in the 1440s). On Cicero and the political virtues, see Schofield 2021, esp. chap. 5. A detailed comparison between the magistracies outlined in Cicero's ideal constitution in *Laws* 3 and Patrizi's order of magistrates would be well worth making but is beyond the scope of the present chapter.

37. Quoted from Sextus Empiricus, *Against the Ethicists* 3.51–56. Patrizi probably intends Crantor's classification to complexify Aristotle's tripartite division of goods (of the soul, of the body, and "external" goods such as wealth and reputation). Patrizi's knowledge of Sextus Empiricus was remarkable for his time; see Schmitt 1972, 49.

38. At *Rep.* 1.5 he claims that *provocatio ad populum* was instituted by the Romans as a remedy for bad magistrates, but there was no need for it as long as magistrates behaved justly. This illustrates Patrizi's wider Aristotelian principle that laws should vary with the times and circumstances (see Chapter 3, 102–103).

39. I defer Patrizi's treatment (*Rep.* 3.4) of "divine magistrates"—church officials—to Chapter 5. It is noteworthy that they are treated after the senate but before the consuls, implying perhaps a subordination of spiritual authority, at least in political matters, to the laity.

40. The role of the second consul is also discussed in *Rep.* 9.3, the book on warfare; see Chapter 3, 124.

41. Hankins 2019, 287–288. The question whether the two consuls should act mainly as a check on each other or exercise distinct functions is later discussed in detail by Guicciardini: see Guicciardini 1994, 102–105.

42. It is possible that Patrizi took the idea of a supreme court of appeal from Hippodamus via Aristotle's account of his legal ideas in *Pol.* 2.8, 1267b. For Patrizi's admiration for Hippodamus, see Chapter 5, 204–208.

43. Cappelli 2012, 2018; see Chapter 5, 234.

44. M, ff. 62v–63r: "Pro omnibus ut labores opus est, quocirca cura ut omnes intelligant liberos coniuges famam fortunasque suas non minori tibi cura esset quam propria ac praecipua, quaeque optimo cuique patrifamilias. Facillimi sint aditus ad te. Audi aequo animo causas ac voluntates omnium. Pateant aures tue miserorum ac calamitosorum hominum querelis, nec feditas ullius nec deformitas nec calamitas nec paupertas aut solitudo tibi obsistat, quominus aeque omnibus facilis in audiendo beni/f. 63r/gnusque in respondendo existas. Est enim opus ut multa audiant qui pluribus imperat, nec te ullius uox senio aut tedio afficere debet."

45. M, 63r: "[Rursusque] qui facile humaneque auditur partem videtur beneficii accipere, si ei etiam quod postulat iuste abnegetur. Nam iniusta roganti neutiquam concedendum est, neque etiam maledictis aut probris secum decertandum, sed sibi quo‹a›d fieri potest suadendum quod poscit aut impossibile factu esse aut minus operepretium aut contra rempublicam aut contra eum ipsum qui id poscit aut contra ius boni et aequi contraque probatissimos mores. Sic facile unumquempiam a te sine acerbitate ulla amolliri poteris."

46. For parallels between More and Patrizi, see the index to More 1965. It cannot (yet) be proven that More read Patrizi's *De republica* (first printed in Paris two years after *Utopia* was published), but it remains possible that he somehow knew the work via its small circulation in manuscript form. It is also very possible that Patrizi's work on republics was read by Francesco Guicciardini, whose *Dialogue on the Government of Florence,* from the early 1520s, presents many parallels with the earlier work.

47. Patrizi's knowledge of Sabaco comes from Diodorus Siculus 2.65.2–3. Patrizi's reluctance to sanction capital punishment is based in part on a philosophical conviction that "the life and spirit of man [is] part of the world, and has a God-given power of reason and perfects the number of living beings."

48. See the account of the magistracy by Lauretana de Libero in *BNP.* The historical Roman officials formed essentially a police magistrate and dealt primarily with non-elite citizens and other inhabitants of Rome. It was the lowest rung on the *cursus honorum.* Patrizi's placement of his discussion, between censors and quaestors, indicates that in his optimal state he would grant it much greater prestige.

49. See Gerber 2006–2007. Gerber attributes the doctrine to John Adams.
50. Probably relying on "The Lives of the Ten Orators," an essay in Plutarch's *Moralia* 832c.
51. *Lex Cincia de donis et muneribus*, later relaxed again in the first century CE by the emperor Claudius, who allowed advocates to receive up to 10,000 sesterces for cases. Patrizi also mentions the Lex Cincia with admiration at *Rep.* 2.4, adding that among the Venetians, the most learned members of the nobility act as barristers "and from their long practice [in law], very many men have become extremely articulate and well-spoken."
52. Patrizi relies here on Tacitus, *Annals* 11.7.
53. Quintilian, *Institutes* 12.1.3.
54. See Appendix A. Examples of humanists who wrote formal judicial orations are hard to find: Leonardo Bruni's *Oratio pro seipso ad praesides* is the only one known to the present writer, although even it seems to deal with an imaginary situation rather than an actual courtroom case.
55. For a detailed discussion of Patrizi's reflection on and use of ancient Athens's political experience in constructing his own ideal polity, see Pedullà 2021a, 114–124.
56. For the belief that Venice, guided by the wisdom of Plato's *Laws*, had succeeded in founding a stable republian constitution where Rome had failed, see Hankins 2019, 377–81.
57. *Politics* 7.2, 1337b. Aristotle's negative view of the working classes is in part a result of his belief in the genetic superiority of the upper classes, a view on which Patrizi remains agnostic. For Aristotle's two constitutions, see Chapter 6.
58. For Dionysius of Halicarnassus's influence on Machiavelli's statecraft, see Pedullà 2018, chap. 6.
59. Hankins 2019, 495–504.

# 5. The Virtuous Society

1. See Grendler 1989; R. Black 2001; Grendler 2002, chap. 6.
2. All are included in Kallendorf 2002.
3. Frulovisi 1932; Quirini 1977; Decembrio 2020.
4. The only substantive study of which I am aware is Sarri 1938.
5. Uberto Decembrio praises the Visconti for their rich palace library but says nothing about establishing public libraries. On the public library of the best city, see further below, 230–231. Pliny the Elder's *Natural History* 35.2 mentions that Asinius Pollio was the first to found a public library in ancient Rome, "and so made works of genius the property of the public."
6. Patrizi's treatment of wifely duties shows careful study of Francesco Barbaro's *De re uxoria* (1415, edited with a study in Barbaro 2021). This treatise, composed by a Venetian patrician, was a humanist classic, ranking among the most widely circulated humanist works of the quattrocento: see ibid., 122.
7. Barbaro 2021, 282–289.
8. Adapting a famous quotation from Cicero (*Tusculans* 1.45.109): *Glory* follows virtue like a shadow.
9. Patrizi quotes from Valerius Maximus (2.10.2b) a famous anecdote about how Scipio during his retirement at Liternum overawed with his personal majesty some thieves bent on robbing him.
10. *Rep.* 2.1.
11. For Patrizi's version of merit citizenship, see Chapter 6, 247–250.

12. *Rep.* 1.9. *Studia bonarum artium* is often a synonym for *the studia humanitatis,* the humanities. On the scope of the humanities in the quattrocento, see Kohl 1992. On the value of work as contributing to social harmony, see Chapter 6, 252–253, 267, for Patrizi's emphasis on commitment to useful work as a marker of the good citizen, even in the case of citizens under a monarchy.

13. *Rep.* 2.Pr. and 8.15. For the promotion of public libraries in the Renaissance, first advocated by Petrarch and Boccaccio, see Celenza and Pupillo 2010.

14. *Rep.* 3.12.

15. *Rep.* 3.12.

16. Bol 2008, 211–212.

17. This theme is also pursued in Patrizi's *Poem.* 3.4.

18. In *Rep.* 9.4, however, he recommends gladiatorial contests to train soldiers for military service. These presumably would not involve public spectacles and the killing of human beings.

19. Rose 1975 discusses mathematical pedagogy in quattrocento humanism (11–18) but does not mention Patrizi.

20. Patrizi's discussion reprises themes from his own long didactic poem on the origins of music, *Poem.* 1.4.

21. See Hankins 2015 on humanist arguments for the public usefulness of music and on the musical modes most apt to support virtue and noble behavior. Many of Patrizi's arguments and authorities regarding the history and moral use of music have parallels in Filelfo's *Convivia Mediolanensia,* on which see Hankins 2021c.

22. *Rep.* 2.4. The definition of the orator is from Quintilian 12.1.1.

23. On the identification of the humanities with eloquence, see further Baker 2015.

24. For the contrast between scholastic logic and humanist forms of persuasion, which is in the background here, see Chapter 2, 81–91. For the humanist tendency to subordinate logic to rhetoric in general, see Nauta 2021.

25. Hankins 1990.

26. *Phaedrus* 245a, a passage translated by Leonardo Bruni in his partial version (ca. 1424) of the dialogue. Bruni translated the pseudo-Platonic letters around 1427/1434; see Hankins 1990, 1:67–72. See also *Apology* 22b–c, *Ion* 533d–534e, and *Laws* 719c–d, for other remarks on the divine origin of real poetic inspiration.

27. Diogenes Laertius 3.29–33; for the poems Socrates wrote during his imprisonment see *Phaedo* 57a–61c. The *Phaedo* was translated into Latin by Bruni around 1404.

28. Patrizi adapts in a negative sense Euhemerus's account of Jove, which he may have known from the fragments of Diodorus Siculus, book 6, preserved in Eusebius, *Praeparatio evangelica* 2.2.59b–61a. The latter work was translated by George of Trebizond in 1448 and dedicated to Pope Nicholas V.

29. For the revival of Roman theater in quattrocento Italy, see Staüble 1968.

30. In *Rep.* 8.14, after discussing in detail how theaters should be built, he proceeds to dismiss the idea of building them in modern times: "But this account of theaters is less necessary in our times. The [ancient] plays have all been rejected and hissed off and ejected from our cities thanks to our severity of mores and holy religion. Hence, it seems entirely superfluous to say more about building theaters, since the ancient theaters are in ruins and new ones are by no means to be built." Theater building was revived in the courts and academies of Northern Italy in the early sixteenth century.

31. For the more comprehensive sense of philosophy, see Patrizi's early speech *De laudibus philosophiae,* discussed in Chapter 1, 21–22.

32. See Chapter 7, 301. Lauro Quirini in his *De republica* (Quirini 1977, 159) had also recommended assiduous reading of history for the sake of the many examples of virtuous

conduct it contains and for its capacity to extend natural memory: "Nothing is more useful for the political man than history."

33. Grafton 2007. The *Actius* with an English translation may be found in Pontano 2012–2020, vol. 2.

34. Patrizi also leaves out the study of theology and natural philosophy. In Italian universities of the period, natural philosophy was studied as part of the medical curriculum, and theology was taught primarily in the studia of the religious orders. See Grendler 2002.

35. Hankins 2019, 9–11, 14, 21–23, 50–51, 202–203.

36. Speroni 1979.

37. Uberto Decembrio, by contrast, writing a half century earlier, before the humanist invasion of the university, rates law highly as a study that a humanist prince should encourage (Decembrio 2020, 237). Tito Livio Frulovisi in his *De republica* also takes it for granted that the prince will support legal studies, though he notes that these need not be taught in every city, whereas every town needs teachers of the liberal arts and ethics (Frulovisi 1932, 352). Quirini recommends that the leaders of his aristocratic republic should study history and rhetoric but says nothing about legal education (Quirini 1977, 159). The humanist Andrea Biglia, in a speech for the opening of Siena's academic year in 1430 (a parallel text to Patrizi's *De laudibus philosophiae* of 1426), includes among the *artes liberales* all the disciplines taught at the Studio from grammar to canon law. Patrizi's pupil Agostino Dati, however, in an academic speech for the conferral of a doctorate in law, includes law in the category of an *ingenua disciplina,* a gentlemanly discipline, and describes it as the first and most important *liberale studium;* for Biglia and Dati, see Fioravanti 1991, 255.

38. Grendler 2002, chap. 6; Lines 2022, chap. 5.

39. Grendler 2002, 214; see Terlizzi 2010 for an overview of universities through the fifteenth century; and Carlino 2010 for debates on the relative prestige of law, letters, and medicine.

40. For the reform of the Florentine Studio in 1473, see Hankins 1994.

41. *Rep.* 4.2. The "certain cities" include Siena, which briefly passed a law in the mid-fifteenth century prohibiting a man from holding public office unless he was married or a widower and the parent of a legitimate child. See Denley 1991, 28. In Alberti's *De iciarchia* a similar case is made for cities to be led by heads of households; see Hankins 2019, chap. 13.

42. Aristotle's *Economics,* translated by Leonardo Bruni, was a Renaissance "bestseller"; Xenophon's *Oeconomicus* was translated by Lampus Birago for Pope Nicholas V; see David Marsh in *CTC* 7:177–178.

43. Tognetti 2005.

44. Minnich 2005, 281.

45. Origo 1955, 335. It should be noted that the scale of the slave trade in the Italian Renaissance was very small. Between 1366 and 1397 a total of 304 slaves were registered in Florence, mostly girls between the ages of nine and twenty-four. The Florentine catasto of 1427 registered 360 slaves, who accounted for less than 1 percent of the Florentine population (Tognetti 2005, 214). The Muslim trade in Christian slaves was far larger; see Davis 2003. Patrizi emphasizes the ungovernable ferocity of "Scythians" from the Black Sea, a trait Tuscan ladies often encountered in trying to manage their Tartar slaves, according to Origo.

46. See below, 210–211.

47. See Grafton 2002, chap. 5.

48. An example drawn from Diodorus Siculus 1.27.

49. For contemporary praise of agriculture in Siena as the best of the arts, see Piccini 2020.

50. In *Rep.* 6.3 Patrizi explicitly prohibits taking interest on a loan and calls for usurers to be punished: "It is shameful and far more abominable to make a loan, then be paid back

a far larger sum than was paid out. Modes of acquisition like this are not only to be abolished, but those who engage in them should be sharply censured."

51. His source is Cicero, *De officiis* 2.25.89.

52. *Rep.* 4.4, 5.3, 5.10, 4.Pr., 3.12.

53. Cardini 1987.

54. Langholm 2003.

55. Nelson 2004.

56. Hankins 2019, 206–215.

57. See Chapter 5 for Patrizi's insistence that the good citizen must engage in an honorable form of employment. On this subject he is closer to Sienese communal values: see Piccinni 2020, 547–548, who discusses Sienese legislation of 1405 requiring all male citizens to engage in commerce, a trade, retail business, or agriculture on penalty of exclusion from political office; see also Piccinni 2021 on praise of work and on work avoidance in Siena in the quattrocento; and Shaw 2006, 7, for legislation of 1451 prohibiting unemployed persons under fifty from holding any communal office.

58. For the problem in quattrocento Siena of rich landowners driving native tenant farmers off their land, requiring the importation of foreign workers, see Piccinni 2009; Piccinni 2020, 546–547.

59. See Chapter 3 for the prudent use of sortition, combined with election, in the appointment of magistrates.

60. His scheme of land reform is presented in *Rep.* 4.1 and 6.2–3. In 3.6, while defending the institution of private property, he also emphasizes the need for the city magistrates to limit the size of property holdings, "lest the rich possess everything and the poor be crowded out."

61. Patrizi seems to be unaware that this was a measure confined to the guardian class; he apparently begins here from Aristotle's misrepresentation of Plato's views in *Politics* 2; this interpretive error argues that Patrizi could not have known Pier Candido Decembrio's translation, which repeatedly draws attention to Aristotle's misrepresentation of Plato (Hankins 1990, 1:144). At *Rep.* 4.1 Patrizi dismisses Platonic *comitas* in fewer words, remarking that "it has been repudiated by Aristotle on excellent grounds."

62. *Politics* 1.7, 1267b1, 5–9 (trans. Stephen Everson).

63. *Rep.* 6.3.

64. Aristotle's teaching in the *Politics* in general relies on philosophical ethics, rather than on legislation, to limit a disordered desire for wealth. The same attitude is also found in the pseudo-Aristotelian *Economics* translated with commentary by Bruni (see above, note 42) and used extensively (following the medieval version) by Giles of Rome in *De regimine principum*.

65. Quirini 1977, 154. George Trebizond makes similar arguments in favor of wealth acquisition in his attack on Plato's fixed socio-economic classes in the *Laws;* see Hankins 2019, chap. 14; and now Monfasani 2021. Giles of Rome reproduces and elaborates on Aristotle's criticism of Phaleas and Hippodamus in *De regimine principum* (Giles of Rome 1607, 439–450 [3.1.15–20]). According to Giles, distributism, apart from its other faults, would destroy the virtues of liberality and temperance, and patrimonies would quickly become unequal again because some fathers would have many children and others none.

66. Patrizi's biographical data on Hippodamus are not attested in modern studies of the Milesian philosopher; see Christoph Höcker in *BNP*. The biographical data may stem from a confusion in Patrizi's reading of sources, or perhaps he is simply embroidering on Aristotle's account. Modern scholars have speculated, without much evidence, that Hippodamus was in fact a radical democrat. He is most famous in modern times as the supposed inventor of urban planning, a fact one would have expected Patrizi, with his interest in urbanism, to mention, especially as Aristotle mentions it twice, at *Politics* 2.8, 1267b, and 7.10, 1330b.

67. See Chapter 4, 137, for Patrizi's argument that peasants in modern republics, lacking the virtue of ancient farmers, should not participate in politics. The attribution to Hippodamus of advice to keep farmers out of politics in larger cities seems to be Patrizi's invention.

68. Aristotle, *Politics* 7.10, 1330a, 9–17. Patrizi's euhemerist description of the goddess Isis as a queen who appropriated land for the priesthood is not to my knowledge found in any ancient source.

69. Dionysius Halicarnasseus 2.7; Livy 1.13; Aurelius Victor, *De viris illustribus* 2.12. The passage has the look of an insertion made after an initial draft of the chapter.

70. See Miskimin 1975, 69. The usual estimate for Europe overall is that the Church owned between a quarter and a third of all land; see Dameron 2014.

71. *Rep.* 6.2, reading *mentiuntur* with V rather than *metiuntur* as in the 1518 edtion.

72. See above, 232–241.

73. For the quattrocento debate among humanists as to whether the city is best defended by hired forces, militias, or citizen armies, see Hankins 2019, chap. 9; for Patrizi's position, see Chapter 3, 120–125.

74. From Plutarch, *Moralia* 194e ("Sayings of the Romans"). Patrizi incorrectly calls him Marcus rather than Manius. Other versions of the story are found in Valerius Maximus, 4.3.5; Pliny 18.4.18; Columella 1.3.10; Eutropius 2.14; Frontinus *Stratagems* 4.3.12.

75. Such leases were not considered usurious by canon lawyers: see Noonan 1957, 154–170.

76. The prudential argument that redistribution rewards laziness and punishes industry is made more fully in the *De regno;* see Chapter 6, 299–300.

77. Patrizi, in this connection, does not mention Lycurgus, the most famous ancient example of the "equal agrarian," possibly because it might undermine his case that successful redistribution of landed property was bound to be unworkable in practice.

78. Nelson 2004.

79. For a similar proposal, though not one worked out in any detail, see Pietro Crinito in *De honesta disciplina* (Hankins 2019, 213).

80. *Rep.* 4.Pr. Both stories are taken from Plutarch's *Lives.*

81. Aristotle, *Politics* 7.12, 1331b, 19.

82. *Iucunditas,* a mental state caused by what is agreeable or pleasant to the senses, is a term that embraces physical pleasure (*voluptas*) but also anything that our bodily nature finds attractive, such as security and recognition by others. See Hankins 2019, 348.

83. *Rep.* 8.8.

84. *Rep.* 7.1.

85. Plato, *Laws* 4, 704d–705a; Aristotle *Politics* 7.6, 1327a–b. Alberti (1988, 95–100 [4.2]) is aware of both sources but follows Aristotle's lead.

86. For Patrizi's arguments for restricting citizenship, see Chapter 6.

87. *Rep.* 7.12.

88. *Rep.* 7.Pr. The surprising reference to Tarsus as a center of literary culture is based on Strabo 15.5.13.

89. Xenophon, *Memorabilia* 1.6.10, quoting Socrates. Aristotle discusses the need for self-sufficiency in *Politics* 7.5, 1326b; Alberti 1988, 86 (4.2), also emphasizes the need for a city to be self-sufficient.

90. The praise of architects here summarizes the long panegyric of their achievements in *Rep.* 1.9, which includes an account of the seven wonders of the ancient world.

91. Building sites: *areae.* For the meaning of this term, see Rykwert's glossary in Alberti 1988, 420. At *Rep.* 1.9 Patrizi warns that a badly designed city gives foreigners grounds for assuming that the city's leaders are uneducated men who lack good taste.

92. Siena's system of aqueducts, fountains, and underground pipes, which dates back to the high medieval city, was being renovated by the Sienese architect Francesco di Giorgio Martini around the time that Patrizi's *De republica* was published (1469–1473), and Patrizi's praise of this convenience may well be an allusion to Martini's work; see below. On Siena's water system, see Nevola 2007, 22–24.

93. Friedman 1988, 5.

94. Ettlinger (1977) 2000; Kostof (1977) 2000.

95. Marchi and Valazzi 2012.

96. In *Rep.* 1.9 Patrizi raises the question whether the architect should be considered an artisan or included among the *disciplinarum professores;* he concludes, following Vitruvius, that if the architect cultivates the liberal arts, he can be considered both, because architecture requires both learning and practical experience. Alberti in the *De pictura* argues in a similar way for the nobility of painting, given painters' need to train themselves in the liberal arts, above all mathematics.

97. *Francesco di Simone Martini:* Patrizi's knowledge of his hydraulic engineering in Siena is likely, given the proud mention of it in *Rep.* 8.Pr. (note 92 above). Also, his discussion of the best shape for the city's pomerium—whether circular, square, or octagonal—may be related to similar questions in Martini's work; see Nevola 2019 and, more generally, Marchi and Valazzi 2012, as well as Frommel 2007, 70–76. Federico of Urbino was Pius II's military champion against Sigismondo Malatesta, and his son was married to Sixtus IV's niece; his natural son Alessandro was commander of the Sienese troops. See Chapter 1, 35, for Patrizi's relationship with *Fra Giocondo.* For *Bernardo Rossellino,* see Frommel 2007, 47–50; he designed the portal in Siena's Palazzo Pubblico at about the same time as he was building the tomb of Leonardo Bruni in Florence; according to Vasari, Pope Nicholas V commanded him to consult Alberti on all his projects for the pope. For *Filarete*'s collaboration with Filelfo on the *Libro,* see Beltramini 1996. Filelfo's correspondence reveals that he and Patrizi spent time together during the latter's embassy to Milan, and a presentation copy of the *Libro* was sent to Alfonso, duke of Calabria. *Luciano Laurana,* the first architect of Duke Federico da Montefeltro's palace at Urbino, was working for Ludovico Gonzaga during the Council of Mantua, which Patrizi may have briefly attended. For Laurana's career, see the article of Francesco Paolo Fiore in *DBI* (2005).

98. Ettlinger (1977) 2000, 119, cites a letter of Federico of Urbino 1468 saying that "Tuscany [was] the source of architects." Siena became a leader a leader in civil and military technology thanks to Francesco di Giorgio, his teacher Vecchietta, and, in an earlier generation, Mariano di Iacopo, called Taccola. A fuller discussion of the relationship between Patrizi's urbanistics and those of contemporary architectural writers would surely be worth pursuing; a start is made in Nevola 2009; see also scattered remarks in Nevola 2007.

99. *Rep.* 8.16. The comment might be read as veiled advice to the Sienese to employ their native architectural talent rather than import Florentines like Alberti and Rossellino.

100. City planning to support a free way of life was not unknown to the ancient Greeks, however; see Paga 2020 on Cleisthenes's reshaping of the urban fabric of Athens at the end of the city's archaic age.

101. Patrizi does not forget aesthetic considerations when discussing fortifications. He recommends, for instance, that turrets should be ornamental as well as militarily effective: "both because they make a city safe and are like an ornamental crown for it." He cites Homer as his authority: "For, as Homer says that knights ornament the plain of battle and ships ornament the sea, so towers seem to crown the city." The idea of city defenses as ornamental, however, probably came from Aristotle, *Politics* 7.11, 1331a, who does not mention Homer. Patrizi may have had in mind something like the beautiful round towers with pyramidal roofs Laurana built for Federico da Montefeltro's castle in Urbino.

102. At *Rep.* 8.7 Patrizi notes that gunpowder artillery has required changes in city defenses. The ancients used earthworks against the blows of the battering ram, but he doubts this will be entirely effective against cannon; he nevertheless recommends moats and low, reinforced rammed-earth walls to defend against *fulmina haec nostri temporis,* "these thunderbolts of our time."

103. For this debate, see Hale 1983 and Rubinstein 1993; the latter briefly mentions Patrizi's contribution to the debate. Patrizi here uses *urbs* in the sense of capital city, as in the *Corpus iuris civilis*—e.g., *Digest* 39.2.4.9, where the *urbs* is contrasted with the *municipium.*

104. Pseudo-Asconius [Pedianus], *In divinationem* 18: "Arx vel sedes tyranni dicitur." Alberti, writing on this subject (*De re archictectura* 5.3, in Alberti 1988, 121), contrasts the good prince who builds a palace in the center of the city with a tyrant who builds a citadel athwart its walls.

105. Sercambi 1892, 1:188, translated in Woods-Marsden 1989, 134.

106. Rubinstein 1993, 6–7.

107. Plutarch, *Moralia* 576a–577d, 807f, 808b; Xenophon, *Hellenica* 5.2.25–36. Note that Xenophon regards the siege as an outrage against heaven. The story of Phoebidas and the Cadmeia is also told in Diodorus Siculus 15.20, but it is not clear that Patrizi had access to book 15, which was not translated in the quattrocento.

108. See Hörnqvist 2000, 112, who quotes a Florentine statesman saying, "Lordship and liberty, for mortal men nothing is more dear nor more welcome than these two things." When the Florentines conquered Siena in 1555, almost the first thing they did was to build an urban fortress in San Martino, the *terzo* of the Patrizi family.

109. *Politics* 5.9, 1313a-b. See Hankins 2019, 104–106. The passage was incorporated into Giles of Rome's *De regimine principum* as well as Bartolus of Sassoferrato's famous treatise, the *De tyranno;* see Hankins 2019, 112–115, where two marks of the tyrant are said to be preventing free association and keeping the city divided.

110. Nevola 2007, chap. 3, and Bowsky 1981, ad indices, for legislation regarding the Campo.

111. Nevola 2007, chap. 4. For the ideological framework of classical architecture in the quattrocento, see Spencer's introduction in Filarete 1965, 1:xxx–xxxvii.

112. Propertius 4.3.57–58 (Loeb translation, slightly altered).

113. Patrizi's advice contrasts with that of Filarete for the princely city of Sforzinda. The latter recommends four gradations in the size of citizen houses: those for the gentleman, merchant, artisan, and wage worker. See Filarete 1965, 1:146–150.

114. Patrizi may have had in mind something like the harbor forum depicted in the famous Berlin "ideal city"; see Marchi and Valazzi 2012, 124–127 (Catalogo 1.3), which shows an oblong forum looking toward a harbor from a colonnade; either side of the forum is lined with three-story houses of approximately equal height.

115. Alberti 1988, 268–278 (8.7).

116. *Moral Epistles* 7. For the technical meaning of *spectacula* or "show buildings" in Alberti to refer to theaters, amphitheaters, circuses, and gladatoria, see Rykwert's glossary in Alberti 1988, 425. For similar Senecan sentiments in Petrarch, see Hankins 2019, 177.

117. See Alberti 1988, 286–287, where Alberti associates the provision of public libraries with the Hellenistic kings and the Athenian tyrant Pisistratus. He calls for libraries to have large collections of ancient books, *mappamundi,* mathematical instruments, and statues of ancient poets. Uberto Decembrio praises the ducal library at Pavia in his *De republica* but does not mention the need for public libraries; the subject is also omitted by Tito Livio Frulovisi and Lauro Quirini in their books on republics. Patrizi may have been thinking of precedents like the Library of San Marco, founded by Niccolò Niccoli and Cosimo de'Medici (1444) and Biblioteca Malatestiana (1452/1454). The latter, founded by Malatesta Novello,

was the first public library belonging to a *commune* rather than a prince or a religious institution. Cardinal Bessarion later (1468) left his large classical and ecclesiastical library to the city of Venice, though the building was not opened to the public until the sixteenth century. For Renaissance public libraries, see Celenza and Pupillo 2010.

118. The detail that the walls of the library should be tinted green may indicate a connection with the Biblioteca Malatestiana. A note on that library's website reads: "Anche il colore riveste un ruolo preciso: il bianco delle colonne mediane, il rosso del pavimento in cotto e delle semicolonne e il verde dell'intonaco, riportato alla luce dai restauri degli anni Venti del Novecento, rimandano ai colori degli stemmi malatestiani" (which featured heraldic green or *vert*). An illuminated volume of Augustine's *City of God* from that library, MS D IX.1 (1450), shows Augustine sitting in a study with green walls. See Pasini 2002, 240. Patrizi's remarks on the design of libraries were excerpted in J. J. Mader's *De bibliothecis atque archivis virorum clarissimorum* (1666, 1702); see Appendix B.

119. For the Casa della Sapienza, founded in 1392, containing dormitories and classrooms for students, see Minnucci and Košuta 1989; Denley 1991, 2006, 2007.

120. This seems on the surface to mark a departure from the practice in Tuscan republics, where citizen committees were, as a rule, in charge of building and maintaining the cathedral fabric. On the other hand, at *Rep.* 3.12 Patrizi says that the principal responsibility of aediles should be taking care of churches along with the other public works like aqueducts, sewers, bridges, and roads. Perhaps Patrizi had in mind a scheme for shared responsibility, although this is nowhere made explicit.

121. In the same chapter Patrizi includes an account of the Doric, Corinthian, and Ionic orders based on Vitruvius. On the diffusion of Patrizi's architectural vocabulary, see Aurigemma 1997.

122. For the text of the oration, see Valla 1994; on this and other of Valla's writings on the Church, see Connell 1996.

123. Cappelli 2012, 2018, and most compendiously, 2016, 10: The humanist state (*stato umanistico*) is "a body [*corpus*] that reflects the natural order of the world, in which each part discharges its proper role, a complex system inspired by justice and oriented to the *bonum commune*, in which *virtus* flows, circulating from top to bottom throughout the body, and that therefore includes a precise series of reciprocal obligations between *caput* and *membra* of the metaphorical organism: [this is] political organicism" (my translation). Cappelli's description applies most aptly to humanist monarchic theory but is also useful for describing the views of humanists like Leonardo Bruni and republican conceptions of the best state.

124. For the term "warlordism" as a feature of weak states, see Marten 2006/2007.

125. Hankins 2019, chap. 10. Such conflicts appear often in Bruni's *History of the Florentine People,* in which Bruni, despite having served as apostolic secretary to four popes, usually shows impatience with citizen politicians who allow their reasoning to be influenced by an excess of loyalty to the popes.

126. *Rep.* 3.4. The text of the 1518 and all subsequent editions is corrupt here; the editor of the 1518 has skipped two lines (the italicized words are restored from *V*): "Humani magistratus hi sunt qui personam publicam gerunt civitatique praesunt *cum imperio ac potestate. Horum alii curam belli pacisque gerunt ex senatusconsulto legibusque; alii praesunt* iuridicundo, qui iura civitatis optime callere debent," etc.

127. On the use of Christian theology and institutions as a basis for civic religion in late medieval Italian communes, see Terpstra 2014.

128. Malcolm 2019, 37–38. Shame-praising means to praise a different culture or people as a way of shaming one's own people and culture into better behavior.

129. See Livy 1.20.

130. Patrizi's careful language here may be compared to the unqualified Erastianism of Uberto Decembrio in his *De republica,* where the prince has full powers to appoint his bishops and to control the ecclesiastical establishment in the interest of the state; see Decembrio 2020, 14.

131. See *Rep.* 1.5, 5.Pr.

132. For Patrizi's role as bishop of Gaeta in founding a cult center of the Immaculate Mary in the town of Itri, see below, 357n91. It is also possible that he would have mentioned such practices and institutions in the separate treatment of religion he promises at *Rep.* 3.1 and 3.4 but did not in the end include in the published work. For Patrizi's discussion of piety and religion in the *De regno,* see Chapter 7.

133. *Rep.* 6.2, also quoted above, where the *opes* of men of religion are to come from the *fructus terrae* and not from commercial activities.

134. Wood 2006, chap. 25.

135. Hankins 2019, 468-474.

# 6. Citizenship and the Virtuous Citizen

1. For the concept of citizenship in modern political theory, see Leydet 2017. For the history of the concept, see Pocock 1992 (reprinted in Beiner 1995); Riesenberg 1992; Heater 2004a; Costa 2005; Ellis et al. 2006; Tristano and Allegria 2008.

2. Buckland 1921, 87-91; Sherwin-White 1973.

3. Bellavitis 2001; Olard 2007. For the history of citizenship in medieval and Renaissance Italy, see Bowsky 1967; Riesenberg 1972, 1974; Quaglioni 1991; Menzinger 2017. Pedullà (2018, 145-180) is the first scholar to draw attention to humanist contributions to the idea of citizenship; he discusses Patrizi's ideas on 156-158.

4. Bowsky 1981, 9-10, 20-22; Piccinni 2013.

5. Cane and Conaghan 2008, describing modern assumptions about citizenship: "Equality among all citizens is an implicit norm; inequality between citizens is presumptively unjust."

6. Heater 2004b. As Frede 2005 shows, Aristotle's concern with virtuous rule leads him to criticize hereditary citizenship and limit the citizen body to those with the capacity to rule; those with extraordinary abilities of rulership were for him more entitled to rule than others.

7. Sherwin-White 1973, 222.

8. Pocock 1992 sees Aristotle as the theoretician par excellence of the participatory model, and the Roman jurist Gaius as the most representative authority on the status model; for Gaius a Roman citizen is above all someone who is under Roman law and able to act *sui iuris* with regard to persons, actions, and things.

9. As late as the thirteenth century, Accursius could write: "I call 'Roman citizens' all who are subject to the empire" (*Cives Romanos dico omnes subjectos imperii*): see Quaglioni 1991, 160.

10. Full political rights were generally confined to citizens *optimo iure;* see Cortese 1960, 137.

11. Kirshner 1973. Crucially, Bartolus validated the right of a *civitas sibi princeps,* a city that is its own emperor (or a sovereign city, as the expression is usually understood), to select its own citizens using its own law (*ius proprium*), independent of imperial authority.

12. Somaini 2012.

13. Marsilius of Padua, relying on Aristotle, was perhaps the first political philosopher since antiquity to define citizenship in a participatory sense: "A citizen I define in accordance

NOTES TO PAGES 246-251

with Aristotle in the *Politics* . . . as one who participates in the civil community in the government or the deliberative or judicial function according to his rank" (Marsilius of Padua 2005, 45–46 [1.12.4]). See Riesenberg 1992, 164–168.

14. Riesenberg 1974, 335. See also Reisenberg 1969, 1972; for reservations, see Quaglioni 1991, 162.

15. Riesenberg 1974, 336: "Nor were these attitudes and needs restricted to the inhabitants of any single form of city state; citizens of princely Milan held them as well as those of republican Florence." See also Riesenberg 1992, 175–176. Herlihy 1995 describes how the expanding number of offices in Florence from the late thirteenth through the early sixteenth century went *pari passu* with a decrease in the political power attached to officeholding.

16. The idea that the excellence of the citizen differs under different constitutions goes back to Aristotle, *Politics* 3.4, 1270b30; see Kraut 2002, 358. Patrizi probably knew the *Politics* via the 1436 translation of Leonardo Bruni, though with his command of Greek he might have read the work in the original.

17. "Royal citizenship" is my term; Heater 2004a discusses but does not identify the phenomenon of citizenship in monarchies as a distinct species of citizenship; Riesenberg 1992 describes "the ambiguities of citizenship under monarchy" (to quote the title of his chapter 7). Modern theorists frequently understand citizens and subjects to be mutually exclusive categories; for example, Kymlicka 2005 states baldly that "citizenship is a distinctively democratic ideal. People who are governed by monarchs or military dictators are subjects, not citizens." Calhoun 2002 traces the prominence of citizenship as a political concept in contemporary theory to the "rise of republicanism" in the early modern period.

18. For the gradual emergence of more "rational"—i.e., centralized, ministerial forms of governance—from the welter of feudal and civic privileges in Naples during the Aragonese period, see Senatore 2012. For the superiority of citizenship to feudal loyalties from the point of view of Renaissance monarchy, see Bodin 1955, 59–65 (1.6–7).

19. The phrase is from Montesquieu 1964, 535 (II, 4).

20. Bodin 1955, 60 (1.6).

21. See Chapter 2, 90–91. In the comparison that follows of Aristotle with Patrizi, the *comparandum* is modern understandings of Aristotle based above all on Kraut 2002; Frede 2005; Rosler 2013; Samaras 2015; and Inamura 2015, chap. 4.2. How Patrizi understood Aristotle is a large question, but one may observe at least that he did not share the widely held view of his day that Aristotle was a monarchist, and his views on citizenship and citizen education show careful study of *Politics* 3 and 7. Patrizi sometimes attributes Aristotelian doctrines, with some *forzatura*, to Homer; for an example, see below, 249.

22. *Rep.* 1.3.

23. *Rep.* 5.1.

24. Cicero refers to the famous doctrine of *duplex patria*, where one can be born and raised in Arpino but also be a citizen of Rome; see Hankins 2019, 223–224. Patrizi's use of *germana patria* is inconsistent here, the result perhaps of employing an inapt comparison.

25. *Rep.* 5.1.

26. The language is not legally precise but Patrizi seems to mean that one can retain citizenship by showing patrilineal descent from a citizen father in an earlier generation.

27. *Rep.* 5.1.

28. Chapter 7, 294–295.

29. Rosler 2013, 149; Samaras 2015, 135–141, citing *Politics* 7.8, 1328b39–41: "a banausic or commercial (*agoraion*) life . . . is ignoble and contrary to virtue." See also Rosler 2013, 166.

30. Frede 2005, 176–178; Samaras 2015, 140.

31. *Rep.* 1.4. For Patrizi's dislike of oligarchic constitutions that reduce the poor to servants of the rich, see Chapter 3, where this passage is also discussed with different questions in mind.

32. *Politics* 3.11, 1281b28: "A state full of *atimoi* would be a state full of enemies." *Atimoi* are citizens without honor, i.e., not permitted to participate in politics.

33. See also *Rep.* 3.1, which treats the duty of private citizens toward their magistrates and the duty of magistrates to private citizens.

34. Aristotle, *Politics* 3.5, 1278a2–3. See Rosler 2013, 150.

35. *Rep.* 1.4. Another definition of the citizen Patrizi employs is more explicitly organic: see *Rep.* 5.2: "virum bonum et reipublicae utilem" (a good man who is useful to the state), a phrase reminiscent of Cato's definition of the good orator, "a good man skilled in speaking." See also below, Chapter 7, 294, for use of the phrase in modeling the best prince and the best poet.

36. *Rep.* 1.4. *Multitudo* here refers, not to all the inhabitants of the city, but rather the mass of the citizen body. Patrizi's knowledge of Solon's constitutional reforms probably came directly from Plutarch's *Life of Solon;* caps. 18–19 in particular describe the measures Solon took to give the people a share in government while leaving magistracies in the hands of the well-to-do (οἱ εὔποροι). But Patrizi would also have had indirect of knowledge of Solon's constitution via Aristotle, *Politics* 3.11, 1281b32.

37. *Rep.* 1.4. See Aristotle, *Politics* 3.11, 1281a16–17.

38. See Chapter 4, 134–135.

39. *Rep.* 1.4. Cf. Aristotle, *Politics* 4.11, 1295a–1296a; and Leonardo Bruni in Hankins 2019, 277–279.

40. See Chapter 5, 180, for Patrizi's condemnation of "leisured and low-spirited youths" who are "the poison of the state."

41. Hankins 2019, 435.

42. Hankins 2019, 40–42; and for Patrizi's understanding of virtue egalitarianism, 60–62.

43. Chapter 4, 131; for Aristotle, see Samaras 2015, 137.

44. See Hankins 2019, 58–60.

45. *Rep.* 5.1. The reference to Romulus's example comes from the passage in Tacitus just below.

46. *Rep.* 5.1.

47. Hankins 2019, chaps. 11 and 14.

48. *Rep.* 6.4. Note that *incola* means "resident alien," contrasted with a citizen; it is the equivalent of the Greek μέτοικος or πάροικος according to Cicero and the *Digest of Roman Law.*

49. *Rep.* 6.4. The rare explicit citation from Aristotle is to *Politics* 5.3, 1303a26–1303b3.

50. *Rep.* 6.4. The story of Spartacus and Crixus (whom Patrizi calls "Chrysus") must be from the *Periochae* of Livy 96, Florus 2.8.20, or Appian, *Bellum civile* 1.14.116.

51. Patrizi's Siena was in fact noted for its "incredibly strong collective identity"; see Ascheri 2020.

52. Quintilian 6.3.102. Giovanni Pontano, another humanist advisor to Alfonso of Calabria, discusses urbanity and rusticity in Pontano 2019.

53. *Rep.* 1.7. Patrizi says of peasants: "Let them exercise their rustic duties and those magistracies that are needed in the countryside. To put them in charge of a citizen would be entirely inhuman, foreign to all urbanity." See Chapter 4, 137.

54. *Rep.* 5.5.

55. *Reg.* 9.10. Compare Plato, *Laws* 5, 731a.

56. Pufendorf 1673 might be considered the first free-standing treatise on citizenship. Hobbes's *De cive* (1642), despite its title, is not a treatise on citizenship, and his usage of "citizen" is indistinguishable from "subject." Pufendorf's *De officio hominis et civis* was a popular compendium of *De iure naturae et gentium* (1672). The latter treatise at 1.3–4 remarks that good citizens are not born but made, a view with which Patrizi would have agreed.

57. But Riesenberg (1956, 134–137; 1992, 144) notes a tendency in some late medieval jurists to equate *subditi* and *cives*.

58. I describe Patrizi's position in the *De regno* as "humanist absolutism," a regime type that precludes any formal constitutional rights to exercise power by persons other than the king; see Hankins 2019, chap. 17, and Chapter 7 following. As in the case of Confucian political theory, however, there are informal constraints on potential tyrants that are exercised by virtuous ministers who refuse to do his bidding when his orders are wicked or unwise. Recent scholars of Confucian political thought have regarded these constraints as a kind of constitutionalism; see Kim 2020.

59. *Reg.* 9.2. In 9.15 he argues that staying on good terms with your prince "may be accomplished in particular through virtue, yet it is greatly aided by *bonae artes* [i.e., the humanities] and the *studia disciplinarum* conjoined with an honorable life: these commend men beyond all other things to kings and princes."

60. See Plutarch, *Moralia* ("Precepts of Statecraft") 816e. Patrizi's ideas about the techniques of statesmanship in general show careful consideration of this essay.

61. The theater analogy is of Stoic and especially Senecan provenance. Patrizi reverses the argument in *Reg.* 9.12: If citizens try to conceal their acts from the king, they are perforce base acts; therefore good citizens should tolerate the king's use of spies to inform on citizens' bad behavior, who bring reports to him "as to a spectator and judge of the most (in)famous actions." People who commit crimes should not be able to act in safety. It is better that the king learn about his people from many sources than from a few, lest he seem to be ruled by the judgment of a clique. This last observation is perhaps indebted to Plato's *Laws* 5, 730d.

62. *Reg.* 9.8. The story embroiders on Diogenes Laertius 4.8. The words Patrizi uses to translate "far away" and "at close range," *eminus* and *comminus,* in their primary Latin sense refer to what is out of range and within range of a sword.

63. *Reg.* 9.8. The story again significantly reshapes its source, Quintus Curtius 4.17–24—for instance, adding the detail, not found in the source, that Abactonius (called Abdalonymus in modern editions of the ancient text) was *studiis bonarum artium eruditus,* educated in the humanities.

64. *Reg.* 9.5.

65. *Reg.* 9.3. To underline his point, Patrizi quotes from a fragment of Ennius's *Iphigenia* preserved in Aulus Gellius 19.10.11–13, excoriating aimless *otiosum otium,* useless leisure.

66. *Reg.* 9.11.

67. See Introduction, 2.

68. There are also what seem to be obvious parallel passages in Isocrates's *Areopagiticus,* a work that, however, seems to have been unknown, at least in Latin, in the fifteenth century. It was first translated by Juan Luis Vives in 1526.

69. Hörcher 2020 discusses the history of prudence as a principle of political action, distinguishing between the "Ciceronian" tradition of the early Renaissance, the realistic prudence of Machiavelli, and the moral realism of "reason-of-state" theorists such as Guicciardini, Botero, and Lipsius.

70. Senatore 2012.

## 7. Virtuous Absolutism

1. Plato, *Republic* 4, 445d. Plato uses the word *politeia*, meaning "constitution," which either Patrizi or the translation he is using renders as *respublica*. See Hankins 2019, chap. 3, for the history of the word *respublica*.

2. *Reg.* 1.1.

3. See *Epg.* 80 (*G, 29v–30r*), written in the voice of King Xerxes. The king makes a generous response to Themistocles, in flight from his own ungrateful Athens. Themistocles has asked him for succor, and Xerxes offers him whatever he needs to live a happy life in his kingdom. Some language in the poem suggests that Patrizi saw in Themistocles's case a parallel to his own situation as a refugee from republican Siena living under the protection of the king of Naples.

4. Chapter 1, 49–50.

5. *Epg.* 147 (*G, 50v*): "Proscribis patriae patres sanctumque senatum/qui tibi tot saeclis libera iura dedit,/moenibus et saepsit legesque ac Pallidis artes/auxit et innumeras accumulauit opes,/eripuit totidem bellis totidemque periclis,/fecit et ut magnis perfruerere bonis." By "the arts of Pallas" Patrizi probably means the University of Siena.

6. *Epg.* 148 (*G, 51r*).

7. *Epg.* 149 (*G, 51r–v*). In *Epg.* 204 (*G, 64r*), probably written about 1487, he addresses Sienese exiles now returning to their city after the populist madness has subsided, urging them to rebuild what has been destroyed and burned down; after all, it is not walls, houses, temples, and the sarcophagi of our ancestors that make a city, but its citizens (*cives patriam faciunt*), wherever they may be located physically.

8. *Epg.* 144 (*G, 49v–50r*), published in L. Smith 1968, 119.

9. *Line 3:* the Sisters; i.e., the Fates. *Line 4:* Apollo, here probably the god of prophecy or foresight, hence prudence; Pallas, here meaning reason. *Line 5:* to whom all things are known; i.e., a well-educated prince. *Line 9:* cruel rods and axes; i.e., the fasces, symbols of magisterial authority in ancient Rome; Patrizi means that the upper classes tend to abuse their power. *Line 10:* flee and return; i.e., unlike the Roman plebs, they accept merely verbal assurances rather than exacting concrete concessions. *Line 12:* Laestrygones; i.e., a tribe of man-eating giants that appears in Homer's *Odyssey*. *Line 13:* the best popular regime, *optima res populi*. Cicero in a surviving passage of his *Republic* (1.39) had famously identified the *respublica*, public affairs, with *res populi*, the people's business. On the meaning of *res populi* in Cicero, Schofield (1999, 183–189) emphasizes, among other things, that *res populi* cannot be straightforwardly identified with popular government. *Lines 13 and 14:* emphasis added.

10. See Chapter 1, 37–46.

11. The sentiment chimes with what Plutarch wrote in *Moralia* 824c ("Precepts of Statecraft"). If the highest goal of the city state is tranquillity and flourishing, it is better off under the protection of a king who banishes civil and foreign wars. The work was translated three times in the quattrocento: by Niccolò Sagundino for the Venetian patrician Marco Donato, by Giovanni Lorenzi, and by Carlo Valgulio (see Hankins 2019, 620n27). Patrizi addressed a late epigram (311) to Valgulio, a follower of Ficino, but probably knew the work already in the 1440s from Sagundino's translation, given its likely use as a source for *De magistratu gerendo*.

12. *Reg.* 9.2–3. I have rehearsed Patrizi's analogies of kingship in more detail in Hankins 2019, 408–412.

13. Discussed in Chapter 3, 113–119.

14. It will be remembered that Patrizi claimed to have derived his constitutional model for republics from Herodotus. A preference for monarchy is also implied by Patrizi's argu-

ment for why citizens of a monarchy should behave with loyal virtue (see Chapter 6, 263–269): see also his explicit statements at *Reg.* 1.13, 9.2.

15. Hankins 2019, chap. 12.

16. For the distinction between generic polity (as a name for constitution) and specific polity (as a name for the legitimate popular regime), see Hankins 2019, chap. 2.

17. As did Cyriac of Ancona, for example; see Hankins 2019, chap. 12, for Cyriac's knowledge of book 6 of Polybius in the 1440s. I am not convinced by the view expressed in Pedullà 2021a that Cyriac derived the term *ochlokratia* from Plutarch's essay *De tribus reipublicae generibus* in *Moralia* 826a. The latter essay was not translated into Latin until the sixteenth century (Hankins 2019, 599n13), and in any case the rest of the constitutional terminology in Cyriac's *Sex modi administrandarum rerum publicarum* (Cyriac of Ancona 2015, 292–299) follows Polybius rather than Plutarch.

18. See Chapter 3, 96–97.

19. For the Aristotelian theory of modes of rule and its history in scholastic political theory, see Blythe 1992.

20. Aquinas and Giles of Rome both accept Aristotle's division of the modes of rule into regal, political, and despotic types, but substitute the master / servant relation for Aristotle's master / slave relation in modeling despotism. See Blythe 1992, 19, 42, 63–65.

21. Patrizi's debt to Isocrates and the ancient tradition of ideal monarchy is discussed in Hankins 2019, 386–398. On the ancient "discourse of monarchy," see now Atack 2020. Note also *Reg.* 2.3 and 4.10, where it is emphasized that the king's magistrates should live on their own income and not make profits from governing the people; this practice too would make royal magistracies superior to republican, in that magistrates of lesser means in republics will always be tempted to profit from their offices.

22. *Reg.* 2.3. Patrizi here contradicts Giles of Rome 1607, 433 (3.1.13), who favored term limits for magistrates.

23. *Reg.* 3.13, 4.9.

24. On modern and premodern forms of sovereignty, see the Introduction as well as Quaglioni 2003, 2007; Lee 2016.

25. See Chapter 3, 102–103.

26. *Reg.* 1.3, where Patrizi gives a summary of Athenian history based on Herodotus, Thucydides, Xenophon, and Plutarch. Pedullà 2021a, 119, calls this "probably the first history of the Athenian constitution written by a modern author."

27. *Reg.* 1.13. Needless to say, he does not use the word "republic" to describe the historical period we moderns call "the Roman republic"; see Hankins 2019, 75–78, 292–296. Patrizi generally uses the term *civitas libera* for Rome in its republican phase.

28. Patrizi helpfully informs us that Greek cities, according to Dionysius of Halicarnassus, had the same institution in the person of an *aesymnetes*.

29. Hankins 2019, chap. 11; and Chapter 4, 111–112.

30. Patrizi cites a letter from Cicero to Atticus, which must be *Ad Atticum* 2.14, where the Roman orator wittily employs (or possibly coins) the Greek word εὐτυραννεῖσθαι, to be "well tyrannized." Cicero was possibly alluding to Plato's judgment that the best vehicle for the reform of city-states would be a "well-behaved tyrant" (*Laws* 4, 710d).

31. Patrizi's judgment echoes that of Dionysius of Halicarnassus, Appian, and the ancient Christian historian Orosius. For Patrizi, those who assassinated Caesar "under the pretense of defending liberty" were fighting against the natural pressure of circumstances that were already trending toward monarchy, and their act merely opened the way to the second triumvirate, marked by the savage cruelty of Octavian, worse than any tyrant's (*Reg.* 4.4).

32. *Reg.* 2.3.

NOTES TO PAGES 283-290

33. Throughout the *De regno* Patrizi sometimes directly addresses his royal reader as "you," presumably meaning the dedicatee, Alfonso, duke of Calabria. Alfonso is also addressed in the prefaces to books 2–6 as well as in the preface to the work as a whole.

34. Patrizi's source for the Lycian League was surely Strabo 14.3.3; he is unlikely to have had access to the Byzantine compilations that preserved the later books of Polybius, which also discuss the Lycian League. Patrizi's target here may be Leonardo Bruni's interpretation of the Etruscan federal league of twelve city-states, which Bruni had used to advocate a new Tuscan league headed by Florence. See Hankins 2019, 231–234. In his early treatise *De gerendo magistratu*, Patrizi had described Siena as the home of Etruscan liberty, a citadel of defense against the tyrannical hegemon, Florence. For Madison's use of the Lycian Confederation, probably based on Montesquieu's *Spirit of the Laws* 1.9.1–3, see *Federalist Papers* 9, 16, and 45.

35. *Reg.* 2.3. Patrizi might have been thinking of Pericles's speech in Thucydides 2.60, where the Athenian empire is described as a tyranny.

36. *Reg.* 2.3.

37. *Reg.* 1.10–11.

38. Herodotus 3.85–86. The image of the primitive king as a shepherd of the human flock may come from Homer, *Iliad* 2.243, etc.; Xenophon, *Cyropaedia* 1.1.2; or Plato, *Statesman* 265b–268d, 274e–277a.

39. See Hankins 2019, 621n35, for references.

40. Walker 1972, 10–21. See also Hankins 1990, 1:283–285 and 2:459–463, on how Ficino's Platonism reverses Aristotle's developmental account of the history of philosophy, privileging the pure source over downstream corruptions. For Patrizi's awareness of and respect for ancient theology, see *Reg.* 8.15, on piety, where Patrizi claims that Homer and Hesiod learned their theology from the Chaldaeans and Egyptians.

41. Hankins 2019, 134–141.

42. For other humanist critics of Poggio's "anti-politics," see Roick 2017, 163–165, who discusses Bartolomeo Facio and Panormita (Antonio Beccadelli).

43. It is worth noting that neither Poggio nor Patrizi considers the possibility that one might do wrong things to accomplish good ends, a view incompatible with virtue ethics. In fact, it is a modern dilemma that begins with the new moral universe of Machiavelli, who famously taught that the prince "must learn how not to be good." Similarly, Guicciardini held that "reason of state," what preserves republics, is incompatible with Christian morality: see Guicciardini 1994, 159. This question is known in modern political theory as the "dirty hands" problem after a famous article by Michael Walzer (1973).

44. *Reg.* 1.7.

45. In *Reg.* 1.5 Patrizi responds to Poggio's argument (again without naming him) that princes have never favored liberal studies and have even persecuted wise and learned men. Patrizi says in reply that it may be all too true that support today for the *studia humanitatis et bonarum disciplinarum artes* is rare, but that was not the case in antiquity. Patrizi then proceeds to drown Poggian skeptics in dozens of counterexamples, noting especially the support of Roman emperors for liberal studies. In return, the *docti viri* gave their patrons prestige in life and preserved their memory in death, which showed that solid interests tied *docti viri* and patrons to each other.

46. *Reg.* 1.7. The negative judgment about Critias comes from Xenophon's *Hellenica*.

47. *Reg.* 1.7. The theme of seeds of virtue in humanist literature has been explored in Horowitz 1998.

48. *Reg.* 4.1.

49. Hankins 2019, 103–107. For Machiavelli's attitude to benign tyranny, see ibid., 450–453.

50. *Agesilaus* 3.13. Compare *Reg.* 3.13: "Scita est enim Agesilai regis sententia, qui ait regiae dignitati non *astutiam,* sed bonitatis excellentiam conuenire." Patrizi's condemnation of cunning is close to Giovanni Botero's later distinction between immoral cleverness (*astuzia*), championed by Machiavelli, and real prudence; see Botero 2007, 62.

51. *Reg.* 1.9.

52. The Catholic theology of grace may be in the background here. Patrizi appears to be giving a naturalized version of the concepts of antecedent, habitual, and consequent grace. Though Patrizi very rarely quotes Christian authorities in his political works, he did have some theological training in 1459 when preparing for the priesthood; see Chapter 1, 33–34.

53. *Reg.* 2.5, quoting Pliny's *Epistles* 3.18.3–4, in which Pliny excuses the sycophantic tone in his *Panegyricus*. I have found no allusions to the *Panegyricus* itself in the *De regno*—not surprisingly, in view of Patrizi's oft-expressed horror of flattery and adulation.

54. An example that Patrizi may have known is the humanist Pier Candido Decembrio's biography of Filippo Maria Visconti, which sometimes praises that tyrant's vices and finds nothing to condemn in the duke's shameful treatment of his wife and his pedophilia; see Hankins 2019, 141–147.

55. *Reg.* 8.6, 4.20. Patrizi's judgement of Augustus reflects Seneca, *De clementia* 1.9.

56. For the Renaissance debate over the character of Caesar, see Hankins 2019, 107–112, 124–134.

57. For the status of Plato's ideal constitutions and the question whether they could serve as practical blueprints in Renaissance polities, see Hankins 1990, 1:228–230.

58. *Reg.* 2.4. The quotation varies from modern texts of *Orator* 8–9 in ways that suggest quotation from memory.

59. Pedullà 2010, 462.

60. *The Prince,* chap. 15 (trans. Russell Price).

61. *Reg.* 2.1.

62. See Quintilian 12.1.3 for the famous definition of the orator, and Strabo 1.2.3 for the moral and intellectual distinction necessary to be a real poet. A similar stipulation of virtue is part of Patrizi's definition of the citizen; see Chapter 6, 250.

63. Hankins 2019, 112–118.

64. See above, 366n12.

65. *Reg.* 3.1: "Those subtle matters about which the dialecticians argue with such fine discrimination do not seem appropriate to the prince. Nor are the matters that go beyond the common views of mankind, called 'off target' by the Stoics, nor the esoteric subjects of Democritus or the dark secrets of Pythagoras, which require many years of silence. The things that should be set in order to educate the prince are those that treat of civil life and teach the best behavior and perfect our reason and our speech."

66. *Reg.* 9.22.

67. Primogeniture was also endorsed by some Renaissance jurists, such as those associated with the Duchy of Milan; see J. Black 2021. Giles of Rome (1607, 461–465 [3.2.5]) also argues in favor of hereditary succession and against any form of election by merit.

68. For the wider effects of Ferrante's illegitimacy on the shape of Aragonese political thought, see Delle Donne 2015; Guido Cappelli, "Cenni sullo stato aragonese nella teoria politica coeva," in Cappelli 2020b, 365–380.

69. Hankins 2019, 391.

70. Patrizi does not name his source, which is Macrobius's *Saturnalia* 3.17.10.

71. See Chapter 3, 102–104.

72. Chiarelli 1932. The view that Roman law had already been brought to perfection by the Roman jurists and did not need further codification is also stated in *Rep.* 1.5.

73. *Reg.* 8.6: "Quod quisque iuris in alterum statuerit, ipse quoque eodem iure utatur."
74. See Chapter 5, 202–213.
75. Nozick 1974. See Chapter 5, 202–213.
76. This rare word is used in Xenophon's *Hiero* 8.10 but may be a corruption there, and the sense in any case is not germane; also in Lucian's *Phalaris* 1.3, where it means impartiality (as between rich and poor). But the probable source is Patrizi's beloved Strabo, at 8.5.4, where in a passage describing early Spartan history it seems to mean an equal right to hold office. The same sense of the word is found in Dionysius of Halicarnassus's *Roman Antiquities* 10.30 (a speech opposing a grant of political rights to the plebs), which could have been available to Patrizi in the Latin translation (finished before 1469, first printing 1480) made for Pope Paul II by the Milanese humanist Lampugnino Birago.
77. *Reg.* 4.10. See also Chapter 3, 104–106, for other inappropriate applications of the principle of equality.
78. *Reg.* 2.10.
79. For the importance of historical study in princely education during the Renaissance, see Grell, Paravicini, and Voss 1998. For the "virtuous environment," see Hankins 2019, 51–54.
80. *Reg.* 2.11–12. The question of whether princes should use Socratic irony (understood as self-deprecation) was considered with similar concerns but rather more nuance by Pontano 2019, 398–401 (*De sermone* 6.4.31–33).
81. See above, note 65.
82. Pliny the Elder, *Natural History* 35.36.
83. See especially *De regimine principum* 1.3 (Giles of Rome 1607, 153–187).
84. For the reception of this collection of moral essays in the Renaissance, see Hankins and Palmer 2008, 14–15. On quattrocento Latin translations of the *Moralia* in general, see Bevagni 1994.
85. Schiera (2007) is to my knowledge the only modern scholar to have commented on Patrizi's highly original theory of civil friendship. Modern surveys of civil friendship such as Scorza 2013 tend to skip from Aristotle, Plato, and Cicero to Montaigne and Rousseau.
86. Diogenes Laertius 3.81 (Life of Plato). Patrizi studiously ignores Aristotle's rival division of friendship in *Nicomachean Ethics* 8.3, 1156a. The Greek word Patrizi (or Ambrogio Traversari, whose translation Patrizi probably used) translates as "civil or social" is ἑταιρική, which Diogenes then glosses: "By the social form of friendship we mean that which arises from intimacy and has nothing to do with kinship; for instance, that of Pylades for Orestes" (Loeb translation). The further subdivision of natural friendship seems to be Patrizi's invention.
87. Cicero, *De amicitia* 47.
88. *Reg.* 8.17–18. On the Renaissance conception of *humanitas,* see further Hankins 2020.
89. See, for example, John 15:9–10: "As the Father has loved me, so have I loved you. Now remain in my love. If you keep my commands, you will remain in my love, just as I have kept my Father's commands and remain in his love."
90. *City of God* 19.24: "Populus est coetus multitudinis rationalis rerum quas diligit concordi communione sociatus," revising Cicero's definition of a *respublica* (*De republica* 1.39): "populus [est] . . . coetus multitudinis iuris consensu et utilitatis communione sociatus" (a people is . . . an assembly of people united by a common agreement about law and a partnership of utility).
91. Kempshall 1999, esp. 145–146, 216–218, 297–299, 312–313.
92. *Reg.* 8.18.
93. See Seneca, *De beneficiis* 4.3.

94. Patrizi relies here silently on Aulus Gellius 13.17.

95. Cicero, *De natura deorum* 1.3.

96. Patrizi's source for the Cambyses story (the son of Cyrus the Great, not the father) is Diodorus Siculus 1.44, 46, 49.

97. On the "inclusivist" approach to religion of the humanists in general, see Hankins 2017.

98. Zorzi 2010, x writes: "In reality, throughout the thirteenth and fourteenth centuries, citizens considered the two forms of government, the communal and the signorial, as alternative resources to which they could have recourse as necessity or circumstances dictated," and notes that signorial power was not infrequently deployed in defense of the *popolo* against oligarchic forces in cities. The corresponding Roman official was of course the dictator, whereas Greek city-states employed the *aesymnetes*, described by Aristotle as an "elective tyranny" (*Politics* 3.14, 1285a).

99. Machiavelli 1989, 1:106. Compare Guicciardini 1994, 19–20.

100. See Chapter 6, 247–250.

101. Hankins 2019, chap. 18.

102. This was one goal of his *Florentine History*, written privately for the use of the Medici. See Jurdjevic 2014; Hankins 2019, chap. 20; and now R. Black 2022, 166–170. For other false prophecies of Machiavelli, see Hankins 2019, 458.

103. Machiavelli 1989; on the design of Machiavelli's improved republic, see Jurdjevic 2014.

104. On defects in Machiavelli's judgments about military affairs, see Hankins 2019, chap. 18.

105. Jacques 2012 chap. 7; Coker 2019.

106. See, for example, Bai 2020; Bell and Wang 2020. The idea of "one country, two systems," however, promised for Hong Kong and proposed for Taiwan, seems more recently to have faded in China, showing that a civilizational state is incompatible with a dogmatic political ideology.

107. *Reg.* 8.10–12; see also above, 303–309.

108. Lee 2016.

109. Bailyn 1993, 2:437. The Anti-Federalist writer James Winthrop wrote in 1787 (ibid., 2:450): "The idea of an uncompounded republick, on an average, one thousand miles in length, and eight hundred in breadth, and containing six millions of white inhabitants, all reduced to the same standard of morals, or habits, and of laws, is in itself an absurdity, and contrary to the whole experience of mankind."

110. Pedullà 2018. For ideological holism, see Rosenblum 2008. See also my comments on Pedullà's book in Hankins forthcoming-b, where I compare at greater length Machiavelli's and Patrizi's relative contributions to political modernity.

111. I have consulted online catalogues of the libraries of Thomas Jefferson, James Madison (with thanks to the staff at the Montpellier Foundation), and John Adams, as well as the Loganian Library in Philadelphia and early catalogues of Yale (1743) and Harvard Colleges, without locating any copies. The Founders in general, in forming their political prudence, seem to have relied mostly on Dutch, English, and French historical writers of the previous two centuries as well as their own reading in classical authors. It is worth noting that the works of Machiavelli were commonly available in American colonial libraries.

112. See Madison's remarks in *Federalist* 18–20. His main defense of constitutional dyarchy comes in *Federalist* 45–46. The Founders' most important theoretical source for federal or confederate republics was Montesquieu's *Spirit of the Laws* 1.9.1–3. Montesquieu had two copies of Patrizi's works in his library (Desgraves 1954, 172, nos. 2420–2421), the

1582 edition of the *De regno* printed in Paris and the epitomes of both the *De regno* and *De republica* compiled by Gilles d'Aurigny and published in Paris in 1459. See Appendix B.

113. As Montesquieu in fact predicted on the basis of the Roman example in *Spirit of the Laws* 1.11.19, possibly following Machiavelli, *Discourses* 2.13.

114. Bailyn 1993 offers a much fuller picture of the rich early debates on the US Constitution than one gets just from the *Federalist Papers*.

115. The most famous claims for the influence of Machiavelli on the American founding generation were made in Pocock 1975, but the literature on this subject is too vast to summarize here.

## Conclusion

1. The most substantial anatomy of this movement of thought is Quondam 2010.

2. For the hermeneutical problems faced by modern political philosophers when reconstructing arguments from early Confucian texts, see Bai 2020, 9–19.

3. See Hankins 2021b, esp. 76–82, for more on the contrast between Machiavelli's and Patrizi's methods.

4. For the idea of tradition as a "golden nugget," see the critique in Appiah 2018.

5. For the positioning of humanists generally between populism and oligarchy, see Hankins 2019, 242–246.

6. Hayes 2012, 57–59.

7. The French revolutionaries of 1789 also defined equality (albeit equality of rights) in terms of political meritocracy and the suppression of privileged access to office; see article 6 of the *Declaration of the Rights of Man and of the Citizen:* "[The law] must be the same for all, whether it protects or punishes. All citizens, being equal in its eyes, shall be equally eligible to all high offices, public positions and employments, according to their ability, and without other distinction than that of their virtues and talents."

# Bibliography

## Sources

Alberti, Leon Battista. 1988. *On the Art of Building in Ten Books*. Edited by Joseph Rykwert, Neil Leach, and Robert Tavernor. Cambridge, MA: MIT Press.

Bailyn, Bernard, ed. 1993. *The Debate on the Constitution: Federalist and Antifederalist Speeches, Articles and Letters during the Struggle over Ratification.* New York: Library of America.

Barbaro, Francesco. 2021. *De re uxoria*. Edited by Claudio Griggio and Chiara Kravina. Florence: Leo S. Olschki.

Beccadelli, Antonio. 2010. *The Hermaphrodite*. Edited and translated by Holt Parker. Cambridge, MA: Harvard University Press (ITRL).

Bodin, Jean. 1955. *Six Books of the Commonwealth*. Abridged and translated by M. J. Tooley. Oxford: Blackwell.

Botero, Giovanni. 2007. *The Reason of State*. Edited and translated by Robert Bireley. Cambridge: Cambridge University Press.

Bottari, Giovanni Gaetano, ed. 1719–1726. *Carmina illustrium poetarum italorum.* 11 vols. Florence: J. C. Tartinius and S. Franchius.

Brandolini, Aurelio Lipp. 2009. *Republics and Kingdoms Compared*. Edited and translated by James Hankins. Cambridge, MA: Harvard University Press (ITRL).

Bruni, Leonardo. 2001–2006. *History of the Florentine People*. Edited and translated by James Hankins. 3 vols. Cambridge, MA: Harvard University Press (ITRL).

Carafa, Diomede 1668. *De regis et boni principis officio*. Naples: Castaldus.

Contarini, Gaspar. 2020. *The Republic of Venice: De magistratibus et republica Venetorum.* Edited by Filippo Sabetti. Translated by Giuseppe Pezzini. Toronto: University of Toronto Press.

Cyriac of Ancona and Francisco Scalamonti. 2015. *Life and Early Travels*. Edited by Charles Mitchell, Edward W. Bodnar, and Clive Foss. Cambridge, MA: Harvard University Press (ITRL).

Decembrio, Uberto. 2020. *Four Books on the Commonwealth: De republica libri IV.* Edited and translated by Paolo Pontù Donato. Leiden: Brill.

Filarete [Antonio Averlino]. 1965. *Filarete's Treatise on Architecture: Being the Treatise by Antonio di Piero Averlino, Known as Filarete*. Translated with an introduction and notes by John R. Spencer. New Haven, CT: Yale University Press.

Filelfo, Francesco. 2005. *Satyrae*. Edited by Silvia Fiaschi. Rome: Edizioni di storia e letteratura.

———. 2009. *Odes*. Edited and translated by Diana Robin. Cambridge, MA: Harvard University Press (ITRL).

———. 2014. *On Exile*. Edited by Jeroen De Keyser. Translated by W. Scott Blanchard. Cambridge, MA: Harvard University Press (ITRL).

———. 2015. *Collected Letters: Epistolarum Libri XLVIII*. Edited by Jeroen De Keyser. Alessandria: Edizioni dell'Orso.

Flavio, Biondo. 2005. *Italy Illuminated*. Edited and translated by Jeffrey A. White. Cambridge, MA: Harvard University Press (ITRL).

Frulovisi, Tito Livio. 1932. *De republica*. In *Opera hactenus inedita*, edited by C. W. Previté-Orton, 287–389. Cambridge: Cambridge University Press.

Garzoni, Giovanni. 2014. *De eruditione principum: De principis officio*. Edited by Alessandra Mantovani. Rome: Edizioni di storia e letteratura.

Giles of Rome [Aegidius Columna Romanus]. 1607. *De regimine principum libri III*. Edited by Hieronymus Samaritanius. Rome: Bartolomaeus Zannettus.

Guicciardini, Francesco. 1994. *Dialogue on the Government of Florence*. Edited and translated by Alison Brown. Cambridge: Cambridge University Press.

Ilarione of Verona. 1473. *Dialogus ad Petrum Sancti Sixti cardinalem*. Rome: Johannes Philippus de Lignamine.

Lipsius, Justus. 2004. *Politica: Six Books of Politics or Political Instruction*. Edited and translated by Jan Waszink. Assen: Royal Van Gorcum.

Machiavelli, Niccolò. 1989. "A Discourse on Remodeling the Government of Florence." In *Machiavelli: The Chief Works and Others*, trans. Allan Gilbert, 1:101–115. 3 vols. Durham, NC: Duke University Press.

———. 2013. *Il principe*. Edited with a modern Italian translation by Carmine Donzelli. Introduction and commentary by Gabriele Pedullà. Rome: Donzelli.

Marrasio, Giovanni. 2016. *Angelinetum and Other Poems*. Translated by Mary P. Chatfield. Cambridge, MA: Harvard University Press (ITRL).

Marsilius of Padua. 2005. *The Defender of the Peace*. Edited and translated by Annabel Brett. Cambridge: Cambridge University Press.

Mercurius Trismegistus. 2011. *Pimander sive De potestate et sapientia Dei*. Edited by Maurizio Campanelli. Turin: Aragno.

Montesquieu, C.-L. de Secondat, baron de. 1964. *De l'esprit des lois*. In C.-L. de Secondat Montesquieu, *Oeuvres complètes*, edited by Daniel Oster, 528–795. Paris: Éditions du Seuil.

More, Thomas. 1965. *Utopia*. Edited by Edward Surtz and J. H. Hexter. Vol. 4 of *The Yale Edition of the Complete Works of St. Thomas More*. New Haven, CT: Yale University Press.

Pannalini, Barnaba. 1979. *Barnaba Senese, Epistolario*. Edited by Giacomo Ferraù. Palermo: Il Vespro.

Pius II (Enea Silvio Piccolomini). 1571. *Opera*. Basel: Henricpetri.

———. 1883. *Opera inedita.* Edited by Josephus Cugnoni. Rome: Salviucci.
———. 1994. *Carmina.* Edited by Adrianus Van Heck. Vatican City: Bibliotheca Apostolica Vaticana.
———. 2001. *De Europa.* Edited by Adrianus Van Heck. Vatican City: Bibliotheca Apostolica Vaticana.
———. 2003. *Commentaries.* Vol. 1. Edited by Margaret Meserve and Marcello Simonetta. Cambridge, MA: Harvard University Press (ITRL).
Pontano, Giovanni. 2012–2020. *Actius.* Vol. 2 of his *Dialogues,* edited by Julia Haig Gaisser, 3 vols. Cambridge, MA: Harvard University Press (ITRL).
———. 2019. *The Virtues and Vices of Speech [De sermone].* Edited and translated by George W. Pigman III. Cambridge, MA: Harvard University Press (ITRL).
Pufendorf, Samuel. 1673. *De officio hominis et civis iuxta legem naturalem libri duo.* London: Adam Junghans.
Quirini, Lauro. 1977. *De republica libri II.* Edited by Carlo Seno and Giorgio Ravegnani. In *Lauro Quirini umanista,* studies and texts edited by Konrad Krautter, Paul Oskar Kristeller, Agostino Pertusi, Giorgio Ravegnani, Helmut Roob, and Carlo Seno; collected and presented by Vittore Branca, 123–161. Florence: Leo S. Olschki.
Rinuccini, Alamanno. 1953. *Lettere ed orazioni.* Edited by Vito R. Giustiniani. Florence: Leo S. Olschki.
———. 2002. *La libertà perduta = Dialogus de libertate.* Edited by Francesco Adorno. Italian translation by Giuseppe Civati. Monza: Vittone.
Scala, Bartolomeo. 2008. *Essays and Dialogues.* Translated by Renée Neu Watkins. Cambridge, MA: Harvard University Press (ITRL).
Sercambi, Giovanni. 1892. *Le Croniche.* Edited by Salvatore Bongi. 3 vols. Rome: Istituto storico italiano per il Medio Evo.
Valla, Lorenzo. 1994. *Orazione per l'inaugurazione dell'anno accademico, 1455–1456.* Edited by Silvia Rizzo. Rome: Roma nel Rinascimento.

## Secondary Literature

Adams, Nicholas. 1989. "The Construction of Pienza (1459–1464) and the Consequences of *Renovatio.*" In *Urban Life in the Renaissance,* edited by Susan Zimmerman and Ronald Weissman, 50–79. Newark: University of Delaware Press.
Alessio, Gian Carlo. 1990. "The 'lectura' of the *Triumphi* in the Fifteenth Century." In *Petrarch's "Triumphs": Allegory and Spectacle,* edited by Konrad Eisenbichler and Amilcare A. Iannucci, 269–290. Toronto: Dovehouse Editions.
Altamura, Antonio. 1941. "Due carmi inediti dell'umanista senese Francesco Patrizi." *Bullettino Senese di Storia Patria* 48: 52–61.
———. 1955. "Una saffica mariana di Francesco Patrizi." *Marianum* 17: 335–338. Reprinted in Altamura, *Studi e ricerche di letteratura umanistica,* 53–59. Naples: S. Viti.
Annas, Julia. 2017. *Virtue and Law in Plato and Beyond.* Oxford: Oxford University Press.

Appiah, Anthony. 2018. *The Lies That Bind: Rethinking Identity*. New York: Norton Liveright.

Ascheri, Mario. 1985. *Siena Nel Rinascimento: Istituzioni e sistema politico*. Siena: Il Leccio.

———. 1986. "Siena nel primo Quattrocento: Un sistema politico tra storia e storiografia." In *Siena e il suo territorio nel Rinascimento: Documenti raccolti*, vol. 1, edited by Mario Ascheri and Donatella Ciampoli, 3–53. Siena: Il Leccio.

———. 1991a. "Un invito a discutere di 'oligarchia': In margine al governo di Siena nel Tre-Quattrocento." In *Esercizio del potere e prassi della consultazione*, edited by A. Ciani and G. Diurni, 263–272. Vatican City: Libreria Editrice Vaticana.

———, ed. 1991b. *L'Università di Siena: 750 anni di storia*. Milan: Silvana.

———. 2001. "La Siena del 'Buon Governo' (1287–1355)." In *Politica e cultura nelle repubbliche italiane dal Medioevo all'età moderna: Firenze, Genova, Lucca, Siena, Venezia: Atti del Convegno (Siena 1997)*, edited by Simonetta Adorni and Mario Ascheri, 81–107. Rome: Istituto storico italiano per l'età moderna e contemporanea.

———. 2007. "Enea Silvio e il suo difficile rapporto con il governo di Siena." In *Pio II Umanista Europeo: Atti Del XVII Convegno Internazionale, Chianciano-Pienza 18–21 Luglio 2005*, edited by Luisa Rotondi Secchi Tarugi, 51–72. Florence: Cesati.

———. 2020. "Siena: A Long-Standing Republic." In *Republicanism: A Theoretical and Historical Perpective*, edited by Fabrizio Ricciardelli and Marcello Fantoni, 129–145. Rome: Viella.

———. 2021. "Siena: The City and Its State throughout Time." In Casciani and Hayton 2021, 11–31.

Ascheri, Mario, and Bradley Franco. 2020. *A History of Siena from Its Origins to the Present Day*. London: Routledge.

Atack, Carol. 2020. *The Discourse of Kingship in Classical Greece*. Abingdon, UK: Routledge.

Aurigemma, Maria Giulia. 1997. "Note sulla diffusione del vocabulario architettonico: Francesco Patrizi." In *Le due Rome del Quattrocento: Melozzo, Antoniazzo e la cultura artistica del '400 romano*, edited by Sergio Rossi and Stefano Valeri, 364–379. Rome: Lithos.

Avesani, Rino. 1968. "Epaeneticorum ad Pium II Pont: Max. libri V." In *Enea Silvio Piccolomini, Papa Pio II: Atti del convegno per il quinto centenario della morte, e altri scritti*, edited by Domenico Maffei, 15–97. Siena: Accademia Senese degli Intronati.

Bai, Tongdong. 2012. *China: The Political Philosophy of the Middle Kingdom*. London: Zed Books.

———. 2020. *Against Political Equality: The Confucian Case*. Princeton, NJ: Princeton University Press.

Baker, Patrick. 2015. *Italian Renaissance Humanism in the Mirror*. Cambridge: Cambridge University Press.

Bassi, Domenico. 1894. "L'Epitome di Quintiliano di Francesco Patrizi Senese." *Rivista di Filologia e di Istruzione Classica* 22: 385–470.

Battaglia, Felice. 1936. *Enea Silvio Piccolomini e Francesco Patrizi: Due politici senesi del Quattrocento.* Florence: Leo S. Olschki, 1936.

Bauer, Stefan. 2006. *The Censorship and Fortuna of Platina's "Lives of the Popes" in the Sixteenth Century.* Turnhout: Brepols.

Beer, Susanna de, Karl A. E. Enenkel, and David Rijser. 2009. *The Neo-Latin Epigram: A Learned and Witty Genre.* Leuven: Leuven University Press.

Beiner, Ronald, ed. 1995. *Theorizing Ctizenship.* Albany: State University of New York Press.

Bejczy, István, and Cary J. Nederman, eds. 2007. *Princely Virtues in the Middle Ages, 1200–1500.* Turnhout: Brepols.

Bell, Daniel. 1972. "On Meritocracy and Equality." *National Affairs* (Fall): 29–68.

Bell, Daniel A. 2015. *The China Model: Political Meritocracy and the Limits of Democracy.* Princeton, NJ: Princeton University Press.

Bell, Daniel A., and Pei Wang. 2020. *Just Hierarchy: Why Social Hierarchies Matter in China and the Rest of the World.* Princeton, NJ: Princeton University Press.

Bellavitis, Anna. 2001. *Identité, mariage, mobilité sociale: Citoyennes et citoyens à Venise au XVIe siècle.* Rome: Publications de l'École française de Rome.

Beltramini, Maria. 1996. "Filelfo and Filarete." *Annali della Scuola Normale Superiore di Pisa,* ser. 4, *Quaderni,* 1–2: 119–125.

Benetti Bertoldo, Paola. 1996. "Francesco Patrizi the Elder: The Portrait of a Fifteenth-Century Humanist." Ph.D. dissertation, Oxford University (Wolfson College).

Bentley, Jerry H. 1987. *Politics and Culture in Renaissance Naples.* Princeton, NJ: Princeton University Press.

Bevagni, Claudio. 1994. "Appunti sulle traduzioni latine dei *Moralia* di Plutarco nel Quattrocento." *Studi umanistici piceni* 14: 71–84.

Black, Jane. 2015. "Medici and Sforza: Breeds Apart?" In *The Medici: Citizens and Masters,* edited by Robert Black and John E. Law, 85–99. Florence: Villa I Tatti. The Harvard University Center for Italian Renaissance Studies.

———. 2021. "The Problem of Succession for the Visconti and the Sforza." In Davies and Monfasani 2021, 17–38.

Black, Robert. 1987. "The New Laws of History." *Renaissance Studies* 1: 126–156.

———. 2001. *Humanism and Education in Medieval and Renaissance Italy: Tradition and Innovation in Latin Schools from the Twelfth to the Fifteenth Century.* Cambridge: Cambridge University Press.

———. 2013. *Machiavelli.* London: Routledge.

———. 2022. *Machiavelli: From Radical to Reactionary.* London: Reaktion Books.

Blythe, James M. 1992. *Ideal Government and the Mixed Constitution in the Middle Ages.* Princeton, NJ: Princeton University Press.

Bol, Peter K. 2008. *Neo-Confucianism in History.* Cambridge, MA: Harvard University Asia Center.

Boschetto, Luca. 2018. "'Uno uomo di basso e infimo stato': Ricerche sulla storia familiare di Niccolò Machiavelli." *Archivio storico italiano* 176, no. 657: 486–524.

Bowsky, William M. 1962. "The *Buon Governo* of Siena, 1287–1355: A Mediaeval Italian Oligarchy." *Speculum* 37: 368–381.

———. 1967. "Medieval Citizenship: The Individual and the State in the Commune of Siena, 1287–1355." *Studies in Medieval and Renaissance History* 4: 193–123.

———. 1981. *A Medieval Italian Commune: Siena under the Nine, 1287–1355.* Berkeley: University of California Press.

Bradshaw, Brendan, and Eamon Duffy, eds. 1989. *Humanism, Reform, and the Reformation: The Career of Bishop John Fisher.* Cambridge: Cambridge University Press.

Briggs, Charles F. 1999. *Giles of Rome's De regimine principum: Reading and Writing Politics at Court and University, ca. 1275–1525.* Cambridge: Cambridge University Press.

Brucker, Gene. 1962. *Florentine Politics and Society, 1343–1378.* Princeton, NJ: Princeton University Press.

Bryce, Judith. 2002. "*Fa finire uno bello studio e dice volere studiare:* Ippolita Sforza and Her Books." *Bibliothèque d'Humanisme et Renaissance* 64, no. 1: 55–69.

Buckland, William Warwick. 1921. *A Text-Book of Roman Law from Augustus to Justinian.* Cambridge: Cambridge University Press.

Calhoun, Craig, ed. 2002. *Dictionary of the Social Sciences.* Oxford: Oxford University Press. Online edition at Oxford Scholarship Online.

Cane, Peter, and Joanne Conaghan, eds. 2008. *The New Oxford Companion to Law.* Oxford: Oxford University Press. Online edition at Oxford Scholarship Online.

Capobianco, Paolo. 2000. *I vescovi della chiesa Gaetana.* Gaeta: Arti Grafiche Kolbe.

Cappelli, Guido M. 2012. "*Corpus est res publica:* La struttura della communità secondo l'umanesimo politico." In *Principi prima del Principe,* edited by Lorenzo Geri, 117–131. Rome: Bulzoni.

———. 2016. *Maiestas: Politica e pensiero politico nella Napoli aragonese, 1443–1503.* Naples: Carocci.

———. 2018. "Lo stato umanistico: Genesi dello Stato moderno nella cultura italiana del XV secolo." In *La determinación de la* humanitas *del hombre en la Crítica del juicio y el humanismo clásico: elementos para la reconstrucción de una tradición desplazada,* edited by Guillermo Villaverde López and Sara Barquinero del Toro, 35–70. Madrid: Escolar y Mayo Editores.

———. 2020a. "The *De republica* by Lauro Quirini between Aristotle and the Roman Tradition." In *Republicanism: A Theoretical and Historical Perspective,* edited by Fabrizio Ricciardelli and Marcello Fantoni, 62–67. Rome: Viella.

———, ed. 2020b. *Al di là del repubblicanesimo: Modernità politica e origini dello Stato.* Università degli studi di Napoli "L'Orientale," Dipartimento di

Studi Letterari, Linguistici e Comparati, Quaderni della ricerca 6. Naples: UniorPress.

Cardini, Franco. 1987. *Banchieri e mercanti di Siena*. With a preface by Carlo M. Cipolla. Rome: De Luca.

Carlino, Andrea. 2010. "Diritto, lettere e medicina: Per una gerarchia delle arti." In Luzzato and Pedullà 2010, 1:235–241.

Casciani, Santa, and Heather Hayton, eds. 2021. *A Companion to Late Medieval and Early Modern Siena*. Leiden: Brill.

Cavenaghi Campari, Paola. 1921. *Un commento quattrocentesco inedito ai "Trionfi" del Petrarca*. Bologna: Zanichelli.

Celati, Marta. 2021. *Conspiracy Literature in Early Renaissance Italy: Historiography and Princely Ideology*. Oxford: Oxford University Press.

Celenza, Christopher S. 2000. "Lapo da Castiglionchio il Giovane, Poggio Bracciolini e la 'vita curialis': Appunti su due testi umanistici." *Medioevo e Rinascimento*, n.s., 14: 129–145.

Celenza, Christopher S., and Bridget Pupillo. 2010. "Le grandi biblioteche pubbliche nel Quattrocento." In Luzzato and Pedullà 2010, 1:313–322.

Chan, Joseph. 2013. "Political Meritocracy and Meritorious Rule: A Confucian Perspective." In *The East Asian Challenge for Democracy: Political Meritocracy in Comparative Perspective*, edited by Daniel A. Bell and Chenyang Li, 31–54. Cambridge: Cambridge University Press.

———. 2014. *Confucian Perfectionism: A Political Philosophy for Modern Times*. Princeton, NJ: Princeton University Press.

Chiarelli, Giuseppe. 1932. "Il *De Regno* di Francesco Patrizi." *Rivista Internazionale di Filosofia del Diritto* 12: 716–738.

Ciccolella, Federica. 2008. *Donati Graeci: Learning Greek in the Renaissance*. Leiden: Brill.

———. 2016. "Epigram." In *Brill's New Pauly Supplements II, Volume 8: The Reception of Antiquity in Renaissance Humanism*. Leiden: Brill: First published online in 2015.

Coker, Christopher. 2019. *The Rise of the Civilizational State*. Cambridge: Polity Press.

Connell, William J. 1996. "Lorenzo Valla: A Symposium—Introduction." *Journal of the History of Ideas* 57, no. 1: 1–7.

———. 2001. "Il cittadino umanista come ufficiale nel territorio: Una rilettura di Giannozzo Manetti." In *Lo stato territoriale fiorentino (secoli XIV–XV): Ricerche, linguaggi, confronti—Atti del seminario internazionale di studi, San Miniato, 7–8 giugno 1996*, edited by Andrea Zorzi and William J. Connell, 359–383. Pisa: Pacini.

Copenhaver, Brian P. 2019. *Magic and the Dignity of Man: Pico della Mirandola and His Oration in Modern Memory*. Cambridge, MA: Belknap Press of Harvard University Press.

Cortese, Ennio. 1960. "Cittadinanza." In *Enciclopedia del diritto*, 7:132–139. Milan: Giuffrè.

Costa, Pietro. 2005. *Cittadinanza*. Bari: Laterza.

Cox, Virginia. 2008. *Women's Writing in Italy, 1400–1650*. Baltimore: Johns Hopkins University Press.

Dameron, George. 2014. "The Church as Lord." In *The Oxford Handbook of Medieval Christianity*, edited by John H. Arnold. Oxford: Oxford University Press. Accessed from Oxford Handbooks Online.

Davies, Jonathan, and John Monfasani. 2021. *Renaissance Politics and Culture: Essays in Honour of Robert Black*. Boston: Brill.

Davis, Robert C. 2003. *Christian Slaves, Muslim Masters: White Slavery in the Mediterranean, the Barbary Coast, and Italy, 1500–1800*. London: Palgrave Macmillan.

De Capua, Paola. 1991. "Francesco Patrizi, Epistolario." Ph.D. dissertation, Università degli Studi di Messina.

———. 2014. *Le lettere di Francesco Patrizi*. Messina: Centro internazionale di studi umanistici.

D'Elia, Anthony F. 2004. *The Renaissance of Marriage in Fifteenth Century Italy*. Cambridge, MA: Harvard University Press.

———. 2016. *Pagan Virtue in a Christian World: Sigismondo Malatesta and the Italian Renaissance*. Cambridge, MA: Harvard University Press.

Delle Donne, Fulvio. 2015. *Alfonso il Magnanimo e l'invenzione dell'umanesimo monarchico: Ideologia e strategie di legittimazione alla corte aragonese di Napoli*. Rome: Istituto storico italiano per il Medio Evo.

Denley, Peter. 1991. "Dal 1357 alla caduta della Repubblica." In Ascheri 1991b, 27–44.

———. 2006. *Commune and Studio in Late Medieval and Renaissance Siena*. Bologna: CLUEB.

———. 2007. *Teachers and Schools in Siena, 1357–1500*. Siena: Betti.

Desgraves, Louis. 1954. *Catalogue de la bibliothèque de Montesquieu*. Geneva: Librairie Droz.

De Vincentiis, Amedeo. 2002a. *Battaglie di memoria: Gruppi, intellettuali, testi e la discontinuità del potere papale alla metà del Quattrocento*. Rome: Roma nel Rinascimento.

———. 2002b. "Papato, stato e curia nel XV secolo: Il problema della discontinuità." *Storica* 24: 91–115.

Dionisotti, Carlo. 1974. "Fortuna del Petrarca nel quattrocento." *Italia Medievale e Umanistica* 17: 61–113.

Doni Garfagnini, Manuela. 2002. *Il teatro della storia fra rappresentazione e realtà: Storiografia e trattatistica fra Quattrocento e Seicento*. Rome: Edizioni di storia e letteratura.

Earle, T. F., and K. J. P. Lowe, eds. 2005. *Black Africans in Renaissance Europe*. Cambridge: Cambridge University Press.

Ellis, Steven G., Guðmundur Hálfdanarson, and Ann Katherine Isaacs, eds. 2006. *Citizenship in Historical Perspective*. Pisa: Edizioni PLUS/Pisa University Press.

Ettlinger, Leopold D. (1977) 2000. "The Emergence of the Italian Architect during the Fifteenth Century." In Kostof (1977) 2000, 96–123.

Ferente, Serena. 2005. *La sfortuna di Jacopo Piccinino: Storia dei Bracceschi in Italia, 1423–1465*. Florence: Leo S. Olschki.

Field, Arthur. 2017. *The Intellectual Struggle for Florence: Humanists and the Beginnings of the Medici Regime, 1420–1440*. New York: Oxford University Press.

Fioravanti, Gianfranco. 1979. "Alcuni aspetti della cultura umanistica senese nel '400." *Rinascimento*, ser. 2, 19: 117–167.

———. 1981. *Università e città: Cultura umanistica e cultura scolastica a Siena nel '400*. Florence: Sansoni.

———. 1991. "Le 'arti liberali' nei secoli XIII–XV." In Ascheri 1991b, 255–271.

———. 1993. "Maestri di grammatici a Siena nella seconda metà del '400." *Rinascimento*, ser. 2, 33: 193–207.

Frede, Dorothea. 2005. "Citizenship in Aristotle's *Politics*." In *Aristotle's Politics: Critical Essays*, edited by Richard Kraut and Steven Skultety, 167–184. Lanham, MD: Rowman and Littlefield.

Friedman, David 1988. *Florentine New Towns: Urban Design in the Late Middle Ages*. Cambridge, MA: MIT Press.

Frommel, Christoph. 2007. *Architecture of the Italian Renaissance*. Translated by Peter Spring. New York: Thames and Hudson.

Fuiano, Michele. 1974. "Un monaco umanista: Ilarione da Verona." *Benedictina* 21, no. 1: 131–163.

Furstenberg-Levi, Shulamit. 2016. *The Accademia Pontaniana: A Model of a Humanist Network*. Boston: Brill.

Gaisser, Julia Haig. 1993. *Catullus and His Renaissance Readers*. Oxford: Clarendon Press.

Gamberini, Andrea, and Isabella Lazzarini, eds. 2012. *The Italian Renaissance State*. Cambridge: Cambridge University Press.

Gambino Longo, Susanna. 2018. "La représentation des origines de la civilisation chez Francesco Patrizi de Sienne." *Revue des sciences philosophiques et théologiques* 102, no. 2: 205–220.

Gerber, Scott D. 2006–2007. "The Political Theory of an Independent Judiciary." *Yale Law Journal* 116. http://yalelawjournal.org/forum/the-political-theory-of-an-independent-judiciary.

Giustiniani, Vito R. 1965. *Alamanno Rinuccini, 1426–1490: Zur Geschichte des Florentinischen Humanismus*. Graz: Böhlau Verlag.

Grafton, Anthony. 2002. *Leon Battista Alberti: Master Builder of the Italian Renaissance*. Cambridge, MA: Harvard University Press.

———. 2007. *What Was History? The Art of History in Early Modern Europe*. Cambridge: Cambridge University Press.

Grant, W. Leonard. 1965. *Neo-Latin Literature and the Pastoral*. Chapel Hill: University of North Carolina Press.

Grell, Chantal, Werner Paravicini, and Jürgen Voss. 1998. *Les princes et l'histoire du XIVe au XVIIIe siècle: Actes du colloque organisé par l'Université de Versailles-Saint Quentin et l'Institut historique allemand, Paris / Versailles, 13–16 mars 1996*. Bonn: Bouvier.

Grendler, Paul F. 1989. *Schooling in Renaissance Italy: Literacy and Learning, 1300–1600*. Baltimore: Johns Hopkins University Press.

———. 2002. *The Universities of the Italian Renaissance*. Baltimore: Johns Hopkins University Press.

Gualdo Rosa, Lucia. 2018. *Lapo da Castiglionchio il giovane e la sua versione delle prime tre orazioni di Isocrate: Con in appendice l'edizione critica dei testi*. Rome: Istituto storico italiano per il Medio Evo.

Gualdo Rosa, Lucia, Isabella Nuovo, and Domenico Defilippis. 1982. *Gli Umanisti e la guerra otrantina: Testi dei secoli XV e XVI*. Bari: Edizioni Dedalo.

Hahm, David E. 2009. "The Mixed Constitution in Greek Thought." In *A Companion to Greek and Roman Political Thought*, edited by Ryan Balot, 178–198. West Sussex, UK: Wiley-Blackwell.

Hale, J. R. (John Rigby). 1983. "To Fortify or Not to Fortify? Machiavelli's Contribution to a Renaissance Debate." In J. R. Hale, *Renaissance War Studies*, 189–210. London: Hambledon Press.

Hankins, James. 1990. *Plato in the Italian Renaissance*. 2 vols. Leiden: Brill.

———. 1994. "Lorenzo de'Medici as a Patron of Philosophy." *Rinascimento*, n.s., 34: 15–53. Reprinted with changes in James Hankins, *Humanism and Platonism in the Italian Renaissance*, vol. 2, 273–316. Rome: Storia e letteratura, 2004.

———, ed. 2000. *Renaissance Civic Humanism: Reappraisals and Reflections*. Cambridge: Cambridge University Press.

———, ed. 2007. *The Cambridge Companion to Renaissance Philosophy*. Cambridge: Cambridge University Press.

———. 2011. "Humanist Academies and the 'Platonic Academy of Florence.'" In *On Renaissance Academies: Proceedings of the International Conference "From the Roman Academy to the Danish Academy in Rome," 11–13 October 2006*, edited by Marianne Pade, 31–46. Rome: Edizioni Quasar.

———. 2015. "Humanism and Music in Italy." In *The Cambridge History of Fifteenth-Century Music*, edited by Anna Maria Busse-Berger and Jesse Rodin, 231–262. Cambridge: Cambridge University Press.

———. 2017. "Marsilio Ficino and Christian Humanism." In *Re-envisioning Christian Humanism: Education and the Restoration of Humanity*, edited by Jens Zimmermann, 54–73. Oxford: Oxford University Press.

———. 2019. *Virtue Politics: Soulcraft and Statecraft in Renaissance Italy*. Cambridge, MA: Belknap Press of Harvard University Press.

———. 2020. "The Italian Humanists and the Virtue of *Humanitas*," *Rinascimento*, ser. 2, 60: 3–20.

———. 2021a. "The King's Citizens: Francesco Patrizi of Siena on Citizenship in Monarchies." In *Habent sua fata libelli: Studies in Book History, the Classical Tradition, and Humanism, in Honor of Craig Kallendorf*, edited by Steven M. Oberhelman, Giancarlo Abbamonte, and Patrick Baker, 282–298. Leiden: Brill.

———. 2021b. "The Virtuous Republic of Francesco Patrizi of Siena." In Davies and Monfasani 2021, 59–82.

———. 2021c. "Vocal Music at Literary Banquets in the Italian Renaissance." In *Basler Beiträge zur Historischen Musikpraxis* 41: 227–243. A special issue, *Stimme—Instrument—Vokalität: Blicke auf dynamische Beziehungen in der Alten Musik*, edited by Martina Papiro.

BIBLIOGRAPHY

———. Forthcoming-a. "Liberty." In *Le parole dei moderni: Continuità e cambiamento fra '400 e '700*, edited by Simonetta Bassi. Rome: Carocci.

———. Forthcoming-b. "Machiavelli and the Humanists: Will the Real Radical Please Stand Up?" Forthcoming in a forum on Pedullà 2018 to be published in *Storica*.

Hankins, James, and Ada Palmer. 2008. *The Recovery of Ancient Philosophy in the Renaissance: A Brief Guide*. Florence: Leo S. Olschki.

Hansen, Mogens H. 2013. *Reflections on Aristotle's Politics*. Copenhagen: Museum Tusculanum Press.

Hayes, Christopher. 2012. *Twilight of the Elites: America after Meritocracy*. New York: Crown.

Heater, Derek. 2004a. *A Brief History of Citizenship*. New York: New York University Press.

———. 2004b. *A History of Education for Citizenship*. New York: Routledge.

Heil, John-Paul. 2022. "Virtue and Vice in the Political World of Renaissance Naples." Ph.D. dissertation, University of Chicago.

Herlihy, David. 1995. "The Rulers of Florence, 1282–1530." In David Herlihy, *Women, Family and Society in Medieval Europe*, edited by Anthony Molho, 353–380. Providence, RI: Berghahn Books.

Hilary, Richard B. 1978. "The Nepotism of Pope Pius II, 1458–1464." *Catholic Historical Review* 64: 33–35.

Hörcher, Ferenc. 2020. *A Political Philosophy of Conservatism: Prudence, Moderation and Tradition*. London: Bloomsbury.

Hörnqvist, Mikael. 2000. "Two Myths of Civic Humanism." In Hankins 2000, 105–142.

Horowitz, Mary Ann. 1998. *Seeds of Virtue and Knowledge*. Princeton, NJ: Princeton University Press.

Inamura, Kazutaka. 2015. *Justice and Reciprocity in Aristotle's Political Philosophy*. Cambridge: Cambridge University Press.

Jacques, Martin. 2012. *When China Rules the World: The End of the Western World and the Birth of a New Global Order*. 2nd ed. London: Penguin.

Jaeger, Werner. 1986. *Paideia: The Ideals of Greek Culture*. Oxford: Oxford University Press.

Jones, Philip James. 1974. *The Malatesta of Rimini and the Papal State: A Political History*. Cambridge: Cambridge University Press.

Jurdjevic, Mark. 2014. *A Great and Wretched City: Promise and Failure in Machiavelli's Florentine Political Thought*. Cambridge, MA: Harvard University Press.

Kallendorf, Craig W. 2002. *Humanist Educational Treatises*. Cambridge, MA: Harvard University Press.

Kempshall, M. S. 1999. *The Common Good in Late Medieval Political Thought*. Oxford: Oxford University Press.

Kim, Sungmoon. 2020. *Theorizing Confucian Virtue Politics: The Political Philosophy of Mencius and Xunzi*. Cambridge: Cambridge University Press.

King, Margaret L., and Albert Rabil Jr. 1983. *Her Immaculate Hand: Selected Works by and about the Women Humanists of Quattrocento Italy*. Binghamton, NY: Center for Medieval and Early Renaissance Studies.

403

Kirshner, Julius. 1973. "*Civitas sibi faciat civem*: Bartolus of Sassoferrato's Doctrine on the Making of a Citizen." *Speculum* 48, no. 4: 694–713.

Knights, Mark. 2021. *Trust and Distrust: Corruption in Office in Britain and Its Empire, 1600–1850*. Oxford: Oxford University Press.

Kohl, Benjamin G. 1992. "The Changing Concept of the *Studia Humanitatis* in the Early Renaissance." *Renaissance Studies* 6: 185–209.

Kostof, Spiro. (1977) 2000. *The Architect: Chapters in the History of the Profession*. Berkeley: University of California Press.

Kraut, Richard. 2002. *Aristotle: Political Philosophy*. Oxford: Oxford University Press.

Kymlicka, Will. 2005. *The Oxford Companion to Philosophy*. Oxford: Oxford University Press. Accessed through Oxford Scholarship Online.

Lambertini, Roberto. 2019. "Giles of Rome." In *The Stanford Encyclopedia of Philosophy*, edited by Edward N. Zalta. https://plato.stanford.edu/entries/giles/.

Langholm, Odd. 2003. *The Merchant in the Confessional: Trade and Price in the Pre-Reformation Penitential Handbooks*. Leiden: Brill.

Law, John E., and Bernadette Paton, eds. 2010. *Communes and Despots in Medieval and Renaissance Italy*. Farnham, UK: Ashgate.

Lee, Daniel. 2016. *Popular Sovereignty in Early Modern Constitutional Thought*. Oxford: Oxford University Press.

Leydet, Dominique. 2017. "Citizenship." In *The Stanford Encyclopedia of Philosophy*, edited by Edward N. Zalta. https://plato.stanford.edu/entries/citizenship/.

Love, Harold. 1998. *The Culture and Commerce of Texts: Scribal Publication in Seventeenth-Century England*. Amherst: University of Massachusetts Press.

Lines, David. 2022. *The Dynamics of Learning in Early Modern Italy: Arts and Medicine at the University of Bologna*. Cambridge, MA: Harvard University Press.

Luzzato, Sergio, and Gabriele Pedullà, eds. 2010. *Atlante della letteratura italiana*. Vol. 1: *Dalle origini al Rinascimento*. Edited by Amedeo De Vincentiis. Turin: Einaudi.

Malcolm, Noel. 2019. *Useful Enemies: Islam and the Ottoman Empire in Western Political Thought, 1450–1750*. Oxford: Oxford University Press.

Marchi, Alessandro, and Maria Rosaria Valazzi, eds. 2012. *La città ideale: L'utopia del Rinascimento a Urbino tra Piero della Francesca e Raffaello*. Milan: Electa.

Marsh, David. 2019. "Francesco Filelfo as a Writer of Invective." In *Francesco Filelfo, Man of Letters*, edited by Jeroen De Keyser, 174–187. Leiden: Brill.

Marten, Kimberly. 2006/2007. "Warlordism in Comparative Perspective." *International Security* 31, no. 3: 41–73.

Menzinger, Sara, ed. 2017. *Cittadinanze medievali: Dinamiche di appartenenza a un corpo comunitario*. Rome: Viella.

Minnich, Nelson H. 2005. "The Catholic Church and the Pastoral Care of Black Africans in Renaissance Italy." In Earle and Lowe 2005, 280–300.

Minnucci, Giovanni, and Leo Košuta. 1989. *Lo Studio di Siena nei secoli 14–16: Documenti e notizie biografiche*. Milan: Giuffrè.

Miskimin, Harry A. 1975. *The Economy of Early Renaissance Europe, 1300–1460*. Cambridge: Cambridge University Press.

Monfasani, John. 2021. "The Impuissant and Immoral City: George of Trebizond's Critique of Plato's *Laws*." In Davies and Monfasani 2021, 39–58.

Mühleisen, Hans-Otto, Theo Stammen, and Michael Philipp, eds. 1997. *Fürstenspiegel der frühen Neuzeit*. Frankfurt am Main: Insel.

Nardone, Francesca Cristina. 1996. *Francesco Patrizi umanista senese*. Empoli: Ibiskos.

Nauta, Lodi. 2021. *Philosophy and the Language of the People: The Claims of Common Speech from Petrarch to Locke*. Cambridge: Cambridge University Press.

Nelson, Eric. 2004. *The Greek Tradition in Republican Thought*. Cambridge: Cambridge University Press.

Nevola, Fabrizio. 2007. *Siena: Constructing the Renaissance City*. New Haven, CT: Yale University Press.

———. 2009. "Francesco Patrizi: Umanista, urbanista e teorico di Pio II." In *Pio II Piccolomini: Il papa del rinascimento a Siena, Acts of the International Conference, Siena, 5–7 May 2005*, edited by Fabrizio Nevola, 179–196. Siena: Alsaba Grafica.

———. 2019. "Ideal Cities." In The *Wiley-Blackwell Encyclopedia of Urban and Regional Studies*, edited by Anthony M. Orum. Hoboken, NJ: Wiley. Accessed online through the Wiley Online Library, 15 April 2019.

Noonan, John T. 1957. *The Scholastic Analysis of Usury*. Cambridge, MA: Harvard University Press.

Nozick, Robert. 1974. *Anarchy, State and Utopia*. New York: Harper and Row.

O'Brien, Emily. 2015. *The Commentaries of Pope Pius II (1458–1464) and the Crisis of the Fifteenth-Century Papacy*. Toronto: University of Toronto Press.

Olard, Ludivine-Julie. 2007. "Venice-Babylon: Foreigners and Citizens in the Renaissance Period." In *Imagining Frontiers, Contesting Identities*, edited by Steven G. Ellis and Ludia Klusáková, 155–174. Pisa: Edizioni Plus–Pisa University Press.

Origo, Iris. 1955. "The Domestic Enemy: The Eastern Slaves in Tuscany in the Fourteenth and Fifteenth Centuries." *Speculum* 30, no. 3: 321–366.

Paga, Jessica. 2020. *Building Democracy in Late Archaic Athens*. Oxford: Oxford University Press.

Paolino, Laura. 1999. "Per l'edizione del commento di Francesco Patrizi da Siena al canzoniere di Petrarca." *Nuova Rivista di Letteratura Italiana* 2, no. 1: 153–311.

———. 2000. "Il fratello di Madonna Laura: Spigolature di biografia petrarchesca dal commento di Francesco Patrizi ai *Rerum vulgarium fragmenta*." *Studi petrarcheschi*, n.s., 13: 243–306.

Pasini, Pier Giorgio, ed. 2002. *Malatesta Novello magnifico signore: Arte e cultura di un principe del Rinascimento*. San Giorgio di Piano (Bologna): Minerva.

Pastor, Ludwig von. 1886. *Storia dei papi nel periodo del Rinascimento (Martino V, Eugenio IV, Niccolò V, Calisto III) fino all'elezione di Pio II*. Vol. 1 of *Storia dei papi dalla fine del Medio Evo*. Translated and edited by Angelo Mercati. Rome: Desclée, 1958.

Pedullà, Gabriele. 2010. "Francesco Patrizi e le molte vite dell'umanista." In Luzzato and Pedullà 2010, 1:457–464.

———. 2018. *Machiavelli in Tumult: The Discourses on Livy and the Origins of Political Conflictualism.* Cambridge: Cambridge University Press.

———. 2020. "Humanist Republicanism: Towards a New Paradigm." *History of Political Thought* 41, no. 1: 43–95.

———. 2021a. "Athenian Democracy in the Italian Renaissance." In Piovan and Giorgini 2021, 105–152.

———. 2021b. "Athenian Democracy in the Late Middle Ages and Early Humanism." In Piovan and Giorgini 2021, 57–104.

Peltonen, Markku. 1995. *Classical Humanism and Republicanism in English Political Thought, 1570–1640.* Cambridge: Cambridge University Press.

Pertici, Petra. 1990. *Tra politica e cultura nel primo Quattrocento senese: Le epistole di Andreoccio Petrucci, 1426–1443.* Siena: Accademia senese degli Intronati.

———. 1992. "Una 'coniuratio' del reggimento di Siena nel 1450." *Bullettino senese di storia patria* 99: 9–47.

———. 1995. "La furia delle fazioni." In *Storia di Siena: Dalle origini alla fine della repubblica,* vol. 1, edited by Roberto Barzanti, Giuliano Catoni, and Mario De Gregorio, 390–393. Siena: Alsaba.

———. 2003. "Il viaggio del papa attraverso il territorio senese: Le tappe di una vita." In *Il sogno di Pio II e il viaggio da Roma a Mantova: Atti del Convegno internazionale, Mantova 13–15 aprile 2000,* edited by Arturo Calzona, Franceso P. Fiore, Alberto Tenenti, and Cesare Vasoli, 143–162. Florence: Leo S. Olschki.

———. 2012. *Siena quattrocentesca: Gli anni del Pellegrinaio nell'Ospedale di Santa Maria della Scala.* Siena: Protagon.

Pertici, Petra, and Gigi Lusini. 1995. *La città magnificata: Interventi edilizi a Siena nel Rinascimento—L'Ufficio dell'ornato (1428–1480).* Siena: Il Leccio.

Piccinni, Gabriella. 2009. "La politica agraria delle città." In *La costruzione del dominio cittadino sulle campagne: Italia centro-settentrionale, secoli, XII–XIV,* edited by Roberta Mucciarelli, Gabriella Piccinni, and Giuliano Pinto, 601–625. Siena: Protagon Editori Toscani.

———. 2013. "Differenze socio-economiche, identità civiche e 'gradi di cittadinanza' a Siena nel Tre e Quattrocento." *Melanges de l'École française de Rome, Moyen Âge* 125, no. 2: 2–15.

———. 2020. "'La più utile et bisognevole arte e exercitio che sia': Il settore primario secondo i senesi del secolo XV." In *Agricoltura, lavoro, società: Studi sul medioevo per Alfio Cortonesi,* edited by Avana Ait and Anna Esposito, 545–557. Bologna: CLUEB.

———. 2021. "Oziosi e sfaccendati: Elogio e rifiuto del lavoro a Siena nel XV secolo." In *Medioevo e Mediterraneo: Incontri, scambi e confronti—Studi per Salvatore Fodale,* edited by Patrizia Sardina, Daniela Santoro, Maria Antonietta Russo, and Marella Pacifico, 741–759. Palermo: Palermo University Press.

Piovan, Dino, and Giovanni Giorgini, eds. 2021. *Brill's Companion to the Reception of Athenian Democracy.* Cambridge: Cambridge University Press.

Pocock, J. G. A. 1975. *The Machiavellian Moment: Florentine Political Thought and the Atlantic Republican Tradition*. Princeton, NJ: Princeton University Press.

———. 1992. "The Ideal of Citizenship since Classical Times." *Queen's Quarterly* 99: 33–55. Reprinted in Beiner 1995.

Prete, Sesto. 1981. "L'epigramma nel Quattrocento: Osservazioni." In *L'ecumenismo della cultura*, vol. 3, *L'umanesimo*, edited by Giovannangiola Tarugi, 215–226. Florence: Leo S. Olschki.

Pritchard, Elizabeth A. 2014. *Religion in Public: Locke's Political Theology*. Stanford, CA: Stanford University Press.

Quaglioni, Diego. 1991. "The Legal Definition of Citizenship in the Late Middle Ages." In *City States in Classical Antiquity and Medieval Italy*, edited by Anthony Molho, Kurt Raaflaub, and Julia Emlen, 155–166. Ann Arbor: University of Michigan Press.

———. 2003. *La sovranità*. Rome-Bari: Laterza.

———. 2007. "Sovranità: Un paradigma premoderno." In *Filosofia del diritto: Concetti fondamentali*, edited by Ulderico Pomarici, 551–561. Turin: Giappichelli.

Quintiliani, Matteo Maria. 2014. "Patrizi, Francesco." *Dizionario biografico degli Italiani*, vol. 81.

Quondam, Amadeo. 2010. *Forma del vivere: L'etica del gentiluomo e i moralisti italiani*. Bologna: Il Mulino.

Richardson, Brian. 2021. "Print and Trust in Renaissance Italy." In Davies and Monfasani 2012, 198–218.

Riesenberg, Peter N. 1956. *Inviolability of Sovereignty in Medieval Political Thought*. New York: Columbia University Press.

———. 1969. "Civism and Roman Law in Fourteenth-Century Italian Society." In *Economy, Society, and Government in Medieval Italy*, edited by David Herlihy, Robert S. Lopez, and Vsevolod Slessarev, 237–254. Kent, OH: Kent State University Press.

———. 1972. "Citizenship and Equality in Late Medieval Italy." *Studia Gratiana* 15: 423–439.

———. 1974. "Citizenship at Law in Late Medieval Italy." *Viator* 5: 333–346.

———. 1992. *Citizenship in the Western Tradition*. Chapel Hill: University of North Carolina Press.

Roick, Matthias. 2017. *Pontano's Virtues: Aristotelian Moral and Political Thought in the Renaissance*. London: Bloomsbury.

Rose, Paul Lawrence. 1975. *The Italian Renaissance of Mathematics: Studies on Humanists and Mathematicians from Petrarch to Galileo*. Geneva: Droz.

Rosenblum, Nancy L. 2008. *On the Side of the Angels: An Appreciation of Parties and Partisanship*. Princeton, NJ: Princeton University Press.

Rosler, Andrés. 2013. "Civic Virtue: Citizenship, Ostracism and War." In *The Cambridge Companion to Aristotle's Politics*, edited by Marguerite Deslauriers and Pierre Destrée, 144–175. Cambridge: Cambridge University Press.

Rossi, Giovanni. 2015. "L'umanista senese Francesco Patrizi e la lezione etico-politica degli antichi: Il trattato *De institutione reipublicae* (ante 1471)." *Acta*

*Conventus Neo-Latini Monasteriensis: Proceedings of the Fifteenth International Congress of Neo-Latin Studies*, edited by Astrid Steiner-Weber and Karl A. E. Enenkel, 440–449. Leiden: Brill.

———. 2018. "Distinzione di compiti produttivi e ruoli sociali nel *De institutione reipublicae* (ante 1471) del senese Francesco Patrizi." In *Città e campagna nel Rinascimento, Atti del XXVIII Convegno internazionale (Chianciano Terme-Montepulciano, 21–23 luglio 2016)*, edited by Luigi Secchi Tarugi, 179–299. Florence: Franco Cesati Editore.

Rubinstein, Nicolai. 1993. "Fortified Enclosures in Italian Cities under Signori." In *War, Culture, and Society in Renaissance Venice: Essays in Honour of John Hale*, edited by D. S. Chambers, Cecil Clough, and Michael Mallett, 1–8. London: Hambledon Press.

Samaras, Thanassis. 2015. "Aristotle and the Question of Citizenship." In *Aristotle's Politics: A Critical Guide*, edited by Thornton Lockwood and Thanassis Samaras, 123–141. Cambridge: Cambridge University Press.

Sarri, Francesco. 1938. "Il piensiero pedagogico ed economico del senese Francesco Patrizi." *Rinascita* 1: 98–128.

Schiera, Pierangelo. 2007. "L'amicizia politica in Francesco Patrizi, senese." In *De Amicitia: Scritti dedicati a Arturo Colombo*, edited by Giovanna Angelini and Marina Tesoro, 61–72. Milan: FrancoAngeli.

Schmitt, Charles B. 1972. *Cicero Scepticus: A Study of the Influence of the* Academica *in the Renaissance*. The Hague: Nijhoff.

Schofield, Malcolm. 1999. "Cicero's Definition of the *Res Publica*." In *Saving the City: Philosopher-Kings and Other Classical Paradigms*, 178–194. London: Routledge.

———. 2021. *Cicero: Political Philosophy*. Oxford: Oxford University Press.

Sciancalepore, Margherita. 2006. "Un copista tra i crociati: *l'Itinerarium classis apostolicae in Turcos* di Pietro Ursuleo." *Annali della Facoltá di Lettere e Filosofia* 49: 329–340.

Scorza, Jason. 2013. "Civic Friendship." In *The International Encyclopedia of Ethics*. Malden, MA: Wiley-Blackwell. Consulted online.

Senatore, Francesco. 2012. "The Kingdom of Naples." In Gamberini and Lazzarini 2012, 30–49.

Shaw, Christine. 2000. *The Politics of Exile in Renaissance Italy*. Cambridge: Cambridge University Press.

———. 2006. *Popular Government and Oligarchy in Renaissance Italy*. Leiden: Brill.

Sherwin-White, Adrian Nicholas. 1973. *The Roman Citizenship*. 2nd ed. Oxford: Oxford University Press.

Skinner, Quentin. 1991. "Machiavelli's Discorsi and the Pre-humanist Origins of Republican Ideas." In *Machiavelli and Republicanism*, edited by Gisela Bock, Quentin Skinner, and Maurizio Viroli, 121–142. Cambridge: Cambridge University Press.

———. 2002. *Visions of Politics*. Vol. 2: *Renaissance Virtues*. Cambridge: Cambridge University Press.

Smith, Christine. 1992. *Architecture in the Culture of Early Humanism: Ethics, Aesthetics, and Eloquence, 1400–1470.* Oxford: Oxford University Press.

Smith, Leslie F. 1966–1968. "The Poems of Franciscus Patricius from Vatican Manuscript Chigi J VI 233." *Manuscripta* 10, nos. 2, 3: 94–102, 145–159; 11, no. 3: 131–143; 12, no. 1: 10–21.

———. 1968. "A Notice of the *Epigrammata* of Francesco Patrizi, Bishop of Gaeta." *Studies in the Renaissance* 15: 92–143.

———. 1974. "Members of Francesco Patrizi's Family Appearing in His Letters and Epigrams." *Renaissance Quarterly* 27, no. 1: 1–6.

Somaini, Francesco. 2012. "The Collapse of City-States and the Role of Urban Centres of the New Political Geography in Renaissance Italy." In Gamberini and Lazzarini 2012, 239–260.

Speroni, Mario. 1979. "Lorenzo Valla a Pavia: Il libellus contro Bartolo." *Quellen und Forschungen aus italienischen Archiven und Bibliotheken* 59: 453–467.

Staüble, Antonio. 1968. *La commedia umanistica del Rinascimento.* Florence: Istituto Nazionale di Studi sul Rinascimento.

Stolf, Serge. 2012. *Les lettres et la Tiare: E. S. Piccolomini, un humaniste au XVe siècle.* Paris: Les Classiques Garnier.

Tateo, Rosa, and Francesco Tateo, eds. and trans. 1990. *Francesco Patrizi: Orazione per le nozze di Alfonso duca di Calabria et Ippolita Maria Sforza.* Bari: Safra.

Terlizzi, Francesco Paolo. 2010. "Istruzione superiore tra Medioevo e Rinascimento." In Luzzatto and Pedullà 2010, 1:258–276.

Terpstra, Nicholas. 2014. "Civic Religion." In *The Oxford Handbook of Medieval Christianity,* edited by John H. Arnold. Oxford: Oxford University Press. Accessed from Oxford Handbooks Online.

Tinelli, Elisa. 2021. "Prolegomeni all' edizione critica del De regno et regis institutione di Francesco Patrizi di Siena." *Critica letteraria* 182: 113–134.

Tognetti, Sergio. 2005. "The Trade in Black African Slaves in Fifteenth-Century Florence." In Earle and Lowe 2005, 213–223.

Tönnesmann, Andreas. 1990. *Pienza: Städtebau und Humanismus.* Munich: Hirmer.

Trexler, Richard C. 1980. *Public Life in Renaissance Florence.* Ithaca, NY: Cornell University Press.

Tristano, Caterina, and Simone Allegria, eds. 2008. *Civis / Civitas: Cittadinanza politico-istituzionale e identità socio-culturale da Roma alla prima età moderna.* Montepulciano: Thesan and Turan.

Turner, Ralph H. 1960. "Sponsored and Contest Mobility and the School System." *American Sociological Review* 25: 855–867.

Waldron, Jeremy. 2002. *God, Locke, and Equality: Christian Foundations of John Locke's Political Thought.* Cambridge: Cambridge University Press.

Waley, Daniel. 1988. *The Italian City-Republics.* 3rd ed. London: Longman.

———. 1991. *Siena and the Sienese in the Thirteenth Century.* Cambridge: Cambridge University Press.

Walker, D. P. (Daniel Pickering). 1972. *The Ancient Theology: Studies in Christian Platonism from the Fifteenth to the Eighteenth Century.* Ithaca, NY: Cornell University Press.

Walzer, Michael. 1973. "Political Action: The Problem of Dirty Hands." *Philosophy and Public Affairs* 2, no. 2: 160–180.

Wilson, Nigel. 2017. *From Byzantium to Italy: Greek Studies in the Italian Renaissance.* 2nd ed. London: Bloomsbury Academic.

Wood, Susan. 2006. *The Proprietary Church in the Medieval West.* Oxford: Oxford University Press.

Wooldridge, Adrian. 2021. *The Aristocracy of Talent: How Meritocracy Made the Modern World.* London: Allen Lane.

Woods-Marsden, Joanna. 1989. "Images of Castles in the Renaissance: Symbols of Signoria, Symbols of Tyranny." *Art Journal* 48: 130–137.

Zorzi, Andrea. 2010. *Le signorie cittadine in Toscana: Esperienze di potere e forme di governo personale (secoli XIII–XV).* Milan: Mondadori.

# Acknowledgments

Research for this volume was made possible by generous grants from the Dean's Competitive Fund for Promising Research, Harvard University, and the SHARP Fund for undergraduate research, Harvard University. These funds enabled me to organize an équipe of researchers to digitize the 1518 edition of the *De republica* and to produce a slightly modernized English version, with glossary, of an Elizabethan translation of an epitome of Patrizi. This work, known as *A Moral Methode of Civile Policie* (1576), will be published in 2023 by the Liberty Fund. The team also identified hundreds of Patrizi's classical sources. The team included Victoria Pipas, Caroline Engelmayer, Molly Goldberg, Carolina Elizondo Moya, and Maya McDougall. Victoria Pipas compiled the list of Patrizi printings in Appendix B. Caroline Engelmayer transcribed the *Poemata* from the Berlin manuscript (*B*) and prepared an edition of the *De laudibus philosophiae,* which we plan to publish jointly in a forthcoming issue of *Rinascimento.*

A number of other scholars and librarians helped me gain access to rare materials during these difficult pandemic years, for which I am most grateful. John Gordan allowed me to consult a digital copy of the unique manuscript (*G*) of the *Epigrammaton liber* from the collection of his mother, Phyllis Goodhart Gordan. I am most grateful to Eric Pumroy, head of the Special Collections Department at Bryn Mawr College Library, where the codex is stored, for facilitating access to the manuscript.

I would like to offer special thanks to my friend Duncan G. Stroik, the distinguished classical architect, for his enthusiastic interest in Patrizi's vision of an ideal republican city. His beautiful digital images, informed by deep knowledge of the classical tradition in architecture, have helped bring to life a lost city of the imagination in Renaissance Italy. Enlargeable color images of the black and white versions printed in this book may be seen on the website of the Patrizi Project: https://projects.iq.harvard.edu/patrizisiena.

In these pandemic years I was grateful indeed to Mario Ascheri, the dean of Sienese historians, for generously sharing his extensive knowledge of all things Sienese with me, including fresh documentation regarding Patrizi's political career from the Archivio di Stato of Siena, and many bibliographical references. Paola de Capua kindly sent me a digital file of her invaluable study of Patrizi's letters. Other scholars who shared their expertise with me include Daniel A. Bell, Robert Black, Guido Cappelli, Allen Guelzo, Thomas Martin, Eric Nelson, and Gabriele Pedullà. Three anonymous readers for Harvard University Press read the entire manuscript and offered many useful suggestions. My esteemed editor at the press, Joy de Menil, offered patience, encouragement, and wise advice.

      ✦      ✦      ✦

In the interests of providing a comprehensive overview of Patrizi's political thought, I have made use of some of my other work. Much of "The King's Citizens: Francesco Patrizi of Siena on Citizenship in Monarchies," included in *Habent sua fata libelli: Studies in Book History, the Classical Tradition, and Humanism in Honor of Craig Kallendorf,* edited by Steven M. Oberhelman, Giancarlo Abbamonte, and Patrick Baker and published by Brill in 2021, is included in Chapter 6. Portions of Chapter 7 first appeared in chapter 17 of *Virtue Politics,* my 2019 book with Harvard University Press.

All translations from Latin or Italian, unless otherwise indicated, are mine. I have not given the Latin texts for any of Patrizi's poems in cases where they were already edited in various articles by Leslie F. Smith, available online, that are cited in the Bibliography.

# Index

*Note:* Page numbers in **bold** indicate passages where subjects are treated in greater detail.

Abactonius (Abdalonymus), 266, 385n63
abortion, 91, 101–102
Academic conspiracy, 47
Academic philosophers, 363n52
Academic Skepticism, 21
academies, 52–53, 359n102
Academy, 79, 177; Neapolitan (Porticus), 52–53; New (ancient), 265; Old (ancient), 289
accountability, 116, 142, 158, 268, 297
Accursius (jurist), 382n9
Achilles, 188
Adriatic Sea, 37, 120
adultery, 198
advisors, humanist, 46, 281, 370n74, 384n52
Aemilius Paullus, 228
Aeschines, 78
Aeschylus, 52
Aesop, 147, 354n53
*aesymnetes,* 387n28, 391n98
Africa/African, 218; slaves/slavery, 194–196
Agamemnon, 198
Alberti, Leon Battista, 7, 61, 220, 230, 354n55, 379n97, 379n99, 380n117; *De iciarchia,* 376n41; *Della famiglia,* 198; *On Architecture,* 56–57, 230, 380n104; *On Painting,* 362n31, 379n96; *Philodoxeos,* 230
Alberto da Perugia, 42–43
Albino, Giovanni, 53–54, 359n106
Alcibiades, 125
Alessandro (son of Federico of Urbino), 379n97

Alexander the Great, 111, 124–125, 161, 188, 265–266, 268, 296
Alexandria, 217
Alfonso, duke of Calabria (Alfonso II of Naples), 15, 46, 48, 51–54, 72, 80, 220, 274, 284, 332–334 (app. A), 357n88, 357n90, 358nn96–97, 359n105, 379n97, 384n52, 388n33
Alfonso I, king of Naples, 30–31, 233, 270, 296, 356n85
ambition (*ambitio*), 99, 129, 132, 152, 154, 276, 292, 325, 361n28, 367n36, 368n48; honorable, 96
America/American, 3, 158, 284, 315, 327–328; Constitution, 316–317; Founders, 316–317, 391nn111–112; Senate, 317
Ammanati, Cardinal Jacopo, 41, 45–46, 357n88, 359n102
Ammianus Marcellinus, 61, 76–78, 164, 218, 352n23
amnesty, 152
Anacreon, 52
Anaximander, 184
Ancona, 60
Andrea, Giovanni, 356n86
Anjou, House of, 270
Antigonids (kings of Macedon), 275, 313
Antiphon of Rhamnus, 163
Antonine Constitution, 243
Antoninus (Dominican archbishop of Florence), 195
Antonio da San Gallo, 232
Apelles, 303

Apennines, 48
Aphrodite (deity), 358n94
Apollo (deity), 275, 350n7, 386n9
Apollonius of Rhodes, 78
Appian (historian), 8, 78, 211, 368n45, 387n31
Appian Way, 227, 356n86
Apuleius, 78; Florida, 78
Aquinas, Thomas, 7, 81, 387n20
Aragon, House of, 30, 270
Aragonese kingdom, 15, 48, 53, 80, 357n90
Archias (poet), 256
architects and architecture, 7, 35, 48, 56–57, 61, 66, 67, 128, 167, 175, 219–221, 321, 356n85, 359n105, 362nn31–32, 378n90, 379n92, 379nn96–98, 380n111, 380n113, 381n121
Areopagus, 310–311
Arezzo, 231
Argos, 50
Argyropoulos, John, 33
Aristides, 213, 262
aristocracy, 12, 114. See also optimate regime
Aristophanes, 189
Aristotelian, 57, 74, 81, 84, 91, 103, 112–113, 118, 182, 280, 305–306, 320, 365n75, 368n50, 373n38
Aristotle, 4, 6, 11, 20, 58, 64, 78, 81–82, 84, 88, 90–91, 95–96, 104, 106, 112–116, 118–119, 128, 133, 135–136, 154, 168, 173, 202, 204, 206, 211, 215–216, 222–223, 245, 247–256, 258, 263, 265, 269–270, 272, 277–280, 284, 289, 299, 305, 308, 310–311, 319, 321, 325, 364n63, 365n7, 366n13, 367n39, 369n67, 373n37, 382n6, 382n8, 382n13, 383n21, 387n20, 388n40; Nicomachean Ethics, 79, 82, 109, 181, 291, 306, 390n86; Politics, 7, 12, 63–64, 66, 71, 82, 85, 101, 109, 114, 127, 149–150, 155, 168–170, 176, 181, 203–205, 214, 225–226, 243, 246, 251, 254, 277–279, 285–286, 305, 365n75, 366n22, 369n52, 369n57, 370n4, 373n42, 374n57, 377n61, 377n64, 377n66, 378n89, 379n101, 383n13, 383n16, 384n36, 384n49, 391n98; Rhetoric, 78, 82
Aristotle (ps.), Economics, 194, 376n42, 377n64

Armenians, 87
armies: mercenary, 6, 121, 122, 152, 209, 222, 370n70; standing, 124, 207, 370n78
Arrian, 8, 78
arts, role of in statecraft, 66–67
Asciano, Abbey of Monteoliveto, 352n32
Ascoli, 351n21
Asconius Pedianus, 223
Asconius Pedianus (ps.), 78; In divinationem, 380n104
Asia, 112
Asia Minor, 126–127, 254
Asinius Pollio, 374n5
assemblies, popular, 5, 65, 99, 100, 108, 119, 131–133, 137, 141–143, 144, 169, 242, 244, 323, 372n20
Assisi, 37
astrology, 113, 184
Atalanta, 359n106
Athanasius, Saint, 354n53
Athena (Pallas), 274–275, 358n94, 386n9
Athenian constitution, 369n54, 387n26
Athenians, 70, 87, 89, 93, 111, 125, 159, 163, 182–184, 190, 200, 213, 224, 262, 276–277, 323
Athens, 87, 90, 118–120, 123, 127, 142, 146–147, 152, 154, 168, 173, 216–217, 228, 251, 253, 260, 273, 275–276, 282, 310, 329, 379n100, 386n3, 387n26
Attalus, king of Pergamon, 265, 356n87
Augustine, Saint, 104, 123, 174, 187, 306; City of God, 78, 381n118
Augustinian Order, 81
Augustinian thinkers, 306
Augustus (Octavian), Roman emperor. See Octavian (Augustus), Roman emperor
Aurigny, Gilles d', 335–342 (app. B), 392n112
Avalos, Costanza d', 359n105
Avalos, Iñigo d', 359n105
avarice, 76, 164, 198, 200–201, 204, 229
Averlino, Antonio (Filarete). See Filarete (Antonio Averlino)
Averroes, 58
Avignon, 38

Babylonians, 76, 87
Badia di Passignano (place), 354n49
Baldus de Ubaldis, 112, 245, 295
Barbaro, Francesco, 224; De re uxoria, 365n68, 374n6

Barbo, Pietro (Paul II). *See* Paul II, pope (Pietro Barbo)
Bartolus of Sassoferrato, 93, 112, 245, 295, 382n11; *De tyranno,* 380n109
Basil of Caesarea, Saint, *Letter to Young Men,* 175
Beccadelli, Antonio (Panormita). *See* Panormita (Antonio Beccadelli)
Becker, Johannes Christoph, 340 (app. B)
Bell, Daniel, 349n13
Belloc, Hilaire, 324
Bembo, Pietro, 350n9
Benedictine Order, 49
Berlin Wall, fall of (1989), 223
Beroaldo, Filippo, the Elder, *Libellus de optimo statu,* 72–73
Bessarion, Cardinal, 49, 52, 355n59, 359n102, 381n117
Bevagna, 37
Bias of Priene, 28
Bible, 82; New Testament, 3, 268
Bichi, Giovanni di Guccio, 31
Biglia, Andrea, 376n37
Birago, Lampugnino, 376n42, 390n76
Black Sea, 194–195, 376n45
Boccaccio, Giovanni, 34, 97, 118, 191, 220; *Decameron,* 232
Bodin, Jean, 2, 8, 113, 262–263
Bologna/Bolognese, 29, 72; university, 21, 192
Borgia family, 318
Botero, Giovanni, 385n69, 389n50
Bracciolini, Giovanni Francesco, *De officio principis liber,* 73
Bracciolini, Poggio, 17, 97, 111, 206–207, 232, 291, 388n43, 388n45; *De avaritia,* 201; *De infelicitate principum,* 286–287
Bramante, Donato, 232
Brescia, 223–224
British, 77, 87; British Commonwealth, 315; British Empire, 314. *See also* Great Britain
Brognanigo, Antonio, 35
Bruni, Leonardo, 16, 19–20, 31, 93, 111, 113, 120, 174–175, 254, 273, 363n52, 365n75, 367n34, 368n43, 368n45, 370n78, 375nn26–27, 376n42, 377n64, 383n16, 388n34; *History of the Florentine People,* 381n125; *Oratio pro seipso ad praesides,* 374n54; *Rerum graecarum commentarius,* 372n32

Brutus, Marcus Junius, 288
Buoninsegna, Duccio di, 23
Byzantium/Byzantine, 56, 58, 244, 388n34
Cadmeia (Theban fortress), 224, 380n107
Calcidius, 78
Calderini, Domizio, 35, 359n102
Caligula, Roman emperor, 28
Calixtus III, pope, 38, 233
Callias and Aristides, story of, 262
Cambyses, king of Persia (father of Cyrus II), 74, 289
Cambyses, king of Persia (son of Cyrus II), 309, 391n96
Campano, Giovantonio, 359n102
Campoli, Val di Pesa (benefice), 34, 37
capital punishment, 161–162
Cappadocians, 111, 273
Cappelli, Guido, 64, 234, 381n123
Capponi, Gino, 29, 33
Capua, 196
Carafa, Diomede, 1, 370n74; *Memoriale sui doveri del principe,* 72
Carthage/Carthaginian, 58, 70, 126, 159
Cassius Dio, 78
Catilinarian conspiracy, 30, 255
Cato (ps.), *Distichs,* 78
Cato the Elder (the Censor), 77, 161, 166, 185, 197, 199, 259, 294, 384n35
Cato the Younger, 250, 353n41
Catullus/Catullan, 51, 351n23
Celsus, 61, 79
Censorinus, 78
Cesena, Biblioteca Malatestiana, 175, 380n117, 381n118
Chaldaean/Chaldaeans, 50, 357n89, 388n40
Charlemagne, Emperor, 244
Charles VIII, king of France, 80, 313
Chesterton, G. K., 324
China, imperial, 12, 131, 133, 170, 181, 329
China, modern, 233, 313–314, 391n106
Chinese people (*Seres*), 77, 218–219
Christ. *See* Jesus Christ
Christendom, 2, 55, 98, 112, 240, 244; of Patrizi's day, 29, 36, 98, 104, 112, 240–241
Christian authorities, 82, 268, 306, 320, 389n52
Christian doctrine, 57, 87–88, 91, 187

Christianity, 3, 18, 36, 55, 59, 84, 90, 195, 229, 240, 246–247, 280, 306, 309, 351n23, 388n43
Christian names, for non-Christian slaves, 194
Christians, 42, 86, 91, 236, 268, 364n66; early, 309; of Patrizi's day, 102, 367n26; resistance to Turks, 357n88; as slaves, 376n45
Christian societies, 87, 186, 252, 306, 308
Chrysoloras, Manuel, 19, 56
churches, in ideal city, 231–232
Cicero, 20–21, 28, 56, 64, 78–79, 106, 116–117, 134, 148, 153, 164, 170, 176, 186, 189, 191, 211, 238, 255, 260, 267, 283, 301, 303–304, 306–308, 328, 383n24, 387n30; *Academica*, 84; *De officiis*, 120, 122–123, 354n53, 369n57, 370n75, 372n30, 372n36; *De oratore*, 175; *Dream of Scipio*, 63, 309, 367n26; *Laws*, 63, 118, 250, 367n25, 369n67, 371n18, 372n36; *Orator*, 88, 293; *Pro Archia*, 256; *Pro Flacco*, 127; *Pro lege Manilia*, 125; *Republic*, 58, 63, 189, 386n9; *Stoic Paradoxes*, 369n57; *Tusculan Disputations*, 374n8
Cicero, Quintus Tullius (brother of Cicero), 372n18
Ciceronian, 26, 28, 84, 113, 228, 367n31, 385n69
Cincius Alimentus, Marcus, 163
Cinna, 260, 371n16
Ciompi rebellion (Florence), 117
citizenship and the citizen body, 6, 106–107, 111, 242–272; civil society (*civilis societas*, i.e., a non-monarchical regime), 118, 217, 250, 279, 282; conceptions of, 242–247; duties of private citizens, 264–269; inclusion of foreigners in, 256–258; inclusion of working men in, 250–254; merit, 6, 256–257; qualifications for, 247–250; royal, 262–270, 383n17
classes, social, 133–140
Claudian, 78
Claudius, Roman emperor, 256–257, 374n51
Claudius Crassus, Appius, 117
Clearchus, "a certain," 212
Cleisthenes, tyrant of Sicyon, 154, 379n100

Clement VII, pope (Giulio de' Medici), 354n49
Clytemnestra, 198
Columella, 61, 77, 207
Commodus, Roman emperor, 296
common good, 114, 369n53
Condulmer, Gabriele. *See* Eugene IV, pope (Gabriele Condulmer)
confidentiality, 372n26
Confucianism, 12, 98, 170, 314, 320, 385n58
Constant, Benjamin, 368n50
Constantinople, 30, 56, 58
constitutional theory, 113–119, 277–281, 368n50; Lycurgus's, 142–144. *See also* aristocracy; democracy; mixed regime; mob rule; oligarchy; optimate regime
Corinthian order (architecture), 381n121
Cornelia (mother of Gracchi), 177
Cornelius Nepos, 77; *Thrasybulus*, 372n32
*Corpus of Civil Law* (Justinian), 101, 380n103
corruption, political, 94, 148–154, 159, 163, 200, 280, 285, 286, 312, 365n7, 366n11
Corsignano (village), 219. *See also* Pienza
Council of Basel, 357n91
Council of Mantua (1459–1460), 36, 60, 379n97
Crantor, 155, 373n37
Crates the Cynic, 136
Crete, 187
Crinito, Pietro, 364n56
Critias, 288
Crivelli, Lodrisio, 48; *Apologeticus adversus calumnias Francisci Philelphi pro Pio II*, 355n59, 356n81
Crixus, 258
crusades, 39
Curius Dentatus, Manius, 209
Curtius Rufus, Quintus, 78, 87, 385n63
Cybo, Giovanni Battista (Innocent VIII). *See* Innocent VIII, pope (Giovanni Battista Cybo)
Cyriac of Ancona, 387n17
Cyrus II, the Great, king of Persia, 74, 90, 94–95, 168, 268, 289, 294, 302–303

Daedalus, 363n47
Damon and Pythias, 86
Danaïdes, 199
Dante Alighieri, 2

Darius, king of Persia, 285
Dati, Agostino, 19, 351n20, 376n37
Dati, Leonardo, bishop of Massa, 62, 354n49
De Capua, Paola, 10
Decembrio, Pier Candido, 273, 377n61, 389n54
Decembrio, Uberto, 174, 374n5, 376n37; *De republica*, 64, 380n117, 382n130
Decii, the, Roman republican heroes, 118
*Declaration of the Rights of Man and of the Citizen*, 392n7
deliberation, 5, 119, 141, 142, **144–148**
dell'Agnello, Giovanni, lord of Pisa, 223
della Marca, Giacomo, 38, 43
della Quercia, Jacopo, 17
della Rovere, Francesco (Sixtus IV). *See* Sixtus IV, pope (Francesco della Rovere)
della Rovere, Giuliano (Julius II). *See* Julius II, pope (Giuliano della Rovere)
della Tacca, Niccolò, 42–44
Delphic maxim, 308
democracy, 114, 349n7. *See also* popular regime
Democritus, 363n47, 389n65
Demosthenes, 78, 147, 280, 301; *Philippics*, 370n78
dialectic (logic), 21, 83–84, 186, 364n65, 389n65
dictators, 110, 154, 155, 157, 168, 283, 372n35, 391n98. *See also* aesymnetes
dignity (*dignitas*), 4, 11
Dio Chrysostom, 8, 58, 78, 116; *De regno*, 369n59
Diodorus Siculus, 8, 61, 77–78, 164–165, 296, 363n47, 373n47, 375n28, 380n107, 391n96
Diogenes Cynicus (ps.), 78
Diogenes Laertius, 77, 117, 187, 190, 352n27, 385n62, 390n86; *Life of Plato*, 304; *Lives of the Philosophers*, 78
Dionysius of Halicarnassus, 8, 78, 117–118, 154, 170, 206, 311, 387n28, 387n31; *Roman Antiquities*, 390n76
Dionysius of Syracuse, Greek tyrant, 44, 52, 224
Dominican Order, 7
*dominium*, 2
Donato, Marco, 386n11
Donatus, 78

Doric order (architecture), 381n121
drama (comedy and tragedy), study of, 189–190
dyarchy, 38, 112, 312–317. *See also* federalism

economy, moral, 6–7
education: civic, 5, **172–193**; curriculum, 21–22, 182–193; legal, 97; military, 124; princely, 300–303; public support for, 5, 179–182; role of mother and father in, 5, 176–178; treatises on, 174–175; value of, 178, 182
Egypt/Egyptian, 13, 58, 77, 87, 164–165, 168, 184, 190, 199, 206, 296, 309, 329, 357n89, 363n47, 388n40
elections, 119, 128–132
eloquence, 11, 20, 56, 173, 185–186; in military leaders, 125
empire, 112, 120, 368n45; republican empires, 120
English language, 9, 80
Ennius, *Iphigenia*, 385n65
Epicharmus, 372n25
Epictetus, 52
Epicureanism, 47
Epicurus, 303, 305
epigram, 51–52, 358nn94–97
Epirotes, 224
equality, 4, 104–110, 115, 138, 392n7. *See also* isonomia
Erasmus, Desiderius, 2, 80; *Education of a Christian Prince*, 9, 335–342
Erastianism, 382n130
Este, Leonello d', marquis of Ferrara, 64
Este family, 172
Etruscan league, 388n34
Eudoxus, 363n47
Eugene IV, pope (Gabriele Condulmer), 38
Euhemerus, 375n28
Eupolis, 189
Euripides, 122–123, 300, 363n47; *Phoenician Women*, 370n75
European Union, 313
Europe/European, 5, 7, 9, 23, 201, 219, 278, 295–296, 314–315
Eusebius, *Praeparatio evangelica*, 375n28
Eutropius, 78
executive power, 157–158
exile, 18, 33, 152, 180, 188, 249

Fabius Maximus, 129
Fabrini, Giovanni, 337–338, 340 (app. B)
Facio, Bartolomeo, 388n42
family and household management, 176–178, 193–200
Fate(s), 290, 386n9
federalism, 284, 315–317, 388n34, 391n112. See also dyarchy
Federalist Papers, 8, 392n114
Federico (brother of Alfonso of Calabria), 53
Federico da Montefeltro, duke of Urbino, 39, 67, 220, 379nn97–98, 379n101
Ferdinand I, king of Naples (Ferrante), 15, 296, 333 (app. A), 357n90, 359n103, 370n74
Ferey, Jean, 341 (app. B)
Ferranti, Matteo di Domenico, da Fucecchio (Franciscan friar), 34
Ferrara, 172, 351n22; university, 192
Ferrara, bishop of (anonymous), 61
Festus, 78
Ficino, Marsilio, 52–53, 79, 232, 286, 291, 359n102, 363n53, 386n11, 388n40; Platonic Theology on the Immortality of Souls, 57–58
Filarete (Antonio Averlino), 220–221, 380n113; Libro architettonico, 220–221
Filelfo, Francesco, 19–21, 26, 32, 47–48, 97, 221, 297, 332 (app. A), 351n20, 352n24, 353n42, 353n46, 356n81, 358n95, 358n101, 379n97; Convivia mediolanensia, 354n56, 375n21; "De exilio," 351n17; Odes, 350n10
Fiorentino, Adriano (sculptor), 358n101
First Lateran Council (1123), 239
Flavio, Biondo, 97–98, 257, 355n59, 362n38, 368n45; Italia illustrata, 55–56; Roma triumphans, 57, 98, 365n70
Florence, 14, 16, 19, 24–26, 29, 53, 79, 113, 117, 120, 172, 200, 221, 226, 248, 311–312, 314–316, 351n20, 351n22, 354n55, 358n97, 371n9, 376n45, 383n15, 388n34; brothels, 16; catasto of 1427, 376n45; church of San Lorenzo, 227; Library of San Marco, 55, 175, 380n117; Medici palace, 227; monastery of San Marco, 227; Ordinances of Justice (1293/1295), 105; Palazzo Vecchio, 14, 231, 312; quarters, 362n36; Sala del Cinquecento, 312; Signoria, 25, 312;

and slave trade, 194–195; Standard-Bearer of Justice (Gonfaloniere della Giustizia; head of state), 158, 310, 312; Studio, 21, 192; tomb of Leonardo Bruni, 379n97; War of the Eight Saints, 235
Florentines, 29–30, 33, 61, 158, 195, 220, 253, 351n20, 365n75, 368n42, 380n108
Florentinus (Roman jurisconsult), 77, 116, 369n57
Florus (historian), 78
Foligno (city/province in Papal State), 10, 15, 37–46, 60–62, 69, 142, 233, 276, 314, 353n35, 357n91, 359n102, 368n48, 370n2; Palazzo Trinci, 45; The Twenty (civic board), 38
Fontanelli, Niccolò (Ilarione of Verona). See Ilarione of Verona (Niccolò Fontanelli)
Forms, Platonic, 89
fortifications, 222–225, 379nn101–102
Fortune, 290
Foscari, Francesco, doge of Venice, 64
France/French, 9, 113, 296
Franciscan Order, 34, 38, 42
Frederick III, Holy Roman Emperor, 17, 29, 36
freedom. See liberty
free speech, 110, 146–148, 153
French language, 9, 80
Friedman, David, 219
friendship, civil, 303–305, 390n86
Frontinus, 78; On Aqueducts, 219
frugality, 6
Frulovisi, Tito Livio, 174, 380n117; De republica, 64, 376n37

Gaeta (city; bishopric), 15, 18, 37, 46–50, 67, 80, 216, 231, 273, 355n57, 356n83, 358n97, 382n132; ducal palace, 358n96; monastery of S. Angelo, 49
Gaius (jurist), 279, 382n8
Gallograecia, 126
Garcés, Henrique, 342 (app. B)
Garzoni, Giovanni: De eruditione principum, 72; De principis officio, 72
Gauls, 77, 126–127, 256–257
Gaza, Theodore, 359n102
Gellius, Aulus, 61, 78, 372n25, 385n65
Genoa/Genoese, 24, 194–195, 357n90
George of Trebizond, 70, 257, 375n28, 377n65

German language, 9, 80
Ghibelline party, 105
Giles of Rome, 79, 88, 91, 94, 114,
    364n63, 387n20, 387n22; *De regimine
    principum*, 63–64, 73, 81–83, 93, 248,
    303, 363n45, 377n64, 380n109
Giocondo, Fra, 35, 48, 220, 356n85,
    360n11
Giovio, Paolo, 10
Giugni, Domenico, 365n3
glory, 22, 27–28, 66, 108, 120, 123, 262,
    283, 288, 374n8
God, 50, 75, 79, 82, 89, 94, 103, 122,
    129, 166–167, 178, 195, 206, 217, 236,
    238, 268, 277, 285, 291, 297, 300, 304,
    306–309, 323, 363nn51–52, 370n74
Gonzaga, Ludovico, 36, 354n55, 379n97
Gonzaga family, 172
Good, the, 270, 295
Gracchi, the (Gaius and Tiberius), 185, 196,
    210–211
Graeco-Roman culture/literature, 55, 76,
    329
grammar, 183–184
Gratian, 239
Great Britain, 315; Government of India
    Act (1919), 314; Parliament, 281, 315
Greece, ancient, 8, 22, 49, 58, 87, 112–113,
    120, 149, 155–156, 168, 184, 216, 224,
    243, 254, 278, 286, 298, 309–310, 313,
    319, 387n28, 391n98
Greek astrologers, 113
Greek authors, 7–8, 20–21, 55, 57–59, 72,
    81, 168, 171–173, 194, 211, 215, 248,
    278, 280–281, 284, 290, 299–300,
    349n7, 351n22, 364n64
Greek language, 19–20, 56, 63, 88,
    278–279, 351n20, 354n55, 356n86,
    369n55, 383n16
Greek model of citizenship, 243–244,
    247, 263
Greek music, 57, 89, 352n24, 358n95
Greek philosophy/philosophers, 2, 20, 27,
    58, 84, 93, 168, 170, 190, 201–202, 211,
    228, 292, 298, 324, 366n17
Greek proverbs, 179, 351n22
Greeks: ancient, 41, 89, 176, 198, 213,
    220, 230, 301, 307, 319, 329, 379n100;
    of Patrizi's day, 56, 58
Greek studies, 19–20, 351n20

Gregorian reform, 239
Grendler, Paul, 21, 192
Grotius, Hugo, 8, 317
Guarino, Battista, 35, 174
Guarino of Verona, 19–20, 172, 175
Guelf Party, 23, 105, 235, 367n30
Guicciardini, Francesco, 2, 6, 385n69,
    388n43; *Dialogues on the Government
    of Florence*, 367n36, 373n46
gymnastics, 182–183

Halley's comet, 31
Hamilton, Alexander, 71, 158, 316
Han dynasty (China), 12
Hannibal, 74, 122, 224
Harrington, James, *Oceana*, 201
Hebrew music, 57
Hellenism, 7, 20, 33. *See also* Greece,
    ancient; Greeks; Greek studies
Hellenistic kings, 275–276, 312–313,
    380n117
Helen of Troy, 95
Heraclea, 212
hereditary rule, 3, 389n67
Hermes Trismegistus, 79, 363n52
Hermogenes, 356n86
Herodotus, 8, 77–78, 87, 115–116, 278,
    280, 285, 310, 369n55, 386n14, 387n26,
    388n38; "Debate on Constitutions," 202
Herodotus (ps.), *Life of Homer*, 77, 351n22
Hesiod, 78, 101, 177, 187, 357n89,
    388n40; *Works and Days*, 351n22
Hippocrates, 79, 184
Hippodamus of Miletus, 204–206,
    208–209, 214, 239, 326, 363n48,
    373n42, 377n66, 378n67
Hippomenes, 359n106
*Historiae Augustae Scriptores*, 78
history: laws of, 88, 97; study of, 190–191,
    375n32; value of, 269–270; whiggish,
    111–112. *See also* method, historico-
    prudential
Hobbes, Thomas, 281; *De cive*, 385n56
Holy Roman Empire/Emperors, 2, 4, 112,
    244, 295, 313
Homer, 19, 78, 94, 116, 129, 176, 187–188,
    215, 249, 278, 285, 290, 300, 357n89,
    363n47, 388n40; *Iliad*, 388n38; *Odyssey*,
    52, 351n22, 386n9
Hong Kong, 391n106

Horace/Horatian, 17, 62, 78, 332 (app. A)
humanities (*studia humanitatis*), 5, 15–16,
21, 74, 180, 186–187, 192, 300, 308,
354n55, 375n12, 388n45
humanity (*humanitas*), 305–308
Hume, David, *Treatise of Human Nature*,
307

Idea, Platonic, 293, 295
ideal cities, 61, 67, 181, 188, 219, 221,
231, 257, 360n10, 380n114
ideal prince, 292–294
Ilarione of Verona (Niccolò Fontanelli), 35,
63, 356n86, 360n18; *Dialogus*, 49
India, 13, 58, 76, 168, 190, 313–314, 329
Innocent VIII, pope (Giovanni Battista Cybo),
15, 333 (app. A), 351n15, 357n90
innovation, 40
Inquisition, the, 233
*institutio*, meaning, 71–72
Ionic order (architecture), 381n121
"Iron Law of Meritocracy," 325–326
irony, Socratic, 390n80
Isabella (daughter of Alfonso, duke of
Calabria and Ippolita Maria Sforza),
53, 359n103
Isis (Egyptian queen, deity), 199, 206,
378n68
Islam/Muslim, 58, 313
Isocrates, 8, 33, 58, 78, 280, 297, 310–311,
387n21; *Ad Nicoclem*, 281, 287, 302;
*Agesilaus*, 290; *Areopagiticus*, 311,
385n68; Cyprian orations, 268
*isonomia*, 115, 278. *See also* democracy
*isotimia*, 300, 390n76
Italian city-states/communes/republics,
56, 70, 92–93, 120, 141, 159, 170, 244,
251, 255–256, 258, 276; and citizenship,
244–246
Italian humanism/humanists, 3, 55, 97, 201
Italian language/literature, 9, 18, 53–54,
80, 332 (app. A), 351n14
Italian regional governments, 38, 312
Italians, 18, 20, 56, 113, 280
Italian universities, 186, 191–192, 376n34.
*See also names of cities*
Italy, 18, 24, 46, 56, 59, 97, 109, 113,
158–159, 206, 210, 243, 263, 267, 313,
350n12; northeastern, 120; northern,
15–16, 375n30; southern, 9, 80, 270, 283

Itri (Hydrum Lemurnum), 356n86;
sanctuary of the Madonna della Civita,
357n91, 382n132

Jay, John, 316
Jerome, Saint, 77–78
Jerome of Prague, 232
Jesus Christ, 79, 236, 297, 306, 363n51,
367n26; Passion of, 354n56
Jews, 42
Johannes Philippus de Lignamine, printer,
356n86
John Paul II, pope, 367n35
Jove/Jupiter (deity), 49, 68, 187, 275, 293,
375n28
Julius II, pope (Giuliano della Rovere), 73
Julius Caesar, 78, 85, 125–126, 154, 161,
198, 283, 292–394, 302–303, 353n41,
370n75, 372n35, 387n31; *Commentaries*, 87
Julius Caesar (ps.), 78
jurisdiction, 2
justice, 60, 75, 103, 119, 138, 156;
arithmetric and geometric, 109
Justin/Justinus (historian), 78, 82, 87,
211–212
Justinian, Roman emperor, 58, 101
Juvenal, 78, 189

Kant, Immanuel, 3
kingship, 74–75, 95, 281–285; divine origin
of, 285–286; virtuous, 286–291. *See also*
ideal prince; monarchy

labor, manual, 136
Labors of Hercules, 188
Lactantius, 306, 308
Lacydes of Cyrene, 265, 356n87
Laestrygones, tribe, 275, 386n9
Lambin, Denis, 80, 340 (app. B)
Landino, Cristoforo, 350n9
Lapo da Castiglionchio, 351n20
Latin language, 9, 16–17, 56, 58, 63, 154,
158, 177, 189, 279, 300, 351n22
Latin literature, 8, 16–18, 20–21, 27, 32,
36, 57, 59, 67, 76, 79–81, 172, 194, 215,
256, 300, 354n53, 364n64. *See also names
of authors;* Romans: ancient; Rome: ancient
Latin translations, 7, 175, 351n22, 365n75,
369n59, 390n76

Laurana, Luciano, 379n97, 379n101
law, 4, 5; backed by divine authority,
100–101; canon, 4, 87, 103, 195, 200,
234, 236, 239; innovation in discouraged, 153; king's power over, 297–298;
popular consent to, 99–100; rule of,
97–104; study of, 191–192, 376n37; of
succession in monarchies, 295–297
Law of the Twelve Tables, 78, 212
leadership, military, 124–125
Le Blond, Jean, 337–338 (app. B), 340
(app. B), 342 (app. B)
legalism, 98–99
legal profession, comportment of judges in,
160–161, 164, 364n63; eloquence in,
164–165; pay of lawyers in, 163–164
legal system, 158–165; foreign officials in,
159–160; independence of judges in, 163
legitimacy and legitimation, 2–4, 26, 92,
327; political, 2–4, 9, 26, 99, 119, 181,
227, 250, 268, 270–271; royal, 294–300
Leo X, pope (Giovanni di Lorenzo Medici),
311
Leto, Pomponio, 47, 52, 359n102
Leuctra (place), 118
Lex Aemilia, 78
Lex Cincia, 78, 163, 374n51
Lex Didia, 78
Lex Fannia, 78
Lex Licinia Sextia, 78
Lex Voconia, 78
liberal arts, 5, 74, 175, 178, 179–180, 182,
376n37, 379n96; the seven, 22. See also
humanities
liberty, 3–4, 92, 106, 110–113, 115, 116,
323–324; civil, 116; negative, 116; as
numen, 110, 133, 323; as self-rule, 3,
38, 107, 110, 112, 116, 244
libraries, 49–50, 55, 230–231, 380n117,
381n118
Libri dei leoni, 353n37
Lipsius, Justus, 8, 385n69
literacy, of citizens, 5, 175, 179–181, 321
Livy, 78, 117–118, 141, 154, 170, 254,
288, 311, 368n50
Locke, John, 3
Locri (place), 224
Lolli, Goro (Gregorio), 30, 34, 39–41, 48
Lombardy, 209
lordship, 2, 368n43; ecclesiastical, 239–240

Lorenzetti, Ambrogio, 23; Allegory of
Good and Bad Government (fresco),
362n32
Lorenzi, Giovanni, 386n11
Lorenzo, Fra, of Fundi, 357n91
Lucan, 78
Lucca, 24, 31, 120, 223, 231, 368n42
Lucian, Phalaris, 390n76
Lucretius, 52, 78
luxury, 7, 201
Lycian League, 284, 388n34
Lycurgus, 96–97, 100, 102, 119, 142, 177,
253, 298–299, 312, 363n47, 378n77
Lydia/Lydians, 76, 87
Lysander, Spartan king, 151, 154, 302

Macedon/Macedonian, 275, 282, 310
Machiavelli, Niccolò, 1–2, 6, 8, 14, 17, 26,
29, 88, 111, 120, 123, 255, 294, 299,
309–311, 314–315, 317–320, 369n53,
385n69, 388n43, 391n111, 392n115;
The Art of War, 9; Discourse on the
Remodeling of the Government of
Florence, 311–312; Discourses, 9, 80,
240, 316; History of Florence, 80;
"Memorandum on the Reform of the
Constitution of Florence," 371n7; The
Prince, 9, 80, 287, 293, 372n30
Macrobius, 78; Saturnalia, 389n70
Mader, Joachim Johannes, 344 (app. B)
Madison, James, 284, 316, 391n112
magistrates and magistracies, 128, 154–167
magnificence, 228–229
Maio, Giuniano, 1; De maiestate, 72
Malatesta, Sigismondo, 39, 41, 355n68,
379n97
Malatesta Novello, 380n117
Malcolm, Noel, 236
Manlius Torquatus, 129
Mantua, 172, 220, 354n55; church of San
Sebastiano, 354n55
Marcus Aurelius, Roman emperor, 95, 296
Mariano di Iacopo (Taccola). See Taccola
(Mariano di Iacopo)
Marius, Roman general, 260, 371n16
Marrasio, Giovanni, 16–17; Angelinetum,
16–17
Mars (deity), 120
Marseilles. See Massilia/Massalia
(Marseilles)

Marsilius of Padua, 7, 382n13; *Defensor Pacis*, 369n69
Martial, 51, 78, 189
Martini, Francesco di Giorgio, 220, 356n85, 379n92, 379n98
Martini, Francesco di Simone, 379n97
Martini, Simone, 23
Marullus, Michael Tarchaniota, 51
Mary (Virgin), 18
Massilia/Massalia (Marseilles), 90, 126–131, 216, 363n48, 370–371n4
Massimi, Pacifico, 351n21
mathematics, 184
Matthias Corvinus, king of Hungary, 365n3
Medici, Cosimo de', 16, 19, 30–31, 33, 55, 351n17, 380n117
Medici, Giovanni di Lorenzo (Leo X). *See* Leo X, pope (Giovanni di Lorenzo Medici)
Medici, Lorenzo de', 192, 354n49, 365n3
Medici family, 26, 310–312, 318, 351n18, 354n49, 371n9
medicine, 21, 185, 192, 220, 376n39
Medici party, 227
Mediterranean Sea, 120, 126–127, 244; and slave trade, 194–195
Megabyzus, 115–116
Melampus, 363n47
Menander, 189
Menenius Agrippa, Marcus, 118
merchants, 118, 137, 143, 216
meritocracy, 60, 73, 75, 80, 126–171, 311, 324–327, 349n13; and equality, 108–109; as regime type, 113–114; as term, 11–12, 60, 75. *See also* optimate regime
Metellus Numidicus, Quintus Caecilius, 86
method, historico-prudential, 8, 81–91
middle classes, 118, 135–136
Milan/Milanese, 15, 30, 46, 48, 120, 220–221, 314, 333 (app. A), 356n76, 359n103, 379n97, 383n15, 389n67
Milesians, 205
Milton, John, 79; *Lycidas,* 354n56
Minerva (deity), 123, 178; "a denser Minerva," 150–151
Minos (judge of the underworld), 68, 163
Minos, king of Crete, 100
Minyas, king of Egypt, 100
mirrors of princes, 72–74
Mithridates, king of the Parthians, 296
mixed regime, 113, 115, 118, 119, 142, 149, 169, 253, 277, 369n67

mob rule (*ochlocracy;* rule by the plebs or lowest classes), 115, 117, 118, 379. *See also* democracy
Modestinus (jurist), 77
Mommsen, Theodor, 244
monarchy, 73–74, 93–95, 97, 272–317; analogies to in natural world, 291; arguments for, 281–286; merits relative to republics, 272–277; military power of, 283–285; sacred authorities and, 298. *See also* ideal prince; kingship
monogamy, arguments for, 84–88
Montalcino (fortress-town), 29, 353n37, 355n58
Montecassino, Abbey of, 356n83
Montefalco, 37
Monte Fusco, 357n91
Montepulciano, church of San Biagio, 232
Montesquieu, 8, 317; *Spirit of the Laws,* 391n112, 392n113
Montughi (villa near Florence), 33
moral economy, 193–213
More, Thomas, 2, 80, 211, 373n46; *Utopia,* 6, 9, 71, 161, 171, 192, 201, 240
*multitudo,* 384n36
Musaeus, 101, 363n47
Muses, 51, 62, 189, 217, 350n7; Polymnia, 275
music, 17, 21, 50, 57, 66, 89, 184–185, 253, 302, 352n24, 358n95, 375nn20–21
Muslim slavers, 194, 376n45

Naples, Cardinal of, 357n88
Naples/Neapolitan (city and kingdom), 15–16, 46–48, 52–53, 216, 220–221, 233, 235, 273–274, 296, 357n90, 358n97, 358n101, 359n105, 383n18, 386n3; and African slave trade, 194; Castel Capuano, 53, 358n96; Porticus Antoniana (now Piazzetta del Nilo), 53
Nature (personification), 94, 97, 102, 112, 116, 121, 217, 290
Navagero, Andrea, 51
Neapolitan academy (Porticus). *See* Porticus (Neapolitan academy)
Nelson, Eric, 211, 366n10
Nemesis, 290
Neo-Confucians, 181. *See also* Confucianism
Neo-Latin poets, 51
Nero, Roman emperor, 197, 229
Nestor, 50

Netherlands, 315
Niccoli, Niccolò, 55, 380n117
Nicholas V, pope (Tommaso Parentucelli),
29, 38, 55, 233, 368n45, 369n55,
375n28, 376n42, 379n97
Nicias, Athenian general, 184
Nicodon, Jean, 341 (app. B), 344 (app. B)
nobility, 134–135; rule by a junta of
hereditary, 115, 117, 118; true, 11
Nocera, 37, 45
non-Christians, as slaves, 194–195
Nonius Marcellus, 78
Nozick, Robert, 299
Numa Pompilius, Roman king, 100, 288

Octavian (Augustus), Roman emperor, 283,
292, 294, 310, 387n31
Octavius, Lucius, 228
Ognibene da Lonigo, 35, 354n53
oligarchy (rule of the wealthy), 115,
116–117, 152–153
Olivier, Richard, 45
opinion, popular, 140
optimate regime, 113–116, 127, 368n50
oratory, judicial, 164, 374n54
organic government and organicism, 118,
119, 160, 207, 234–235, 239, 252, 253,
255, 369n65, 369n69, 381n123, 384n35
Orosius, 387n31
Orpheus, 188; and Eurydice, 86, 363n47
Otanes, 115–116
Otranto, battle of, 274, 357n88
Ottomans, 56
Ottonian emperors, 244
Ovid, 78

Pacini, Pacino, 40
Padua, university of, 192
Palladius, De re rustica, 82
Pallas. See Athena (Pallas)
Pannalini, Barnaba, 19, 365n75
Panormita (Antonio Beccadelli), 52,
358n101, 388n42; The Hermaphrodite,
16, 51, 350n9
Papal State(s), 10, 15, 39, 43, 248
Papinian (jurist), 77
Parentucelli, Tommaso (Nicholas V). See
Nicholas V, pope (Tommaso Parentucelli)
Parleo, Petrus, 351n22
Parliament, British, 281, 315
Parthenopaeus, 351n21

Parthians, 76, 87
participation, 105, 142, 382n13; graded,
140–141; popular, 142, 372n20
passions: building types that inflame,
230; danger of, 75–76, 122, 159, 303,
357n88; eloquence as a cure for, 186;
study of, 27, 190
patria potestas, 197–198
"Patritio, il gran'," 10
Patrizi, Agostino, 47, 61–62
Patrizi, Francesco di Giovanni: accusations
of corruption against, 43–46; ancestry
and family, 16; as commentator on
Petrarch, 53–54; conspiracy against,
42–44; as court poet, 36; criticism of
scholastic method, 83–84, 88; exile,
32–33, 35, 36, 37; as diplomat, 29–30,
41; interest in architecture and town
planning, 48–49; interest in political
psychology, 107–108; knowledge of
Greek, 19–20, 351n22; later reputation
of, 9–10, 13, 18–19, 79–81; as Latin poet,
16–19, 36–37, 50–52, 350n9, 351n23,
357n93; literary network, 52–53; love of
Gaeta, 48, 356n83; love of Siena, 35–36;
no good at subservience, 357n88; originality of, 2, 63–64, 150, 320; political
career of, 14–15, 26, 29, 31–33, 37–46;
popularity in print, 9; praise of a quiet,
rustic life, 34–35, 49–50; preference for
life under a good prince, 49; as priest
and bishop, 33–34, 37; as private tutor,
27–28, 33, 35; as professor of rhetoric,
26; relations with Alfonso of Calabria,
46, 48, 51–54, 101, 357n88, 357n90,
358nn96–97, 358n101, 359nn103–105,
362n41, 388n33; as student of Francesco
Filelfo, 19–21; as student of philosophy,
20–22; as Themistocles, 386n3; and
utopianism, 71; views on religion and
the Church, 233–241, 357n91, 363n51,
367n26, 382n130
Patrizi, Francesco di Giovanni, works
—Commentary on Petrarch's Canzoniere,
xv, 53–54, 332 (app. A), 351n14
—"De Christi Natali" (Poemata 2.2), 18,
36, 332 (app. A), 351n15, 354n56, 357n90
—"De exilio" (Poemata 4.7), 33, 152
—De gerendo magistratu, 27–29, 160–61,
333 (app. A), 352n35, 366n18, 370n2,
370n73, 372n26, 388n34

INDEX

Patrizi, Francesco di Giovanni, works
(*continued*)
—*De institutione reipublicae* (*De republica*),
ix–x, 35, 41–42, 49, 349n7, 351n22,
355n58, 356n86, and passim; aims in
writing, 67–72; dating, 59–60, 61;
models and predecessors, 63–64;
patrons and dedicatees, 59, 62;
sources, 76–79; structure, 64–66
—*De metris Horatii*, 332 (app. A), 350n10
—*De origine et antiquitate urbis Senae*, 333
(app. A), 353n41
—*De regno et regis institutione*, ix–x, 58,
71–81, 83–84, 89, 113, 190, 246, 250,
261–71, 272–317 (chap. 7), 321, 334
(app. A), 349n7, 351n22, 367n26,
378n76, 385n58, 385n61
—"De vita quieta" (*Poemata* 3.3), 34
—*Epaeneticorum libri V*, anthology in
honor of Pius II, contributions to, 36–37
—*Epigrammaton liber*, 10, 17–19, 50–52,
332 (app. A), 358n94, 360n14, 386n3
—Epitome of Priscian's *Institutes of
Grammar*, 332 (app. A)
—Epitome of Quintilian's *Institutes*, 332
(app. A)
—*Letters* (Foligno Corpus), 331 (app. A),
355n63
—*Letters* (*Lettere sparse*), 331 (app. A),
333 (app. A)
—"On the Injustice of Peoples" (*Poemata*
2.5) 18
—*Oratio ad Hippolytam Mariam Sforzam*
(*De matrimonio*), 15, 46, 333 (app. A),
356n76
—*Oratio ad Innocentium VIII*, 15, 333
(app. A), 357n90
—*Oratio de laudibus philosophiae*, 21–22,
173, 332–33 (app. A), 376n37
—*Poematum libri IV*, 10, 17–19, 35–37,
60, 152, 188, 331–32 (app. A), 351n23
—"What Would Make Me Happy"
(Epigram 14), 49–50, 345–46 (app. C)
Patrizi, Giovanni di Franchino (Francesco's
father), 22
Patrizi, Niccolino di Buonaventura
(Francesco's ancestor), 24
Patrizi, Tino and Tizio (Francesco's
ancestors), 24
Patrizian republic, the, 167–171

Patrizi family, 23–24, 350n3, 352n32,
380n108
Paul II, pope (Pietro Barbo), 45–47, 390n76
Paulus (jurist), 77
Paulus Diaconus, 78
Pausanias, 78
Pavia: ducal library, 380n117; university, 191
Pazzi conspiracy, 235, 274, 358n97
peasants, 137, 139, 205, 218, 259, 378n67,
384n53
peculation, 106, 153, 166, 200, 213, 325
Pedullà, Gabriele, 92–93, 152, 315–316,
349n7, 349n13
Pelagianism, 232, 291
Peloponnesian War, 184, 260
Pergamum, 49
perfectionism (political), 104
Periander (tyrant), 117
Pericles, 125, 184, 388n35
Peripatetic philosophers, 229, 363n52
Perotti, Niccolò, 279, 359n102
Persia/Persian, 13, 58, 74, 76, 90, 115–116,
161, 168, 173, 190, 197, 268, 285, 310, 329
Persius, 78
Peter, Saint, 297
Petrarca, Francesco (Petrarch), 1, 8, 16,
34, 49, 55, 97–98, 118, 126, 191, 193,
220, 233, 240, 247, 270, 292, 295, 319;
*Canzoniere*, 53–54; *On His Own Ignorance
and That of Many Others*, 84; *Sine
nomine* letters, 232; *Trionfi*, 359n107
Petreius, Marcus, 353n41
Petroni, Ludovico, 31, 367n34
Petrucci, Achille, 15, 27, 40–41, 79–80, 333
(app. A), 353n35, 353n37, 370n2
Petrucci, Andreoccio, 17, 19, 22, 26, 352n30
Petrucci, Antonio di Ceccho Rossi, 26,
30–32, 353n41, 367n31
Petrucci, Pandolfo, 26, 80
Petrucci family, 23, 26–27, 30–32
Phalaris (Greek tyrant), 44
Phalaris (ps.; epistographer), 78
Phaleas of Carthage, 204, 209
Phidias (sculptor), 293
Philip II, king of Macedon, 111, 146–147,
213
Philip IV, king of France, 82
Philip of Macedon (ps.), 78
philosophy, as university subject, 190
Philostratus, 33; *Heroicus*, 78

424

INDEX

Phocaeans (Ionian Greeks from Asia Minor), 126–127
Phocion, 148, 213
Phoebidas (Spartan general), 224, 380n107
Phoenicia/Phoenician, 190, 266, 329
Phormio, 74
Phraates, king of the Parthians, 296
Piccinino, Jacopo, 31–32, 39, 370n70
Piccolomini, Agostino Patrizi, 355n58, 357n91
Piccolomini, Enea Silvio (Pope Pius II), 15, 17, 29, 31–33, 36, 174–175, 227, 350n8, 351n23; Chrysis, 350n9; Cinthia, 51. See also Pius II, pope (Enea Silvio Piccolomini)
Piccolomini, Francesco Todeschini (Pius III). See Pius III, pope (Francesco Todeschini Piccolomini)
Piccolomini family, 23–24, 47, 68, 220, 227, 231, 352n32, 358n97
Pienza (Corsignano), 61, 219–221, 231, 355n58, 360n11
piety, 103, 156, 308–309
Pindar, 78, 351n22
Piraeus, 205
Pisa, university center in, 192
Pisistratus (Athenian tyrant), 125, 200, 380n117
Pistoia, 33
Pius II, pope (Enea Silvio Piccolomini), 1, 7, 18, 30, 33, 35, 37, 39, 44–47, 59–61, 63–64, 66, 68–69, 105, 195, 219–220, 233, 331 (app. A), 333 (app. A), 350n12, 354nn56–57, 355n58, 355n68, 359n102, 364n65, 367n31, 379n97; Commentaries, 31, 354n54; Epistolae familiares, 353n40
Pius III, pope (Francesco Todeschini Piccolomini), 50, 59, 62–63, 357n93, 360n14
Platina, Bartolomeo, 1, 47, 354n55, 355n59, 359n102; De optimo cive, 72; De principe, 72; Lives of the Popes, 232
Plato, 4, 8, 20–21, 47, 78–79, 88–89, 93, 96–97, 104, 114, 169, 173, 187, 216, 237, 260, 270, 272, 289, 293, 299, 303–304, 360n14, 363n47, 363nn51–53, 365n7, 366n13, 367n26, 377n61, 387n30; Laws, 63, 66, 68, 79, 109, 122, 181, 211, 243, 268, 310–311, 364n66, 366n10, 374n56, 377n65, 385n61; Phaedo, 260, 375n27;

Phaedrus, 187, 260, 363n52; Republic, 63–64, 71, 85–86, 96, 101, 114, 186–187, 202–203, 260, 270, 272, 287, 300, 363n52, 364n66, 368n50, 386n1; "Speech of the Laws" (in Crito), 261; Statesman, 366n12, 388n38; Symposium, 52, 79, 363n53
Plato (ps.), 78; Seventh Letter, 187
Platonism/Platonists/Platonic, 21, 57–58, 79, 96, 155, 184, 308, 363n52, 388n40
Plautus, 52, 78, 189
plebs, 100, 117, 118, 136–139, 140, 141, 208, 210, 212, 254, 257, 278–280, 360n9. See also mob rule
Pliny the Elder, 66, 78–79, 88, 303; Natural History, 219, 359n102, 374n5
Pliny the Younger, 109, 292; Epistles, 389n53; Panegyricus, 389n53
Plusiopolis (port city; ideal city), 221
Plutarch, 8, 33, 77, 119, 148, 170, 211, 224, 288, 292, 352n27, 365n68, 387n26; De tribus reipublicae generibus (in Moralia), 387n17; Life of Aristides, 262; Life of Camillus, 354n53; Life of Lysander, 372n30; Life of Pyrrhus, 224; Life of Solon, 384n36; Lives, 146–147, 170, 310; Moralia, 78, 303, 372n36, 386n11; Precepts of Statecraft (in Moralia), 170, 372n36, 386n11
Plutarch (ps.), On the Education of Children, 175
poetry: Christian Latin, 18, 36; as university study, 7, 21, 186–190, 192, 230, 300, 328
Poggio Bracciolini. See Bracciolini, Poggio
political theory, modern Chinese, 12
Poliziano, Angelo, 20, 51, 56–57
Polyaenus, 78
Polybius, 8, 78, 96, 114, 365n7, 366n13, 369n67, 387n17, 388n34; Histories, 279–280, 311
Pompeians, 126
Pompeius Trogus, 212
Pompey the Great, 85, 293
Pomponius (jurist), 100
Pomponius Atticus, Titus, 229, 387n30
Pomponius Mela, 78
Pontano, Giovanni, 1, 52, 358n101, 359n104, 384n52; Actius, 191; De principe, 72

poor, public support of, 6
Poppaea Sabina (wife of Nero), 197
popular regime, 115, 353n42. *See also*
democracy
Porticus (Neapolitan academy), 52–53
Porto Ercole, 48
Portuguese, 93; slave markets, 194
Priscian, 353n47
Proclus, 78
profits, 6
Propertius, 51–52, 78, 86, 228
property: church, 6; distribution of, 6;
private, 6
proscriptions, 152
Protestant reformers, 240, 262
Providence, Divine, 97, 295
*provocatio ad populum* (appeal to the
people), 103, 156, 158, 169, 373n38
prudence (practical wisdom, *phronesis*) in
politics, 4, 82–84, 88–91, 96–97, 102,
372n36; royal, 299
Ptolemaic kings of Egypt, 313
Ptolemy of Alexandria, king, 180
Pufendorf, Samuel, 263, 317; *De officio
hominis et civis*, 263, 385n56
pursuit of happiness, 3
Pylades and Orestes, 86
Pythagoras/Pythagorean, 184, 260,
360n14, 363n47, 389n65

Quintilian, 22, 78, 164, 177, 259, 354n53,
359n102; *Institutes of Oratory*, 175,
293, 389n62
Quirini, Lauro, 204–205, 376n37,
380n117; *De republica*, 64, 174, 375n32

Radicofani (fortress-town), 29, 353n37
*ratio Solonis*, 142, 253. *See also* Solon
reason of state, 388n43
reform, institutional, 5
religion and the Church, 4; humanist views
of, 232–233
republic: best (*optimus status reipublicae*),
5, 71, 90, 126, 141; Roman, 112
republics: defense of, 92–97; fame of, 112;
perpetuity of, 95–96, 114, 282–283.
*See also* monarchy: merits relative to
republics
revival of antiquity, 16–17, 55–56

revolution, political, 13, 94, 107, 138,
148–154, 156, 206, 327
Rhadamanthus, 68
Rinuccini, Alamanno, 33; *De libertate*, 371n9
Robinson, Richard, ix, 80, 341 (app. B)
Romagna, 235
Roman authors, 56, 223, 361n29
Roman Catholic Church, 2, 4, 55, 104, 200,
232, 238–240, 297, 378n70, 389n52;
and enslavement of non-Christians, 195;
religious orders, 233 (*see also names of
orders*)
Roman citizenship, 242–244, 246–247,
250, 256–258, 382nn8–9; model of, 263
Roman constitution, 156, 311
Roman customs, 84, 86–88, 136, 140–141,
155–156, 162–163, 165–166, 183,
197–198, 230, 372n20, 373n38
Roman decemvirs, 154
Roman drama, 189
Roman emperors, 94–95, 295, 388n45;
"Caesars," 240. *See also names of
emperors*
Roman Empire, 8, 58, 243, 257–258, 282
Roman history, 58, 125, 283, 303, 317
Roman institutions, 212; Senate, 25, 118,
156, 207
Roman jurists, 249–250, 389n72. *See also
names of jurists*
Roman law, 2, 22, 58, 97–100, 170, 198,
210, 245, 297–299, 366n17, 382n8,
389n72
Roman music, 89
Roman officials, 166–167, 373n48, 391n98;
aediles, 166–167; censors, 165–166;
consuls, 157–158; quaestors, 166
Roman precedent, 93, 155, 165–166
Roman republic, 93, 112–113, 122,
157–158, 168–170, 244, 260,
282–283, 309–311, 316, 387n27
Romans: ancient, 7, 16, 41, 70, 86–87, 89,
97–98, 100, 111, 118, 120, 123–124,
134, 141, 159, 161–163, 184–185, 204,
209–210, 213, 220, 224, 227, 256–258,
273, 275–276, 283, 288, 293, 298, 301,
310, 313, 319, 329, 371n16; patricians,
141; senators, 156; and slavery, 195–196
Romans (biblical book), 268
Roman virtue, 55, 201

# INDEX

Rome: ancient, 4, 49, 57–58, 65, 90, 97–98, 103, 111–112, 120, 123, 126–127, 134, 155, 158, 168, 173, 206, 210, 224, 247, 254, 283, 319, 350n3, 363n48, 364n63, 365n70, 368n45, 386n9; of Patrizi's day, 15–16, 18, 29, 36–37, 40, 43, 45–48, 52, 59–60, 62, 192, 220, 233, 333 (app. A), 351n22, 355n59, 362n36. *See also* Papal State(s); Vatican

Romulus, 206, 237, 256, 372n20

Rossellino, Bernardo, 61, 220, 379n99

Rousseau, Jean-Jacques, 3

Rubinstein, Nicolai, 224

Sabaco the Ethiopian, king of the Egyptians, 161

Sacchetti, Franco, 195

Sagundino, Niccolò, 372n36, 386n11

Salic Law (France), 296

Sallust, 78, 201, 354n53; *Bellum Iugurthinum,* 366n11

Salutati, Coluccio, 193

Samnite Wars, 209

Sannazaro, Jacopo, 51

*Santissima Unione* (Foligno), 38, 42

Savigny, Jean de (Joannes Savigneus), ix, 81, 335 (app. B), 336 (app. B)

Savonarola, Michele, 312; *De esse verae republicae,* 361n21

Scala, Bartolomeo, 80; *Defense of Florence,* 364n56

Schiera, Pierangelo, 390n85

Schifaldo, Tommaso, 332 (app. A)

Schmidt, Joseph Andreas, 344 (app. B)

Schmitt, Charles B., 21

schools and universities, 172–173, 192–193. *See also* education

Scipio Aemilianus, 198, 229

Scipio Africanus, 67, 178, 189, 374n9

scrutiny for office (*scruptinio*), 371n6

Scylla and Charybdis, 136

Scythians, 124, 190, 376n45

Second Punic War, 126

senate/senators/senatorial order, 128, 131, 132, 133, 135, 136, 139, 141, 144–146, 149, 155–157, 236, 242, 279, 298

Seneca the Younger, 78, 189, 385n61; *De clementia,* 73, 389n55; *On Crowds,* 230

servants, indentured, 196–197

Servile Wars, 196

Sextus Empiricus, 78; *Against the Ethicists,* 373n37

Sforza, Francesco, duke of Milan, 30, 32–33, 333 (app. A)

Sforza, Gian Galeazzo, 359n103

Sforza, Ippolita Maria, 15, 46, 53, 333 (app. A), 359n103, 359n105. *See also* Alfonso, duke of Calabria (Alfonso II of Naples)

Sforza family, 30

Sforzinda (fortress-city; ideal city), 221, 380n113

"shame-praising," 236

Sicily/Sicilian, 16–17, 184

Sidon, 266

Siena, 10, 14–18, 24, 29, 30–32, 35–37, 41–42, 48, 50, 52, 60–61, 67–69, 80, 93, 105, 112, 120, 129–130, 140, 144, 158–159, 172, 200, 217, 221, 227, 234, 252, 272–274, 276, 315–316, 333 (app. A), 350n3, 350n10, 351n18, 351n20, 354n54, 357n93, 358n94, 376n41, 377n57, 379n92, 379nn97–98, 384n51, 386n3, 388n34; anti-magnate act (1277), 105; *Buon governo* of, 23–24; Capitano del Popolo, 25–26, 353n37; Casa della Sapienza (university), 231; as a center of Latin poetry, 16–17; church of San Giorgio, 354n49; citizens and citizenship in, 16, 19, 21, 25–26, 67–69, 243, 248–249, 253, 274, 364n64, 379n99, 386n7; Communal Palace, 23; Concistoro, 25, 68, 128, 353n37; Council of the People, 25, 29, 68, 128, 144; deliberation in, 144; Duomo, 23; Fonte Gaia, 17, 350n7; judicial system, 25; meritocratic elements in government of, 24–25; Nine (*Nove, Noveschi*), 14, 22–26, 105, 226, 274, 353n37, 358n97; Nobles (*Gentiluomini*), 23, 68, 105; oligarchy in, 24–25; one-man rule in, 25–26; Opera del Duomo, 167; Palazzo Pubblico, 17, 23, 220, 226, 379n97; People (*Popolo*), 23, 105; Piazza del Campo, 17, 23, 226, 231; political system of, 22–26; popular revolutions in, 273–276; Priorate, 14, 21, 26–27, 29, 370n2;

Siena (continued)
Reformers (Riformatori), 23, 105, 358n97;
Sala del Concistoro, 220; San Martino
terzo, 353n37, 380n108; Studio (university), 15, 19, 21, 26, 192, 332 (app. A),
352n28, 381n119, 386n5; terze, 362n36,
371n14; Torre della Mangia, 226; Twelve
(Dodici), 23, 25, 105
Sienese territory, 31, 217, 284, 358n97,
370n70
Silius Italicus, 78
Sixtus IV, pope (Francesco della Rovere), ix,
58–60, 62–63, 68, 101, 219–220, 234,
333 (app. A), 356n86, 357n93, 360n18,
362n41, 379n97
skepticism, Academic, 21
slander, 153
slavery, 87, 91, 195–196, 280–281, 321,
376n45
Smith, Adam, 368n50
Socrates/Socratic, 21, 87, 89, 93, 113, 136,
187, 288, 301, 368n50
Solinus, 78
Solon, 102, 119, 142–143, 170, 197, 253,
273, 312, 360n14, 363n47, 384n36
Sophocles, 300
Soriano (castle), 38
sortition (selection by lot), 128–132, 371n7
sovereignty, 3
Spanish language, 9, 80
Sparta/Spartans, 51, 70, 87, 89–90, 96,
100, 118, 120, 123, 148, 151, 154, 159,
168, 173, 182–183, 185, 203, 216, 253,
264, 310, 329, 366n11
Spartacus, 196, 258
sponsored mobility, 371n10
Statius, Silvae, 17
Stoic philosophers, 3, 95, 102, 155, 228,
291, 363n52, 385n61, 389n65
Strabo, 52, 78, 87, 127, 215, 294, 388n34,
389n62, 390n76
Struggle of the Orders, 141
Suetonius, 77
Sulla, Roman general, 260
sumptuary legislation, 153, 361n29
Switzerland, 315

Taccola (Mariano di Iacopo), 379n98
Tacitus, 78, 94; Agricola, 127; Annals,
256–257

Taiwan, 391n106
Talamonte (port), 48
Tarento (place), 224
Tarquin the Proud, Roman king, 283, 288
Tarsus, 217
taxes, 28, 38, 39, 48
Terence, 78, 189, 302
Tertullian, 78
theaters, 229–230, 375n30, 385n61
Thebes/Theban, 118, 136, 370n4
Themistocles, 125, 129, 386n3
Theocritus, 78
theology, 376n34, 389n52
Theopompus, king of Sparta, 154,
264
Thermopylae, 51
Thirty Tyrants (Athens), 152, 154
Thrasybulus, 152; letter to Periander,
117
Thucydides, 8, 78, 280, 310, 387n26,
388n35
Tigeou, Jacques, 342 (app. B), 343
(app. B)
Timoleon, story of, 224
Tinctoris, Johannes, De inventione et usu
musicae, 57
Tithonus, 50
Tizio, Sigismondo, 31
Todi, church of Santa Maria della Conso-
lazione, 232
Tolomei, Francesco, 352n30
Tolomei family, 23–24, 352n32
Tranchedini, Francesco, 33, 35, 332
(app. A), 353n42, 353n46
Tranchedini, Nicodemo, 33, 352n23
trattatistica, 72–73
Traversari, Ambrogio, 21, 369n62,
390n86
Trecento, 6
tresviri capitales (court for capital
punishment cases), 162–163, 168,
373n48
Trevi, 37; Castello Piccolomini, 39
tribunes of the people (tribuni plebis), 65,
118, 141, 155, 168, 371n18
Trinci, Corrado, III, 38
Trinci family, 38
truthfulness, 75–76, 151
Tudeschi, Niccolò de', 16
Turks, 30, 39, 59, 350n12, 357n88

Tuscan cities/communes/republics, 157, 194–195, 220, 248, 276, 381n120
Tuscan league, 388n34
Tuscany, 15–16, 27, 30, 37, 69, 235, 274, 379n98
Tusculum, 250
tyranny, 11, 52, 116, 225–226
Tyrtaeus, 300

Ulpian, 77
Ulysses, 178; and the Sirens, 302
United States. See America/American
urban planning, 7, 61, 66, 214–232, 321. See also architects and architecture
Urbino, 67, 220–221
Ursuleus, Petrus (scribe), 360n18
usury, 6, 199–200, 202, 376n50

Valerius Flaccus, 78
Valerius Maximus, 78, 82, 127, 354n53, 374n9
Valgulio, Carlo, 358n95, 359n102, 386n11
Valla, Lorenzo, 191, 232, 369n55; On the Donation of Constantine, 232–233
Valturio, Roberto, De re militari, 57, 370n82
Varro, 77–78, 189
Vasari, Giorgio, 379n97
Vatican: College of Abbreviators, 47; Library, 29, 47, 55
Vecchietta (Lorenzo di Pietro), 379n98
Vegetius, 78; De re militari, 82
Vegio, Maffeo, Six Books on the Education of Children and Their Fine Deportment, 174
Venetian government, 131–132, 159, 281, 310
Venice/Venetians, 24, 45, 70, 97, 120, 127, 131–132, 158–159, 168, 174, 216, 223–224, 242–243, 253, 314, 362n38, 366n10, 374n6, 374n51, 374n56, 381n117, 386n11
Vergerio, Pier Paolo, the Elder, 174, 332 (app. A), 353n47
Vergil, 78, 176, 188, 300; Aeneid, 163; Fourth Eclogue, 36
Vergil (ps.), Priapeia, 51
Verginia (rape of, by Appius Claudius Crassus), 117

Verona/Veronese, 35, 354n55, 356nn85–86, 359n102
Verres, 44
Vespasian, Roman emperor, 94, 292
Vibius Sequester, 78
Vicenza (city), 35, 354n53
virtue/virtues, 4–5, 11, 27–28, 51–52, 75, 76, 96, 168, 319; citizen, 259–262; of the common people, 371n16; potential for virtue in all classes (virtue egalitarianism), 118–119, 384n42
virtue politics, 1, 26, 118, 181–182, 268–269
virtuous environment, 7, 66, 301, 362n31
Visconti, Filippo Maria, duke of Milan, 16, 223–224, 389n54
Visconti family, palace library, 374n5
Vitelleschi, Cardinal Giovanni, 38
Vitruvius, 35, 48, 61, 66, 79, 175, 215, 220, 229–230, 360n11, 379n96, 381n121; Ten Books on Architecture, 219
Vittorino da Feltre, 172
Vives, Juan Luis, 80, 385n68
Voconius, 204
voting rights, 143

Walzer, Michael, 388n43
Wanckel, Johannes, 343 (app. B)
war, 28, 120–125, 140, 321, 370n74; defensive, 121; for empire, 122–124; for honor, 121–122; offensive, 121; for the sake of peace, 121
warlordism, 39
wealth, 321, 377nn64–65; distribution of private wealth, 202–205; distribution of public wealth, 205–209; inequalities in, 6, 201–202; limitations on private wealth, 209–210, 212–213; in mature polities, 210–212, 299–300; redistribution, folly of, 210–212, 299–300, 324, 378nn76–77
West/Western, 3, 7, 13, 58, 131, 133, 181, 243–244, 268, 315, 321
William of Moerbeke, 7
Wilson, James, 316
Winthrop, James, 391n109
Wollstonecraft, Mary, 198
women, role of, 83–89, 127, 172, 176–177, 183, 194, 198–200, 223, 228, 231, 242, 258

work, importance of, 7, 107, 180, 202, 252–253, 255, 267, 371n13, 377n57

Xenophon, 8, 78, 93–96, 119, 218, 272, 294, 303, 380n107, 387n26; *Agesilaus*, 366n11; *Cyropaedia*, 161, 173, 268, 297, 388n38; *Hellenica*, 224, 310, 372n32; *Hiero*, 289–290, 390n76; *Oeconomicus*, 194, 376n42; *On Hunting*, 354n53; *The Spartan Republic*, 366n11

Xerxes, king of Persia, 273, 386n3
Xunzi (Confucian philosopher), 98

Young, Michael, 11, 349n13

Zalmoxis (Getae), 100
Zetzner, Lazare, 343 (app. B)
Zeuxis, 95
Zhu Xi, 181
Zorzi, Andrea, 391n98